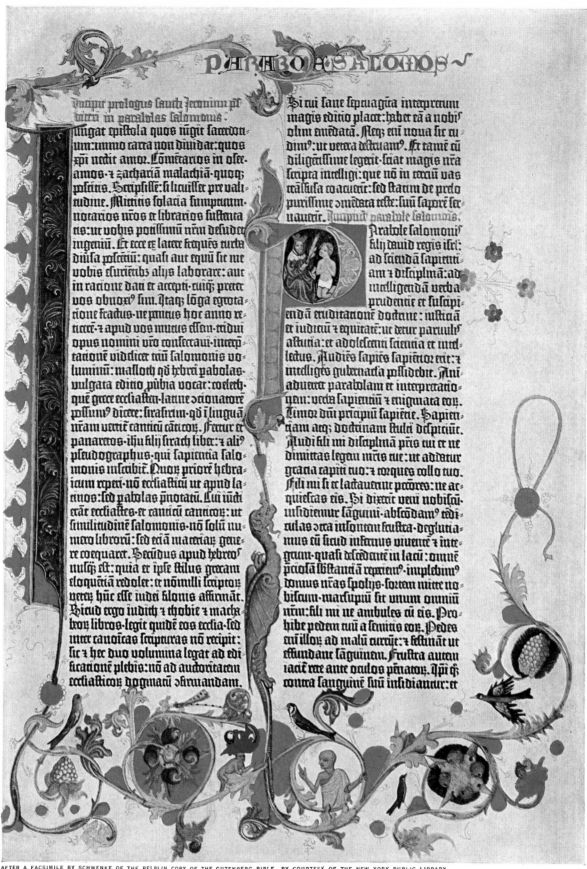

ILLUMINATED PAGE FROM THE GUTENBERG BIBLE

The Gutenberg Bible, traditionally accepted as the first book printed from movable type, was issued at Mainz, Germany, about 1454. The illustration shows page one of the Proverbs of Solomon. The pages are illuminated to give the effect of a hand-copied manuscript, as desired by the printers, who did not wish their invention discovered. The book was probably printed in 10 sections on 6 presses working simultaneously. Of nearly 300 copies, only 45 are known to be in existence to-day

GRAPHIC ARTS

By the Following Authorities

PAUL BEAUJON

MUIRHEAD BONE

FRANKLIN BOOTH

PERCY V. BRADSHAW

EDWARD C. BRIDGMAN

GEORGE B. BRIDGMAN

EGERTON CASTLE

WARREN E. COX

MAJOR CYRIL JAMES DAVENPORT

RANDALL DAVIES

CAMPBELL DODGSON

HUGH FERRISS

FREDERICK R. GRUGER

ARTHUR HASELOFF

ARTHUR M. HIND

ROLLIN KIRBY

PAUL G. KONODY

W. H. LAWRENCE

JOHN LECKIE

WILLIAM R. LETHABY

E. LUMSDEN

ARTHUR B. MAURICE

DOUGLAS C. MCMURTRIE

FRANCIS MEYNELL

STANLEY MORISON

F. J. MORTIMER

RALPH PEARSON

ELIZABETH ROBINS PENNELL

ALFRED E. POPHAM

E. S. PRIOR

JOHN R. RIDDELL

MALCOLM C. SALAMAN

MARION H. SPIELMANN

ALEXANDER STODDART

G. C. MILLER

HENRY TONKS

ARTHUR YOUNG

GARDEN CITY PUBLISHING COMPANY, INC.

Garden City, New York

\# 669589

PUBLISHERS' FOREWORD

THE MATERIAL of this book is presented through the courtesy of the publishers of the Encyclopædia Britannica. The text is composed of a selection of articles from its pages. To its editors we are indebted also for the use of the illustrative material.

Probably between no other two covers could such a mass of authoritative and enlightening material on the subject of Graphic Arts be found. The work is a composite production of artists, critics, editors and curators both here and abroad, and represents a cross section of the best informed and least prejudiced modern opinion.

We are proud of having received the opportunity to present such a valuable compilation at a price which nothing but the complete co-operation of the publishers of the Encyclopædia Britannica could make possible.

PREFACE

To THOSE who collect prints or drawings of any kind, to the artists who make them and to the laymen who would like to know a little more about them, this book is dedicated. Collectors need every book on the subject, and I believe they will find this the most generally useful one in their whole library. Artists will find that their fellow artists have written a large part of this booklet and I doubt whether anyone, no matter how experienced, can read it without gleaning some new theory or some technical point which he had not known before. To the man who is not familiar with these subjects there is a wholly new and fascinating world of adventure and many possibilities for the development of hobbies that will afford a lifetime of beneficial pleasure.

It will be noted that there are some contending opinions and where these occur both sides are presented so the reader can form an idea as to wherein the issue lies and perhaps make up his mind as to which is the more true as time goes on. Such a development of the theories of art would, of course, be quite impossible in any book written by a single commentator; it is in this diversity of expert opinion here expressed that the reader will find a unique and quite true picture of what is going on in the world of art.

Many of those who write on the theories and all of those who write on the practice of the various arts are themselves successful artists, and consequently the information which you receive from them is first-hand and practical. Where the technique of an art is described, there is a discussion of the tools needed, the way to set up one's studio, what kinds of paper to use, etc., I can truthfully say that a number of excellent artists have learned all that

PREFACE

was necessary for them to begin their work from such articles as those on etching, lithography, batik and wood engraving. Such men as Muirhead Bone, E. Lumsden, Arthur Young, Hugh Ferriss, Geo. B. Bridgman and Stanley Morison have had many years of experience and have found many short-cuts and above all have perfected a correct technique which is just as easy to learn as an incorrect and less useful one.

I would suggest that the student, after he has read the articles on general theory, follow this sequence: First read and adopt in continual practice all the material under the heading Drawing. Next, read Design, Perspective and Drawing (Anatomical), practising always. And at this point the student is prepared to take up the various articles on the different arts and may make up his mind whether he would prefer to work with the Japanese brush, the burin, the etching point or any other tool. Most artists find that one medium suits them better than any other, but this is no reason why they should give up completely all others. Each medium will present a different viewpoint and it is an excellent experience to try them all from time to time. Most of these arts can be practised at little expense and, if they are practised seriously, there is a good chance of their paying in real money for the effort expended in study. The chief reason, however, why a man may profitably practise them lies in the personal satisfaction of having created a thing with his own hands. No other sense of accomplishment is so secure in this world and none can be more pleasant.

It seems to me that the collector also should attempt to practise the type of art he is interested in. No one can possibly understand the mastery shown in a fine etching, for instance, until he has himself experienced the hazards that endanger a plate from the time it is conceived to the pulling of the last print. I believe, too, that if collectors practised the arts there would be far better taste shown, for they would then the more easily detect those insincerities which spoil the beauty of a work, and they would understand the almost magical touch of the great masters. This might keep their interest from becoming too limited by what I call the stamp collector's attitude; that is, the valuing of things on the basis of rarity alone. Art is a very difficult thing to describe because it has so many possible attributes, but rarity is certainly not one of them, and the man who thinks he has a beautiful or great work of art simply because he has the only one, may be deceiving himself. It is true that the very nature of painting makes it impossible to have two exactly alike, but on the other hand a score of etchings

viii

can be of equal value and all so nearly alike that you could not tell the difference between them.

There are some other articles in this book written by experts who are not practising artists but who have handled so much of one or another type of art that they are well qualified to discuss their subjects. These men have had much to do with museums and some of them have written a number of books of their own. What they have to say is of great interest because they know what they are talking about and are writers of merit.

WARREN E. COX, ART DIRECTOR
Encyclopædia Britannica

CONTENTS

CONTENTS

xii

CONTENTS

CONTENTS

xiv

CONTENTS

ILLUSTRATIONS

COLOUR PLATES

HALFTONE PLATES

ILLUSTRATIONS

ILLUSTRATIONS

DRAWING

Drawing, the art of delineation or of portrayal by means of lines, is so primitive that its history is practically that of man. Its beginnings must have been early, for one of the first things a child will busy its hands with is the making of marks in the dirt, and the walls of many a schoolhouse or home stand as mute witnesses to the inherent tendency of man to draw. It is a deep-rooted instinct whose satisfaction gives great pleasure.

Early Art.—In the beginning the primitive mind with its usual groping for essentials was satisfied with simple structural lines and, at times, outlines of those objects wherein the structure was less evident. The cave-man drew his pictures of men just as the child does—with the inverted Y for the body and legs, a crosspiece for the arms and a circle for the head, part of his drawing showing structure and part outline. The first of these drawings of the child are always without consideration of motion but it does not take long before, with the addition of feet, the figure is walking and soon the arms are brought to the front. Thus we see the early beginnings of the three elements which are essential to all drawing, if it is to please man who has for thousands of generations and from childhood up been trained to expect them: structure, outline and motion. (*See* fig. 1.)

Fig. 1.—Child drawing showing natural development of motion

In order to draw the human figure successfully the artist must first learn about its bony structure. But his work does not cease in this study of structure. Trees spread their branches in certain characteristic ways. Rocks must be closely examined and their origin understood or they cannot be given the proper structure.

GRAPHIC ARTS

The artist must spend much time in finding out how things were put together or how they grew and why.

In speaking of outline we should think first of line itself. It has been contended that "It cannot be reasonably held that one purely abstract line or curve is more beautiful than another, for the simple reason that people have no common ground upon which to establish the nature of abstract beauty." This is, of course, false, for if there were no common ground in beauty there

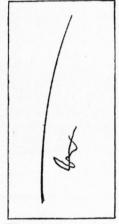

FIG. 2.—LINES WHICH ARE ESSENTIALLY BEAUTIFUL AND UNBEAUTIFUL

would be very little incentive to draw other than as a simple record. But to put into words just what this beauty consists of, is a difficult task. Fig. 2 illustrates two lines. It will be agreed that one is more beautiful than the other. One has a sureness and sensitive taper while the other wanders in a hesitant and aimless manner without object, without character. Perhaps a line can have character and therefore can show those beauties and weaknesses which we see in the characters of our fellows. This is undoubtedly possible, for no two men can draw a line exactly alike and certainly into the lines of each must creep something of the man himself (*see* TECHNIQUE IN ART, page 157). Therefore, beauty of line does exist but is difficult to analyze, as it is dependent upon the personality of the artist. It may be as difficult to tell why you like one line better than another as why you like one friend better than another; nevertheless, there is no doubt of your preference.

Besides this beauty of abstract line we find the age-old necessity for outlining objects, and when asked to describe a thing our minds at once turn to its shape. Its consistency, its structure, its movement are all often secondary unless they assert themselves strongly. The artist has only his eyes to

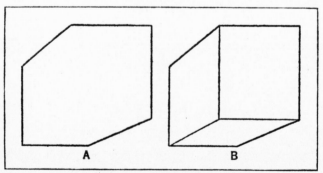

FIG. 3.—DIAGRAM SHOWING (A) DEFICIENCY OF OUTLINE ALONE (B) NECESSITY FOR STRUCTURE IN ORDER TO MAKE FORM UNDERSTANDABLE

2

LITHOGRAPHIC CRAYON DRAWING BY WARREN E. COX

This drawing was especially prepared by the author of this article to show the appeal which is obtainable through the proper observance of the fundamental laws of structure, movement and composition. The structure of the old tree clearly suggests its struggle against the prevailing winds. The movement of the foliage and grasses is immediate and vital. This movement is aided by the slower movement of the clouds and the even slower movement of the sand dunes and is opposed by that of the tree branch to the right, the dead stick in the sand and the boulder to the left, all of which only help to indicate the strength of the wind. The composition is well balanced but made dynamic by the small tree placed at the extreme left just disappearing off the picture as does the crow described on the Japanese screen in the text. By the use of these elements the artist has attempted to give the feeling that the sea is just out of sight over the dunes

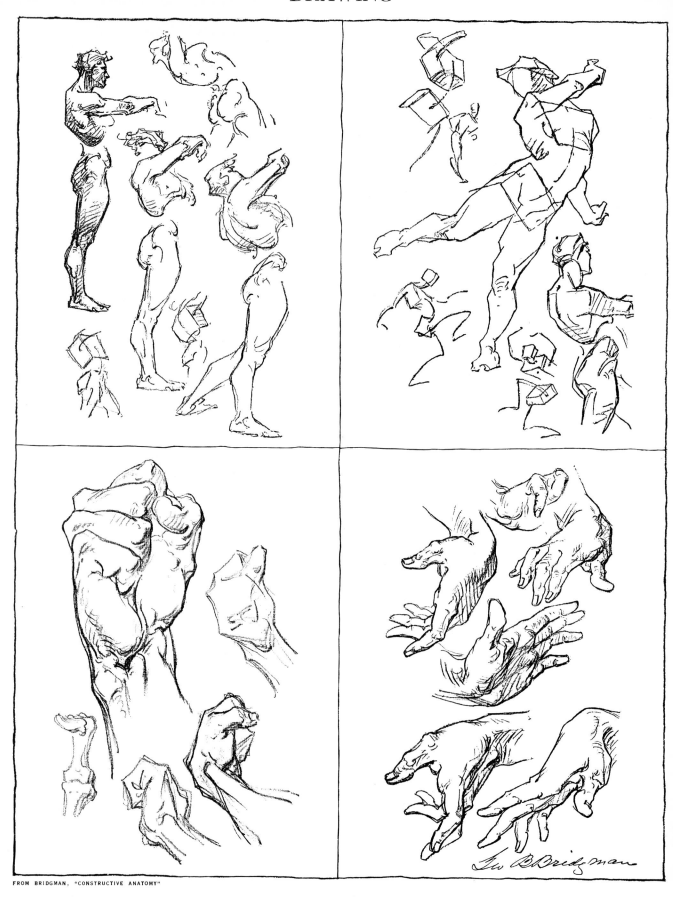

DRAWINGS OF THE FIGURE IN MOVEMENT AND STUDIES OF THE HAND

Upper left. Unchanging masses of the head, torso and pelvis, to be conceived as blocks, and the turning or twisting of these blocks or masses

Upper right. Blocked movements of the figure, showing tilting of the masses

Lower left. Studies of the hand on the wrist indicating power or force

Lower right. Studies of the hand showing rhythm

help him in this work but a knowledge of what lies within is also an aid to him. The author on drawing in the eleventh edition makes use of an illustration given herewith, to show how hard it often is to guess the shape of an object by its silhouette alone. (*See* fig. 3.) As soon as the three lines are added which indicate its structure it is obvious in shape.

It is sometimes possible to erect an imaginary structure which is of assistance and artists frequently resort to this method. For instance, in the drawing of a vase (*see* fig. 5) the straight lines might be sketched in lightly and would be of some assistance in judging both curves and proportions. In other words a sort of scaffolding is first erected and then the outline drawn upon it. After a little practice the scaffolding need not be drawn for the artist can visualize it without the aid of actual lines. Another help in drawing the silhouette of an object is to reverse the idea and look at the silhouette of the background instead. But all of these are simply suggested aids to seeing, and it takes practice to be able to draw what one sees. (*See* fig. 4.)

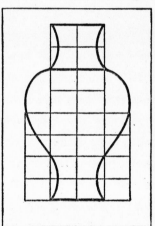

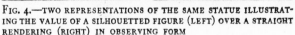

FIG. 4.—TWO REPRESENTATIONS OF THE SAME STATUE ILLUSTRATING THE VALUE OF A SILHOUETTED FIGURE (LEFT) OVER A STRAIGHT RENDERING (RIGHT) IN OBSERVING FORM

FIG. 5.—DRAWING OF VASE SHOWING METHOD OF TAKING MEASUREMENTS

THE REQUIREMENTS OF A DRAWING

EVEN MORE PRACTICE and observation are necessary to catch the movement which is also one of the fundamental appeals of good draughtsmanship. First it must be understood that there is movement in everything. Trees, when well drawn, seem to show how through years they have twisted and grown up out of the ground. Rocks show the bending of their hot masses by volcanic eruptions and the splitting and eroding of their surfaces. Just as each thing has characteristic structure and outline so too has it characteristic movement, and this movement must be caught in the drawing and should be emulated to a degree in the very movement of the lines. One does not draw the placid sea of a summer night with the same quality of line and movement as one would use to portray its raging strength in a storm. Without typical movement a drawing lacks life and therefore interest. The savage all over the world typifies a snake by a simple wavy line showing its motion, and he feels that an animal is "not himself" in a drawing, if not shown in typical movement.

Composition.—Closely related to these three fundamental requirements in good drawing is a fourth which came into the consciousness of man undoubtedly at a later date, but thousands of years ago, that is, composition. No doubt the first artists drew without any consideration of a boundary or limitation to their work, but at some time in the dim past, in the decoration of a clay vase or some other object, a discovery was made that the design was related to the space in which it was executed. Slowly through thousands of years drawings were developed which seemed to be a part of the structure of the limitations or borders themselves; outlines were so related that the eye of the observer was held within the limited area and led from one important detail to another, and it was found that movement was somewhat assisted by the proper placing of figures in the surrounding border.

Much has been written about composition. The Far Eastern artist is perhaps its greatest master. After observing carefully the object to be drawn, he sits and looks at the piece of silk or paper upon which he is to work and plans where he is to place the main features. He does not start at once to sketch as do many of our western artists, for he has found that once the pencil or brush is touched to paper one's ideas crystallize and it is difficult to get away from the slightest commitment. It is, therefore, much better to keep the mind at first in a fluid state so that the final arrangement can be unhampered and things can take their proper relationship.

Simple proportions in composition are easy to grasp and have more meaning than have those proportions which the eye does not understand. Rhythmical or parallel movements are interesting methods of accenting what seem to be the most typical lines and are often used. Perfect symmetry is tiring. It is as though one were to sit upright in a chair for a long time. The balance should then be thrown to a greater or lesser degree away from the centre to indicate the movement of the picture and give it ease. The story is told of a famous artist in Japan who was asked to paint a screen for the emperor, showing crows in flight. He at length painted one crow just disappearing off of the fourth panel, leaving the other three untouched. Thus composition helped the movement of the drawing, and the finished work is famous.

If these four simple laws of drawing are observed, it is possible that the finished work will be excellent, but, if any one be omitted, this is impossible. Man has for so long learned to observe structure, outline, movement and composition that the most casual observer feels a lack, if the work does not show them all. Good modelling, perspective and all other considerations can be neglected, and yet a drawing may be a masterpiece aesthetically, though there is no doubt that these do add to its appeal. But these four elements do not in themselves make a great work of art but rather their proper balancing and expression, which may be called taste.

Good Taste.—In considering taste it is first necessary to understand what enters into a good drawing, or any outstanding work of art. The personality of the artist or his style is a great part of it and this may be dashing and strong or delicate and sensitive; it may be keen and light, or ponderous and powerful. There are as many styles as there are artists and much of the love that people have for some works of famous artists is due to the fact that these works give some idea of the man himself. There is also the medium used, be it drypoint, graphite, etching, lithographic crayon or brush, and each medium has advantages and disadvantages. The drypoint line is strong and delicate without much flexibility but with a burr which is distinctive. The etched line has a sure clean-cut quality, but neither admit the soft shading possible with the pencil and the crayon or the flexibility of the brush. The appropriateness of the medium and its adaptation to the subject expressed are considerations often neglected, for artists sometimes become used to one medium alone and never find out the possibilities of the others. Finally there are the mood and character of the subject to be expressed. The woodlands which Corot chose to paint seemed to be a part of an enchanted world. The jagged rocks crashing into heaven which Li Lung Mien so deftly rendered with his brush are like flames crackling against the sky. These artists added much of their own imagination to what already existed; but it is nevertheless necessary to have something to start with, and without having seen the elms of France Corot would have found it difficult to paint, as would Li Lung Mien without the rough mountains of China.

Good taste is the perfect fusion of the personality of the artist through long years of practice into a skilful wielding of the tool, which in turn expresses the vital and inner meaning of the object portrayed with all due attention to its structure, its typical silhouette and motion, with appropriate and reasonable composition. When a thing is drawn in good taste one can see what the artist felt while drawing and what his reactions were to the subject shown. Each mark on the paper not only tells how he felt and what his mood was, but what he saw in the mood of the subject. If his subject be a gladiator he may have felt the glory of battle, the vigorous strength, the cruel beauty of the contest; or on the other hand he may have felt the pity and pathos of the inevitable destruction of so beautiful a body. In the one case his strokes would be sharp and vigorous; in the other heavy and dull. Moreover the composition, structure and movement would also reflect both the artist's feelings and those of the subject; both the artist's soul and that of the subject for it is only in this dual expression finely balanced that we ever find the really great works of art.

Some artists fail in good taste because they are so self-centred that they portray everything with too much of themselves and too little of the subject in the work. Others fail because they are so weak that they attempt a totally different treatment for each subject and have nothing to say about any. A drawing may also be in good taste in its expression of line, in its balance of the subjective and objective, but fail because the composition has not been studied to express this condition and is therefore not appropriate. Drawing is like music: it has tempo, key, pitch and many other elements, all of which, when perfectly handled by a master, make for beauty; but which, in the hands of one untrained or unfeeling, may prove terrible pitfalls.

Three Dimensions.—In this discussion nothing has been said of the attempt to portray three dimensions on a two dimensional surface (*see* PERSPECTIVE, page 16). It is the consensus of opinion that a work of fine drawing can be just as great in two as in three dimensions. Nay, it has often been pointed out that drawing is fundamentally two dimensional art and that the introduction of the third dimension savours of trickeries, and either builds lumps on the two dimensional surface or pushes holes into it. However, since the discovery of perspective, such superb trickery is it that a great vogue for its use has sprung up, and in the development of realistic painting which found its apex in the early 19th century much was done to make man expect the third dimension in drawing. Others, led perhaps by Cézanne, have attempted to give an even greater feeling of solidity to objects by the use of

6

exaggeration and distortion.   This is all interesting and may, in thousands of years to come, grow so into the consciousness of man that children drawing in the sand with a stick will spontaneously depict the third dimension, but at present it is a comparatively new development and has not yet penetrated deeply enough to make it one of the fundamental requisites.   A work of art can be a masterpiece if drawn in only two dimensions and does not gain an appreciable aesthetic advantage, if drawn in three.

The Teaching of Drawing.—Owing to a faulty understanding of terms and a general misunderstanding of the underlying principles of art there has been a great effort in the last generation to teach "originality" and individual expression in all the arts.   One might as well try to teach character or soul. These are things which grow through the years and which cannot be taught. The result is a chaotic condition hampered by the belief that artists are born, and that they express their "gift" suddenly and without the work which a careful study of the lives of all great masters proves to be necessary.   Some schools do not feel it is necessary to teach the pupils the fundamentals of art, so cautious are they in the foolish effort to protect their pupils' freedom. Therefore it seems necessary to consider the sane and proper method which should be followed in the instruction of others or of self.

First of all, become friendly with a ruler.   A large part of the artist's work consists in measuring with the eye, and it is imperative that the eye be trained to accuracy.   Only by judging distances and proportions and then checking one's judgment by measurement can this accuracy be obtained.   A good plan for the beginner is to purchase a drawing board, T square, triangles, compasses and pair of medium size calipers.   With these instruments an attempt should be made to draw vases of simple form so that the eye may be trained to see curves and proportions.   For example (*see* fig. 5) after the piece of paper is fixed to the board with thumb-tacks (drawing pins) so that its lower edge is in line with the T square when pressed in place at the left side of the board, a line is drawn near the bottom to act as base line and upon this line a portion is measured off with a ruler, equal to the diameter of the base. This line is then divided in half and a perpendicular is erected at its centre, upon which the height of the vase is laid off; at this point another horizontal line is drawn, upon which is laid off the diameter of the lip centred immediately above the base.   The ruler is then stood perpendicular to the table upon which the vase stands and moved until it touches the side of the vase at a point where it is widest, and another horizontal line is drawn with the T square, the same distance from the base line as this point is from the table. With the calipers this widest diameter is found and it is laid off on this line. Similar measurements are taken of the narrowest diameters and of their height from the table, and finally the curves are drawn in, touching those points which have been established.

It will be surprising to the beginner to find how accurate his first drawing is, if done in this manner. It will also be surprising to find how quickly he can grasp the amount of concavity or convexity of a curve no matter in what position it may occur; and to grasp its changes into another curve after he has drawn a number of vases. He will begin to see where one curve becomes more abrupt and another more gentle in its course. Looking back upon his first drawing, he will see all the slight delicacies of line which he missed, and will begin to appreciate the fine innuendoes the potter had put into the vase, which had at first completely escaped his eye.

The modernist may criticize this method and say that it will make the student a slave to the ruler. This is not true, for as time goes on the student needs fewer and fewer actual measurements, until at length he can draw a vase on any scale accurately. It is then time to attempt more complicated forms and these too should be measured at first. The greatest sculptors do not entirely trust their eyes for this work, and it is only by long training and much hard though interesting work that real efficiency can be accomplished, but new beauties will reward the student at every turn as he begins to train his eye to see. There is time enough later to try certain distortions or caricatures of the objects, to gain points which it is wished to stress. These distortions must be based upon correct drawing, or they will not be convincing. During this training the student should constantly observe masterpieces of various kinds, and remember that masterpieces are not only paintings which hang in museums but vases, sculpture, furniture and all of the thousand and one other things which show the touch of real art. The East should be studied as well as the West and every thing which especially appeals should be copied; for it will be found that one sees into a thing much more, if it is actually copied, than one can by any amount of mere looking at it. Through all of this study, the principles which were first pointed out should be kept in mind and an attempt should be made at all times to incorporate them in the actual work as it goes along.

8

ANATOMICAL DRAWING

THE STUDY of the anatomy of the human body is approached by the artist and the anatomist from different points of view. The former, by a process of artistic selection, seeks the ideal and adopts the proportions which give the most pleasing effect, while the latter desires to know only the mean, or average, of a large series of measurements.

ARTISTIC ANATOMY

THE REPRESENTATION of the anatomical form of man as applied to the Graphic Arts may be called *Artistic Anatomy*. This form of illustration may be divided into three groups: (1) The schematic, (2) That which represents the subject exactly, (3) The ideal conception or the ideal figure, constructed from the mean proportion of several types.

The schematic drawing is one which represents in outline the main characteristics of the object. It may be drawn with little or no regard as to the exact knowledge of the form. It has been of use in setting forth certain physiologic principles by the general form and location of the organs of the body, and especially used in post-mortem and zootomic comparisons.

The true drawings occur particularly in pathologic anatomy, where various and unknown forms are sought and where certain organs have to be shown in the individual, as in the case of human embryology and comparative anatomy.

The representation of the ideal is the only form suitable for teaching— and the very development of this figuration corresponds with the growth of the science of anatomy in all its periods. This type of drawing presupposes a vast amount of previous study of the human figure. It cannot come out of a period in which the artistic development overshadows that of the science of anatomy. This vague feeling for beauty, with a corresponding neglect of the real, was evidenced in an early period of anatomical illustration, when conditions favoured an artistic point of view, as was the case in the first half of the 16th century. This, however, changed as the cold scientific and extensive dissection was practised during the 17th and 18th centuries. It is only the combination of these two tendencies which can satisfactorily serve the advanced science of anatomy and the modern art of drawing, bringing to perfection through exactness of detail and ceaseless observation a comprehension of beauty in the entire figure.

GRAPHIC ARTS

In artistic anatomy, nothing else is of value to the artist but the idealized drawing. The more he eliminates unessential, the better; the keener his eye for the unnecessary, the bigger his vision of the true needs of the artist. The unnecessary is harmful, and the artist's presentation of too much anatomy makes of him a professional anatomist. Of immediate necessity is the study of the antique, or the older plaster models of Greek figures, for in drawing the nude the young artist visualizes the actual healthy form in all its fulness of life and movement, thus adding an element which can never be supplied by purely anatomic delineation.

HISTORY

THE DEVELOPMENT of artistic anatomy was not of outstanding consequence before the 16th century. Only a few anatomical engravings and woodcuts are found to that date. Even the drawings that Aristotle used in supplementing his works on anatomy have been lost. Figurations of skeletons and representations of bodies on cameos, seals and bronzes were common, but these delineations never served the purpose of anatomic instruction; they were rather of an emblematic nature: symbols of death, magic amulets, references to the fable of Prometheus, etc. In view of this, artistic anatomy may be divided into the following periods:

To the 16th Century.—Anatomical drawings of the Classic Period and the Middle Ages were known, and even mentioned by Aristotle, but so few have come to us for study that the subject cannot be adequately covered. Before the time of Berengario, commonly called Berenger of Carpi, about 1521, most of the attempts were schematic drawings for medical observation, artistic anatomy remaining in the background as a private study and depending largely upon professional anatomists for its development.

The 16th Century.—Although the name Berengario belongs only to the annals of medicine and will be remembered as the most zealous and eminent in cultivating the anatomy of the human body, it was his day, and that of Vesalius (1514–64), that marked the beginning of the attempt to free the anatomical drawing from schematic and arbitrary features and recognized its place in art. This artistic anatomy, was promoted by both artist and anatomist for the sole purpose of instruction. It was during this period that the Italian School of Anatomy reached its height of interest in the woodcut; it was during this period that sculpture and painting adopted proportions of the human body never before developed; it was during this period that Michel-

10

PLATE III   DRAWING

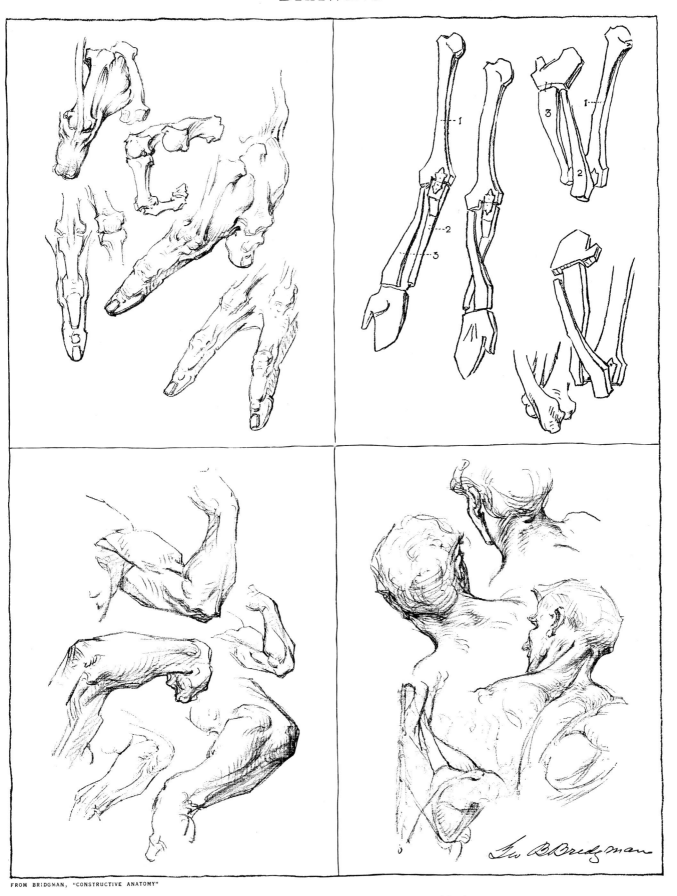

MECHANISM OF ARM AND FINGER JOINTS
AND DIAGRAM OF THE BACK OF THE NECK

Upper left. Mechanism of finger joints and knuckles. *Upper right.* Wooden device used to illustrate the crossing of radius over ulna. (1) Humerus, armbone. **(2)** Ulna, forearm, little finger side. (3) Radius, forearm, thumb side. *Lower left.* Flexing of forearm on arm. *Lower right.* Diagram of muscles of back of neck

STUDIES IN CONSTRUCTION OF THE HEAD, EYE, NOSE AND MOUTH

Upper left. Blocked construction of the head

Upper right. Heads seen in different perspectives

Lower left. Construction of the eye

Lower right. Construction of the mouth

angelo lived. Other 16th century artists who contributed to the study of anatomical figures were Leonardo da Vinci, Raphael, Titian and Dürer.

The 17th Century.—A comparative study of the antique, a clinging to Vesalian patterns, and the advent of independent publications on artistic anatomy mark the development of the study in the 17th century. A closer training in details and an effort toward the artistically perfect reproduction may also be included.

18th–19th Century.—Albinus (1697–1770) was one of the most famous teachers of anatomy in Europe, his classroom at the Leyden School of Anatomy being frequented not only by students but by many practising physicians. The Leyden school exerted untold influence in creating a greater exactness in all details. The styles of both Vesalius and Albinus were used as patterns in anatomical drawing, many independent attempts proving unsuccessful.

About 1778 combinations of utmost anatomic truths with artistically beautiful reproductions were brought out. The adoption of the steel engraving, lithography, the daguerreotype, as well as the revival of the woodcut in an improved form, meant an advance in the art; the exclusive use of the Albinian patterns gave rise to a greater independence. In fact, 1778 may be given as the beginning of the period in which the most valuable material on artistic anatomy was produced. Modern scientific medicine had gained its stride and was already moving swiftly toward the goal of a well-organized body of real knowledge capable of continuous growth. And this development may be shown in the bibliographic list as given below, the chain running from the first half of the 18th century to the present day. This bibliographic account gives the distinctive examples of anatomic illustration, including the modern work in both the technical and the artistic.

TECHNIQUE

FOR THE YOUNG STUDENT of anatomy as applied to art the simple drawing is the most effective in learning to construct the human figure. The eye must follow a line or a plane or a mass, which in construction becomes a moving line, a moving plane, a moving mass. But the mental construction must precede the physical, and in this the concept of mass must come first, that of the plane second, that of line last.

Certain laws enter into the functioning of the various organs of the body, just as pronounced as they are in controlling any other machinery. To the bones, for example, which make up the pressure system, belong the laws of architecture, as in the dome of the head, the arches of the foot, the pillars of the legs, etc.; also the laws of mechanics, such as the hinges of the elbows, the levers of the limbs, etc. Ligaments constitute the retaining or tension system, and express other laws of mechanics. Muscles produce action by their contraction or shortening and are expressed in the laws of dynamics and power, as well as the laws of leverage.

In giving herewith only an outline of the construction of the main parts of the body, the author presupposes a rudimentary knowledge of drawing, on the part of the student, and offers the following, in connection with the illustrations only as a further guide in studying the elements of anatomy and becoming more adept in the art of drawing.

The Hand.—In drawing the hand the artist must realize that, as in the human figure, there is an action and inaction side. When the thumb side is the action side the little finger is the inaction side. The inaction construction line runs straight down the arm to the base of the little finger. The action construction line runs down the arm to the base of the thumb at the wrist, from there out to the middle of the joint, at the widest part of the hand; thence to the knuckle of the first finger, then to that of the second finger, and then joins the inaction line at the little finger. However, with the hand still prone, when it is drawn *from* the body the thumb side becomes the inaction side and is straight with the arm, while the little finger, corresponding previously to the thumb, is at almost right angles with it. The inaction construction line now runs straight to the middle joint of the thumb, while the action line runs to the wrist on the little finger side, thence to the first joint.

The Fingers.—Each of the four fingers has three bones. The middle finger is the longest and largest, because in the clasped hand it is opposite the thumb and with it bears the chief burden. The little finger is the smallest and shortest and most freely movable for the opposite reason. The middle joint of each finger is the largest, and, like all the bones of the body, the bones of the finger are narrower in the shaft than at the ends. In the clenched fist it is the end of the bone of the hand that is exposed to make the knuckle. Each of the three joints moves about one right angle except the last, which moves slightly less. The movements of the joints are also limited to one plane, except the lower one, which has also a slight lateral movement, as shown when the fingers are spread.

The Thumb.—The centre of all the activities of the fingers, the hand, and the forearm, is the thumb. The fingers, gathered together, form a corona around its tip. Spread out, they radiate from a common centre at its base; and a line connecting their tips forms a curve whose centre is the same point. This is true of the rows of joints also. The thumb has three joints, and its bones are heavier and its joints more rugged than those of the fingers. It is pyramidal at the base, narrow in the middle, pear-shaped at the end. The ball faces to the front more than sideways. The thumb reaches to the middle joint of the first finger. The last segment bends sharply back, its joint having about one right angle of movement, and only in one plane. The middle segment is square with rounded edges, smaller than the other two, with a small pad. Its joint is also limited to one plane. The basal segment is rounded and bulged on all sides. The joint of its base is a saddle joint, with the free and easy movement of one in a saddle.

The Arm.—The forearm has two bones, lying side by side. One, the radius, is large at the wrist and the other, the ulna, is large at the elbow. Diagonally opposite the thumb, on the ulna, is a bump of bone which is the pivot for both the radius and also the thumb. Muscles must lie above the joint they move, so the muscles that bulge the forearm are mainly the flexors and extensors of the wrist and hand. The flexors and pronators form the inner mass at the elbow, the extensors and supinators form the outer mass.

Both the above masses arise from the condyles of the humerus, which is the bone of the upper arm. The part of the humerus near the shoulder is rounded and enlarged, where it joins the shoulder blade. The lower end is flattened out sideways to give attachment to the ulna and radius, forming the condyles. The shaft itself is straight and nearly round, and is entirely covered with muscles except at the condyles.

The Shoulder.—The deltoid muscle, triangular in shape, gives form to the shoulder. Just below the base is a ripple which marks the head of the arm bone. The masses of the shoulder, arm, forearm and hand do not join directly end to end with each other, but overlap and lie at various angles. They are joined by wedges and wedging movements. Constructing these masses first as blocks, we will have the mass of the shoulder, or deltoid muscle, with its long diameter sloping down and out, leveled off at the end; its broad side facing up and out; its narrow edge straight forward. The mass of the forearm overlaps the end of the arm on the outside by a wedge that rises a third of the way up the arm, reaches a broad apex at the broadest part of the forearm and tapers to the wrist, pointing always to the thumb; and on the inside by a wedge that rises back of the arm and points to the little finger. In the lower half of the forearm, the thin edge of the mass, toward the thumb, is made by a continuation of this wedge from the outside. In the back view of the arm, the mass of the shoulder sits across its top as in the front view.

The Neck.—Curving slightly forward, the neck rises from the sloping platform of the shoulders. The strength of the neck is at the back of the head, this portion being somewhat flat and overhung by the base of the skull. The sternomastoid muscles descend from the bony prominences back of the ears to meet almost at the root of the neck, forming a triangle whose base is the canopy of the chin. In this triangle below is the thyroid gland, larger in women, and above it the angular cartilage of the larynx, or Adam's apple, larger in men.

The Head.—Both the oval and the cube have been used by artists as a basis for drawing the head, but the cube seems preferable in that the oval is too indefinite and offers no points for comparison, no basis for measurement, and the eye does not fix on any point in a curved line. The block not only carries the sense of mass, but provides a ground plan on which any form may be built, as well as its perspective and foreshortening. The element of bilateral symmetry enters the drawing of the head. A vertical line in the centre divides the head or the trunk into parts equal, opposite and complemental. The right eye is the counterpart of the left; the two halves of the nose are symmetrical; the limbs, except for changes of position, are nearly exact though reversed duplicates of each other.

The cranium, the skeleton of the face, and the jaw constitute the masses of the head. Into the rounded mass of the cranium sets the narrower mass of the forehead bounded by the temples at the sides and by the brows below. From the lower outer corners of the forehead the wedge of the cheek bones begins, moves outward and downward until it just passes the curve of the cranium, then down and in, in a long sweep, to the corner of the chin. The two cheek bones together form the central mass of the face, in the middle of which rises the nose.

The planes of the head are those of the forehead, sloping upward and backward to become the cranium. The sides turn sharply to the plane of the temples. The plane of the face, divided by the nose, is broken on each side by a line from the outer corner of the cheek bone to the centre of the upper lip, making two smaller planes. The outer of these tends to become the plane of the jaw, which is again divided, etc. The relations of these

14

DRAWINGS ILLUSTRATING THE MECHANISM OF MOVEMENT

Upper left. Back of hand, showing movement of the hand on the wrist. *Upper right.* The muscles of the arm and forearm: (1) Coraco-brachialis, (2) Biceps, (3) Brachialis anticus, (4) Pronator radii teres, (5) Flexors grouped, (6) Supinator longus. *Lower left.* Flexing of leg on thigh. *Lower right.* Comparative movements of hands and feet

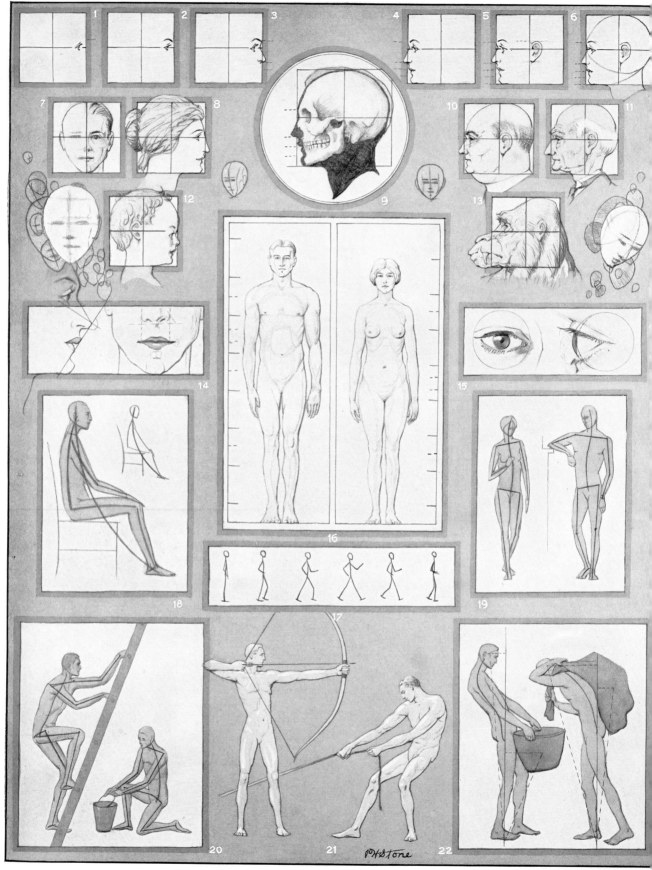

ANATOMICAL STUDIES FOR ELEMENTARY DRAWING

1–6. Illustrate the method of applying the egg-shape to a profile by means of a square

7–13. Are variations controlled by the principle of the egg-shape and square

14–15. Show the construction of nose and eye

16. Shows the proportional measurements of male and female forms

17. Shows six stages in a single step illustrating balance in walking

18–22. Illustrate distribution of weight in figure at rest and in action

masses and planes is to the moulding of a head what architecture is to a house. They vary in proportion with each individual and now must be carefully compared with a mental standard.

The Eye.—Below the eyebrow, on the lid, are three planes, wedging into each other at different angles. The first is from the bridge of the nose to the eye. The second is from the brow to the cheek bone, which is again divided into two smaller planes, one sloping toward the root of the nose, the other directed toward and joining with the cheek bone. The lower lid is stable; it is the upper lid that moves. It may be wrinkled and slightly lifted inward, bulging below the inner end of the lid. The cornea is always curtained by the upper lid, in part. The immovable masses of the forehead, nose and cheek bones form a strong setting for the most variant and expressive of the features.

The Nose.—The bony part of the nose is a very clear wedge, its ridge only half the length of the nose. The cartilaginous portion is quite flexible, the wings being raised in laughter, dilated in heavy breathing, narrowed in distaste, and wings and tups are raised in scorn, wrinkling the skin over the nose.

The ears, the mouth, the lips, and the chin, all offer variations in construction, and it is through comparison with others that the art of drawing them can best be acquired.

The Trunk.—The upper part of the body is built around a bony cage called the thorax, conical in shape, and flattened in front. The walls of this cage are the ribs, twelve on each side, fastening to the spine behind and to the sternum or breast bone in front. The first seven are called true ribs, the next three false, and the last two floating ribs. The masses of the torso are the chest, the abdomen or pelvis, and between them the epigastrum, the first two comparatively stable, the middle one quite movable. The shoulders are also movable, changing the lines of the first mass and bulging the pectoral muscles, but the mass itself changes little except the slight change in respiration. The mass of the abdomen is even more unchanging.

The Torso.—In profile the torso presents three masses: the chest, the waist and the abdomen. The mass of the chest is bounded above by the line of the collar bones; below, by a line following the cartilages of the ribs. This mass is widened by the expansion of the chest in breathing, and the shoulder moves freely over it, carrying the shoulder blade, collar bone and muscles. The back view of the torso presents numerous depressions and prominences, due to its bony structure and the crossing and recrossing of a number of thin layers of muscles. The outside layers manifest themselves only when in action, and for this reason the spine, the shoulder-blade, and the hip-bone are the landmarks of this region.

The Lower Limbs.—The thigh, the leg, and the foot constitute the lower limb. The thigh bone is the longest and strongest bone of the body, and the mass of the thigh is inclined inward from hip to knee, and is slightly beveled toward the knee from front, back and outside. Below the knee is the shin bone, the ridge of which descends straight down the front of the leg, a sharp edge toward the outside, a flat surface toward the inside, which at the ankle bends in to become the inner ankle bone. The outer bone of the foreleg soon overlaid by a gracefully bulging muscular mass, emerges again to become the outer ankle bone. Two large muscles form the mass on the back of the leg.

The Foot.—In action, the foot comes almost into straight line with the leg, but when settling upon the ground it bends to keep flat with the ground. A series of arches form the symmetry of the foot, the function of these arches being that of weight-bearing. The five arches of the foot converge on the heel, the toes being flying buttresses to them. The balls of the foot form a transverse arch. The inner arches of the foot are successively higher, forming half of a transverse arch whose completion is in the opposite foot.

PERSPECTIVE

Perspective deals with the phenomena of appearance; usually applied to the construction of drawings intended to represent objects as seen from some definite point of view. In appearance an object may seem very unlike what is known to be in reality. A railway track is of the same width throughout its length, yet in appearance the rails seem to approach one another as they recede, as the reader may see by looking at Plate I., fig. 2. A cube is known to have 12 edges all equal in length and to have a perfect square for each face, but when viewed the edges do not appear to be by any means equal, nor do the faces appear to be squares, as may be seen in Plate I., fig. 6.

Isometric Drawing.—A method of representing objects is sometimes used in which dimensions in three directions are shown in their true size to the

scale of the drawing.   A cube constructed by this method is given in fig. 6.
Every line in the direction of *ab*, of *ac*, or of *ae*, is drawn at its true scale.
Thus all the edges of the cube as shown are of equal length.   Such a drawing
is known as an *isometric*.   It is useful in indicating the size of an object, as
three dimensions at right-angles to one another can be shown upon a single
plane surface.   It is a purely arbitrary method of representation, however,
gives a distorted picture of the object, makes no pretence
of reproducing its appearance, and should never be confused with true perspective.

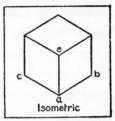

FIG. 6—AN ISOMETRIC
PRESENTATION OF A
CUBE, ALL EDGES HAVING
SAME DIMENSIONS AS
ACTUAL

True Perspective.—In true perspective three lines at
right-angles to one another cannot all appear in their true
lengths.   Lines and forms seem to change in size and
shape as they occupy different positions in the picture.
Colours and lightings seem to change as well.   In the foreground objects appear brilliant with distinct details, clear
colours, dark shadows and strong contrasts.   As one looks farther into the
distance objects seem less brilliant, contrasts less marked, colours gradually
lose their clearness and tend to merge into a purplish monotone.   This is
caused in part by minute specks of dust or moisture held in the atmosphere
which reflect a soft hazy light into the picture.   These lighting effects are
outside the scope of the present article.   The apparent changes in form, however, are dealt with as an exact science known as *linear perspective*, by means
of which it is possible to construct, from the actual dimensions of an object,
its apparent shape and size at any point in space.

The camera is an instrument by means of which perspective views can
be produced mechanically.   On Plate I., figs. 2 and 6 are so produced.   Rays
of light reflected from any object, as *ab*, fig. 7, pass through the lens of the
camera and fall upon the sensitive plate forming an image which will represent the appearance of the object to one who views the photograph.

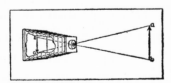

FIG. 7.—PERSPECTIVE PROJECTION
PRODUCED PHOTOGRAPHICALLY

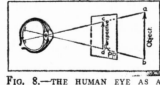

FIG. 8.—THE HUMAN EYE AS A
CAMERA

The human eye, fig. 8, is, in effect, a little camera with a lens, *o*, and a sensitive surface, the retina, which receives the image, *fe*.   If a transparent

17

GRAPHIC ARTS

plane, *PP*, be placed between the object and the observer's eye, the rays of light coming from the object will pass through the plane and project upon it an image, *cd*, of the object. The image on the plane would be a *perspective* of the object and would represent to the observer its appearance.

Wherever one looks he sees a perspective view. An expert draftsman before a group of objects might record on paper exactly what he saw. The result would be a perspective drawing reproducing the appearance of the objects and might conceivably be made without any understanding of the laws of perspective. Some of the ancient peoples, the Chinese for example, developed an interesting technique in drawing, and their pictures often showed a strong sense of perspective. Whether they understood the underlying science or merely copied what they saw is open to argument. It was probably not until the early part of the 15th century that the governing principles of the science began to be understood by western civilization. The names of Brunelleschi, Alberti, Ucello, Leonardo da Vinci, Piero della Francesca and Albrecht Dürer are all connected with its development. To Francesca has been attributed the conception of the vanishing point which is the key to modern perspective construction.

FUNDAMENTAL PRINCIPLES

Apparent Diminution in Size.—The complete theory of perspective can be developed from a single basic phenomenon; viz., the apparent decrease in size of an object as it recedes from the eye. A railway train moving over a straight track furnishes an example. As the train becomes more distant its dimensions apparently become smaller. Its speed also seems to diminish, for the space over which it travels in a given time appears to be shorter and shorter as it is taken farther and farther away. Plate I., fig. 8, is another example, showing posts of equal height and with equidistant spaces between.

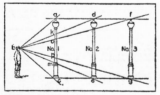

FIG. 9.—CAUSE OF APPARENT FORESHORTENING

The reason for the apparent diminution in size is readily understood from fig. 9. The size of any object is estimated by comparing it with some standard. As the observer looks along the line *ba* at the top of the first post, the top of the second post is invisible. It is apparently below the top of No. 1, and in order to see it he must lower his direction of sight until he looks along *bd*. He now sees the top of No. 2, but No. 3 is still invisible and in order to see No. 3 he must lower his gaze still further until he looks along *bf*. Con-

18

sidering the bottoms of the posts he finds the same apparent shrinkage. Compared with No. 1, No. 2 seems to have a length only equal to *km*, No. 3 only equal to *op*, and so on. The posts thus appear relatively smaller and smaller as they are taken farther and farther from the eye. If the line of posts could be extended an infinite distance, the last post would evidently appear incalculably small or of zero length.

Similarly the two parallel lines, *adf* and *ceg*, running respectively along the tops and bottoms of the posts must, owing to the apparent decrease in the lengths of the posts, appear to approach one another as they recede. Could they be of infinite length they would evidently appear to meet in a point at an infinite distance from the observer. This imaginary point which parallel lines seem to approach is called a *vanishing point*. Plate I., fig. 3, shows a perspective of the interior of an aqueduct in which the parallel lines of the stone courses can easily be imagined to meet in a vanishing point.

Systems of Lines.—If any object bounded by planes, *e.g.*, a cube is examined, its edges can be grouped into several series or systems of parallel lines. Each system will have its particular vanishing point. In fig. 10 there are three such series, one apparently converging or *vanishing* toward the right, one toward the left, and a vertical system. It is important to be able to locate the imaginary vanishing point of any system of lines. This can always be done by looking along one of the lines or *elements* of the system. Whatever the position of the observer, every element of a given system appears to converge towards the vanishing point of that system and, if extended indefinitely, to meet the vanishing point. Hence if the observer looks along any element, he will be looking directly at the vanishing point of the system. The line along which he sights will be seen endwise, as a point, exactly covering the vanishing point toward which all other elements of the system will appear to converge. Thus, an observer might sight directly along one of the course lines in Plate I., fig. 3, and discover the vanishing point for the other course lines directly in front of his eye.

This principle is further illustrated by the model shown in Plate I., fig. 1, which consists of a series of rods representing straight lines and arranged in a parallel system. Let the observer look directly along any one of the rods, as the one at the lower left corner. This rod will appear as a dot, and apparently cover the imaginary infinitely distant vanishing point of the system. All the other rods or elements will appear to converge toward the vanishing point which the observer has located. Again if he sights along the centre rod,

Plate I., fig. 4, he will see it as a dot covering the imaginary vanishing point towards which the other elements of the system appear to converge. Let him choose which rod he will the result will evidently be the same. The line along which the observer sights is called the *visual element* of the system. Plate I., fig. 9, shows the use of this method to locate the vanishing point of the horizontal lines in the view that are parallel to the curbing. The observer sights along the fence rail which being parallel to the curb leads his gaze to the desired vanishing point. All other horizontal lines in the view belonging to this system seem to converge towards the infinitely distant vanishing point covered by the fence rail.

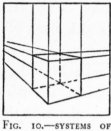
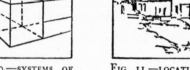
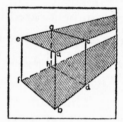

FIG. 10.—SYSTEMS OF LINES   FIG. 11.—LOCATING A VANISHING POINT   FIG. 12.—APPARENT CONVERGENCE OF PARALLEL PLANES

It is evident that the view of the scene as well as the apparent position of any vanishing point must change with every new position of the observer. Therefore a perspective drawing can only attempt to represent the view as it will appear from one point of view. This is a limitation inherent in every perspective drawing.

Instead of sighting along an actual element, the observer can look in a direction parallel to an element. The direction in which he looks may be considered as an imaginary element which will lead his eye to the desired vanishing point. In fig. 11, the observer is looking in a direction parallel to the two edges *ab* and *cd* of the roof plane. These two edges appear to him to converge towards a point infinitely distant from him in the direction of his gaze.

Rule A.—From the method of locating a vanishing point it follows that if a system is horizontal its vanishing point must appear to be on a level with the eye. If a system vanishes upward its vanishing point will be located above the eye; if downward, below the eye; if toward the right, to the right of the eye; or if toward the left, to the left of the eye.

Theoretically every system of lines has two vanishing points, for, if the observer can locate one by looking along an element in one direction, he can also locate a second by looking along the same element in the opposite direction. For any given position of the observer one of these vanishing points will usually lie before and the other behind him. The one lying in the direction of his gaze is the only one considered, except in certain special problems.

Systems of Planes.—Plane surfaces which are parallel appear to approach one another as they recede. This will be evident from fig. 12. Since the horizontal edges of the cube appear to converge, the top and bottom planes must appear nearer together at *cd* and *gh* than at *ab* and *ef*, and must seem to approach one another as they extend into space. Parallel planes extended an infinite distance appear to meet in a straight line known as the *vanishing trace* of the planes. Each system of planes will have its own vanishing trace which can be located by looking along any one of the planes. The plane will appear edgewise, as a line, and cover the vanishing trace which every plane of the system will appear to approach.

The method of locating a vanishing trace is illustrated in Plate I., figs. 5 and 7. The plane along which the observer looks is known as the *visual* plane of the system. It appears as a straight line and the other planes of the system seem to approach it. The vanishing trace of the system of horizontal planes will evidently be a horizontal line on a level with the observer's eye. To this vanishing trace is given the special name of *horizon*. The visual plane of a horizontal system is called the *horizon plane*.

If the observer while locating a vanishing trace should slowly turn completely around still looking along the visual plane, at every instant he would see the vanishing trace as a straight line directly in front of him. The vanishing trace therefore may be considered as a circle of infinite radius which is theoretically the same thing as a straight line. In practical work so small a field is usually visible that a vanishing trace is always treated as a straight line.

Axioms.—The foregoing discussion may be summarized in five axioms and one rule.

Axiom 1. Parallel lines appear to converge as they vanish, and to meet at an infinite distance from the observer in an imaginary point called the vanishing point of the system.

Axiom 2. Parallel planes appear to approach one another as they recede from the eye, and to meet at an infinite distance from the observer in an imaginary straight line known as a vanishing trace.

Axiom 3. A line lying in a plane must have its vanishing point in the vanishing trace of the plane.   This is evident from the manner of locating the vanishing point of a line and the vanishing trace of a plane.

Axiom 4.   The vanishing trace of a plane must contain the vanishing points of all lines which lie in the plane.   This is the converse of number 3.

Axiom 5.   A line which forms the intersection of two planes, since it lies in both, must have its vanishing point at the intersection of the vanishing traces of the two planes.

Rule B.   To locate the vanishing point of a system of lines, look along any real or imaginary line of the system.

APPLICATION TO PERSPECTIVE DRAWING

The Picture Plane.—The five axioms just formulated apply to conditions which are apparent but which do not really exist.   In a perspective drawing these apparent conditions in space must be represented by actual conditions on paper.   The perspectives of parallel lines are represented by converging lines which actually meet at a point which is the perspective of their vanishing point.   Fig. 13 illustrates this.   An observer stands before an object. Between him and the object is a plane called the *picture plane.*   The object becomes visible to him by rays of light known as *visual rays* reflected into his eye from each point on its surface.   Each point is projected upon the picture plane by its visual ray and the result is a perspective view.

Rule C.   The perspective of any point is where the visual ray from the point intersects the picture plane.

A perspective is really a *conical projection* of the object on the picture plane, the projecting cone being made up of visual rays.   In order to locate the imaginary vanishing point of the roof lines ab and $a_1 b_1$, the observer looks in a direction parallel to ab and $a_1 b_1$ (Rule B).   The direction in which he is looking becomes the visual ray passing between the imaginary vanishing point and his eye.   The point in which this visual ray intersects the picture plane is the perspective of the vanishing point (Rule C), and to this perspective vanishing point the perspectives of the roof lines ab and $a_1 b_1$ actually converge.

Rule D.   To find the perspective of the vanishing point of any system of lines, pass a line parallel to the system through the observer's eye and find where the line pierces the picture plane.

Planes of Projection.—In making a perspective drawing three planes are used: first, a vertical plane, the picture plane, which receives perspective view; second, a horizontal plane, the horizon plane which must always contain the observer's eye; third, a second horizontal plane called the ground plane on which the object always rests, fig.14. Since the horizon plane always contains the observer's eye, or *station point*, and the object always rests upon the ground plane, the relation between these two planes determines the kind of view to be produced. If the distance between them equals the height of a man (to the scale of the drawing) the view obtained will be as though seen by an observer standing on the ground plane. Increasing this distance is equivalent to raising the observer's eye, and if the distance is great the result is a

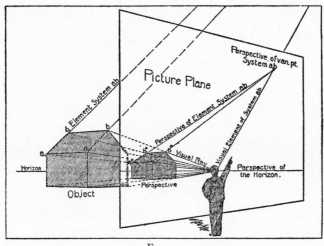

Fig. 13

bird's eye view. The ground plane may be taken above the horizon plane and the resulting view will show the object as though the observer were looking up at it. The picture plane and the horizon plane are known as the *co-ordinate planes of projection* and on them is performed all the work of constructing the perspective view.

Orthographic Projection.—As already stated the perspective view is a conical projection on the picture plane. This conical projection is in practice not found from the actual object in space, but from a plan and an elevation of the object. The plan is essentially a top view and the elevation a front view or sometimes a side view.

A plan is constructed by projecting each point in the object to a horizontal reference plane by lines or projectors which are perpendicular to the horizontal plane. An elevation is constructed by projectors perpendicular to the vertical plane. Such views are known as orthographic or right-line projections in contrast to the conical or perspective projection, and are the

GRAPHIC ARTS

ordinary means of representing objects on paper. Fig. 15 shows a conical and an orthographic projection. Fig. 16 illustrates the construction of a plan and an elevation. Fig. 17 shows the two views as they are represented on paper. Each point in the object, has two projections, both being necessary to locate accurately the relations of the point to the two planes. Thus

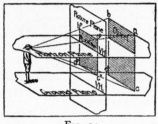

FIG. 14

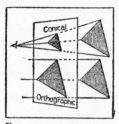

FIG. 15.—COMPARISON OF CONICAL AND ORTHOGRAPHIC PROJECTIONS

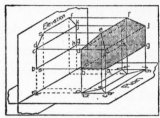

FIG. 16.—CONSTRUCTION OF PLAN AND ELEVATION

the point *a* is above the horizontal reference plane, a distance equal to *am* as indicated in elevation, and in front of the vertical reference plane a distance equal to *an* as shown in plan. The elevation shows vertical distances, the plan shows horizontal distances. The object in space may be above the horizontal plane as in figs. 16 and 17, or it may be below the horizontal plane as in fig. 18. It may be behind or in front of the vertical plane, or it may lie partly behind and partly in front of the vertical plane or partly above and partly below the horizontal plane.

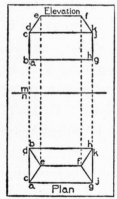

FIG. 17.—PLAN AND ELEVATION, ORTHOGRAPHIC PROJECTIONS

Any point in space may have three different but related projections, a plan or horizontal projection, an elevation or vertical projection, and a conical or perspective projection. This is illustrated in fig. 19 where two points in space *a* and *b* are shown, each with its vertical, its horizontal and its conical projection. The horizontal projection is indicated by an index *h*, the vertical projection by an index *v*, and the perspective projection by an index *p*. The point *a* is shown behind the picture plane and above the horizon plane. The point *b* is shown in front of the picture plane and below the horizon plane. The conical projection or perspective is always on the vertical or picture plane.

Fig. 20 shows the planes of projection with the ground plane indicated by its intersection (VH_1) with the picture plane. The point *a* is shown in space behind the picture plane and below the horizon plane, with its horizontal projection (a^h) and its vertical projection (a^v). The station point is

24

represented by its two orthographic projections just as every point in space. Since it always lies in the horizon plane its horizontal projection, SP^h, must always coincide with the point itself. Its vertical projection will be directly in front of SP^h, on the picture plane as SP^v. SP^v must always lie in the line VH which represents the vertical projection of the horizon plane.

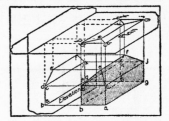

FIG. 18.—CONSTRUCTION OF PLAN AND ELEVATION

Just as a point in space has a horizontal projection and a vertical projection, so the visual ray which passes from the point a to the observer's eye has two projections, one on each plane. Its projection is seen on the horizon plane passing through a^h_1 and SP^h. Its vertical projection is seen on the picture plane passing through a^v and SP^v. The visual ray pierces the picture plane at a^p which is the perspective of the point a (Rule C).

Rule E. The intersection of a visual ray with the picture plane must always lie upon the vertical projection of the visual ray, and must be directly in line with the point where the horizontal projection of the visual ray crosses the horizontal projection (HPP) of the picture plane.

In practice both the picture plane and the horizon plane must be represented on one sheet of paper. One can imagine the picture plane to be revolved about its intersection with the horizon plane in the direction indicated by the arrows s_1 and s_2, fig. 20, until the two planes lie coincident as shown in fig. 21. In this position the group of projections on the picture plane will overlap the group on the horizon plane. To avoid the resulting confusion the two planes can be pulled apart

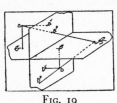

FIG. 19

as shown in fig. 22. After these movements of the planes the horizon plane will still contain all of the horizontal projections, which will remain undisturbed in all aspects of their relations to one another.

HPP is the horizontal projection of the picture plane and is the reference line for all horizontal projections. Similarly the picture plane will contain all of the vertical projections. VH is the vertical projection of the horizon plane, and is the reference line for all vertical projections. VH_1 represents the intersection of the ground plane with the picture plane. The distance between VH and VH_1 shows the height of the observer's eye above the plane on which the object rests.

The two groups of projections are usually represented as in fig. 23. The

25

only relation between the two groups is that the two corresponding ortho-graphic projections of any point as a^h and a^v, or SP^h and SP^v, must always be vertically in line with one another. Horizontal projections show distances back and front. Vertical projections show distances up and down.

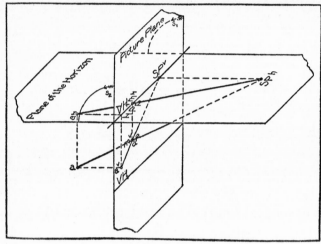

Fig. 20

Distances are never measured between a horizontal and a vertical projection. The relation of a^h to HPP shows the point a to be behind the picture plane. The relation of a^v to VH shows it to be below the plane of the horizon. The

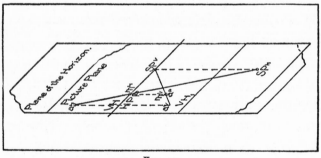

Fig. 21

two projections of the visual ray through the point a are shown (R^h and R^v). By Rule E, the point p can be determined.

Measure Lines.—Fig. 24 shows a rectangular block resting upon the ground plane in plan and elevation. The perspective of each point has been found by Rule E. Connecting these points by straight lines, the perspective of the block is determined. Since the object lies some distance behind the picture plane, as seen by comparing the plane with HPP, the perspective is smaller than the object. Any line which lies in the picture plane will show

26

its true length in the perspective view, and is called a *measure line*. It can be drawn at once to scale and used to determine the dimensions of other parts of the object which do not lie in the picture plane and consequently appear larger or smaller than their real dimensions, according to whether they are in front of or behind it. Any vertical plane if extended will intersect the

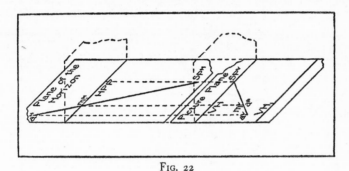

Fɪɢ. 22

picture plane in a vertical line. The intersection will be a measure line on which true vertical dimensions may be scaled. Thus, in fig. 24, the left vertical face of the block can be extended forward until it intersects the picture plane in a measure line on which the distance $a^v m$ will show the true height of the block. The right vertical face if extended will also give a measure line, on which $b^v n$ shows the true height.

The Construction of a Perspective Projection.—Fig. 25 illustrates the fundamental method of constructing a perspective from which all other methods are derived. A plan and elevation are given on the left, an end view on the right. *HPP* determines the picture plane in horizontal projection, *VH* determines the plane of the horizon in vertical projection. *VH*₁ determines the plane of the ground on which the object is to rest. The observer's eye, *SP*, is given in vertical and horizontal projections. The resulting perspective is to show the house with the vertical corner *ae* lying in the picture plane, and with the face *aefb* making an angle of 45° with it. This position is indicated by the diagram, which is a plan of

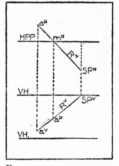

Fɪɢ. 23.—ELEMENTARY PROBLEM IN PERSPECTIVE

the house revolved about a vertical axis until the side *aefb* makes the specified angle of 45° with *HPP*, and placed with the corner *ae* touching *HPP* in accordance with the specification. The point *a* will thus lie both in the picture plane and on the plane of the ground. Its perspective must be at a^p on *VH*₁ and directly under the point *a* in the diagram. As the front corner lies in the

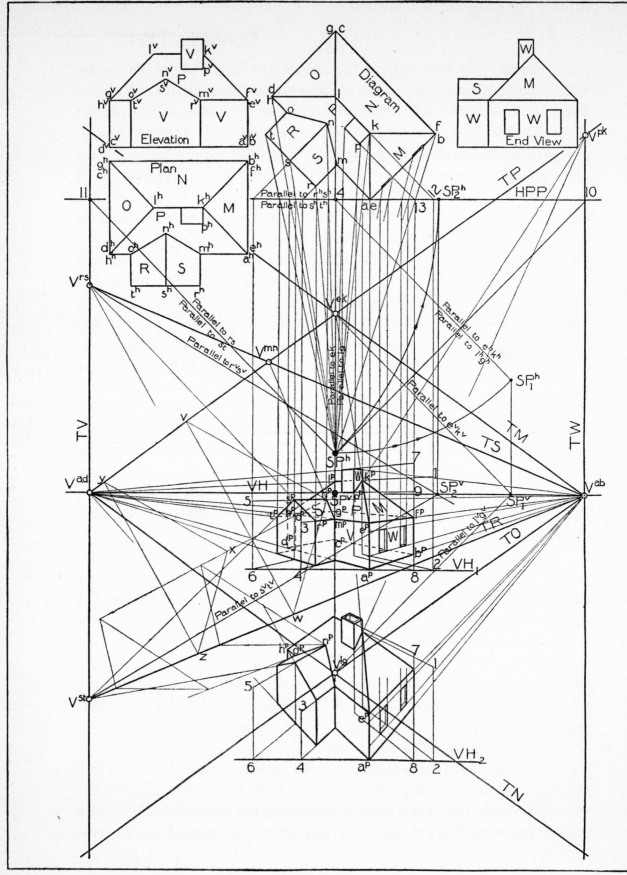

FIG. 25

28

picture plane it will be a measure line and its true height taken from the elevation can be laid off directly from a^p, determining e^p as indicated. Next, by Rules D and E establish the vanishing point for the system of lines parallel to ab, as follows: the horizontal projection of the visual ray will pass through SP^h parallel to ab in the diagram, and will cross HPP at the point 10. Since

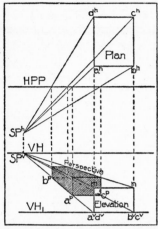

FIG. 24.—MEASURE LINES

ab is a horizontal system the vertical projection of the visual ray will pass through SP^v and coincide with VH. The desired vanishing point must be on VH directly below 10, at V^{ab}.

Similarly the vanishing point for the horizontal system parallel to ad will be found on VH at V^{ad}. The upper and lower edges of the right face run from e^p and a^p respectively and vanish at V^{ab}. The observer sees the rear edge of the right face projected on the picture plane directly below the point where a visual ray from fb in the diagram crosses HPP. As the perspective of a vertical line upon a vertical picture plane is always a vertical line, the rear edge will be found at $b^p f^p$. In a similar way the upper and lower edges of the left face vanish at V^{ad}, and the rear edge of this face is found at $d^p h^p$. The rectangular portion of the house is completed by lines running from b^p and f^p vanishing at V^{ad}, and from d^p and h^p vanishing at V^{ab}, establishing by their intersections c^p and g^p.

To find the roof of the main house, extend the ridge (lk) in the diagram until it intersects HPP in the point 12. Imagine a vertical plane to pass through the ridge. It will intersect the picture plane in a vertical line dropped from the point 12. This will be a measure line for the ridge and the true height of the ridge above the ground, 2–1, taken from the elevation, can be laid off on it. A horizontal line through l vanishing at V^{ad} must contain the ridge which will be located on this line at $k^p l^p$ directly below the points in which visual rays through the extremities of the ridge in the diagram, intersect HPP. From k^p, lines to e^p and f^p respectively, and from l^p, lines to h^p and g^p respectively will complete the roof.

The chimney can be located in a similar manner. Extend the front face through p in the diagram until it intersects HPP in 13. The plane of this face will intersect the picture plane in the vertical line dropped from 13, which will be a measure line for this face. Lay off on this measure line the true height of the top of the chimney 8–7, and the true height of the bottom line of the front face, 8–9. Through 7 and 9 lines vanishing at V^{ad} will contain the top and bottom edges of the front face which will be located vertically below the points where visual rays from the front face of the chimney in the diagram intersect HPP. The construction of the rest of the chimney is obvious from the drawing.

A measure line for the right vertical face of the porch is found by extending this face in the diagram until it intersects HPP and dropping a vertical 3–4. On this vertical shows the true height front face, 8–9. Through 7 and 9 lines vanishing at V^{ad} will contain the upper and lower edges of the right hand face. The points r^p and m^p can be located by visual rays drawn through r and m on the diagram. 5–6 shows the true height of the ridge of the porch laid off on the measure line for the ridge. A line through 5 vanishing at V^{ab} will contain the ridge. Points s^p and n^p on this ridge can be located by visual rays through s and n in the diagram. The construction of the remainder of the porch can be readily understood from the drawing.

The heights of the tops and bottoms of the windows can be taken directly from the end view and laid off on $a^p e^p$ which is the measure line for the right hand face of the main house. Horizontal lines through these heights will establish the top and bottom lines of the windows. The vertical sides can be located vertically below where visual rays from the windows in the diagram cross HPP. In this way the entire perspective can be completed.

Vanishing Points of Oblique Lines.—The vanishing points for the inclined lines in the roof ek, kf, lg, lh, etc., are not absolutely necessary for the construction of the perspective. The method of determining them, however, should be understood as in some problems the vanishing points of oblique lines form an important part of the solution. The construction for their determination is shown on fig. 25.

First consider ek. A line drawn through the station point parallel to ek will establish the vanishing point by its intersection with the picture plane (Rule D). The horizontal projection of such a line will pass through SP^h parallel to ek in diagram, and will cross HPP at 14. The vanishing point will be vertically in line with 14 and on the vertical projection of the line through SP^v parallel to ek (Rule E). But since the diagram containing ek has been revolved from the original position of the given plan, no vertical projection is given which corresponds to the revolved direction of ek. The line ek must therefore be revolved back into its original direction, i.e., parallel to $e^h k^h$ in

ILLUSTRATIONS OF PERSPECTIVE

1. Method of locating a vanishing point
2. Apparent convergence of parallel lines
3. Apparent vanishing point of parallel lines
4. Element at centre used to locate vanishing point
5. Method of locating vanishing trace

6. Appearance of object contrasted with reality
7. Plane at centre used to locate vanishing trace
8. Apparent diminution in size with increasing distance
9. Location of vanishing point

PLATE II

PERSPECTIVE

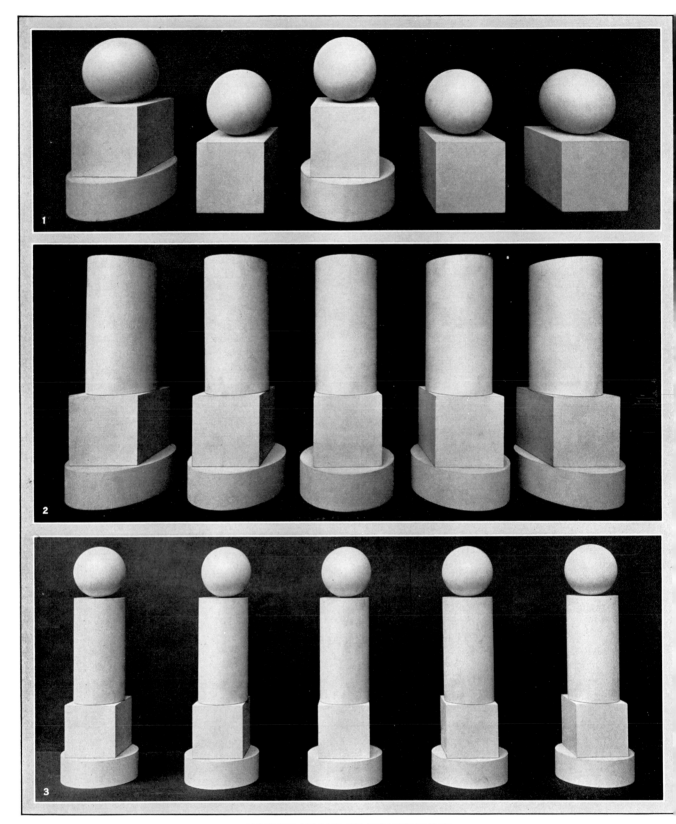

ILLUSTRATIONS OF PERSPECTIVE

1. Example of apparent distortion
2. Example of apparent distortion
3. Effect of increased distance between object and picture plane

the given plan, in order that the given vertical projection $e^v k^v$ may be used to establish its vanishing point. As the vanishing point must lie in the vertical through 14, the vanishing point will not be disturbed if the vertical line through 14 is used as the axis about which the revolution takes place. During the revolution, the horizontal projection of any point in the line, as SP^h, will describe a circle with the point 14 as its centre. The vertical projection, SP^v, of the same point in the line, will move in a horizontal path along VH, and at any instant during the revolution will be found directly under SP^h. The revolution will be continued until the horizontal projection of the line is parallel to $e^h k^h$ in the given plane. The line will now be in its original direction, SP^h will have moved to SP_1^h, SP^v will have moved to SP_1^v, and the given elevation $e^v k^v$ can be drawn through SP_1^v, determining by its intersection with the vertical through 14, the desired vanishing point V^{ek}. Since the line ek slopes upward as it recedes, V^{ek} is found to be above VH (Rule A).

In a similar manner the vanishing point for lg can be found. The line through SP^h parallel to lg coincides with the one parallel to ek. This is swung back about a vertical axis through 14 until parallel to $l^h g^h$, in which position it will coincide with the line parallel to $e^h k^h$, and SP^h will have revolved to SP_1^h, SP_1^v will be on VH directly below SP_1^h and a line parallel to the given elevation $l^v g^v$, drawn through SP_1^v will, by its intersection with the vertical through 14, determine V^{lg}. Since the line lg slopes downward as it recedes, its vanishing point is found below the horizon (Rule A).

To find the vanishing point for rs draw a line parallel to rs, in the diagram, through SP^h, crossing HPP at 11. V^{rs} will be found somewhere on a vertical through 11. Swing the line about a vertical axis through 11 until parallel with $r^h s^h$ in the given plan. SP^h will revolve to SP_2^h and SP_2^v will be found on VH vertically in line. Through SP_2^v draw a line parallel to $r^v s^v$ in the given elevation which will determine by its intersection with the vertical through 11, the vanishing point rs. This will be found above VH as rs vanishes upward. A similar series of steps will determine the vanishing point for st at V^{st} below the horizon.

Vanishing Traces.—With the vanishing points that have now been determined it is possible to locate a vanishing trace for each plane in the object. The roof planes have been lettered on the diagram. The vanishing trace for the plane M will be a line lettered TM containing V^{ab} and V^{ek} (Axiom 4). Similarly TO, the vanishing trace of the roof plane O, must contain V^{ab}

and V^{lg}. TN must contain V^{ad} and V^{lg}, TP must contain V^{ad} and V^{ek}, TS will pass through V^{ab} and V^{rs}, and TR will pass through V^{ab} and V^{st}. The vanishing trace of a vertical plane must always be a vertical line and can therefore be determined by a single vanishing point. TW will be a vertical line through V^{ab} and TV a vertical line through V^{ad}. A vanishing trace is thus found for each plane in the object and, by virtue of Axiom 5, the vanishing points for the remaining oblique systems can now be located. Thus mn being the intersection of the planes S and P will have its vanishing point, V^{mn}, at the intersection of TS and TP. Similarly pk, the intersection of the right hand face of the chimney with the roof plane P will have its vanishing point at the intersection of TW and TP.

V^{no} must be situated at the intersection of TP and TR, but these two vanishing traces do not intersect within the limits of the paper. A line may be drawn through n^p to meet TP and TR at their intersection in the following manner. Draw any triangle as n^pvw with its apex at n^p and its base, vw, stretching between TR and TP. Draw any other triangles as xyz with its sides respectively parallel to n^pvw and its base vz stretching between TR and TP. A line from n^p through x will meet TR and TP at their intersection.

Lines Parallel to the Picture Plane.—It has been stated that the perspectives of vertical lines on a vertical plane are always vertical and not convergent. The reason for this follows directly from Rule D. If a vertical line is drawn through the observer's eye it cannot pierce a vertical picture plane within finite limits. The perspective of the vanishing point of such a system will theoretically be vertically over SP^v at an infinite distance. As the perspectives of all vertical lines must meet at the perspective of their vanishing point they cannot meet within a finite distance and must be drawn parallel and vertical. The parallel vertical lines drawn in perspective are themselves, however, subject to the laws of appearance, as are all lines in space, and, though actually drawn vertical, will appear to the observer to converge in just the right degree as they recede in the picture from his eye. This is true not only of vertical lines but of all lines which are parallel to the picture plane; .i.e, all lines whose projections in the diagram are parallel to HPP. From this truth three additional and very useful axioms may be deduced.

Axiom 6. Lines in space which are parallel to the picture plane will have their perspectives drawn parallel to one another and not convergent.

PERSPECTIVE

Axiom 7. Any line parallel to the picture plane must have its perspective drawn parallel to the vanishing trace of every plane in which it lies.

Axiom 8. If the line in which two planes intersect is parallel to the picture plane, the vanishing traces of the two planes must be parallel to one another.

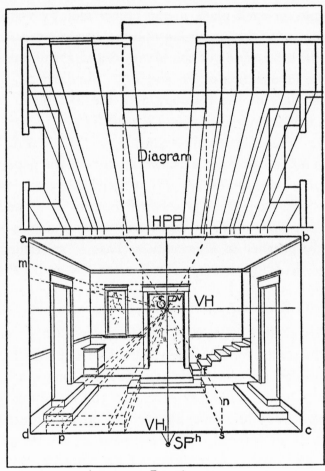

Fig. 26

These axioms are exemplified in the vertical lines in the drawing and also in the lines *kf* and *lh* whose projections in the diagram show them to be parallel to the picture plane. *kf* being the intersection of *M* and *N*, *TM* and *TN* should be parallel to one another (Axiom 8) as they are found to be, and *kf* should be drawn parallel to *TM* and *TN* (Axiom 7). Similarly *lh* is drawn parallel to *TO* and *TP*, and these two vanishing traces are parallel to one another.

Vanishing Point Diagram.—The more or less geometrical figure composed of the vanishing traces of the planes, the vanishing points of the lines,

33

VH, *HPP*, and the projections of the station point form the vanishing point diagram. This vanishing point diagram is quite independent of the particular location of the revolved plan, provided the directions of the lines in the revolved plan are not changed. It would serve to determine the perspective of the house were it placed to the right or the left of its present position, or it might be brought forward or moved backward in relation to the picture plane. It might also rest on a ground plane higher or lower than the one used, provided always that the lines in the object do not change their direction. The vanishing point diagram would therefore serve for a number of similar objects placed at different positions but always having the same angular relation to the co-ordinate planes. As an illustration of this a second perspective projection has been drawn in Plate III on a ground plane represented by VH_2 some distance below VH_1. The same vanishing point diagram serves for both perspectives. Should, however, the angular relation between the diagram and the picture plane be changed it would be necessary to construct a new vanishing point diagram.

Parallel Perspective.—Sometimes instead of the diagram being turned with its principal horizontal lines oblique to the picture, it is placed with one of its principal systems of horizontal lines parallel and the other perpendicular to the picture plane, as in fig. 26. The result is often referred to as a *parallel* perspective and is frequently used in showing interior views. The picture plane may be taken coincident with the nearest wall of the room. The horizontal system perpendicular to the picture plane will have its vanishing point coincident with SP^v (Rule D). The horizontal system parallel to the picture plane will, in perspective, show as true horizontal lines (Axioms 6 and 7). This is simply a special case under the general method already explained, and involves no new principles. The vertical and horizontal edges of the room, *ab*, *bc*, *cd* and *da* being lines in the picture plane will be measure lines and true lengths can be laid off on them directly, as *dm* the height of the door and *dp* the projection of the lower step from the wall; or any line as *ef* can be extended forward into the picture plane where it will show its true height *sn*, above the ground plane.

CURVES

As MUST BE EVIDENT from the foregoing discussion, linear perspective is essentially a science of straight lines. When curves appear in the plan or elevation their perspectives are usually constructed by reference to straight

AN ARCHITECTURAL DRAWING IN AERIAL PERSPECTIVE

A rendering by Claude Bragdon showing an interesting use of aerial perspective

A Birdseye View of the NEW YORK CENTRAL STATION AT ROCHESTER, New York

CLAUDE BRAGDON AND THE NEW YORK CENTRAL ENGINEERING DEPARTMENT, ASSOCIATE ARCHITECTS

BY COURTESY OF (1, 2) RIJKS ETHNOGRAPHISCH MUSEUM, LEYDEN, (4) KOLONIAAL INSTITUUT, AMSTERDAM, (3) ROUFFAER AND JUYNBOLL, FROM "DE BATIKKUNST IN NEDER-LANDSCH-INDIE," (N. V. A. OOSTHOEK UITGAVE MIJ)

SCULPTURED ORIGINALS OF BATIK DESIGNS

1–2. Figures 1 and 2 show side and front views of the goddess Prajnap-aramita, the Buddhist personification of supreme wisdom, with a lotus resting behind her left shoulder. The book containing the quintessence of Buddhist wisdom is in her hands

3. Detail of a design taken from a figure of a stone Ganeśa, showing its similarity to Javanese batik designs

4. The back of a seated Ganeśa, the god of wisdom and justice in Indian mythology

lines. If the curve is of regular form it can be enclosed in a polygon, usually a rectangle, the perspective of the rectangle found and the curve then constructed within the perspective rectangle. Fig. 27 shows a curve so enclosed, the perspective of which has been found. The diagonals of the perspective rectangle locate its centre. Lines drawn through the centre respectively parallel to the adjacent sides give by their intersections with the sides, points at which the curve is tangent. The sides of the rectangle give the directions of the curve at the points of tangency. Fig. 28 is another illustration of curves of regular form

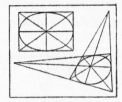

Fig. 27

constructed in perspective. If the curve is not regular in form the enclosing rectangle can be subdivided into smaller rectangles, as shown in fig. 29, as a further aid to locating the curve.

Although methods can be devised for constructing the exact perspective of any curved object, they are complex and seldom used in practice. A few important points are usually located and the outline sketched in freehand, if in a position corresponding to that in the picture.

Apparent Distortion.—It is evident from the statement in connection with Plate I., fig. 3 that an object in space is exactly represented by its perspective prospective projection, or in other words, no distortion or exaggeration can exist in correctly constructed perspective projection.

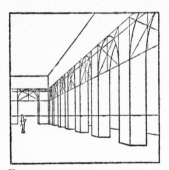

Fig. 28.—Semi-circles enclosed in rectangles

Notwithstanding this fact, very disagreeable effects and very apparent distortions are often noticed in perspective projections, the accuracy of which cannot be questioned. A few examples will suffice to show what is meant. Plate II., fig. 1, is a true perspective. It is supposed to represent a number of perfect spheres of equal size. The view as seen does not convey this impression. A sphere in space always appears as a perfect circle and never as the oval-shaped areas seen near the edges of the photograph. Again, Plate II., fig. 2, is a correct perspective of five circular cylinders all having the same diameter. The ones farthest to the right or left should appear smaller than the nearest one at the centre. In the photograph just the opposite is true and the farther from the eye the larger they appear. The explanation of these seeming anomalies is as follows: Before any perspective projection is constructed the position of the observer's eye

35

is definitely fixed, and, in order that the perspective shall represent the view in space, the observer must close one eye and place the other exactly in the predetermined position. It is seldom that an observer looks at a drawing with one eye only, or places either eye even approximately in the correct relation to the drawing. This limitation of a perspective view and the failure to understand it is the cause of all apparent distortion. In Plate II., figs.

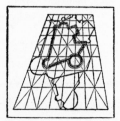

FIG. 29.—IRREGULAR CURVES REFERRED TO RECTANGLES

1 and 2, the station point has purposely been chosen so close to the paper that it is impossible for the observer to see the view from the correct position. Should either of these views be enlarged so that the distance from the paper to the station point became considerably greater, and should the observer examine the enlarged view with one eye only, placed exactly at the station point, the elliptical projections of the outside spheres would be foreshortened by the obliquity of his line of vision and would appear as perfect circles, representing to him perfect spheres. The cylinders would also appear in their proper relations.

When the eye is not in its proper position all parts of the drawing show more or less distortion. This is most noticeable in regular curved forms or in the human figure, especially when these are located near the edges of the drawing. The disagreeable effects are much more pronounced when the station point is taken too near the picture plane. Thus the apparent distortion seen in a correctly constructed perspective is due, not to inaccuracies in the perspective theory, but to an unwise choice in the station point, a faulty arrangement of the view, and the failure of the observer to recognize the limitations of a perspective projection. In making a perspective, the station point should always be chosen in such a position that the observer will naturally place his eyes approximately at the chosen point when viewing the drawing. An arbitrary rule sometimes given is to assume the station point directly in front of the centre of the drawing, at the apex of an equilateral triangle the base of which just covers the width of the view. The station point may be chosen farther away than this without much danger but not nearer, and never nearer than eight or ten inches. Curved forms of regular shape and human figures or animals should be kept as near the centre of the drawing as possible. Plate II., fig. 3, shows a view of the same cylinders and spheres seen in the two previous figures but with the station point much farther from the picture plane. The result is a vast improvement in the view obtained, though the spheres on the outskirts of the picture still appear slightly elliptical. After all precautions have been taken, if disagreeable effects still persist in the drawing it is customary to introduce certain so-called corrections such as making the perspective of the spheres in Plate II., fig. 1, all perfect circles. These are really not corrections but actual transgressions of the rules of perspective which alter the view so that it will not be exactly correct at any point, yet it may not be noticeably disagreeable from any position likely to be taken by the observer.

BINOCULAR PERSPECTIVE

FINALLY, mention should be made of the most perfect form of perspective representation, the binocular. When a single perspective drawing is viewed with both eyes the image on the retina of each eye is practically the same. When, however, an object in space is viewed with both eyes two slightly different images are received, one by the right and one by the left eye. It is the fusion of these different views which gives to the observer the impression of relief or solidity.

In binocular perspective two slightly different views are made of the same scene from two slightly different points of view some $2\frac{3}{4}$ in. apart, to correspond with the views seen by the two eyes. This is most easily done with a camera having two lenses, known as a stereoscopic camera. The two views are then presented to the observer in such a way that the right eye sees only the view taken by the right-hand lens and the left eye only the view taken by the left-hand lens. An instrument designed for showing these double pictures is called a stereoscope, and gives a result that is startling in its realistic reproduction of distance and relief.

AQUATINT

AQUATINT, a variety of etching (q.v.) in which effects are obtained by the action of acid through a porous ground of sand or some powdered resinous substance (Lat. *aqua*, water, and *tincta*, dyed). The plate is first covered with a ground over which the resinous powder or sand is evenly dusted by some mechanical process, the portions of the plate which are to appear white when printed being covered with stopping-out varnish. The plate is then covered with the mordant which bites into the interstices between the minute particles and produces a granulated surface. The process is repeated and the different tones obtained by the varied depths to which the different portions of the plate are bitten. In theory therefore aquatint is not capable of producing even graduations of tint, but may be compared in effect to a contour map where each particular elevation is indicated by a flat tint ending abruptly. In skilful hands, however, the series of bitings can be so manipulated as to make these contours almost invisible; the process can be used in conjunction with etching, drypoint, mezzotint and crayon.

The invention of aquatint is generally credited to Jean Baptiste Le Prince (1734–81), but there seems little doubt that some form of it was known and used almost 100 years earlier. A certain Jan van de Velde seems to have combined aquatint with roulette work in some of his portraits about 1658. In the hands of F. Janinet, P. L. Debucourt and other French artists of the end of the 18th century the process was brought to a technical perfection which has never been surpassed. It was used by them, with extraordinary skill and success, as a vehicle for printing in colour. In England in the last quarter of the 18th century and the first half of the 19th century the method was used by such artists as Paul Sandby, Thomas Malton, the Daniells, R. Pollard, J. C. Stadler for reproducing water-colour drawings. English aquatints were not printed in colours, but were usually coloured by hand. The process during the latter part of the 19th century fell into disuse but was revived and successfully employed by Sir Frank Short, Theodore Roussel, Oliver Hall, W. Lee Hankey, W. P. Robins and others. (*See* Etching, page 133.)

BATIK

Batik, a Javanese word meaning wax painting—the application of a wax "resist" to various materials which are afterwards dyed, and certain portions of which are protected by the wax so that they do not absorb the dye, leaving

FROM ROUFFAER AND JUYNBOLL, "DE BATIKKUNST IN NEDERLANDSCH-INDIE," (N.V.A. OOSTHOEK UITGAVE MIJ)

NATIVE BATIK MOTIFS

Top row: 1 (left). Pattern and colouring of design made in Surakarta, central Java. 2. Colouring and design from Sumenep, Madura

Middle row: 1 (left). Pattern in red from Lasem, on the northern coast of Java. 2. (Centre). Two patterns from Kain Kapala, coast region of Java. 3. Blue batik made in Indramaju, Java

Lower row: Three designs from Surabaya, Djokjakarta and Batavia, Java

BATIK HANGING, "THE LAND OF PLENTY"

An example of modern batik executed with the brush by Arthur Crisp on heavy silk. The delicate design, though original, shows traces of Eastern influence

as a result a pattern or design on them. The resist is usually composed of bees-wax, paraffin and sometimes a little resin, which makes it adhere more securely to the material. This resist is applied hot so that it flows easily and sinks into the material, protecting from the dye that part which it covers.

History and Uses in Java.—Little is known of the origin of this art; it is, like many others, lost in antiquity. Some believe that it originated in China, while others claim that it is a natural outgrowth of the methods employed for centuries in India. Probably the latter is more nearly correct. There have been found ruins of temples in Java about 1,200 years old, among

FIG. 30.—NATIVE JAVANESE DANCERS, DRESSED IN COSTUMES OF BATIK, PERFORMING AN ANCIENT DANCE

which were fragments of stone figures wearing garments similar to those worn to-day by the natives and decorated with similar patterns, and it is likely that these same designs have been handed down for centuries. Batik is used almost entirely throughout Indonesia for the decoration of the very simple clothing which the people wear. This clothing consists, in the main, of only four pieces:—

(1)   The *Sarong*, a strip of cloth from 9 to 14 ft. long by about $3\frac{1}{2}$ ft. wide, which is worn twisted about the body in various ways. (*See* fig. 33.)

(2)   The *Slendang*, a piece of cloth about 9 ft. long and only 18 in. wide, which may be twisted about the head or used by the women for carrying their babies or other burdens on their backs.

(3)   The *Kemban*, a narrow girdle or band, worn only on occasion by the women, twisted tightly about their waists or breasts.

(4)   The *Sarong Kapala*, a square piece of material not unlike a large bandanna handkerchief, worn by the men, twisted about their heads like a turban in some particular way which designates the locality from which the wearer comes and his station in life. After this piece has been arranged on

39

the head it is removed and starched on the inside so that it will hold its shape.

Each of these pieces is decorated with a design and in colours which indicate the part of the country from which it comes. The designs and colours are all similar, but, on the other hand, they have very definite variations. In all parts of the country, however, there are in use two types of sarong; the usual type, decorated with an all-over pattern, and the dress type, worn on ceremonial occasions. The latter is enhanced by the addition of a wide band,

FIGS. 31, 32.—JAVANESE WOMEN IN DRESS COSTUME OF BATIK

across one end, more ornately decorative than the body of the piece, and also by a surrounding border made up of a number of various-sized smaller borders of different widths, making a beautiful frame similar to that seen on oriental rugs. In all of the sections the designs are based upon the same origin and consist of conventionalized objects of nature, such as flowers, butterflies, birds, fruits, foliage, cuttlefish and shells and occasionally of a conventionalized Malay kris or knife. These designs are passed from generation to generation and taught by each mother to her daughter, for it is the women who draw them while the men do the dyeing. (*See* figs. 40 and 41.)

Javanese Practice.—In Java batik is done, as a rule, upon cotton cloth or sometimes silk. Whatever the material, it is first carefully prepared by several washings in hot water, alternating with steepings in coconut oil or castor oil (fig. 35). These washings are done in water containing an alkali,

40

such as a weak solution of soda or the ashes of burnt rice stalks, and after each washing, before it is steeped in the oil, it is dried in the sun until it finally assumes the soft creamy tone so beautiful in the finer pieces. After the washing process it is hemmed and then starched or sized in a solution of rice water, again dried in the sun and then rolled up into a loose roll, placed on a board and gently pounded with a hammer or rolled with a wooden roller until it becomes soft and pliable, when it is ready to be suspended upon a frame. Sometimes the artists block in the designs with charcoal (*see* fig.

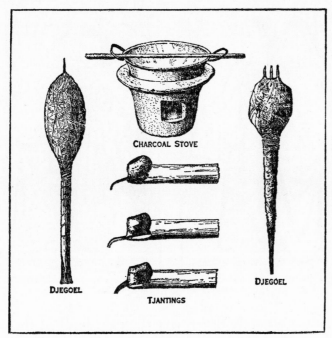

CHARCOAL STOVE

DJEGOEL

DJEGOEL

TJANTINGS

Fig. 34.—NATIVE IMPLEMENTS USED IN MAKING BATIKS
The wax is melted on the charcoal stove and applied to the lines of the design with various types of tjantings, which will be noted as having different kinds of spouts. The larger areas are covered by the use of djegoel, two types of which are shown

39), but many of them are so sure in their art that they are capable of drawing the intricately involved patterns without this aid.

Instruments.—The *tjanting* is the instrument used for applying the wax. It is a small copper cup, from the bottom of one side of which curves outward and downward a delicate spout or capillary tube, and from the opposite side of which projects a bamboo handle, cut in such a way that a spur follows the lower line of the cup. These tjantings are of various forms: some have large spouts and some very slender ones; some, called *penembok*, have wide flat spouts, while others may have as many as two, three, four or even six, all springing from the same cup, so that it is possible to draw with them, simultaneously, a number of parallel lines. Besides the tjanting, there is a primitive instrument called the *djegoel*, which is simply a stick of wood with a wad of cotton attached to the end, forming a sort of crude brush which is used for filling in the large areas with wax. (*See* fig. 34.)

Native Practice.—Seated on the ground, the material hanging over a frame before her (fig. 40), the artist covers that part of the design which is to remain the natural colour of the material with a wax consisting of about six parts animal fat to one part resin and to which is sometimes added one

FIG. 33.—NATIVE WOMAN SHOWING METHOD OF TWISTING SARONG ABOUT THE BODY

FIG. 35.—WASHING THE CLOTH AS A PRELIMINARY TO BLEACHING AND DRYING IT IN THE SUN

part of pure bees-wax and a little of the old wax which, owing to carbonization and former contact with the indigo dye, has become dark, making the whole resist more easily seen upon the fabric. When this first step is finished the piece must be turned over and carefully waxed on the back so that there is no possibility of the dye entering the fabric from that side. It is then immersed in cold water, which thoroughly hardens and solidifies the wax, so that it is ready to enter the dye which has been prepared for it. When it has been satisfactorily dyed, the wax is removed and the piece rewaxed, leaving exposed other parts which are to be dyed a different colour.

In sharp contrast to the East Indian, and even more so to modern European methods, stands this "Javanese practice" of carefully waxing the back of the fabric and of removing the wax and replacing it in a different section of the design each time a new colour is to be dyed. In Europe and America the custom is to dye one colour over another, removing the wax only when this becomes impossible. It is, as has been said, the native cus-

PLATE II

BATIK

FROM ROUFFAER AND JUYNBALL, "DE BATIKKUNST IN NEDERLANDSCH INDIE" (N. V. A. OOSTHOEK UITGAVE MIJ)

THE SIX STAGES IN THE PREPARATION OF BATIK

1. The fabric after the first application of wax, before being dyed
2. The fabric dyed for the first time
3. The wax removed, showing the first stage of the pattern

4. The fabric after the second application of wax
5. The fabric dyed a second time
6. The wax removed and the design completed

LITHOGRAPHS OF THE 19TH AND 20TH CENTURIES

1. "The Boxers," printed between 1817 and 1821, by Théodore (Jean Louis André) Géricault (1791–1823), French
2. "Christ as a Child in the Temple," 1852, by Adolf von Menzel (1815–1905), German
3. "The Thames," by James A. McNeill Whistler (1834–1903), American
4. "Souvenir de Sainte-Pélagie," by Honoré Daumier (1808–79), French
5. "Il se composa une armée," by Marius A. J. Bauer (1864–   ), Dutch. This is one of a series of illustrations for *La Légende de Saint Julien l'Hospitalier*, by Flaubert
6. "Ils grognaient, et le suivaient toujours," 1836, by Denis Auguste Marie Raffet (1804–60), French
7. "Rome, the Café Greco," 1913, by John Copley (1875–   ), English

tom to confine themselves almost entirely to cotton and silk, while in the West batik is also done upon woollens, velvets, ivory, straw or any other material which can be stained with dye. Sometimes batik is employed upon metal or wood, the exposed surface of which is etched away with acid, giving the effect of low relief carving.

The dyes used by the natives were originally, without doubt, vegetable, but nowadays they are making use of some of the anilines brought to them from Holland. Indigo provides blue, and the other colours, such as red from madder and yellow from the bark of mangosteen, are typical. Secondary colours are produced, at times, by dyeing one of these colours over another, and black is produced by the dyeing of brown over the indigo-blue; the range of colours, however, is not very great, and the native is far more interested in the intricacy of the design than in the delicacy of colour.

Figs. 36, 37.—Laying out cloth for sun-bleaching and pounding the cloth to soften it

Tjap Printing.—Although this is not true batik and is looked down upon by the natives themselves, it is a similar process, and one with which beautiful results have been obtained. There is little doubt that the method originated in Madras, where it has at any rate been used extensively since the 15th century.

A *tjap* is a wooden block which has had set into the end of the grain small copper strips, similar to the *cloissons* which divide the different enamel colours in the well known *cloisonné* of China and Japan. These strips are carefully bent with tiny pliers until they assume the desired curves and are then fastened into the wood block. For the application of the wax, the tjaps are made in pairs, one for each side of the material. They are simple to use, for the process consists of dipping the block into the molten wax (which, in this case, must be somewhat stiffer than that used for true batik, and made of resin, paraffin and varnish gums) touching the block to a pad to remove the excess wax, and then printing the wax on to the material, after which the process is repeated for the back and the dyeing is proceeded with exactly as in the case of real batik.

Tjap printing is not considered equal to batik, but as the tjaps must be made in pairs so as to correspond perfectly in the printing of the front and

43

back of the fabric, and as the making of the tjaps is, in itself, a most exacting and delicate craftsmanship, the work must not be neglected by the student, who should realize that sometimes really good specimens of tjap printing are fully as valuable as batiks.

European History and Uses.—Batik was introduced into Europe by the Dutch, who, returning from Java, described the beautiful costumes of the natives. It was lectured about, and in due time some specimens were brought home by travellers, but very little attention was paid to them as

FROM JASPER, "DE INLANDSCHE KUNSTNIJVERHEIT IN NEDERLANDSCHE INDIE"
FIG. 38.—NATIVES MAKING BLOCKS FOR USE IN TJAP PRINTING

FIG. 39.—NATIVE DRAWING THE DESIGN WHEN THE BORDER HAS BEEN DYED

works of art or to the method of execution pursued. Sporadic interest did occur, but when the Dutch acquired the islands, an industry was started in the printing of imitation batiks for sale and trade with the natives. This had an ill effect, as many people did not understand the difference between these printed atrocities and the beautiful creations of the natives, and it was not until the latter part of the 19th century that the great strides made in the production of dyes led artists to experiment with them as a medium and to the revival of this 2,000-year-old art.

Some batik in Europe and America is executed like that in Java, for the purpose of wearing apparel, but the length of time involved in producing these fabrics makes it impossible to compete with the beautifully printed and woven fabrics done by machinery and therefore the art has been driven a step higher. Artists found that they could not spend the time to design and execute a batik gown unless they could first find patrons willing to spend large sums of money for their work; therefore, the application of this art to the more permanent elements of decoration such as wall hangings,

44

lamp shades, table runners or throws, etc., for which comparatively higher prices could be asked, was necessary. The first artists who awoke to the possibilities of this medium of expression were those in Holland; then followed such artists as Arthur Crisp, Pieter Mijer, Bertrand Hartmann and Ethelyn Stewart in America, who developed batik to a higher standard.

These artists, equipped with an almost unlimited range of colour, produced by modern dyes, have created designs of a beauty never before realized. Improved instruments have also aided them in obtaining good results. For instance, they now use heavier cups for the tjantings, so that the heat can be held longer, and tapering spouts which allow the wax to stay hot until it reaches the tip. These spouts extend about half way up into the cups so that the sediment sinks to the bottom and does not clog them. The technique of the brush, which was never properly developed in Java, has been borrowed from Japan and has given its fluent vigour to the lines of these modern artists. The dyes are not only more varied, but infinitely clearer and purer in colour, and the removal of the wax by gasolene has facilitated the cleaning process. Not only is the art itself undergoing improvement; the materials upon which it is executed are becoming, due to modern machinery, more and more beautiful in their varied textures. And so batik has come to be thought of as an art comparable to painting in oils or water colours or to drawing with pastels, with the lithographic crayon or the etching point. In comparison with other arts batik has some limitations, but it has also many well-defined advantages over the other graphic arts and should, without doubt, eventually take its place among them. Swift, vigorous sketches can be executed with it. An utmost delicacy of colour is obtainable, and flat areas of rich tone as well as subtle variations of mottling and "crackling" can be had when required. Besides all these and many similar advantages, there is the possibility of the feel of material, the creation of that texture which not only appeals to the eye but to the sense of touch as well. (*See* TECHNIQUE IN ART, page 157.)

Modern Technique and Practice.—Modern technique varies only a little from that which has been practised in Java for centuries, the chief difference being that the Western artist prefers as a rule to do the application of wax on a horizontal or only slightly inclined table rather than on the rack which is preferred in Java. The design is generally sketched in pencil on the material, though some artists trust their ability sufficiently to do it direct with the wax itself. The application of wax is done with an improved type of tjanting or with a brush which may be pointed or wedge-shaped. The brush is usually a good type of water-colour brush made of tapered hairs, because it is necessary constantly to keep a large amount of wax in it, in order to maintain the heat that the wax may flow freely, and yet a fine point is necessary. It has become the practice to dip the brush in wax, touching it very gently to the edge of the pan so as to remove only a little, and then to take a razor blade or sharp knife and carefully trim it to a point. This practice, however, does not always produce a brush capable of the best work, especially where a line of variable width is desired, for when it is allowed to rest a little more heavily while painting in order to produce a broader line, the short trimmed hairs are sure to spread unevenly. A different type of brush, preferred by some artists, is one with a wedge-shaped arrangement of hairs. This brush will, when held properly, produce a very fine line, one that can be made broader by the simple turning of the brush in the fingers. Of course, it has the disadvantage that in drawing a fine sharp curve one must learn how to twist it in the fingers in just the right way to keep the line uniform. When a brush is first put in the hot wax the bristles spread into a great bunch and it takes a few moments' manipulation to slowly press the air and moisture out so that it will resume its natural form. This process should be done slowly and with care, as it determines the form the brush will take in future use. One should always avoid touching a brush to the bottom of the pan, or for any longer than a second to the edge of the pan, as the metal is so hot that it will burn and curl up the hairs.

Cleaning.—The modern tjanting is so well made that one does not need to exercise the precautions that used to be required in the care of the more fragile native instruments. When it becomes clogged through impurities in the wax, a fine wire, such as can be obtained on a spool at any hardware store, will quickly remove the dirt, though care should be taken in inserting the wire at the point of the spout as it is likely to cause rough edges, which may catch in the fabric and cause an unpleasant stuttering of line or even an upsetting of the tjanting, which might destroy many days' work.

Use of Tjanting.—In using the tjanting one must, first of all, take the utmost precaution to see that no wax clings to the outside of the cup after it has been dipped in the wax pot. The usual method is to keep in the left hand a small bit of cloth or cotton waste with which the cup is gently wiped off over the wax pot each time it is filled. Another method which has worked out satisfactorily is the scraping of the bottom of the cup with a small frag-

GOTHIC BATIK HANGING

Executed on woollen cloth after a 13th century tapestry design representing King Arthur. This is a fine example of the direct technique of Miss Ethelyn Stewart, as shown in the treatment of the high-lights of the robes and the delicate but vigorous architectural ornamentation

ment of cardboard which has been torn or cut into a square form. Some artists use for this purpose old laundry shirt boards, the backing to blocks of paper, etc. This same cardboard may be used to advantage in taking another precaution. It is often well to cover the material between the wax pot and the part of the design being worked on with two or three pieces so that in case of a spill, due to the jogging of one's elbow, they will protect the fabric. In using the tjanting one should hold the hand with the back up and allow it to slide on the nails of the small and third fingers, if such support

FIG. 40.—JAVANESE WOMEN, AS A RULE, APPLY THE WAX. IT WILL BE NOTED THAT, CONTRARY TO THE EUROPEAN PRACTICE, THE FABRIC IS HUNG OVER A RACK, AS SHOWN HERE

is necessary. The tjanting should be held delicately and without tension, and the drawing should be done with a free arm movement. It is better not to move the fingers at all, and some artists, whose nerves are not sufficiently well under control, find a wrist rest of help. When it first touches the material it is likely to leave a small globule at the beginning of the line. To avoid this it will be found that if a small piece of cardboard or a piece of paper is held in the left hand with its edge exactly where the line is to begin, and the tjanting is brought down on this paper and carried forward so that it slides off at the proper place on to the fabric, the line will commence with its usual width. It must of course, be understood, that in good work with the tjanting it is possible to make all lines of a uniform width, for any attempt to make the lines narrower or wider is likely to result in a lumpy uneven quality not to be desired. Dots of various sizes, however, can be obtained with the tjanting by the simple process of allowing it to rest a shorter or longer time on the spot and it will not be found difficult to produce these dots in perfectly round form. Under no conditions should the tjanting be held over a flame to reheat the wax, causing clogging and even melting of the solder with which the small spout is attached to the cup, thus ruining the instrument. Fine, even lines can also be obtained with the brush, and the advantage to the

47

skilled artist is that he can make these finer or broader with a sure, even touch. Added to this advantage is that of the technique of the almost dry or cooled brush which deposits the wax in the various textures so often desired. We may say, therefore, that for finer works of art in which the artist wishes to vary the line, the brush is better adapted, while for decorative works of art where an even unbroken line is desired, the tjanting will give a more structural effect.

Wax.—The kind of wax used depends upon the result desired, but it is usually a mixture of one-half bees-wax and one-half paraffin, to which is sometimes added a little resin, for the purpose of making it cling more securely to the fabric, and sometimes a little old wax, which makes the mixture darker. The more paraffin used the more brittle the mixture becomes when cooled, and therefore in producing the sometimes desired "crackle," the proportion of paraffin is increased. "Crackle" is an accidental texture which can be governed by the artist only with difficulty. Therefore, though it is perfectly characteristic of this art, it should not be made use of indiscriminately, and the best artists avoid it almost entirely. It is produced by the cracking up or crushing of the fabric after the wax has cooled and stiffened and then immersing it in a dye which is thus permitted to sink through the cracks and which produces irregular lines, wandering in a haphazard way wherever the wax has been broken. It is not easy to avoid crackle and in dyeing large pieces, a sufficiently large dye bath should be used to avoid crowding. It is advisable also to have the dye sufficiently warm so that the wax does not become too brittle.

The first step in treating the fabric is to wash it, as they do in Java, so as to remove all weighting or sizing, though certain craftsmen do not make use of oil, preferring to leave the fabric as clean and white as possible. It is then pressed, after having been rinsed thoroughly, and stretched either upon a frame, a piece of glass, or an enameled table-top. Sometimes this is done by painting a band of wax at the top which adheres to the surface beneath it when cooled, and then stretching the fabric evenly and painting a band at the bottom following this by the same treatment of both sides. At other times the artist, preferring to move the material into different positions, may stretch it by means of weights placed along the edges. The advantage of the frame is that the wax sinks through and is not broken, as is sometimes the case when the cooled finished piece is removed from glass or enamel. Thus it often saves re-waxing the back.

48

Methods of Obtaining Colours.—After the first waxing is completed, the dyeing can be proceeded with and in this, again, the western method differs from the eastern, for while the eastern craftsman dyes a colour and then removes the wax, re-waxing other portions of the design to prepare it for the dyeing of another colour, the western craftsman through his knowledge of

the mixing of colours need never recommence his waxing more than three times, once for each of the three primary colours whose combinations give all other hues. It may be well to recall at this point that there are three primary colours—red, yellow and blue—and that through the proper mixing of these colours any other colour in the spectrum can be obtained. By mixing these colours secondary colours are obtained, for red and yellow produce orange; yellow and blue, green; red and blue, purple. Making use of this fact, the western craftsman usually begins by reserving (covering with wax) that part of his design which he wishes to keep white and also that part in which no yellow is needed. When this waxing is completed he dyes the fabric

FIG. 41.—THE DYEING OF BATIK IN JAVA IS USUALLY DONE BY THE MEN

a very pale yellow. Should he have use for a yellow red in his design or a yellow blue, that is a green blue, he now blocks out the sections where these

colours would occur as well as the sections where he wishes to keep the shade of yellow just applied, and then dips the fabric again in a deeper yellow, reserving with the wax those sections which he intends to have orange and green or deeper yellow, and so on, keeping in mind exactly what hues he wishes to produce in each part of the design and thinking always of their intensity. When he has completed the dyeing of the yellows he may take up the reds or blues by first removing all the wax

FIG. 42.—AFTER THE DYEING, THE WAX IS REMOVED BY WASHING THE FABRIC IN HOT WATER

and then again covering those parts, which in the final fabric are to appear white or clear yellow. When this is completed he begins perhaps with a light red, dyeing it over white in certain places where he wishes the exact colour to appear, over a pale yellow where he wishes it to take this tint and over a deeper yellow where he wishes it to be orange. Thus it will be seen that modern batik

49

makes use of colour principles not unlike those employed in the process of four-colour printing, and it may also be seen that the artist must not only be an excellent draughtsman or painter with the wax but must have a perfect knowledge of colour and of the analysis of colour, otherwise his work is sure to be a haphazard jumble of unrelated hues and values.

The batik artist must also have a knowledge of the chemistry of modern dyes, which is a separate study (*see* DYES). As to the technique of this side of the art, it is sufficient to state here in general that for the beginner's use there are no better dyes than those sold by reputable firms in small packages. From these or from the other acid dyes, obtainable in larger quantities wholesale, can be made concentrated solutions by boiling them in the required amount of clear water. When the experienced artist sets out to procure a certain colour he cuts a strip of the same material on which his design is to be worked and tests the colour carefully, adding a little at a time this concentrated solution to a bath of clear water, made properly acid, before immersing his work of art. In making these tests it is necessary that the small fragment of material be kept in the bath for a given length of time, as under certain conditions the longer it stays the deeper the colour. It is also necessary that this test piece of material be rinsed just as carefully and thoroughly as the artist intends to rinse his work of art, and finally, of course, the sample must be dried before it can be determined whether or not the colour is correct. The experienced artist is most careful in his testing and is never satisfied until he has obtained the exact hue desired. It is in this work alone that many amateurs fail, sometimes ruining what might otherwise be a fine piece of craftsmanship. In testing the sample, the temperature of the dye-bath, the length of time it is immersed and all other conditions must be exactly similar to those which the batik itself must undergo. When the sample is ready and seems perfect, the material should be wetted in clear water so that the dye can enter it at once, then immersed and kept moving gently through the dye solution. Some artists do this with sticks, but many prefer using their hands in spite of the discomfort involved, because in order to avoid crackle the motion must be gentle though constant. It is often wise to remove the material in just a little less time than has been given the sample, for it will be found easy, if the colour is slightly pale, to give it one or two more brief dippings, rinsing it each time thoroughly, and thus arriving at the proper result. This system of gentle approach is infinitely more satisfactory than the careless attempt at procuring the desired colour in a single opera-

PLATE II   LITHOGRAPHY

AMERICAN AND ENGLISH LITHOGRAPHY, 20TH CENTURY

1. "Approaches to Gatun Lock, Panama Canal," by Joseph Pennell (1857–1926), American

2. War Poster by Frank Brangwyn (1867–   ), English

3. "A Stag at Sharkey's," 1917, by George W. Bellows (1882–1925), American

4. "Hooley's Arches," c. 1912, by G. Spencer Pryse (1881–   ), English

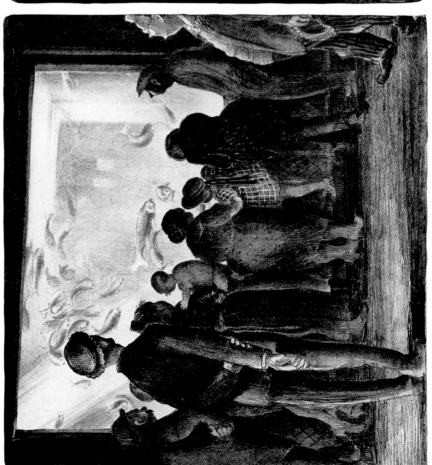

TWO LITHOGRAPHS

1. "Goldfish" by Mabel Dwight, an interesting genre subject taken from the aquarium and showing dark figures silhouetted against a light motif

2. "The Crypt" by Mabel Dwight, showing a suggestive use of black shadows which are cast against a light wall and give relief to the figures

tion, only to find that one has overdone it, and must resort to unsatisfactory bleaching.

Bleaching can be done with soda, ammonia or any of the well-known powders on the market, but it is very likely to attack the wax, and to work upon one colour more than another, giving the result, not of a simple paling of the hue, but of changing it to a distinctly different hue.

Removing Wax.—After the fabric has been properly dyed, the wax must be removed. This can best be accomplished by giving it a preliminary ironing between sheets of newspapers, which absorb a good deal of the wax. Then it is immersed in petrol and left to soak for some time so that a good deal of the remaining wax is dissolved. It is then carefully wrung out and placed in another clean bath of petrol. This work should be done most carefully, away from all flames, and with no quick movements, for even a spark of static electricity, such as may be caused by a shake or flip of the material, has been known to ignite the fumes. It is advisable to have good ventilation where this cleaning is undertaken, for gasolene fumes are poisonous when concentrated and one should breathe as little of them as possible. Often an electric fan, properly placed, will solve this difficulty. When the cleaning by petrol has been accomplished the fabric should be rinsed and washed lightly in warm water and soap-suds, to remove all traces of the acid, and then pressed.

It will be seen that proper technique in batik is quite as difficult as that of etching or painting. It must be realized that this technique involves even surer understanding of line and colour, for it is practically impossible to correct a mistake in drawing once it has been made, and it is also very nearly impossible to correct a mistake in colour. This is no art for those who work with trial and error methods. It must be carried on by those who conceive clearly and completely their finished result before undertaking the first step.

In permanence, batik compares favourably with the weaving of rugs, for modern dyes are sufficiently fast to make it proof against ordinary light conditions and easily cleaned without risk. Used as lamp shades or hangings against windows, it is second only to stained glass in its brilliancy and exceeds stained glass in its delicacy and variety of texture. This is then an art centuries old, little understood, demanding the utmost in technique, lasting and varied in its possibilities.[1]

[1]All drawings in this article are from Jasper & Mas Pirngadie, "*De Inlandsche Kunstnijverheit in Nederlandsch-Indie*" (Boek & Kunstdrukkery).

LITHOGRAPHY

LITHOGRAPHY, the art of drawing with a greasy substance, usually crayon, on a stone, metal or paper surface, and then printing, is based on the fact that grease attracts grease and is repelled by water. It is the most direct of all the graphic arts, for in practising it the artist first sees the exact value of each line that he draws and then has his drawing reproduced so accurately that it may truly be said to have been multiplied. Whereas in making an etching, a process in which a drawing is engraved on a metal plate through a thin film of wax, or a woodblock (one in which the drawing is carved in wood) the artist must wait for a print to estimate his work fairly; in making a lithograph his drawing grows in definite values under his eyes and he can make changes in it as he works. Lithographic crayon yields broader tones than the etching needle, which is limited to a solid line; it makes and retains finer lines than can be obtained in a woodblock. Lithographs can be made from pen drawings on a plate or on a stone; they can even be painted with a brush in what are called lithographic wash drawings or, sometimes, lithotints. A stone can be made solid black and a drawing produced with a knife by scratching, ripping out and reducing. This method of procedure gives fine lines, greys and jet blacks. Engravings on stone print well.

THE PROCESS

Drawing Materials.—The best medium on which to draw is Kelheim stone, that on which Senefelder was by chance working when he discovered the art. There are three grades of lithographic stone in use to-day: blue (hard), grey (medium), and yellow (soft). The blue is used for engraving, the grey for very fine work, and the yellow for work relatively unimportant. Lithographic stones are grained by rubbing two together with a sifted layer of flint or carborundum between; the grain, therefore, is not native to the stone but is made up of innumerable, minute dots that can be varied by changing the quality of the flint or carborundum. Erasures may cause irremediable damage to such a fine surface and are best effected by means of a small piece of lithographic stone rotated with sand and water; defects may be picked out with a needle; a knife may be used to scratch out, but if the grain is removed the part shows scratchy if drawn on again. After being ground the stone is washed thoroughly with clean water and is then ready to receive a drawing.

Zinc and aluminium plates are bought with prepared surfaces of a coarseness depending on the size of the flint grains struck against them. The disadvantages of using a plate are that its surface easily becomes greasy, corrections are hard to make and its colour may at first confuse values for the artist. In drawings made direct on either a stone or plate the composition known as "tusche" can be applied for solid black lines or large black areas.

Despite its excellence as a drawing surface, the inconvenience of carrying lithographic stone about has caused it to be most used as a receiving surface for drawings transferred from paper. Not only can paper be easily carried in the artist's portfolio, but, since a drawing made on paper has to be transferred to another surface before being printed, it appears as it will when printed and does not have to be made in reverse like those made direct on a zinc or aluminum plate or on stone. Good lithographic paper, made by hand in Germany, France, Scotland and Austria, has a specially prepared chalk surface that is very good to draw on, permits scraping out with a knife and transfers well. In the United States artists usually employ a fine quality of tracing paper. In drawing a lithograph on paper it is not necessary to develop the design with lithographic crayon. A Conté sanguine pencil can be used for the preliminary design over which lithographic crayon is passed later; or charcoal, or a lead pencil can be used, since neither these nor the Conté contain grease to interfere with transference; but the Conté marks, being red, can be easily distinguished from those of the black lithographic crayon, while the black marks of charcoal or lead pencil are likely to confuse the artist. Changes in a drawing on paper can be made by painting out with Chinese white, which, if applied smoothly, can be drawn over; or they can be made on the stone or plate after transference. Since transferring has a tendency to intensify, the drawing should be kept slightly lighter than it is wanted to appear in the finished print.

Lithographic crayon is a composition of soap, wax, oil and lampblack. A No. 0 crayon is very soft, No. 1 soft, No. 2 medium, No. 3 hard, No. 4 very hard and No. 5 copal. In warm weather a No. 3 or No. 4 crayon should be used; in cold weather any may be used but it is advisable never to use a No. 5.

GRAPHIC ARTS

Great care should be taken to keep the drawing surface absolutely clean, free from dust, crumbs, etc. In all cases, the artist should be careful not to touch it; perspiration, which contains grease, will reproduce in smudges, marring the finished print. A piece of paper or light felt should be kept between the drawing surface and the artist's hand and arm.

Transferring.—Generally, drawings transferred soon after being finished yield the best results, but drawings protected by a film of gum may be preserved indefinitely. Some printers prefer to transfer to a zinc or aluminum plate rather than to stone, believing that the plate reproduces fine tints better. Transferring a drawing on paper to either involves the same method, but a stronger acid solution is used for stone. The drawing is first placed in a "damp book," which consists of damp blotters with a rubber cover, and if the paper tends to wrinkle it is stretched with thumbtacks. It is left between the blotters from 20 to 60 minutes, until the printer believes it ready to transfer. It is then dropped on the stone or plate, already on the press, and left in the position in which it lands; to move it is to smudge. It is covered with "backing"—a sheet of clean paper and a sheet of compressed fibre-board whose upper surface is greased to further the passage of the scraper over it. In running the stone or plate through the press care should be taken that the scraper runs entirely across the drawing but not to the edge of the stone or plate, which the scraper slipping off under pressure would damage. To facilitate this a margin of at least one inch should be allowed for every stone or plate; and this holds whether the drawing is made direct on these surfaces or transferred to them. The bed of the press is slid forward, normal pressure is applied, the bed is turned through the press, the pressure is released and the bed is returned to its original position. If special transfer paper has been used it should be soaked off; ordinary tracing paper should be pulled off without dampening. The plate or stone is then fanned dry and allowed to stand for about 30 minutes.

The Etch.—What has happened is that some of the greasy lithographic crayon has been forced off the paper onto the plate or stone. If the printer is satisfied with the transfer he gives it what is known as an "etch," *i.e.*, a solution of, for a stone, gum arabic and nitric acid, or, for a zinc plate, gum arabic, chromic acid and phosphoric acid, or, for an aluminum plate, gum arabic and phosphoric acid, flowed over the surface with a brush or a piece of absorbent cotton. The gum arabic desensitizes the surface not drawn on, decreasing any affinity for grease that it may have, and also is so absorbed

54

by the pores of the stone or plate that it serves to "hold the drawing in place"; the acid eats away any invisible particles of grease that may be on the surface, but when in the correct solution (*see* formulas appended), does not affect the drawing itself, which is protected by the wax in the lithographic crayon. If the printer thinks the transfer poor, he coats the surface with pure gum arabic, washes it off with water, inks it up until the drawing appears, dusts the inked drawing with rosin and then gives it an "etch."

For a stone, after the "etch" has dried the surface is washed with clean water, sponged with a pure solution of gum arabic, rubbed down as smooth as possible with a clean rag and fanned dry. For a plate, the acid solution is washed off without being allowed to dry. For both, the crayon is next washed off with turpentine, leaving the drawing invisible, apparently destroyed; but it is preserved, of course, in the grease that the stone or plate has absorbed. A little asphaltum is rubbed in and fanned dry. The stone or plate is then again washed with water so that when the ink, which contains grease, is applied it will take only on the grease and be repelled by all parts of the surface not drawn on. It is then damped over with a sponge and inked up with a roller. It is advisable, finally, to dust the stone or plate with rosin dust, to clean it up, polishing out all dirt, and to repeat the process, after which it is ready for printing.

Drawings made direct on a stone or plate are given an "etch," and then prepared for printing in the same way. Lithographic engraving, or intaglio printing, is done with a needle on stone desensitized by a solution of gum arabic and nitric acid. Such engravings are inked with a dabber that pushes the ink into the engraved lines; otherwise they are treated like a lithograph drawn direct on stone.

Printing.—Lithographic ink is made from the best dry colour and linseed oil. It is generally sold stiff so that the printer can soften it with varnish to the consistency demanded by his working conditions and the results that he wants. It is available in various colours, but, no matter what colour or combination of colours is wanted in the print, all drawings are made in black, one stone being prepared for each colour desired. It is applied by means of a roller made of wood covered with grain leather; during the operation, difficult because the ink must be applied evenly until judged strong enough, the stone or the plate rests on the bed of the press in order that an impression can be made at once.

The pressure used in printing a lithograph is sliding pressure. The scraper, which is made of box or apple wood sharpened to a blunt edge and covered with well greased leather, is set by a screw. Hand-made paper is generally used for lithographic prints and the best grades come from Italy, Sweden, France and Japan; machine-made paper, however, gives good results in practice. The paper is generally moistened to give it a greater affinity for ink and to enable it to print very fine tints in full value. It is then placed on top of the plate or stone as it rests in the centre of the press bed, and is covered with backing. The pressure is applied and, the same precautions being taken as in transferring, the stone is cranked through the press; the pressure is released and the bed of the press is returned to its original position. The first prints pulled have a tendency to be light; the proper strength is built up gradually. If, after a few prints have been pulled, the drawing has a tendency to grow too dark it is advisable to repeat the "etching" process; if the stone is in colour, before being given an "etch" it is washed with turpentine, rolled up with black ink and dusted with rosin. As many prints as are wanted can be had, but, when taken from the press, the stone or plate, to keep the drawing in place, should be rolled up with ink, gummed down with gum arabic and rubbed down very smoothly with a clean rag.

Formulas.—The proportions of gum arabic and acid used in the solution known as the "etch" vary with the quality of the stone or plate, the type and age of the drawing, and the temperature of the room. Only the following approximate proportions can be given: For a stone, one half glass of gum arabic to one teaspoonful of nitric acid. For a zinc plate, one half glass of gum arabic to one teaspoonful of chromic acid to from 12 to 15 drops of phosphoric acid. For an aluminum plate, one half glass of gum arabic to from 15 to 20 drops of phosphoric acid. (*See also* ETCHING, page 133).

HISTORY

THE HISTORY of the invention of lithography leaves no chance for ingenious theory and learned speculation. Art authorities may argue over the origin of etching and wood-engraving, but the inventor of lithography, Alois Senefelder (1771-1834), himself gave the facts of his invention in *A Complete Course of Lithography—Der Steindruck* (1818)—a book which is half autobiographical, half technical, and wholly absorbing. He was a Bavarian actor and dramatist. Not over successful, he endeavoured to be his own printer and publisher as well and, to that end, experimented with metal plates and Solenhofen stone, acids and inks. According to his often-quoted story, his mother asked him, one day when he was at work, to write her week's washing list and, paper not being handy, he wrote it with his greasy ink on a smooth stone upon which he practised writing in reverse. Later, instead of cleaning off the writing, he was curious to see what would happen if he etched the stone and pulled a proof. What happened was his discovery of relief engraving on stone (1796). But only after "thousands of experiments" did he make the further, the all-important discovery (1798) that without etching the writing or design in relief, he could prepare the stone so as to get a print from the surface. This is lithography-chemical surface printing.

Germany.—Senefelder did not start out to benefit the artist, nor did the business men who took him up and launched his invention. The first patents were mostly for printing music and calico. However, artists and their patrons quickly saw the possibilities of lithography as an art. In Germany, royalty patronized Senefelder; Baron Aretin went into partnership with him (1806) and their printing shop in Munich was shown as one of the sights of the town to the many distinguished strangers who passed through in those Napoleonic days. Less came of royal condescension than of the first work of note issued by the Senefelder-Aretin Press (1808): the reproduction of Dürer's Missal of Maximilian from the copy in the Munich Royal Library, the drawings made by N. Strixner. German artists grew enthusiastic, got to work on stone, less often as original lithographers than as faithful copyists of the Old Masters. Their reproductions were extraordinary, especially when it is remembered that they had no camera to aid them. Strixner, Piloty, Mitterer, Hanfstängl were the most accomplished. Their prints were large, and large portfolios of national and private collections were issued, became immediately popular, and the fashion quickly spread to other countries. Technically, artists could scarcely carry lithography further, but no artist of genius or talent can make himself a mere machine, the Old Masters necessarily lost something in their interpretation, and, eventually, photography did away with the artist as copyist.

England.—Already, in 1801, Senefelder had taken out patents in England, where he was personally overshadowed by Philip André and Hullmandel, who seemed inclined to appropriate all the credit, and the profit too. Fortunately he was recognized by the Royal Society of Arts as the

inventor, a gold medal was bestowed upon him, and artistic lithography—
"Polyautography" the English then called it—was encouraged. The interest of artists was roused, and an album of *Specimens of Polyautography* was
published by André in 1803, with Benjamin West, Stothard, Barry, Fuseli
among the contributors. For some years, however, little was heard of the
new invention. Now and then an experiment was made by artists, notably
by Blake and Bewick. But Géricault had made his lithographs in London
and Bonington his in France before lithography acquired the least popularity, before royal and titled amateurs, Queen Victoria and Count d'Orsay
of the number, began to amuse themselves with it, before albums of "Views"
of architecture and landscape were "on the town." Artists like Prout and
Harding went to France to work for Baron Taylor's colossal, never-finished
Voyages Pittoresques which no doubt stimulated the British fancy for such
publications as Wilkie's *Tour in the East*, Lewis's *Sketches in Spain and the
Orient*, Roberts' *Holy Land*, and many of the huge books so long in vogue.
As a rule, the artists did not make the lithographs for these English publications. They simply supplied sketches from their sketch books which professional lithographers reproduced on stone and printed. Under such conditions
it is small wonder that lithography languished as an art, that the artist
who practised it for pure love of the medium was the exception. Catter-
mole's lithotints remain, the few by Cotman, and John Linnell Jr.'s copies,
especially one of Mulready's *The Sonnet* which the most skilled German
never surpassed. By 1850 lithography in England was really a *Finished
Chapter of Illustrative Art*, as it was later described by William Simpson,
whose *India* was the last of the big travel books.

France.—Lithography as an art met with the most immediate, the most
splendid response in France. There also it received early official recognition
and honours, was patronized by amateurs, was for a time the mode in modish
drawing-rooms—a fashionable plaything. But in France this period was
short. General Baron Lejeune's famous *Cossack*—result of his visiting Senefelder's Munich shop with the crowd—inaugurated the fashion, and was
also, no doubt, the first inspiration of the cheaply got up, cheaply priced
albums of military subjects that did so much to popularize the Napoleonic
Legend. Good printers multiplied rapidly—Engelmann, Lasteyrie, Del-
pech, Gihaut, Motte, Lemercier. The Vernets, Charlet and Raffet were
quick to see in Napoleon and his armies a motive for their lithographs.
Charlet contributed not only to the subject but to the art, experimenting

LITHOGRAPHY

THREE MODERN AMERICAN LITHOGRAPHS

1. "Entrance to a Village" by Ernest Fiene. The massing of dark foliage and the angular light areas makes an effective design
2. "Cows" (drypoint on stone) by George Biddle. Strong in design and original in technique
3. "Washington Square" by Ernest Fiene, in which a sense of light is produced by leaving areas exposed, and an impression of mistiness by blurring thin edges

TWO POLITICAL CARTOONS OF THE LATE 19TH CENTURY FROM PUCK

1. "Why they dislike him—He will not prove himself a cat's-paw in the enterprise" by Bernhard Gillam. This cartoon, printed in September 1884, shows Cleveland defying corruption during his campaign against James G. Blaine for the presidency

2. "They Hate the Light but they can't escape it" by J. Keppler, published March 26, 1890. The Press is represented as throwing the light of publicity on the secret executive sessions of the U. S. Senate

tirelessly, getting amazing effects out of *la manière noire*—"mezzotint applied to stone." Raffet on a few inches of paper could make a romance of war, turn it into beauty, in such prints as *Le Réveil* and *Ils grognaient mais le suivaient toujours*. Other artists used lithography for portraits, none more notably than Achille Devéria, above all in his renderings of R. J. Lemercier, founder of the great printing house, and of Alexandre Dumas, *Père*, slim, elegant, with a mop of black hair to betray the colour in his blood. Painters were attracted by the medium and the variety of its resources. There were few who did not give it at least a trial. Géricault went further than a mere trial, his boxers and horses among the best known prints of those early years and, later, the most sought after by collectors. Delacroix mastered the method triumphantly in his *Lion de l'Atlas* and *Tigre Royal*, less strikingly in his illustrations for *Faust* and *Hamlet*. Isabey's triumph was in his little towns for Baron Taylor, his shipping and harbours for himself. But the list is endless—the prints published sometimes separately, sometimes in magazines and papers. Much of the best work came out in *L'Artiste*, the most successful of the magazines, or in Philipon's two papers, *La Caricature* and *Le Charivari* with Daumier and Gavarni for regular contributors. From the beginning French lithographers had devoted themselves to caricature and fashion plates, records of social life and political satire with as much zest as to war, portraits and "picturesque views," but Daumier and Gavarni excelled them all. Daumier overflowed with fun in providing adventures for Robert Macaire, but he could invent political cartoons so deadly that he was sent to prison for them, and he was tragedy itself, when it came to drawing the murders in the *Rue Transnonain*. Gavarni lent charm to fashion, grace to *grisettes*, but Achille Devéria's portraits have not more character than his Edmond and Jules de Goncourt, no doubt modelled on Gigoux's Alfred and Tony Johannot; nor was Daumier ever more tragic than Gavarni in his horrible *Thomas Vireloque*.

Other countries lagged far behind Germany, England and France in the first half of the last century. Spain gave us Goya, the brilliant, the romantic, the grim; Manet, with paint or canvas, did not get more life and colour out of the bull-ring than Goya with greasy chalk on stone. The rest of Europe was practically barren. In America lithography was entirely commercial, with nothing to show that Americans appreciated it as an art save for a stray print by Lafarge or William Morris Hunt and the *Campaign Sketches* of Winslow Homer, made during the Civil War and remembered now because of his fame as a painter. By the middle of the century, the first great period of the art of lithography was everywhere at an end.

Decline of Lithography.—Already in 1840, etchings were competing with lithographs in *L'Artiste* and Beraldi was announcing the decline of lithography. In 1864 Burty declared the art *en pleine décadence.* Both were right. The reasons are not far to seek. The swing of the pendulum for one, lithographs had been almost too popular. French lithographers, warned to be serious like the Germans, began to copy pictures which they did, though with distinction, at the sacrifice of original design. Photography became a serious rival in all countries, bringing its disastrous gift of cheapness. Photographic processes replaced lithography, as well as wood-engraving, for the illustration of magazines and papers. In the '60s photo-lithographs were finding their way into Baron Taylor's monumental work. The commercial lithographer soon preferred the camera to the artist. The horrors of chromolithography demoralized the public. A mystery was made of the actual printing. Artists, not allowed near the press—and few had presses of their own—were kept in an outer room waiting for proofs. The earlier transfer papers were abominable. Dealers fought shy of lithographs and collectors hesitated to follow where dealers feared to lead. Under the new conditions the art threatened to disappear.

Modern Revival.—But an art with such possibilities for the artist could not altogether die. Adolf Menzel, trained in a Berlin printing shop, was the chief link between the first great period and the revival. In the '40s and '50s, those dark decades for lithography, he was doing his *Uniforms of the Army of Frederick the Great,* issuing his *Sketches on Stone* in a portfolio, bringing out occasional prints, none more famous than his *Christ in the Temple.* His lithographs are marvels of technical knowledge and accomplished drawing, an inexhaustible mine for the intelligent student. In France, the new generation was discovering lithography for itself through the work of the French masters. In the '60s Manet experimented, also Bracquemond, Legros, Fantin-Latour, who began his well-known series with Wagner as inspiration. In London in the '70s the printer Thomas Way interested Whistler, who, enchanted with so autographic a medium, produced little masterpieces that made a talk in the studios. Several appeared in *Piccadilly, The Albemarle, The Whirlwind,* publications which his contributions could not save from an early death. And so, little by little, lithography as an art came into its own again, especially in France where a retrospective exhibition of lithographs was held at the École des Beaux Arts in 1891. Beraldi now talked of the revival in the air and the French, ever leading in such movements, prepared for a more important, more complete exhibition to celebrate the centenary of Senefelder's invention.

The '90s were the years when the Champ-de-Mars *Salon* opened its doors wide to the new school of lithographers, and the black-and-white section was a place to linger in—the years when Toulouse-Lautrec, Steinlen, Odilon Redon, Valloton, Ibels, Anquetin were at work, and Chéret made the walls of Paris gay with his posters. Painters returned to the stone—Besnard, Blanche, Gandara, Puvis de Chavannes and Carrière who never did anything finer in any medium than his portrait of Paul Verlaine. Lithographs again appeared in papers and magazines, again were issued in series, gave the chief interest to such collections as *L'Estampe Originale*, for which Toulouse-Lautrec made the memorable poster in colour. The excitement reached its climax with the wonderful Centenary Exhibition at the Champ-de-Mars, opening in 1895, three years in advance of the actual date as if France could not wait to pay its tribute to Senefelder.

In England only a few shared Whistler's enthusiasm. C. H. Shannon set up his own press, lithographed much the same subjects he painted, with much the same delicacy and grace. Joseph Pennell used lithography for the illustration of Macmillan's new edition of *The Alhambra* and the *Devon and Cornwall* volume in the *Highways and Byways* series. He had no press, the printing was done at Way's where mystery prevailed, and the pale grey prints gave no idea of his powerful Panama and War Work lithographs that were to come later. William Rothenstein published portfolios of portraits. Charles Conder's lithographs, in their subjects, seem like his fans, but even vaguer in design, more elusive in charm. William Strang, like Rothenstein, turned to portraiture—grave serious studies. A few more artists could be named but, in all, so few that when Great Britain was asked to contribute to the Champ-de-Mars Exhibition, Alfred Gilbert, the sculptor who had begun his career in a lithographer's office, and Charles Goulding, the lithographic printer, scattered transfer paper, chalks and washes wholesale among Royal Academicians and prominent outsiders before any sort of contemporary representation could be made. England held a retrospective exhibition at the Victoria and Albert Museum three years later, 1898, the correct date, with not much more to show in the British Section than the collections sent to the Champ-de-Mars.

61

GRAPHIC ARTS

Düsseldorf chose the same year for its Centenary Exhibition as Paris (1895–96), and German and Austrian artists played their part in the revival. Hans Thoma and Max Liebermann, Greiner, Unger and Fischer, one woman of power and distinction, Kathe Kollwitz, had revived the traditions of the great days in Germany. A few lithographs were published during its short life by the magazine *Pan* and excellent work has been done at the Pan Printing Press in Berlin. *Jugend* opened its pages to the men of the younger generation, reproducing their lithographs. And a number of other magazines and papers have, with more or less success, looked to lithography for their principal attraction. Belgium has contributed to the chronicles of lithography, and Félicien Rops, Henri de Groux, Emil Claus, Fernand Knopf are among the masters. In Holland, Bauer, Von Hoytema, Van Toroop, Van s'Gravesande, Jacob Maris, Veth, are names to be remembered. In New York the Grolier Club arranged an Exhibition in 1896 which probably was an influence in awakening American artists, so long lukewarm. Arthur B. Davies, experimenting in colour, Albert Sterner, George Bellows, Charles Locke, a much younger man, are the most prominent of the too small group of artists who have as yet practised the art in America. J. McLure Hamilton also is an American, but his work has been done mostly in England. Factors in arousing this new interest were the improvement of transfer paper, the use of aluminium plates, the growing tendency of the artist to print his lithographs himself on his own press.

Since 1900 lithography has been more alive and active in England than elsewhere. Public interest dwindled after the Victoria and Albert Museum Exhibition but not the interest of artists. Certain magazines even in the '90s opened their pages to lithographers, whose work may be found in *The Pageant, The Savoy, The Studio, The Magazine of Art, The Art Journal*. But 1907–08 brought the boldest venture of all, *The Neolith*, a quarterly which lithographed text and illustrations alike. It ran for only four numbers. But almost immediately three men associated with it, A. S. Hartrick, F. Ernest Jackson, J. Kerr Lawson, to whose number Joseph Pennell, who had been living in England for years, was promptly added, established the Senefelder Press, which was soon abandoned, and organized the still prosperous Senefelder Club with Pennell as president. The first exhibition was given in the early winter of 1909 and since then annual exhibitions have been held in London and many others throughout Europe and America. Most of the distinguished lithographers of the day became members: J. McLure Hamil-

62

ton, C. H. Shannon, John Copley its first secretary, E. J. Sullivan, Ethel Gabain, Spencer Pryse, Frank Brangwyn, the second president. The club already in the first quarter of the century did much to restore lithography to its rightful place among the graphic arts, and upon it the future of the art, in a large measure, now rests.

COMMERCIAL PROCESSES

Lithographic Printing.—The work of the lithographic printer commences at the point where the lithographic artist completes the drawing. When a stone with a design drawn upon it is sent to the press, the printer has a delicate task to perform in order to prepare the work for printing. It has to be etched with a weak acid, covered with gum arabic, and rolled up with printing ink, and during this work extreme care has to be taken that the delicate lines in the drawing are not destroyed. A proof is then pulled on the press and submitted to the artist, who may find it necessary to add further work or to delete some of the work he has already put on to the stone. When the artist is satisfied, finished proofs are pulled and submitted to the customer. When it is a colour job, cross-lines called "register marks" are included on the margins of the "key" and printed on the sheet of paper, each printing having to register to these marks. When printing on the press, needles are put through the marks on the paper, and registered to similar marks on the stone. When printing on the machine the sheet of paper is "fed to lays," and great care has to be exercised to place the sheet accurately into the "lays" each time it passes through the machine.

When the work is finally passed, transfers on special paper are pulled in a greasy ink upon the hand-press from the original stone. These are patched up and fixed on to a sheet of the paper on which the job is to be printed, this having previously been ruled to the size required. The sheet of transfers is then placed face downwards on to a stone or plate and run through the press until the design adheres to the printing surface. This is followed by a series of operations of gumming, rolling up, cleaning and etching. It is by printing a number of designs together on one sheet that large editions can be economically produced. After printing, the prints are cut up singly.

In a large measure, thin sheets of zinc and aluminium have taken the place of stones during the last quarter of a century, but the same principles of preparation apply, with the distinction that a different etch may be used

63

for the various surfaces. It is doubtful, however, if an equivalent quality of work can be obtained from a plate as from a stone. The call of the age for a speedier method of production made plates necessary. The principal advantages of plates are that they do not occupy the same space as a stone when storing and that they can be fixed round the cylinder of a rotary machine, which produces at least three times as many impressions in a given time as those used for stone printing.

Photo-lithography.—This is a photo-mechanical process for placing on a planographic printing surface a reproduction of an original design without the intervention of handwork by the lithographic artist.

Vandyke.—Various copying methods are employed, the simplest being a process known as Vandyke, a method whereby line drawings and tracings on ordinary paper can be reproduced without the aid of a camera. The drawing is used as the negative for photographically printing the image on to a metal plate coated with a solution containing fish-glue, ammonium bichromate and ammonia. This has to be filtered, care being taken that the plate which is to be coated is chemically clean. When the coating is dry the plate is placed in a photographic printing frame and the copy placed in contact with the prepared plate. This is exposed to light for a predetermined time. It is then removed from the frame and the plate washed in running water, after which it is dyed with a methyl violet solution, when a transposition of the copy appears upon the plate: the bare parts of the metal represent the black lines of the original. The plate is then dried and inked over with a special transfer ink, when it is allowed to stand for some time and then developed in a weak solution of sulphuric acid. The film, acted upon by light, is easily removed, leaving the design outlined on the plate, which is printed in the ordinary way.

Typon.—Another copying process now in general use is known as Typon. This process is extremely useful and especially adapted to the reprinting of old books. In this form of reproduction a specially constructed frame with a glass top and lights placed beneath is employed. On the glass, a yellow filter is placed, then a sheet of "typon paper," of special manufacture, with the emulsion side uppermost, the page or design being placed face downwards on to the paper. A sheet of rubber is stretched over this and clamped securely in a frame, the air being extracted until a close contact is obtained between the original and the photographic paper. The lights at the bottom are switched on and the necessary exposure given. The photographic record of the original is obtained by means of reflected light. The paper is developed and fixed, and when dry becomes the negative from which a design is photographically printed on to the printing machine plate.

Photo-litho Transfers.—These are usually supplied to printers who do not possess photographic equipment by firms specializing in the work. The method of production is as follows. A sheet of suitable paper is coated with gelatine, sensitized by potassium bichromate. This is dried in a dark room and is then ready for exposure through a negative taken from the original to be reproduced. After being rolled up with transfer ink until it is covered evenly all over the surface, it is placed into water, then carefully rubbed over with a piece of cotton-wool, those parts which the light has not affected dissolving and washing away, leaving the design in a greasy ink upon the sheet of coated paper, which is then ready for transferring to the printing surface.

Direct Photo-lithography.—This is the modern method of placing a design on a printing plate. A negative is obtained and when developed and dried is photographically printed on to a lithographic plate coated with albumen and ammonium bichromate. The negative and plate are placed in a printing down frame, the air being extracted by a pump and the plate and negative exposed to light for a certain period of time. The plate is then rolled up solidly with printing ink and placed under running water. A piece of cotton-wool is rubbed over the surface and where the light has not passed through the negative such parts of the coating are washed away, leaving the design on the plate, which after rolling up with ink, etching and gumming is ready for the press. Remarkable progress has recently been made in preparing photo-litho plates, especially where a number of duplicates have to be placed on the same plate.

Step-and-repeat.—A machine has been invented which will project on to a sensitized glass plate a photographic record of a design from a master negative. This machine automatically and accurately projects on to the plate any number of duplicates of the original with the pre-determined space between each. When developed, this large negative is printed down on to a machine printing plate.

Negative Printer.—Another type of duplicating machine, known as a negative printer, automatically "steps up" and repeats the design in accurate register on to a sensitized printing plate. In this instance, however, the photographic image is not made by projection, but the master negative is brought into direct contact with the printing plate and both are exposed to artificial light. This is also known as the "Photo-Composing" machine.

Lithographic Machines.—The hand-press is used for proving and transferring and, in some cases, for printing a job of small numbers. This may be said to be composed of a frame with a roller upon which a movable bed rests, supported by the frame. At the head there is an upright section with a movable bar, actuated by a screw or lever to impart the necessary pressure. The bar is so made that a "scraper" made of boxwood can be fitted into a slot on the underside and secured by a screw. On the end of the bed there is a hinged frame upon which a sheet of metal or leather is stretched. This is called a tympan and is turned down on to the top of the stone placed on the bed and run through the press under the scraper. It is by this means that an impression is obtained on a press. Small presses are usually operated by hand but the larger sizes are run by power.

The method of obtaining a print on a hand-press is to damp the stone, pass a roller charged with ink several times over the surface, and place a sheet of paper on to the stone to marks which determine the position of the print upon the sheet. A few sheets of packing are then placed on the top, the tympan turned down, and the bed containing the stone propelled under the scraper. Thus, an inked impression of the design is made upon the paper. The bed is then returned to its normal position, the tympan raised, the packing removed, and the printed sheet carefully taken from the stone. These various operations have to be repeated for each impression.

Flat-bed.—Flat-bed machines are power driven and are mainly used for printing from stone. They are of a heavy build and comprise a frame held together by cross-stays. Running within the sides of the frame is a bed with racks fixed on the underside and supported by runners, the machine obtaining its to-and-fro motion by means of a system of gears connected with the main driving shaft. Geared into the upper side of the bed is a cylinder which is driven by the bed and held in position by brackets. The impression exerted by the cylinder is obtained by springs or levers with weights. The inking apparatus consists of a duct or trough which holds printing ink. This can be regulated by screws and the required quantity of ink supplied by means of a roller to a slab attached to one end of the carriage. As the carriage moves to and fro the ink is distributed by means of a number of rollers. The inking rollers take their supply of ink from the slab and in turn transfer it to the printing surface. At the back of the cylinder there is a damping

PLATE II

CARTOON

SOCIAL AND POLITICAL CARTOONS

1. "Why don't they go to the country?" a cartoon by George Bellows, which appeared in *The Masses,* Aug. 1913; an example of the starker form of cartooning which was used widely in this magazine. The meaning is evident at a glance and all details contribute to the impression. Cartoons of this type are usually propagandist, intended to sway popular feeling and bring about reforms

2. "Discrimination" from a drawing by Alice Beach Winter, published in *The Masses,* Feb. 1913

3. "Betriebsstörung" (the Strike) by Heinrich Kley, a contemporary German cartoonist, showing the use of symbolism which is characteristic of the cartoons of that country. A giant satanic figure is stopping production completely by crushing the mill and blocking the smokestacks with his hand

4. "Fiume," drawing by O. Gulbransson which appeared in *Simplicissimus,* a Munich weekly, following D'Annunzio's occupation of Fiume in 1919. D'Annunzio, the figure on the horse, is brandishing his sword and defying President Wilson, who protested that the Italian had no right in Fiume. The picture when published carried the legend, "How easily even the smallest Europeans manage to ride over the greatest American ideas."

5. "The Bachelor Girl," by John Sloan. *The Masses,* Feb. 1915

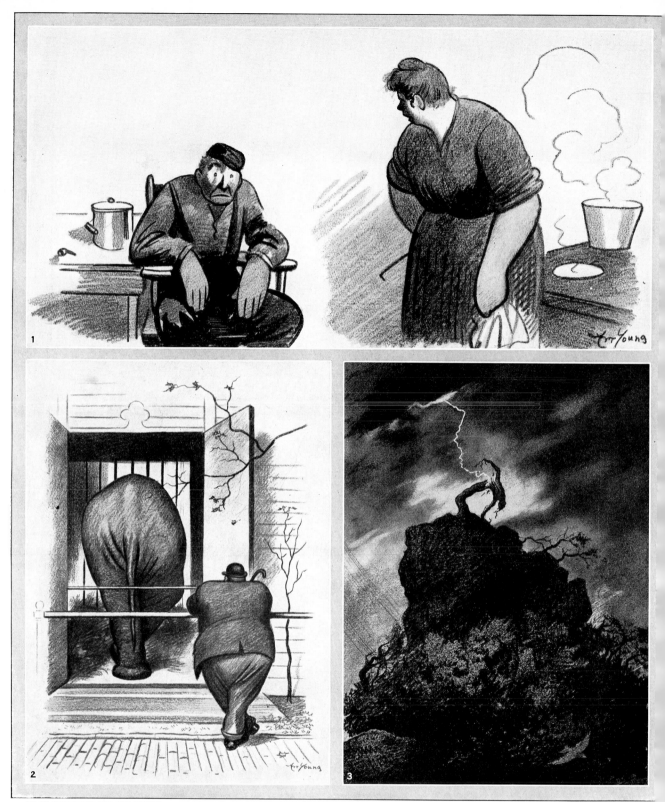

THREE CARTOONS BY ART YOUNG

1. Cartoon first printed in *The Masses* in May 1913 and since reprinted widely. The picture carried this dialogue, "I Gorry, I'm tired." "There you go! You're tired. Here I be a-standin' over a hot stove all day and you workin in a nice cool sewer." 2. "Beast and Man" and 3. "The Price of Prominence" illustrate the satirical manner of cartoon drawing, as distinguished from the cruder method of the "comic strip"

equipment where water is taken from a trough, transferred to a slab (fixed on the opposite end of the carriage to that of the ink slab), from which the damping rollers obtain a regular supply of water to moisten the stone.

On the crown of the cylinder is a feed-board upon which the paper is placed and from which a feeder takes a single sheet at a time and places it in lays, usually fixed on the inside of the grippers which are connected with the cylinder. As the cylinder rotates it takes the sheet and presses it on to the stone, and in this way an impression of the design is placed upon the paper which is then taken off at the back of the machine either by hand, or by a mechanical device called "flyers." This type of machine is rapidly being superseded by the rotary.

Direct Rotary.—This machine, on which plates only can be used, gives a larger output than a flat-bed stone printing machine. In this type there are two cylinders, one of which carries the plate with the design, the other supplying the pressure. The inking and damping apparatus are so arranged that the plate is automatically damped and inked as the machine rotates. In this machine the sheet to be printed is placed to lays, fixed on to a bar, which automatically rise as the grippers on the impression cylinder take the sheet from the feed-board to receive the impression from the plate, the sheet being automatically delivered at the rear of the machine. It is on this class of machine that pictorial posters are usually printed.

Offset.—In most printing processes the sheet of paper is brought into direct contact with the plate on which the design is placed. This is known as direct printing, but in the offset method an intermediate cylinder covered with a sheet of rubber is included. The same method of printing has been applied to the printing of tin for a number of years, but it is only comparatively recently that it has been adopted for printing upon paper.

The construction of the offset machines mostly in use may be likened to that of the direct rotary, with the addition of a third cylinder. As the machine operates, an inked impression of the design on the plate cylinders is transferred on to the rubber sheet and this, in turn, is transferred to the sheet of paper. A flat-bed offset machine is sometimes used. This is similar to an ordinary stone litho printing machine, but fitted with an additional drum for pressing the sheet against the main cylinder covered with a rubber blanket, which takes the impression from the stone.

The advantage of this method lies in the fact that a printer can otherwise only get the best results when a paper with a smooth surface is used, but by the offset method, a paper with a rough surface, or material such as fabric or leather, can be printed with remarkable results. The reason is that a sheet of paper has an undulating surface and, when printing by the direct method, the highest "points" on the paper receive the impression; but in offset, the resiliency of the rubber does not only allow for the printing of the highest points but will go down into the hollows, which are naturally more pronounced in a rough paper than in that which has been calendered or coated. Offset printing is used not only for the highest grade of work—such as art subjects, show-cards, calendars—but also for the production of newspapers and magazines. In the latter instance the paper is fed into the machine from a reel instead of a single sheet at a time. The development of this section of lithographic printing is still in its infancy and its possibilities have not yet been fully investigated. In time, however, with a fuller knowledge of the capabilities of the process, difficulties will be surmounted, making it possible to produce illustrated papers with a result equal to that of other processes.

Tin Printing.—This is a branch of the lithographic art in which a few firms specialize. The beautifully decorated tin containers used for confectionery and household requisites are printed by this method. The method is similar to offset printing, but instead of a sheet of paper, a sheet of prepared tin is "fed" into the machine which receives an impression of the design from a rubber blanket. This sheet of tin is then "stoved," i.e., dried in a high temperature, this being done for each printing until all the colours necessary to complete the design have been printed: a separate stone or plate is required for each colour.

Remarkable developments have taken place since 1910 in the lithographic branch of the printing industry. Reproductions by lithographic draughtsmen of original drawings in monochrome and colour are rapidly being superseded by photographic methods; whilst the printing by slow-running flat-bed machines is being supplanted by high-speed rotaries fitted with automatic feeders and the latest mechanical devices, ensuring better and quicker production. It was not uncommon under the old method, when reproducing a colour printing, to have as many as 20 printings, each of a different colour or tint. The modern method (a photo-mechanical one) whereby colour negatives are secured by scientific photographic dissection of the colours of an original, has been made possible by the development of photography and the progress of mechanical science.

The rapid growth of planographic printing has put printing engineers on their mettle, and it is generally acknowledged that available processes and machines are far in advance of the craftsmen. Machines are now produced to deal with every phase of lithographic printing, even to the printing of two, three or four colours simultaneously, and the perfecting of the sheet, i.e., printing on both sides before delivery.

CARTOON

CARTOON, originally a preliminary drawing, executed to full scale and often in colour, of the design to be carried out in tapestry, mosaic, mural painting, or other work of art, and usually upon a heavy or durable paper. The cartoon when used for tapestry is usually placed in the loom so that the weaver can see it clearly just below his work, for which it acts as a guide.

To-day, the word means also a drawing, distributed publicly, which crystallizes some current thought into pictorial form often humorous and derisive.

UNITED STATES

THE POLITICAL CARTOON has come into greater general use in the United States than in any other country. Almost every daily paper uses either a syndicated cartoon or one drawn by a staff artist. The cartoon's worth is based on its instantaneous exposition of an idea. The very specific character of the drawn picture precludes anything except a direct attack. There is no qualification in it—it says but one thing and that at a glance. Herein lies its virtue and its limitation. The cartoon of approbation is rarely successful. To say a man is a good man in a cartoon carries little force; but if the artist can say that he is corrupt or unworthy, then he is wielding a weighty club. All cartoons, however, need not be bitter to be effective. Humour plays an important part in their appeal. Ridicule is one of the most potent weapons in the world when turned into social and political channels.

The cartoon in America roughly divides itself into two schools. In one, the homely, quasi-rural setting and characters are presented somewhat in the manner of the comic "strip." John McCutcheon of the Chicago *Tribune* is the chief exponent of this, by far the more numerous, group. The chief characteristics of these artists are usually a cheerful humour, a multitude of little figures engaged in violent action, comic animals and a generous labelling of persons and objects. In these pictures the sudden impact of the idea is diffused through the multiplicity of incident. "Balloons," those bits of conversation surrounded with a wire line, must be read as well as the labels attached to the figures in order that the artist's idea may be comprehended. The other school deals in a starker form of pictorial representation. Here the meaning explodes at first glance. Everything exterior to the single idea is eliminated. This method is derived from the French of which Forain is the leading exponent. Also, it may be noted that the execution of this second group is of higher artistic merit or at least aspiration. There is a greater sophistication, both in conception and execution in these cartoons, and they imply an audience of more mature thought than do those of the cheery, bucolic nature which abound in the country's press.

Through syndication, cartoons reach even the smallest papers so that the country is thoroughly supplied with its daily picture. The syndicate, however, having to serve all sorts of papers in all sorts of communities, has softened the "attack" quality in most of this product so that the result has been a more or less negative, qualified picture which is guaranteed to offend no one and therefore has lost most of its pungency. Lacking that virility, it has come to be simply a thing of entertainment wherein the annals of the great middle class are set forth in terms of simplicity.

There is growing up in the daily press a social cartoon which is based upon a close observation of urban life—a sort of picture which has no relation to politics or public affairs, but sets forth some phase of life with either sympathy or satire. Dennis Wortman of the New York *World* is the best representative of this interesting form.

One of the handicaps which confront the cartoonist is the paucity of symbols through which he must express himself. Through repetition the various devices become worn and threadbare; yet there is no escape from them for they have become established in the public's mind and any variant or change would obscure the meaning of the message the cartoonist wishes to convey. The G.O.P. elephant; the Democratic donkey (both originated by Thos. Nast in the days when he fought the Tweed ring); the weedy individual labelled "Prohibition"; the round Nihilist bomb with the sputtering fuse; the apoplectic, silk-hatted individual who becomes "Wall Street" or "The

70

Interests" or "The Trusts"; the meek, side-whiskered, spectacled creature who receives the brick Labour hurls at Capital and who is labelled "The Common People"—all these and more form the standardized little group of puppets with which the cartoonist must work. The figure of Uncle Sam is the most overworked of all. Each day he looks sternly out at the world from his place on the editorial page and views with alarm, warns, dictates, with pontifical fervour. Rarely does he laugh, for he is the Federal voice, and as such, deals only in weighty matters. He tells kings, potentates, labour unions, corrupt office-holders, swindling trusts (depending on whether he is a Republican or Democratic Uncle Sam) where they "get off." In his gayer moments he welcomes transatlantic flyers and channel swimmers and, in his sadder moments, stands with bowed head at the death of a public man of importance. He is ubiquitous, untiring and a good deal of a bore. Yet the management of a daily cartoon would be difficult without his valuable services.

The influence of the cartoon is doubtless a very considerable one in the formation of public opinion; for the public at large can comprehend the simple message of the drawn picture, whereas the reading of long editorials entails a much greater sustained effort on their part. A few of the weekly magazines use a political cartoon; but here we find the methods of the comic "strip" used rather than the sterner forms of satire. It would appear that, on the whole, the editors of the United States feel that a cheerful, simple, innocuous appeal is preferable to a more mordant presentation of pictorial ideas. Many of the cartoons of the extreme left wing of the Socialist party are of great force, full of bitterness and class antagonism. Because of the restricted circulation of the papers in which they appear, they are little known to the public. On the whole, the cartoons of the daily press fairly well represent the mind of the American public in its tolerant, non-critical, excessively partisan point of view.

THEORY OF DESIGN, TECHNIQUE AND MATERIALS

THE WORD CARTOON will no doubt be associated mainly and lastingly with such drawings as have a political or social significance and which, unlike the ordinary run of picture comicalities, stimulate thought on public affairs.

Materials and Methods of Reproduction.—To account for the material that cartoonists have used to get the best results one's field for investigation dates from the first Philipon publications (Paris 1830) to the present time.

71

GRAPHIC ARTS

The instruments used for drawing cartoons determine to a large extent the technique. The pencil and the pen have been the favourite tools of the cartoonist all along, the pencil holding first place in order of practicability. The pencil is used in learning to draw, and thus pencil drawings have a more intimate appearance than those done with a pen. Pen drawing is more of an acquired art, and is preferred by some masters of the cartoon because of its directness. In a sense, it is short-hand. A line must suggest more than is there; moreover, it must convey the feeling of substance—not merely the edge of something. Take for example the pen drawings of Gulbransson of *Simplicissimus* and "Phil May" of *Punch*, the former extremely grotesque, the latter but mildly exaggerated. Both cartoonists give the impression of knowing all about their subject, though they express it with the minimum of linear simplicity.

Forain in his early work was another master of brevity, though he used a fine brush much as one would use a pen. Some cartoonists play sketchily with the pen, while others prefer a rigid outline. Caran d'Ache drew pen and ink outline cartoons that strongly resembled the lines made by an etching needle on copper plate. On the other hand Heinrich Kley of *Jugend* tossed his pen lines like a juggler, making gestures as if about to miss, but always impressing one with his facility in creating amazing fantasies of nudes and animals. Charles Dana Gibson uses the pen as if cutting his way through his composition, the lines falling casually all about; many go part of the way only, leaving the rest to the imagination of the observer.

Two political cartoonists, Tenniel of *Punch* and Nast of *Harper's Weekly*, produced much of their work on wood-blocks. When it was later discovered, however, that a cartoon drawn on paper could be photographed on the wood, paper was used almost exclusively. Wood-cut cartoons were line drawings executed with a pen or sharp pencil, the latter quite similar to a pen point. Both Nast and Tenniel, who were contemporary, put a good deal of shading on their drawings. Nast used the cross-hatch abundantly, a method of shading produced by drawing a lot of more or less parallel lines and then going over them with other lines at right angles. Tenniel cross-hatched sparingly and shaded faces less than Nast. Tenniel had more knowledge of accurate draughtsmanship, whereas Nast had a clumsy way of drawing all his own. Much of his work was comedy, but he had a biting satire and naturally the Democratic press sometimes referred to his work as "those nasty cartoons."

72

What cartoonists draw with or what they draw on is of course not so important as what is drawn and how well it is done. A real artist can produce very good results with an old piece of charcoal on a barn door, but to have his work widely circulated, and that after all is what a cartoonist desires, he has been led to many experiments in reproduction. Daumier was doing his political cartoons and caricaturing life all about him, on stone; Cruikshank, at the same time, was producing his pictorial satires on copper and steel plates, ploughing through the lines of his drawing with an etching needle, making him both designer and engraver. William Blake at an earlier date did most of his work in the same way. Both processes have long since fallen into disuse except for exclusive reproduction. A remarkable facility was acquired by these artists on wood, steel and stone, in spite of the fact that mistakes made on these surfaces were hard to correct. However, the wood could be dug out and another piece glued in, the metal could be burnished and the stone could be scratched, but obviously with tedious effort and loss of time.

Most cartoons seen in the publications of the 20th century are drawn with a black crayon pencil or pen. Some cartoonists use both instruments on the same drawing. A brush is sometimes used for ready distribution of blacks. When the crayon pencil is employed the paper used has a surface similar to the lithograph stone, to all appearances quite smooth, but with a slightly rough surface (in the technical term, a "tooth" to it). Both pen drawings and those drawn with a crayon lend themselves to that most widely used process of engraving called zinc-etching (*q.v.*). This is also called the direct process as distinguished from the half-tone process, which is the popular way of reproducing drawings having soft gradations of light and shade, executed with a brush and water colour or rubbed in with the thumb or cloth. Zinc-etching is the universal process for making plates ready for printing cartoons done with a black crayon or pen and ink.

Theory of Design and Technique.—In the handling of pen and ink there are no rules, except those born of the artist's own feeling. The trite remark, "It is merely a matter of taste," describes the various degrees that artists go go in modelling, shading and the other requirements within the main outline of their pen and ink composition. Materials and methods of reproduction are merely incidental in the world of successful cartooning; the main factors lie in the ability to invent ideas, to compose pictures and to understand the value of emphasis. Creating ideas can become habitual. As the cartoonist

73

looks about him he sees in the every-day walks of life scenes that he thinks might apply to political situations. These ideas he notes and stores away in his subconscious mind, some day to develop and release as cartoons. Like the poet and the dramatist, he gets suggestions from the natural scene, from wide and purposeful reading, or from cartoons that have been produced in another era, endeavouring to improve them. We might say that the cartoonist is like the dramatist and, carrying the simile further, that the surface on which he draws is at once his stage-floor and proscenium arch. Within this area he creates a scene.

Doré was one of the most dramatic draughtsmen of any period of art. Had he succeeded Daumier as a cartoonist instead of becoming the illustrator of literary classics there can be no doubt he would have been an extraordinary propagandist, a great portrayer of affairs, for in the realm of both tragedy and comedy and in composing pictures that get "over the footlights," his work was always "cartoony."

The public will not admit that an actor can be both a tragedian and a comedian, but they expect this duality in a cartoonist. Keppler, Tenniel, Nast, Daumier, Doré, Steinlen, Félicien Rops, John Leech and many other draughtsmen of the past were skilful in depicting both humorous and serious ideas. The ideas of these early notables in black and white drawing, with few exceptions, also reveal minds with cultural backgrounds. Most of the political cartoonists of the 19th century, especially Tenniel, Leech, Nast and C. G. Bush of the New York *World*, often illustrated ideas that were suggested by their reading of Shakespeare, Greek mythology, Aesop's Fables and other classics, which were made analogous to situations in the English parliament, the U.S. Congress, or other seats of legislation.

Later the ideas, especially in America, became less "high brow." Ideas that were supposed not to be "above the heads of the people" were thought by editors to be more popular. As if the common man had to know all about Macbeth before the cartoonist could dress up a politician in a Macbeth costume and put a Macbeth quotation underneath his picture! Once the cartoonist has decided on his idea, then comes the composition of the cartoon. Good composing also is something one must feel, as there are no set rules. But just as in literature and all of the arts, to compose well is to feel a balanced harmony or completeness, which means that the cartoonist has relegated to second place the less essential features of the scene and stressed the most important, that he is alive to the value of contrasts and above all knows

POLITICAL AND HISTORICAL SATIRE, 16TH–18TH CENTURIES

1. "The Scots Holding Their Young Kings Nose to Ye Grinstone," a print from a broadside in prose, July 14, 1651, ridiculing the severe conditions exacted by the Scotch before offering Charles Stuart (later Charles II.) the crown. The central figure, Jack Presbyter, represents the church; Jockie (left), the laity. 2. Presentation of the Bible to Henry VIII.; from a woodcut, 1570. Henry (1491–1547), on his throne, is receiving the Bible from Thomas Cranmer, archbishop of Canterbury, and Lord Cromwell, and is trampling on Pope Clement VII., who denounced him. Cardinals Pole and Fisher are endeavouring to raise the Pope. 3. The European Powers throwing dice for the fort of Schencken, Holland; Dutch caricature, 1636. It represents the enemies and allies of the United Provinces, the gamblers being Prince Frederick Henry of Orange, Protestant leader, and Prince Cardinal Ferdinand, governor of Spain. Standing are Richelieu and Louis XIII. of France, supporting Frederick; Emperor Ferdinand II., Philip IV. of Spain, the Pope and the Bishops of Cologne and Mayence support the governor. The peasants await the result in terror. 4. "Taste in High Life," one of William Hogarth's (1697–1764) satires on London society in the 18th century. 5. "Prenez des Pilules, Prenez des Pilules."—"Dr. Misabin." This French caricature by Antoine Watteau (1684–1721), engraved by Arthur Pond, 1739, shows "Dr. Misabin," a Huguenot in London, who prescribed his pills with disastrous result. 6. "The True Portrait of Martin Scribbler," by George Duckett. The ape represents Alexander Pope (1688–1744), who was small and deformed; the donkey his friend William Cleland, who signed Pope's "Letter to the Publisher," in defence of "The Dunciad" (1729)

POLITICAL AND HISTORICAL SATIRE IN CARICATURE,
LATE 18TH AND EARLY 19TH CENTURIES

1. "The Plumb-pudding in Danger." An English caricature, dated Feb. 26, 1805, by James Gillray (1757–1815), showing Pitt and Napoleon dividing the world, Napoleon taking all Europe for France, Pitt the whole ocean and the rest of the world for England

2. "We Three Logger-heads be," a satire on the Court of Appeal by Thomas Rowlandson, England (1756–1827)

3. "Why hide them?" an etching by Francisco Goya y Lucientes, Spain (1746–1828), from his best-known satirical series, Los Caprichos

4. "Old Bumblehead the 18th trying on the Napoleon Boots," Louis XVIII. of France vainly trying to put on Napoleon's boots. This English political cartoon by George Cruikshank (1792–1878) satirizes the Spanish campaign, undertaken by Louis XVIII. in 1823. The figure, right, trying to snatch the falling crown of the Bourbons is Napoleon's son, Napoleon II. commonly known as the duke of Reichstadt (1811–32), who was twelve years old at this time

when it is time to leave off, having said enough. How much caricature or exaggeration to put into one's cartoon is also a matter of individual preference. What might be called the excessive grotesque appeals to some cartoonists. Others incline more toward a slightly emphasized naturalism, for example Braakensiek of *De Amsterdammer*.

If a public man is fat and his nose is long, good caricature in the opinion of some caricaturists is to magnify these characteristics very much—to pile Pelion on Ossa. To others the natural is almost funny enough and needs but a subtle emphasis.

Cartoon Publications.—From about 1870 to 1890 the political cartoon printed in colours was popular in Europe and became so in the United States during the late '70s, when Joseph Keppler started *Puck*. Keppler first experimented with *Puck* in St. Louis, at that time printing it from the stone in black and white only. When the St. Louis *Puck* was abandoned Keppler came to New York and drew cartoons on wood for *Leslie's Weekly*. In a few years, Adolph Schwarzman, a foreman printer of Leslie's, joined Keppler in organizing the Keppler and Schwarzman Company, and revived the name *Puck* for the humorous weekly that later became famous, popular and a financial success. The new *Puck* resembled the general *format* of the coloured cartoon papers of Europe, especially *La Flaca* in Madrid and Barcelona and *Humoristische Blätter* in Vienna.

In Australia, where Phil May started his career and that droll caricaturist Hopkins, "Hop," was a pioneer, the production of cartoons has been mostly in black-and-white. However, the tendency of these later years on the weekly humorous magazines is the use of one or two colours over pen and ink or crayon cartoons—the result of which is posterized attractiveness. Steinlen was one of the first draughtsmen to use red as an accompaniment to black crayon drawings. Wilke, Heine, Thöny and others of *Simplicissimus* use flat colours, as do other cartoonists of Europe, especially in Russia. In Mexico also much of the cartooning is simply coloured.

The coloured cartoons of Keppler, like Gillam's and others on the staff of *Puck*, were drawn on and printed directly from the stone. The first printing, in black ink, was called the key-plate. Then followed the printing on this key-plate impression from other stones to register reds, blues and other colours in facsimile to the cartoonist's water-colour design. The decline of the coloured political cartoons and weekly cartoon magazines in general was due, no doubt, to the fact that daily newspapers had begun to employ cartoonists

GRAPHIC ARTS

(this was about 1890) and to print coloured comic supplements. These supplements were "thrown in" for the price of the newspaper. This innovation in newspaper publishing was made possible by the invention of the fast multi-coloured printing press. In the beginning, these supplements sometimes printed coloured political cartoons in imitations of those in *Puck* and *Judge*.

As a result of all this the principal humorous weeklies of that day were not so much in public demand. But just as interest in the wood-cut and the lithograph is being revived, so the political cartoon in colours may have another day. The cartoon magazine *Life* was born a decade later than *Puck* and *Judge*. It opened a somewhat different field for artists. This magazine never had a staff in the sense that *Punch* and *Puck* were produced by a staff of artists regularly employed. John Ames Mitchell, the founder and first editor, was an artist himself, and in the first numbers of the magazine can be seen his pen and ink drawings. However, he is better known as an author. *Life* was not as political as its older contemporaries and was printed for many years without the use of colour. It indulged mostly in ridicule of social foibles and surveyed the American scene from the editor's amiable viewpoint, but not without occasional thrusts at the evils of commercialism, the law, the medical profession and other institutions.

While the Latin Quarter artists of Paris issued protesting magazines in the beginning of the present 20th century, it is generally conceded that one of the most artistic and at the same time shocking magazines was published in America. The magazine was called *The Masses*, the first number appearing in 1910 and the last in 1918. Its existence was due largely to one fact: an artist is an individualist; he wants to express himself in his own way. Many artists who believed that the sordid and the vulgar, the cruelties and hypocrisies that manifest themselves in this age of the industrial machine, should be ridiculed and caricatured without stint, joined the staff of *The Masses*. Then, too, the conventional magazine with its trite and formal make-up and its many taboos, was sooner or later doomed to become a target for the iconoclast artists. The pretty girl cover was the vogue when *The Masses* was started. One of its earliest cover designs was a picture of two poor, homely girls. One of them is saying: "Gee, Mag, think of us being on a magazine cover." On the art staff of *The Masses* were John Sloan, George Bellows, Charles A. Winter, Cornelia Barns, Maurice Becker, Glenn O. Coleman, H. J. Glintenkamp, K. R. Chamberlain, Boardman Robinson and Art Young.

With a natural aptitude for pictorial expression, with patience and hard work, the cartoonist creates ideas, composes pictures and puts exaggeration or mere emphasis where he thinks they belong.   But a cartoonist cannot produce convincing cartoons that will live, more than an author can produce good books, unless he feels the truth of his work.

CARICATURE

CARICATURE, a general term, adopted from the French, for the art of pictorial ridicule or satire of any kind, whether personal, social or political, derived from the Italian word *caricatura* in the sense of a portrait in which characteristic features are ludicrously exaggerated.

The practice of personal caricature is at least as old as to be recorded by Aristotle and Aristophanes, both of whom tell us something of an artist named Pauson who made pictorial fun of people, and was made to suffer for it.   Again, Pliny mentions two sculptors, Bupalus and Athenis, who, by way of a joke, exhibited a portrait of the poet Hipponax, who was very ugly, for public ridicule: the poet is said to have retaliated in satirical verse with such effect that the sculptors hanged themselves in despair.   That none of these three appears to have benefited by his activities in this direction very possibly accounts for the fact that the line of their successors, if they had any, is not traceable, and that among all the stories related by Vasari there are none that point to any survival of their baneful influence.   Leonardo da Vinci made many wonderful drawings of distorted heads, but these we are told were life-like portraits carefully studied from actual freaks, and it is not until the close of the 16th century that we can begin to trace a regular unbroken pedigree for the art of *Caricatura* (the "ritratto ridicolo di cui siansi esagerati i difetti" as it is defined in the *Nuova Enciclopedia*) from the Carracci and their school in Bologna, through Ghezzi, Townshend, Daumier, Dighton, "Ape" and "Spy," to its supreme living practitioner Max, and the very numerous brood of stinging birds whom his revival of the art in the closing years of the last century undoubtedly did much to encourage.

RISE OF CARICATURE

Early Italian School.—In Bologna *caricatura* was the natural result of its artistic and popular "atmosphere." So at least says Count Malaguzzi-Valeri in a recent brochure, and he quotes with approval the opinion of Ludovico Frati (from an article in *La Villa Cittadina*, Nov. 1919) that when the history of caricature in Italy is studied as it has been in England, France and Germany, Bologna will have one of the first places in it. The foundation of the vivacious *Papagallo* in the '80s of the last century proved that the old spirit was not extinguished, and a glance at its activities in the 17th and 18th centuries reveals a considerable amount of material for such a history, which has somehow escaped the attention both of the historians of caricaturists and of the Magnasco society. So far from being *tenebroso*, the school—the actual studio of the Carracci—appears to have sparkled with continuous outbursts of artistic humour. "I Carracci stessi amavan lo scherzo," says Malaguzzi, and they habitually indulged in artistic frivolities in the intervals of serious work. They began by introducing the use of linear symbols and asking their friends to guess what they represented—a practice possibly foreshadowing those of some of the modernists—and visitors to the studio were regarded as fair game for caricature, and saw themselves portrayed under the guise of dogs, pigs, beasts of burden, and even of inanimate objects like jugs or loaves of bread. Annibale Carracci himself was responsible for some of these, and his followers included Pietro Facini, Lionello Spada, Giuseppe Maria Crespi and, most prolific of all, Giuseppe Maria Mitelli. Eight large volumes of Mitelli's drawings, many of them caricatures, are in the library at Bologna, and a pair presented to the British Museum by Lawrence Binyon are of a quality that induces a strong desire to see some of the others.

None of these names is familiar—at least as a caricaturist—but thanks to the English engraver, Arthur Pond, who published a series of 24 prints in 1743, we have examples from drawings in private collections by Guercino, Francesco Mola and Carlo Maratti. Most of Pond's subjects, however, are by the then "famoso cavaliere delle caricature," namely, Pietro Leone Ghezzi, who was renowned in Rome, not only among his fellow-countrymen, but also among foreigners for his caricature portraits.

To Pond we are also indebted for what is possibly the earliest example of pure caricature in Great Britain, a drawing made by Antoine Watteau when

CARICATURES OF CELEBRITIES AND PERSONAGES

1. "It is truly painful to see how these wretched shopkeepers get themselves up." Gavarni. 2. "M. Prudhomme." Henri Monnier. 3. "A Young Poodle." H. Heath. 4. "The Rising Generation in Parliament" (Disraeli and Peel). John Leech. 5. "England v. Prussia." Virginio. 6. "Dropping the Pilot" (Bismarck). John Tenniel. 7. "Statesman No. 48" (Sir John D. Coleridge). J. J. Tissot. 8. "The Story of Cruel Joseph" (Chamberlain). Gould. 9. "The Baron of Oakland." "H. B." (John Doyle)

PLATE IV

CARICATURE

LATE NINETEENTH AND EARLY TWENTIETH CENTURY CARICATURE

1. "Robert Browning taking tea with the Browning Society" by Max Beerbohm, one of the first satirical artists to break away from the conventional Victorian style of caricature

2. "Gladstone" from "The Phil May Folio"

3. "The Railways" by Honoré Daumier, showing third-class passengers frozen during a train trip

4. "Jules Renard" by "Sem" (George Goursat)

5. "S'r 'enry" (Sir Henry Wood) "refusing an encore" by Low

6. Yvette Guilbert, from "Stage Folks" by Alfred J. Frueh, an American born in Lima, Ohio

7. "Austen Chamberlain" by A. B. Sava

8. "Kruger and John Bull" by Caran d'Ache (Emmanuel Poiré), a satire on the Boer War. John Bull is rifling the pockets of President Kruger

9. Drawing by Daumier, published in *Charivari*. "Why the devil should this great red creature, only half-dressed, too, be called Olympia?" "But, my dear, it is the black cat they mean by that!"

10. "Old Bill. Full of determination and plum & apple." Central figure in a series of World War cartoons created by Bruce Bairnsfather

11. Cécile Sorel, by André Rouveyre

he was in London in 1720, of Dr. Misaubin, a French refugee who was so suc-cessful in his profession as to be branded by posterity as a quack. This draw-ing is said by Mariette to have been made in a coffee house, and it is not straining probability to suggest that the place may have been Button's, where Hogarth in his younger days made portrait sketches from the life. None of the work mentioned so far, it should be noted, was intended for publication, for *caricatura* was essentially personal, and it was only the vogue created by Ghezzi that led to the publication by Pond of his portraits of this class, and by Oesterreich of another series of about 40 at Potsdam in 1766. There is little if any malice in them, and they seem to have been done simply for the amusement of the subjects and their friends.

Rise of Political Caricature.—For the employment of this gentle art as an adjunct to political satire, it is not so easy as it may sound to find any abso-lute authority earlier than the middle of the 18th century. There may be one or two examples, but the prints of Chancellor Finch with a pair of wings behind him, in allusion to his flight from the country, or of Bishop Williams with a large blunderbuss, etc., and indeed of whole packs of cards representing individuals, in the 17th century, are purely symbolical in their satire, and cannot be said to attack the personal appearance of the victim. This wicked practice would appear to have been introduced by George (afterwards Mar-quis) Townshend, and even if he cannot be discredited with the sole responsi-bility for such a monstrous extension of a private artistic diversion, we can at any rate produce illuminating evidence of it in his case. In June 1765 a letter appeared in *The Public Advertiser* dealing banteringly with Townshend's ac-tivities of this kind. After referring to the use of the rolling-press in produc-ing satirical prints, the writer proceeds thus: "He has dealt his grotesque cards from house to house, from Town's End to Town's End. Is there a great general of the highest rank and most eminent military abilities . . . ? If the size of his person as well as fame should be larger than ordinary, this malicious libeller at three strokes of his pencil scratches out his figure in all the ridiculous attitudes imaginable (Duke of Cumberland). Is there a noble-man distinguished for wit, eloquence and learning? If his person be long and lank, lean and bony, he also is in the like manner exposed to ridicule (Lord Lyttleton). If the name of a Scotch peer bears the least resemblance of Boot, and his Christian name be John, a huge jack-boot serves for him on copper-plate (Lord Bute). And if another lord bears the name of some animal (a fox, for instance) his features are assimilated perforce to those of the animal, and aggravated or distorted in the most ludicrous manner in order to produce a likeness between them."

The personal note has made "caricature" in the broader, modern sense, a living thing. The older satirists merely personified institutions. The papacy was figured as a monster with the trunk of a woman, the head of a donkey, and a different symbol lurking in every limb. The Dutch prints that were so effective against Louis XIV. show us merely dolls representing the various crowned and coroneted heads of the period, and the English ones simply dummies with labels issuing from their mouths, inscribed with the right thing. There is no human interest in any of these designs, valuable as they are to the student and the collector.

Pictorial Satire.—For pictorial satire in general, claims have been advanced to an even greater antiquity than for *caricatura,* which cannot be lightly dismissed, although they must necessarily be accepted with considerable reserve. With the very old as with the very new, it is not always obvious to the spectator whether a joke is intended or not, and it is a dangerous subject on which to be too positive. Champfleury, who ransacked every corner of antiquity for materials for his *Histoire de la Caricature antique,* turned away in despair from the Assyrian bas-reliefs; but are they a whit less solemn than those on the Albert Memorial? Man, as he declares, has laughed, as he has wept, in every age: so why should we deny the possibility of the existence of Assyrian satirists who worked in less enduring materials than granite or marble?

As it happens, the oldest example of pictorial humour put forward by Thomas Wright in his *History of Caricature* is of a religious, not a political, subject and, what is still more interesting, there is good *a posteriori* evidence for accepting it for inclusion in the gallery of the satirical. For, whatever difficulties the extension of the term "caricature" in modern times has occasioned in deciding what is and what is not to be properly included within its limits, there is one strain constantly recurring in the modern family which is also prominent in antiquity, and which may therefore be accounted as of some genealogical significance, namely the representation of human beings with the heads of animals, or, more generally, investing them with animal characteristics.

It is in Egypt that we find the example in question, a painting in the tomb of King Rameses V., presumably as early as 1100 B.C. It represents a soul condemned by Osiris to return to earth in the form of a pig, accompanied by two dog-headed monkeys. It may be that this is simply religious symbolism, but that need not exclude it from consideration here, for there is a definite historical, or, at least, traditional link between it and the famous Roman *graffito* of the Crucifixion, of the 3rd or 4th century A.D. In this the figure on the cross has the head of an ass, and a man contemplates it in an attitude which is interpreted by the legend in Greek characters "Alexamenos worships God." At first sight this might seem to be a scoff directed against the Saviour Himself, but it probably has a more general significance. There was a definite belief among some of the Gentiles that the Jews secretly worshipped the image of an ass, or of an ass's head, but the Gnostics, who were possibly nearer the mark, maintained that the Jewish God Sabaoth was figured in the form of a man with the head of an ass.

Little less than religious belief was the Roman tradition of descent from Aeneas, and at Herculaneum we find something very similar to the Crucifixion *graffito* in an exact parody of a well-known group of Aeneas carrying Anchises and leading Ascanius from Troy, in which the figures are drawn with the heads and extremities of animals. Titian, some 1,200 years later, went even further than this in converting "the Laocöon" into a group of monkeys. In the animal strain, James Goupy satirized Handel "with a snout of a hog playing on an organ, with many symbols of gluttony round him," and Newton drew Wilton, the sculptor, with the head of an ass. None of these examples answers to the definition of *caricatura*—all are symbolic.

Conversely, Tenniel put the British Lion into trousers, while Landseer invested dogs of all sorts with every variety of human sentiment, whether he meant to or not. For this also there is good historical precedent, though hardly as ancient as the days of Rameses V. In some later Egyptian papyri are whole groups of animals performing human actions—notably a lion and a gazelle playing chess together, who are doubtless intended to typify a king and one of his ladies. The fox and the goose were taken to satirize monks and their dupes in the middle ages, and in later times apes for the admonition of humanity at large. Claude Gillot, and his more famous pupil, Antoine Watteau, festooned the way for the Victorian scientists with orgies of artistic anthropoids. "La Grande Singerie" and "La Petite Singerie" at Chantilly are developments of Gillot's numerous engravings, and Watteau, whether or not he actually painted these, has left us two simian satires, "La Peinture" and "La Sculpture." Christophe Huet, J. Gueland and Le Mire followed the lead, and even Chardin in 1740 exhibited "Le Singe Peintre" and "Le

Singe Antiquaire." Seeing how many and how obvious are the resemblances between certain types of humanity and animal creation in general, it is no wonder if satirists of all ages have availed themselves freely of these opportunities. It is the same in literature, from Aesop to Gulliver, and on to Dr. Dolittle, while in conversation it is so common as to escape notice altogether. Is there any social circle that does not include a goose, an ass or a cow?

The Effect of Printing.—But whether or not caricature and pictorial satire had even a single ancestor in common in remote ages, it is certain that the latter, unlike the former, depends chiefly for its existence on circulation; and so we have to wait for the invention of the art of block printing on wood and of engraving and etching on copper before we can begin to trace its history with any success. The earliest example mentioned in the British Museum catalogue of Italian engraving, which dates from about 1460, is neither religious nor political, being known as "The battle for the hose." It represents a group of richly attired ladies scuffling for the possession of a pair of trunk hose held aloft in a garland by two winged genii. Dr. Warburg has suggested that the specific idea is a popular illustration of the text of Isaiah iv. 1, thus bringing the prophets of Israel again within our range. Somewhat similar in subject is a slightly later German woodcut of a duel between a man and a woman, which is supposed to symbolize the eternal marital question: "Who shall wear the breeches?" Less abstruse are one or two satires against the Jews; but the surviving examples of the 15th century (probably a mere percentage of such perishable and ephemeral material) are very few, and it is not until the Reformation, when Luther organized whole arsenals of pictorial artillery for his campaign against Rome, that we speak of it as fairly established.

Once the Reformation was established there may have been a less regular demand for satirical prints, though there was still intermittent firing; a contemporary Italian print of Diana and Calisto was altered by Peter Miricenys to represent the young Queen Elizabeth and the pope, the latter "uncovered by Time and Truth." Not until the end of the 17th century, when the Dutch followed Luther's example and employed Romeyn de Hooghe to satirize Louis XIV., did the stream begin to flow regularly and to swell into the great river it became in the time of the Georges.

CARICATURE

EARLY BRITISH CARICATURE

17th and Early 18th Century.—The catalogue of satirical prints in the British Museum, compiled by F. G. Stephens, is unfortunately only carried down to the year 1770. Its contents, numbering over 4,000 items, with copious notes, are an indespensable commentary on the history of the period they cover, and a veritable museum of literary and social curiosities. In his preface to the second volume Stephens emphasizes the importance attached to political satire in the time of William III., when Romeyn de Hooghe and his school were producing print after print directed against Louis XIV. One of the most famous of these was "The Reported Death of William III.," occasioned by the public rejoicings in Paris over the false news of William having been shot in 1690. Of this there were four editions, two of them made in Paris, in order to show the "folies extravagantes" of those who produced the original; and in a later print, "Pantagruel agonisant," one of the most elaborate and interesting satires connected with the history of England, the "Reported Death" is introduced as an accessory to the mortification of the French king. These prints continued into the next reign, another effective piece being "Vacarme au Trianon," occasioned by the battle of Ramillies.

British royalties had, up to this time, escaped personal attack in prints, but with the advent of the house of Hanover any restraint in that direction soon melted away. As Stephens observed in commenting on a print entitled "Aeneas in a Storm," not only is George I. hinted at without much respect, but the personal habits of his successor are vividly described, and his peculiar practice of kicking hats, if not larger and living objects, is laughed at. "The Festival of the Golden Rump" deals vigorously with this subject, and has wider bearings of very great importance, social as well as political and personal; it shows that royalty had become an object of stage satire, and indicates the parliamentary origin of the restraints on theatrical representations which were then newly imposed, and have been maintained.

Hogarth, whose period of activity coincides almost exactly with the reigns of the first two Georges, stands alone in the history of caricature. Champfleury calls him "le premier roi" and "le véritable père de la caricature," while Fielding, as we shall see, distinguishes his "comic painting" from *caricatura*, as, save for a few notable examples, he was quite right in doing. Hogarth rarely availed himself of personalities in his satires, and the identification of any of his characters with actual people must be taken with the

83

greatest reserve. Nor did he, as a rule, take any particular event as a subject, looking much more widely over the whole range of human frailties, and selecting and staging them like a theatrical manager. Hogarth's great serial works were "not of an age, but for all time," whereas the satirical prints of the 18th century are merely squibs which light up some ephemeral extravagance or political brawl, brightly enough, but without any permanent illumination of the world's stage.

By the time George III. had ascended the throne the issue of satirical prints had become a regular institution. As already mentioned, a new species now first appeared, invented by George Townshend; they were caricatures on cards. The original one, which had an amazing success, was of Newcastle and Fox looking at each other, and crying, with Peachum in *The Beggar's Opera*, "Brother, brother, we are both in the wrong." Another of Townshend's masterpieces, published in 1762, was "The Scotch Hurdy-Gurdy or The Musical Boot," signed "D. Rhezzio inv., G. Oh! Garth scratch-avit." Further activities against Bute are reflected in another advertisement of a Political and Satirical History.

Stephens claims rather too much for Townshend in saying that he may fairly be styled the inventor of the most modern form of artistic satire, but it may be allowed that he raised the tone of it, and that his skill, though often mercilessly employed and subject to political passion, was not disgraced by the unscrupulous frankness and licence of some of his predecessors or successors.

Later 18th Century Caricature.—In his fourth volume, which deals with the years 1761–70, Stephens writes that a very striking attestation of the growing importance of artistic satire which, by this time, was partly personal, partly political, is afforded by the fact that many magazines, illustrated by satirical prints, were published during this period. Previous to this date such work could hardly be said to exist. These publications were essentially arsenals of satirical weapons of which the cuts enriching them were the most efficient. The *London Museum* was one of the more prominent. The *Political Register* supplied a considerable number of satirical prints, notably one of Bute as Colossus with Pitt between his feet (1767). The *Oxford Magazine* was enriched by a series of very cleverly designed prints such as "The Siege of Warwick Castle," a satire on physicians (1768) and "The Rape of the Petti-coat." Even the decorous *Gentlemen's Magazine*, which in 1746 had published a version of Hogarth's portrait of Lord Lovat, issued among its few illustrations with figures the satirical print of "John Wilkes Esq. before the Court of King's Bench." The *Universal Museum* printed "The Present State of Surgery or Modern Practice" (1769). The *Town and Country Magazine*, the most prolific of satire-bearing works, had numerous illustrations, many of which were directed against men of note, and women of ill-fame. The former were nearly all politicians opposed to the popular leaders, and these prints may fairly be called the arrows of their party directed against the king and his court. These weapons showed that the dignified and honourable modes of English political warfare had given place to a coarser and meaner system of attack; the *Town and Country Magazine* spared neither the public nor the private lives of the courtiers, and their wives and daughters, living and dead, chaste or unchaste, had no more mercy at the hands of the satirists than was vouchsafed to their mistresses or the harlotry of the stage and opera. The common object of attack in these cases was that order of society which hung like a fringe about the court, and of which the most extravagant front comprised those *"macaronies"* whose vagaries occupied the *Universal Magazine* and other publications.

If Stephens could say as much as this of social satire down to 1770, one wonders how he would have expressed himself had he continued till the end of the century, the last quarter of which was enriched by a steadily growing production of caricatures of every sort, and not always of the nicest. But the establishment of the Royal Academy had certainly raised both the quantity and the standard of artistic work in Great Britain, and until the Regency there is much more in the comic part of it to be praised than blamed. Gillray and Rowlandson, in the work of their early prime, had no rival but each other, though the field was a large one, and included such men as Henry William Bunbury, Paul Sandby, P. J. de Loutherbourg, James Sayer, John Raphael Smith, James Hamilton Mortimer and others less known but hardly less worthy. The demand for caricatures continued to increase, and on some of the prints issued by S. W. Fores—the founder of the still extant firm in Piccadilly—it was advertised that folios of caricatures were lent out for the evening, and that his gallery might be inspected for one shilling. The range of subjects also increased, and while politics continued to take first place, social subjects became much more numerous and more absurd. Rowlandson drew every class of society, in every sort of occupation, and as there was little or no "mixture" of the social classes in his time, his variety is enormous.

Disappearance of the 18th Century School.—By the end of the 18th century the rose had become somewhat overblown, and during the first quarter of the 19th, caricature sank into exceeding coarseness. The artistic reputation of its two gifted exponents, Rowlandson and Gillray, has suffered irreparable damage from the atrocious and often revolting quality both of their subjects and their interpretation of them; it is only in recent years that the former has been recognized from his immense output of beautiful drawings as one of our finest artists, while the latter, surviving only in his caricature prints, has still to wait for a recognition of his true powers which were so grossly employed in disgusting satire. Isaac Cruikshank, who with his still more gifted son, George, forms a link between the older order and what was to come, was never offensively coarse, though like Newton, Heath and one or two more, he was too fond of being funny to have much regard to artistic excellence. The extravagances of this school may be excused to some extent by the opportunities offered them in the ridiculous fashions, both sartorial and social, of their time, and they may very possibly be more appreciated in time to come than they are at the moment.

FRENCH CARICATURE

Effect of Censorship.—Meanwhile, our attention may conveniently be turned to France, where personal caricature, even if it had established itself as soon as in England, was hardly likely to be allowed the same liberty in connection with political satire. The rarity of satirical prints of the earlier part of the 18th century is due rather to the extreme rigour with which they were suppressed than to their numbers, and apart from politics there was a large and varied supply of very interesting material for Grand-Carteret's volume *L'Estampe Satirique*, etc., and the more recent and fuller works of André Blum on the same subject. Among the earliest examples is another medical satire by poor Watteau who, in the short interval between his return from England and his death in 1721, burlesqued the whole faculty in a drawing which was engraved by Comte de Caylus. Caylus himself appears to have caught the infection of pure caricature from Ghezzi, and he made some very curious *portrait-chargés* of the frequenters of Madame Doublet's salon. Of more public interest were the satires against literary and artistic personages; in 1728 the *Almanac de Parnasse* had a frontispiece introducing portraits of Rousseau, Voltaire, Racine le jeune, Crébillon and other figures, which was suppressed by the police and the *Almanac* sold without it. Voltaire in later years was bombarded with caricatures, one of which had the interest for us of showing Urania offering him a pair of spectacles to help him in reading New-ton's *Principia*. Jacques Saly produced a series of caricatures when he was at the French Academy in Rome in 1750, thus carrying on the true Carrac-cian tradition. The lighter side of social satire is represented by Jeurat, J. B. Huet and Gabriel St. Aubin, all of whom had a kindly eye for *les filles de joie*, and later by Duboucourt, some of whose works have more than a little in common with the best of Rowlandson's. With *Vauxhall Gardens* and *La Promenade de la Galerie du Palais Royal*, published in 1785 and 1787, Eng-land and France, the only two countries in which a continuous development of caricature is traceable, were within measurable distance of each other. In the years of the Revolution and Napoleonic Wars such an approach could hardly be expected to be continued; no later than 1791 the rift was wide enough for the following legend beneath a very telling print:—"La grande aiguiserie royale des poignards anglais: Le fameux ministre Pitt aiguisant les poignards . . . Le gros Georges Dandin tournant le roule en haletant de fatigue." The very numerous satires of these years are of the greatest interest historically, but are not of an attractive nature. It is, however, all the more interesting on this account to note that when the two countries were, so to speak, starting afresh in the second quarter of the next century, they did so on remarkably similar lines. Let us, therefore, continue with France.

The Reign of Louis Philippe.—Champfleury begins his *History of Modern Caricature* with the reign of Louis Philippe in 1830. In his preface he re-marks that the book might well be styled "The demolishers of the *bour-geoisie*," for they had no more determined adversaries than Daumier, Traviés and Henri Monnier; and that whatever satirical characters might be created in the future to succeed those of Mayeux, Robert Macaire and Mon-sieur Prudhomme, those three types would subsist as the most faithful rep-resentatives of the *bourgeoisie* from 1830 to 1850. The king himself, he adds, was the first *bourgeois* in the realm, and seemed to think that he could govern it with an umbrella for a sceptre, and that he only had to open it to protect himself from political storms. Certainly that strikes the dominant note of modern caricature, which henceforth, not only in France and England, but generally everywhere, became gradually less rude and savage, and more "refined" and domesticated. As both politically and socially the world set-tled down after the Revolution and the Napoleonic Wars, so caricature, save for occasional necessities, assumed a more polite, if more sarcastic, tone, and monsters and deformities gave place to subtler rendering of human weaknesses or excesses. In France, at first, the satire was none the less biting, the ridicule none the less stinging for its artistic excellence, and personal, physical caricature was used by Daumier and others with terrific effect. The king's heavy physiognomy was transformed into a symbol—*la poire*—and there was no public character who escaped merciless caricature of his features, gestures and habits. At the same time, however, the artistic sense predominated, and when the bitterness had somewhat abated, survived as an example to be followed, a standard to be maintained. Even if this improvement was, so to speak, in the air, it was actually precipitated by one man, namely Charles Philipon. Whether or not he influenced John Doyle in the course of their lithographic studies, who, as we shall see, was doing something of the same sort for English caricature, he was certainly the great general who organized and led to glory the noble army of French satirical artists, and thereby furnished an example which has been followed more or less closely in every country in the world.

Philipon's Career.—Philipon was born at Lyons in 1800 and settled in Paris in 1825, where he took to lithography for a living and produced some very charming caricatures; but he soon realized his ambition to found a paper. This was *La Caricature*, which made its appearance on Nov. 4, 1830, and after braving a continuous deluge of legal actions, was suppressed in 1835. Its chief artists were Honoré Daumier, Henri Monnier and J. T. Traviés, above mentioned.

On Dec. 1, 1832, was born Philipon's second child, *Le Charivari*, which still survives in a new series, having only temporarily succumbed to the World War in 1915. This was a daily paper, "publiant chaque jour un nouveau dessin." Its birthday vignette, designed by Tony Johannot, the public were informed, required such special preparation that it could not appear in time. When no more than eight years old, it stood godfather to another lusty, and still thriving paper, *Punch, or the London Charivari*. In 1838, on Nov. 1, *La Caricature Provisoire* donned the shoes of its deceased brother, dedicated "aux amis de l'ancienne Caricature politique," and adorned by its artists Daumier, Grandville, Forest, Bouchot, etc.; and when asked about the adjective *provisoire*, Philipon replied: "Si elle n'est pas politique, elle sera non politique . . . elle sera morale, littéraire, théatrale, artistique, sociale, medicale, chirurgicale, agricole, somnambuliste, anabaptiste, etc." In the following June it received a new sub-title, "revue morale, judiciaire, littéraire, artistique, fashionable et scénique," having abdicated its title of *provisoire*, "désormais trop sûre de vivre longtemps, et bien, pour ne pas se proclamer définitive." In Jan. 1842 its subtitle was further modified, and it broke out into coloured plates of a most distressing brilliance.

Philipon's third child to attain public importance was *Le Journal pour Rire*, a specimen number of which was issued in Dec. 1847, and No. 1 on Feb. 5 following. This was on large newspaper sheets and full of wood-cut illustrations by some of the older artists, and also some new ones. Among these one of the most brilliant was Gustave Doré, who furnished *Punch* with the idea for at least two of his most successful features, namely, the "Bird's Eye Views of Society" and "The Royal Academy Guyed." Besides these, Philipon was responsible for *Le Musée Philipon* and was also the godfather of a great many occasional publications. In No. 5 of *Le Journal pour Rire* is a list of "Caricatures par les principaux dessinateurs du *Musée Philipon*, du *Charivari*, du *Journal pour Rire*, et de la maison Aubert," some of them consisting of as many as 70 or 80 plates, a glance at which will give us a fair idea of what purely social caricature had become under the fostering influence of Philipon. First place is given to Gavarni, with "Le Carnaval," "Le Carnaval à Paris," "La Boîte aux Lettres," "Les Maris vengés," "Les Artistes," "Les Impressions de Ménage," "Les Lorettes," "Les Enfants terribles." Next is Daumier with "Les Beaux Jours de la Vie" (80 plates), "Les Croquis d'Expression" and "Les Robert Macaire" (with Philipon). Then Bouchot's 70 "Bonnes Fêtes Musicales"; Jacques's "Militariana"; Behr's "L'Amour à Paris"; "Croquis parisiens" and "L'Opéra au 19ᵉ siècle" by E. de Beaumont; "Au Bal de l'Opéra," "Les Troupiers Français," "Croquis militaires," "Les Grisettes," and "Physiologie des bals publics" by Vernier. The anonymous remainder is not long, and is necessary to complete the survey:—"Nos Gentilshommes," "Turlupiniades," "Souvenirs de Garnison," "À la Guerre comme à la Guerre," "Mœurs Algériennes," "Mœurs britanniques," "Les Chargés parisiens," "Le Conservatoire de danse," "Ces bons Parisiens," "Prophètes charivaques."

For one man such an achievement, of which the above is the barest outline, was prodigious, and its effect on caricature, both in France and other countries, has been decisive. He raised caricature from the precarious issue of occasional prints to the regular position of an indispensable auxiliary to journalism. To his recognition of the practical and artistic possibilities of lithography combined, we owe the magnificent series of drawings that await resurrection in the forgotten or neglected volumes above mentioned, and his undying ardour in political ridicule is still traceable in these days of milder expression.

Among the brilliant and very numerous band of his artists, three names only are familiar to the public in Great Britain or the U.S.A. Daumier, who stands head and shoulders above the rest; Doré, who might have rivalled him had he been prevented, as Daumier was, from evaporating into popular painting; and Gavarni. The first has now been recognized, like Rowlandson, as a serious factor in the history of art; the second had his popular triumph and must wait for reinstatement until the effects of it have cleared off. The third is still hovering. But none of the three can be fairly appreciated, until much more of their work is brought out into the light. Of the rest, Traviés and Monnier stand out conspicuously as the creators of two almost historical characters—the hunchback Mayeux and Monsieur Prudhomme—characters like Philipon's and Daumier's Robert Macaire and Bertrand (feebly imitated in "Ally Sloper" and "Ikey Mo"); and Grandville, who is best known for his ornithological whims, though they were but a part of his excellent works, deserves equal rank.

WORLDWIDE SPREAD OF CARICATURE

Doyle and Seymour.—In England, as in France, modern caricature may be fairly dated from 1830, when McLean, the printseller, commenced the issue of his *Monthly Caricature Sheets*, a series which outlasted Philipon's first venture by a year. These sheets were entirely covered with lithographs, mostly by Robert Seymour, but also by John Doyle who in the previous year had begun the famous series of political cartoons, also in lithograph, over the mysterious signature "H. B." These, too, were published by McLean, and although it would be paying him too high a compliment to style him the English Philipon, he is certainly to be congratulated on having brought out two such notable caricaturists as Doyle and Seymour, and also on having realized the practical and artistic possibilities of lithography for the purpose. Doyle was an Irishman who came to London to paint portraits, but turning his attention to lithography, like Philipon, found it an equally efficient and delightful means of improving and refining the artistic qualities of political caricature. George Cruikshank, not content to follow in his father's footsteps, but still using the needle, was also a great, and certainly a wider, influence in the general refinement upon the monstrous and extravagant fancies of the older school which is apparent in the work of John Leech, Richard Doyle, Hablot Browne and the rest. But there is a softness and a gentle spirit of raillery in the elder Doyle's political sheets—numbering in all over 900—and at least equally discernible in the work of his son, that inclines one to place Doyle as high as Cruikshank among those to whom the spirit of modern caricature is most indebted for its high tone and gentle demeanour, no less than for its artistic excellence.

Robert Seymour, whose name and work are now entirely forgotten, was really one of the older school. Like Woodward and Bunbury, he was a born caricaturist. It was his suggestion of *Cockney Sporting Plates* to be issued monthly that was altered by Charles Dickens, whom he asked to supply the letterpress, into *The Pickwick Papers*, and he was their first illustrator. His art was not of the highest order, or he might not have achieved such a wide popularity in his inartistic period. It was in *Figaro in London*, edited by Gilbert à Beckett, that Seymour was described, in 1833, as the Shakespeare of caricature, and in the same year was announced *The Terrific Penny Magazine* with cuts by Seymour and other artists of celebrity, and later, *The Wag*, and a new supply of Figaro's caricature gallery. In this sort of company one might observe, like Dr. Primrose, that if there was not more wit than usual, there was certainly more laughter. But the dominating figure of this period was, undoubtedly, George Cruikshank, who, if we allow for the difference in time and circumstances, occupied very much the same place in the 19th century as Hogarth did in the 18th.

The untimely death of Seymour, by his own hand, in 1836, and a diminishing output of H. B.'s lithographs, may possibly have accelerated the foundation in 1840 of *Punch or the London Charivari*. Certainly the time was ripe for such an event, thanks to the efforts of the preceding decade, and although neither the elder Doyle nor George Cruikshank had any hand in it, and its origins were of the humblest, it soon established itself, and only needed Richard Doyle and John Leech to make its success the more sure and more glorious.

But the success of Philipon's papers in Paris was bound to be attempted, sooner or later, in other countries than England, and for even a glance at the history of caricature during the second half of the 19th century we must look all over Europe—to say nothing of America, north and south—where in every capital the press was being requisitioned to provide a regular weekly service of vehicles for comical and satirical expression of feeling, which had hitherto had to go on foot or hire a conveyance for any particular occasion.

91

GRAPHIC ARTS

Bismarck in Caricature.—Such a consummation was, perhaps, dimly foreshadowed by the publication, in 1890, in Paris, of a little volume entitled *Bismarck en Caricatures*, illustrated by 140 cartoons, etc. from the more important periodicals since 1862. Its author, J. Grand-Carteret, was already well known for his work on caricatures in earlier periods, and he followed it some years later with volumes dealing similarly with Leopold II., Nicholas II., Alphonse XIII. and Edward VII., which bring us nearer to present days. But the first volume, in itself marking a distinct advance in the importance of caricature as an aid to history, and also emphasizing, as it happened, the beginning of a new epoch with the dismissal of the great Chancellor, is for many reasons the most valuable. Allowing for Bismarck being its only subject, with the stage all to himself, one cannot fail to see how clearly the mirror of caricature reflects the events, and the subtleties with which they are developed, throughout the whole quarter of a century in which Bismarck was violently, yet always respectfully attacked, both in his own country and in many other States. A French author might be pardoned for a little bias in dealing with such a subject, but throughout the volume there is hardly a cartoon which Bismarck himself could not have regarded with pleasure or pride. All are tributes to his incessant activity and efficiency, even those of the little Munich *Punsch*, which never ceased to sting him till it ceased to appear in 1870. The occasional issue of single caricatures to a very limited clientèle was now superseded by the regular publication of illustrated periodicals which were read by thousands, and the foundations of a permanent and world-wide alliance between caricature and journalism were firmly laid. On its social side this alliance was no less fruitful in its developments than in politics, and the gain to both parties to it became more and more apparent as the century advanced to its close. To posterity the gain is immeasurably greater, in having a live record of manners and customs in place of the haphazard fragments from which its knowledge of earlier periods is alone derivable. Astronomers contemplate the heavens in a pool of mercury, and the reflections of human action in the mercurial element, though the gaiety of nations may ripple the surface, are not so distorted as to impair their interest or their value. Rather do the ripples add that relish to matter of fact which, as we presently shall see, is at the root of the derivation of the word caricature, and, we may almost say, of a really spiritual understanding of anything human.

Eastern Europe.—Beginning with the remotest and least prolific of the nations, we find in Russia *Strekoza* and *Palimet*, in Cracow *Djabel* and in Warsaw *Mucha*. None of these is available for perusal in England, but the Buda-Pest *Borsszem Janko*, by some strange chance, though not mentioned by Grand-Carteret, is in the British Museum library. It began with the New Year in 1868, and had an excellent artist in Karl Klič. It is amusing to find scraps of English here and there; there is "Lord Jockeymorland" in Janko's *Museum*, remarking on a bottled specimen "indeed very curious," while outside Queen Victoria is sitting attended by a Scotch piper. In 1887 the paper was still well illustrated, by Klosz and others unnamed, a really fine cartoon being a grim rendering of "Cholera," and a more amusing one showing Bismarck in the prompter's box dismissing the old year down a stage trap, and calling on the new, armed to the teeth. More surprising is a group of politicians in the disguise of Gilbert and Sullivan's *Mikado* and the "Three Little Maids from School." *Caviar*, another Hungarian paper, had a good caricaturist in C. Sieben.

Vienna, as might be expected, was far more prolific. *Kikeriki*, founded in 1861, is still crowing; *Figaro*, a name adopted by numerous papers and in all lands—there was even a *Sheffield Figaro*—was most famous in Vienna; and there were also *Der Floh*, *Lucifer*, *Die Bombe*, *Die Auste*, *Wiener Caricaturen* and *Die Muskete*. At Innsbruck, too, was *Der Scherer*, and at Prague *Humoristiche Listy*.

Spain and Portugal.—In Lisbon, *Os Puntos nos ii* (the dots on the i's) had a notable cartoonist in Raphael Pinheiro. In Madrid the only considerable illustrated paper in the last century was *El Motin*, and the work of Spanish caricaturists must be looked for in North and South America. But there is now quite a long list including *El Liberal*, *España*, *Gil Blas*, *Gedeconcito*, *Blanca e Nera*, *La Espera*, *Gedéon*, *El Mundo Humoristico*. In Barcelona two excellent caricaturists, Bracons ("Apa") and Inglada, work for *Iberia*, and Picarol for *La Campana de Gracia*.

Switzerland, Belgium, Holland.—Switzerland was fortunate in having two caricaturists at a much earlier date, Rudolf Topffer and Martin Bisteli. Both were dead before 1850; but their influence may have contributed to the success of the Geneva *Carillon* and the Zurich *Postheiri* and *Nebelspalter*, the last of which attained first rate importance in political caricature and is still flourishing.

In Belgium, the grotesque and somewhat fearful expressions of Breughel, Bosch, Wierz and Jan van Beers found a remarkable exponent in Félicien

Rops, whose contributions to the Brussels *Uylenspiegel* in the '50s and '60s are among the *rariora* of modern prints. On one occasion, in 1863, he paid Grandville the compliment of a new version of that artist's famous cartoon of 1831, "Order is established in Warsaw." In the '80s, the eccentricities of "Popold" had begun to afford opportunity for the caricaturists which were not neglected. At Liége, there were Lemaître in *Le Rasoir* and Lapièrre in *Le Frondeur;* and in Brussels, Boum-Kelkou in *Le Clairon*, Sebranc in the *Moniteur du Congo*, Levy in *Le Gourdin*, and Zarib in *Clair de Lune*. With the new century appeared G. Julio in *Le Cri du Peuple* and *La Réforme*, C. de Busschera in *Le Flirt*, Sicambre in *Le Zwanzeur*, besides others in *Le Sifflet*, *La Trique* and *Les Corbeaux*.

From the colder genius of Holland, where Romeyn de Hooghe established pictorial satire as a serious contribution to politics, we need not expect very much on the lighter side of caricature, but can appreciate all the better the extraordinary manifestation of the old spirit in Louis Raemaekers' war cartoons; and even forgive the Amsterdam *Weekblad von Nederland* and *De Kroniek* for their sharpest hits at the British Government in the Boer War. The magnificent conception of Cecil Rhodes in his coach, in 1897, needs no forgiveness. *De Notenkraker*, Amsterdam, and *De Nederlandische Spectator* at The Hague are also to be remembered.

Scandinavia, Greece, Italy.—Scandinavia, in an atmosphere comparatively free from the political smoke or social scents of its neighbouring countries, has produced numerous caricaturists whose delightfully fresh and simple touch proclaims their kinship with Grieg and Ibsen. With the exception of Olaf Gulbransson and "Blix" who became famous on *Simplizissimus*, their names and their works are little known abroad. Among the earliest were Wilhelm Marstrand, Constantin Harrisen and Fritz Jürgensen in Copenhagen and Wilhelm Petersen, the illustrator of Hans Andersen. In the Danish *Punch* we find excellent work of Hans Tegner and Knud Gamborg, in *Blaeksprutten* and *Klods-Hans* of Alfred Schmidt, and in *Vort Land* of Axel Thiess.

In Norway and Sweden the principal artists were Th. Kittlesen in *Tyrilhaus*, E. Schwart in *Sondags Nisse*, Knud Stangenberg in *Strix*, and Albert Engelström.

At the present time Copenhagen maintains a good display but of no special merit. "Blix" contributes on Sundays to the venerable *Berlingske Tidende* (no connection with Berlin), now in its 180th year. *Politiken*, ap-

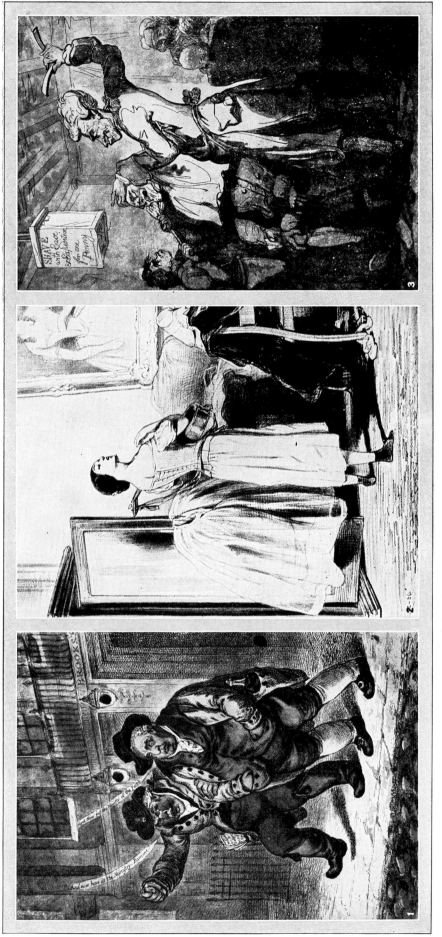

ENGLISH AND FRENCH CARICATURE, 19TH CENTURY

1. "Pillars of the Constitution—Three o'clock and a Cloudy Morning," by James Gillray (1757–1815). Gillray, one of the best known satirists of the 18th and early 19th centuries, made Georgian politics and manners the target of his scathing humor. Here Sheridan and the Duke of Norfolk are shown reeling out of Brooks's. (The Duke is stammering, "And now for the Majesty of the People," while Sheridan calls out, "And now have at the Ministry, Damme!")

2. "Rien n'est si joli que la fa-a-a-ble-e-e, si triste que la vérité!" This is one of a series of 79 sketches, "Les Lorettes," by Gavarni (1804–66), nom de plume of the French caricaturist, Hippolyte Sulpice Guillaume Chevalier

3. "A Sufferer for Decency," by Thomas Rowlandson (1756–1834). Rowlandson, a contemporary of Gillray, produced landscape paintings as well as drawings and etchings of many types of subject, the fine quality of which gave to them a definite place of importance in English art. He was a keen satirist of the social life of his era

PLATE VI　　　　　　　CARICATURE

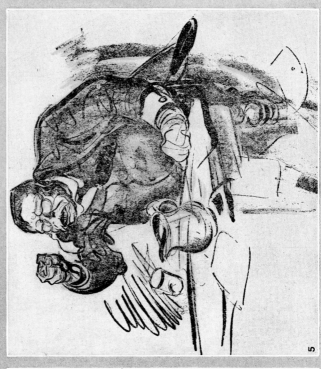

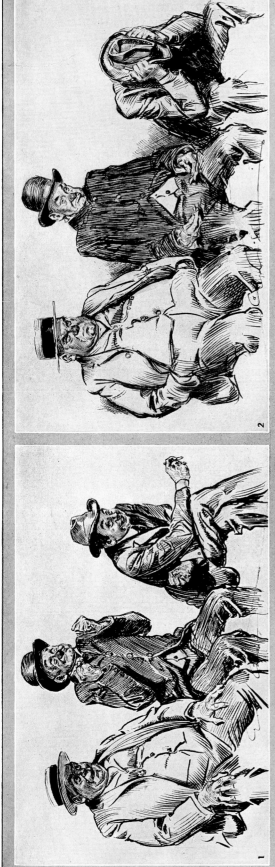

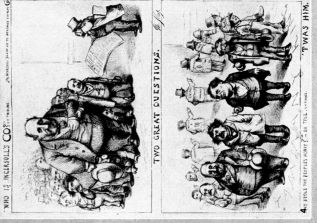

CARICATURE IN THE UNITED STATES

1, 2. "Two Strikes and the Bases Full," and "Fanned Out," two caricatures by Charles Dana Gibson of types among the spectators at a base-ball game

long series in which he attacked "Boss" Tweed and the Tweed Ring. The firm of J. H. Ingersoll and Co. was used by Tweed to cover fraudulent transactions

5. "The Boss" by Oscar Cesare, caricature of Theodore Roosevelt, published in May 1912. The legend

proaching its jubilee, is wonderfully vivid and varied, as are the morning *Dagens Nyheder*, the noonday *B.T.* and the weekly *Hjemmet*.

If Greece was somewhat outside the European circle in the last century, and if her language and written character are still beyond the casual intelligence, her recent contributions to our subject are fuller and more certain than in the days of Pauson. *Romeos*, the most famous of all Greek comic papers, which first appeared in 1883 and was read by every Greek from Marseille to Trebizond, was the work of one man, Soures, the Aristophanes of modern Greece, who wrote the whole of it (including the advertisements) in verse. It ceased, with his death, in 1918. *Asty* was more remarkable for its caricatures (a volume of which has been published) by its editor Themistocles Anninos (d. 1906). *Eleutheron Bema*, the present leading morning paper, exhibits a daily cartoon (Γελοιογραφία) by Ph. Demetriades; and *Proia*, another daily, rivals it in the productions of El. Koumetakes and N. Kastanakes. *Gatos* (the Cat), a weekly paper, supplies the only coloured caricatures in this country.

In Italy, modern caricature began with the establishment of *Il Fischietto* in 1848, at Turin, as a very small paper with one or two crude woodcuts. But it soon enlarged itself, and early in the '60s it was admirably, one is almost tempted to say superbly, illustrated by three artists, Virginio, Teja and Redenti. If Virginio's lithographs lacked the genius of Daumier, as any but Daumier's must, they lacked little else to recommend them both to the collector and to the historian. Had Grand-Carteret included Napoleon III. in his series, the Italian artists would have had a preponderating share of the illustrations, for as he points out in his *Bismarck*, French influence was predominant in Italy right up to 1870, and it seemed that the caricaturists were violently protesting against it. After 1870, he adds, there is a complete change; the kingdom of Italy, having now attained her unity and territorial integrity, began to look abroad, and the press admirably reflected the new state of affairs. Italian comic papers might be those of a neutral country with cosmopolitan ideas, and *Papagallo*, soon afterwards established in Bologna, was a veritable European picture gallery, unfolding week by week in a succession of coloured cartoons the broadest outlines and most important questions of European politics. So great was the success of *Papagallo* that it was soon imitated by *Il Trottola* and *Il Rama*. *Il Pasquino* was already established at Turin and *Il Pulchinella* in Naples. *Il Fischietto* was later managed and illustrated by Camillo Marietti, who signalized the retirement of

95

Bismarck in 1890 by a cartoon which may take rank with Tenniel's "Dropping the Pilot." It was entitled "L'Armoire aux retraites," and showed Tisza and Bismarck each occupying a cupboard, and the hand of history pointing out a third to Crispi. *Il Travaso* in Rome, *Il 420* in Florence, *L'Uomo di Pietra* and *Guerin Meschino* in Milan, are lively younger brothers of the still flourishing *Pasquino*. Among the modern caricaturists none is finer than Musacchio, and none more effective than Sacchetti.

Germany, France.—The extent and diversity of modern Germany, apart from her great place in Europe, precludes more than a very scanty tribute in our space to the very large and accomplished family descended from Luther and Cranach as also from Gutenberg and the early block printers. Between the homeliness of Adolf Oberlander and the mordancy of Th. H. Heine there is a wide gulf, but it is by no means a void; and from *Fliegende Blätter* of 1845 to *Des Junggeselle* of 1928 one cannot step as through a desert. Berlin and Munich were naturally the two most prolific centres, and they were not long in following England in Philipon's train with *Kladderadatsch* (1848) and *Fliegende Blätter* (1845). Munich was first in point of time, and has certainly never been eclipsed by Berlin in point of quality. The miniature cartoons of E. Schleich from 1862 to 1870 in the Munich *Punsch* are a most valuable commentary on the story of the rise of Prussia under the influence of Bismarck. *Jugend* and *Simplizissimus* in later times have developed the artistic possibilities of caricature, and if with more vigour than charm, it may be added that even their most cruel and brutal satire has something about it which compels laughter. In Berlin, besides *Kladderadatsch*, there were soon *Der Ulk* in 1868, *Wespen* in 1870, *Lustige Blätter*, and *Humoristiche Blätter*. The Frankfurt *Latern*, the Stuttgart *Wahre Jacob*, the Düsseldorf *Monatschafte*, the Danzig *Bunte Blätter* are all of them to be reckoned with the Berlin and Munich papers.

In France, the school of Philipon continued to flourish, and also to expand. Daumier lived on to 1879, and his cartoon "After Sedan" was one of his most impressive. Doré had abandoned caricature, or "Cham" would not have been Daumier's next of kin. The foremost names or pseudonyms of the next generation were Nadar, André Gill, Draner, Sahib, Stop, Luque, Félix Regamey, Alfred le Petit, Moloch and Pilotell. Of the many new papers before 1890 were *L'Eclipse*, *Le Trombinoscope*, *La Chronique Parisienne* and *La Chronique Amusante* (all containing cartoons by Moloch), *Le Journal Amusant*, *Le Cri de Paris*, *La Lune*, *La Charge*, *Triboulet*, *La Journée*, *Le*

CARICATURE

Figaro Illustré, *La Silhouette*, *Le Carillon* and *Le Sifflet*. The last named, which began in 1872, was peculiarly vivacious, and its large coloured cartoons by Le Mare and others, though of little artistic merit, and vulgar in their extravagant outlines, were still very amusing and informing. It was thoroughly radical, and the ex-emperor, the royalists and the church cut very sorry figures in it. Certainly there was a decline in artistic illustration, not in France alone, towards and during the '80s; and though we can hardly drag in Bismarck here, it is noticeable that after 1890 there were signs of a very potent revival. The appearance of *Gil Blas* in the kiosques in 1891, and of *Le Courrier Français*, if not a challenge to the inanities of "Mars" in *La Vie Parisienne*, was truly a relief. Though Steinlen was even less a caricaturist than Gavarni, and Forain little more, both were great artists, and it was a pity that so much of their subject matter being "the unmentionable," their really fine qualities, like those of Rowlandson and Gillray, had to wait to be discovered.

The first appearance of *Le Rire* on Nov. 10, 1894, may fairly be regarded as an event of some importance in the history of caricature, at any rate as to its lighter side, and its opening number, with a coloured plate by J. L. Forain, is a document of considerable interest. In the first place, there is its list of artists, which, even without the further promise "d'autres noms, aimés du public, et d'autres encore qui seront des surprises," is surprising enough:— J. L. Forain, Willette, Caran d'Ache, Fernand Frau, Dépaquit, Paule Crampel, Courboin, Jossot, Georges Delaw, G. Darbour, D'Espagnet, Gyp, Heidbruck, Jean Veber, Léandre, Louis Anquetin, Ch. Maurin, H. de Toulouse-Lautrec, P. Bonnard, Hermann-Paul, Marc Mouclier, Vallotton, Rupert-Carabin, Roedel, Louis Morin, A. Schlaich, Alphonse Lévy ("Said"), Grellet, Gumery, Verbeck, Vavasseur, Guydo, Charly, Lebègue. Even without Steinlen, Guillaume, Gerbault, Abel Faivre and many more, there are names in this list to which none of the previous generation, with the great Cham, Moloch, Sahib, Bac, etc., can deny at least equal places in the niches of fame. Of no less interest, and of considerable historical significance, is the introduction of two features, "Le Rire d'Autrefois" and "Le Rire à l'Étranger," the latter still continuing. The former was distinctly homage to Philipon, the first item being a double page reproduction of Daumier's famous "Le Ventre Legislatif," with the mischievous parenthesis added "Ça n'a pas beaucoup changé depuis 1834." Later numbers reproduced still older caricatures, by Isabey and others. The foreign section had a distinctly English flavour, being introduced by a note signed "Globe-Trotter," and two out of its three items (nowadays it contains a dozen) were English—one by Sambourne from *Punch*, and the other by Phil May from *The Sketch*. The third was from the Vienna *Floh*, but still with a Gladstonian allusion—Bismarck as "The Grand Old Man" trying to fell Capriva personified as a tree. Of more recent date were *L'Assiette au Beurre*, *Le Canard sauvage* (subsequently *Le Canard enchaîné*), *L'Intransigeant*, *L'Indiscret*, *Mon Dimanche*, *D'Artagnan*, *Fantasio* and many others.

Great Britain.—Returning at last to England, it is interesting to observe that *Punch*, though dominating the realm of caricature from its very inception, and for over a quarter of a century almost alone in its glory, was always equal to the occasion, sustaining with dignity and charm the whole responsibility of an ancient and most honourable inheritance. Victorian conditions inflated the popular love of monarchy, and the public at large came more and more to regard established institutions like the Royal Academy, Covent Garden theatre or the Langham hotel as all-sufficient, and to look askance at any attempt to supplement them with new ones. So that when *Judy*, *Fun*, *Moonshine* and *Ally Sloper's Half Holiday* were successfully established, they were never in any sense rivals to the legitimate monarch. It is rather surprising that half-a-dozen artists in a single journal, of so small a size, and with no coloured illustrations, should for half a century more or less have been the only representatives of the great family with its ramifications that flourished in former days. But *autres temps*, *autres mœurs* and the extraordinary vulgarities with which the domestic life of the young queen and her consort was made fun of soon gave place to the refinement introduced by the Doyles and established by their successors, Leech, Tenniel, Keene, Du Maurier and Sambourne. For Victorian England this must be allowed to have sufficed, and Dr. Primrose might now have observed that if there was not more laughter than of yore there was certainly as much wit. At the same time it must be admitted that the Victorian climate was not suitable for the development of rude health in caricature. Heavy academical foliage absorbed the sun, and the pungent undergrowth of Pre-Raphaelitism only succeeded in forcing its way up by virtue of its deadly earnestness. *Punch* alone enjoyed the free air.

One plant, however, appeared in 1869, which by its fruits we know must have been from a seed of the original tree, namely *Vanity Fair*. Here, at last, was a revival, and in its pleasantest form, of personal caricature. Though

(1 — manuscript page of text)

(2 — bestiary page)

(3 — facing pages from the Gospel of St. John)

SPECIMEN PAGES FROM TWELFTH AND THIRTEENTH CENTURY MANUSCRIPTS

1. Page with vulgate text and Latin gloss from Bible ms. containing the minor prophets and the Book of Job, probably written at Christ Church, Canterbury, towards the end of 13th century

2. Page from an illuminated bestiary, written in Latin. England, early 13th century

3. Two facing pages from the Gospel of St. John, the capitula on the left, and the first page on the right, with miniatures and illuminated initials. This is from a vulgate version of the Bible, written for the Abbey of Floreffe, near Namur, in Belgium, about 1160

PLATE II   BOOKS

1

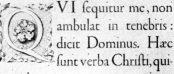

2

3

FUGITIVE PIECES
IN
VERSE and PROSE.

Pereunt et imputantur.

PRINTED AT STRAWBERRY-HILL.
MDCCLVIII.

4

FUGITIVE PIECES.

VERSES
IN MEMORY OF
KING HENRY the SIXTH,
Founder of KING's-COLLEGE, CAMBRIDGE.

[*Written February 2, 1738.*]

WHILE Superstition teaches to revere
The sainted Calendar and letter'd
year;
While Bigots joy in canonizing Shades,
Fictitious Martyrs, visionary Maids;
Haste, Gratitude, and hail this better day;
At HENRY's shrine present thy votive lay;
If this peculiarly for His be known,
Whose Charity made ev'ry day his own.
B   But

5

TYPES OF 17TH AND 18TH CENTURY PAGE DESIGNS

1. *A Midsommer nights dreame*, by William Shakespeare. The edition was printed by James Roberts and published by Thomas Pavier, who is alleged to have annotated it falsely. The date on the book is 1600 but the real date is supposed to have been 1619

2. *De Imitatione Christi*, by Thomas à Kempis, 1642. The first publication was a folio text of the *Imitation* which was printed in Garamand's *Caractères de l'Université*

3. The *Médailles sur les Événements du Régne de Louis Le Grand*, 1702. The book has an engraved frontispiece by the elder Simonneau after Coypel fils. Its borders and fleurons are by Berain; the head of the king on the medals is from the burin of Gerard Edelinck

4. Title page from *Fugitive Pieces in Verse and Prose*, by Horace Walpole, published by the Strawberry-Hill Press in 1758

5. First page of *Fugitive Pieces in Verse and Prose*

"Ape" and "Spy" (Carlo Pellegrini and Leslie Ward) were the only two of its artists whose names are familiar to the general public, it is significant that many of the finest portraits in the earliest numbers were by J. J. Tissot, so that the success of the paper was really established by Italian and French artists. Historically this is quite as it should be, just as "Punch" is named after the mythical "Polchinello" whose characteristics were illustrated by Ghezzi, and one of its most successful artists, Du Maurier, was of French extraction. Not until the last decade—*la fin du siècle*—did the Victorian glaciation give any sign of loosening. Among the first, in 1890, and of itself insignificant, was a little paper called *The Whirlwind* edited by Herbert Vivian and Stewart Erskine and illustrated by some of the founders of the New English Art club—another sign. A little later *Pick me up* made a gallant bid for popular favour, but was before its time. In 1894 there was a more decided crack, and *The Yellow Book*, published by Matthews & Lane, threw up two volcanoes in the shape of Aubrey Beardsley and Max Beerbohm, whose molten streams combined to flow with ever increasing effect on the artistic and literary climate. Widely different as they were, both these young men achieved the same result in bursting the shackles that were cramping the arts of illustration and caricature. Reed's caricature in *Punch*, "Britannia à la Beardsley," was far too witty and too clever to have been designed in derision of so fine an artist; but there was something so entirely new to the Victorian in Beardsley's uncanny grotesque, that he was for long looked at askance. His influence on "black and white" in general was enormous, and in caricature it is traceable everywhere. Max, on his part, being a caricaturist in the strict Carraccian tradition, loosened the buttons, shook out the folds and generally disorganized the growing trimness of personal caricature as exemplified in the *Vanity Fair* cartoons, which in the '80s were becoming more and more suitable for *The Tailor and Cutter*. The most baffling thing about his marvellous gift of spiritual portraiture seems to be that the farther he gets from actuality the nearer he gets to truth.

Recent Developments.—With the most recent developments of caricature it is impossible for the staid historian to keep pace. He can only shout after the caricaturists, not to stop, but to wish them still more activity in still wider fields. As it is they have rushed in at the studio doors opened to them by the cubists, vorticists, post-impressionists and their imitators, and rushed out again with their arms full of fancies which they have twisted up and thrown, like confetti, into the most unexpected places. Some have stuck to the hoardings, others have got into the circulars of the most respectable and stately commercial firms, and the least humorous of the weekly papers. This great and surprising expansion is due, in no small measure, to the World War, when they were employed with Lutheran vigour and insistence, both as propaganda and as a relief to the feelings. Posterity may perhaps decide which were the most successful (for either purpose) among such as King George reviewing the British fleet in a diving suit (German), the Bolsheviks at the telephone (Musacchio), or "What did *you* do in the Great War, Daddy?" (English); but there is no doubt that all of them contributed something to the very general extension of the employment of caricature for artistic and commercial, no less than for satirical purposes, in these present days. Instead of being destroyed, or reserved for private circulation, as in the old times, the careless rapture of the modern artist now finds a place on the hoardings. These modern artists are a determined lot of fellows, a large and exceedingly fierce tribe, and they are doing much more for caricature than any one before them. Adopting the most advanced and highly artistic tenets, they have imposed significant form alike on the commonest objects of the ideal home and the rarest flowers in the garden of public affairs. They know to a hair's breadth how far a statesman's face can be stretched without snapping, they have the bursting strain of every bulge in his figure calculated to a decimal point. With a few strokes of the pen they can visualize an international situation or a social tendency in a manner that saves us reading whole columns of print. Finally, notwithstanding every excess, they have shown themselves equal to the delicate task of sustaining the traditions of the very oldest of the comic papers under the double disadvantage of the devastations of the World War and the complete change of outlook on many subjects resulting therefrom. *Charivari*, past its 87th year, has in Soupault, Bib and Cyl, cartoonists as lively as ever, and if an artistic comparison with their earliest predecessors is impossible now, it is probably only because it is too soon to make it. *Punch*, the next oldest, having enjoyed uninterrupted prosperity with a sound constitution and no incitement to change, is still an old friend with a young face. *Kladderadatsch* and *Fliegende Blätter* are oftener quoted by *Le Rire* than any others, and side by side with them we find *Nebelspalter, Simplizissimus, Mucha, Ulk, Jugend, Pasquino, Lustige Blätter* and *Wahre Jacob*, most of them past their jubilee and all well up to date. If the tight-lacing of the '80s was finally abolished by the War, and if the reaction seems a little too startling just at the moment, it must be accepted nevertheless as a very healthy symptom in an art which to be an art at all, must always be allowed its own way.

United States.—Political caricature in the United States began with William Charles, a Scotsman who, forced to leave Great Britain, emigrated to America, and, in the War of 1812, used his pencil and invention with great bitterness against his renounced country. Pencil and invention were both crude. Charles was an imitator of James Gillray, and his most widely-circulated cartoon, "John Bull Making a New Batch of Ships to Send to the Lakes," bore a close resemblance, in conception and detail, to Gillray's "Tiddy-Doll (Napoleon) Making a New Batch of Kings." Gillray, influencing Charles, also influenced the work of Charles's successors for several decades. The basis of the early American cartoon was the Gillray group of many figures. A school of distinctively American caricature came in with the first administration of President Jackson. These lithographs told their stories by means of legends enclosed in balloon-like loops issuing from the lips of the various members of the groups. The anonymous artists were most productive in the heat of political campaigns, during the Mexican War, and with the rising slavery agitation. The Civil War naturally let loose a flood of cartoons; among them the early work of Nast.

Thomas Nast (1840–1902) remains the dominant figure in the history of American caricature. Lincoln called Nast's cartoons the best recruiting sergeants on the Union side. His picture "Peace," originally called "Compromise with the South," first made his reputation. It appeared just after the election of 1862, and was circulated by the million as a campaign document. Nast's later influence was both national and local. He was the inventor of the "donkey" used as the symbol of the Democratic Party, the Tammany "Tiger," the "rag-baby" of inflation, and the cap and dinner pail emblematic of labour. More than any other man he was responsible for the overthrow of the notorious Tweed Ring that long held New York City in its clutches. Such cartoons as "The Brains of Tammany" and "The Tammany Tiger in the Arena" proved the siege guns in the battle for civic reform. Finally it was a Nast picture that led to the capture, in Spain, of the fugitive Tweed. The traditions of Nast were carried on in the late '70s, '80s and '90s by Keppler and Gillam. The series of "Tattooed Man" cartoons, depicting James G. Blaine in the title rôle, contributed to Cleveland's victory in 1884. They were the work of Bernard Gillam, who, upon leaving *Puck*, drew equally vindictive caricatures of Cleveland and the Democratic Party on the rival pages of *Judge*. A cartoon with a story was Gillam's "Where Am I At?" of 1892. It was originally drawn to commemorate an expected smashing Republican victory. When the election returns showed that Cleveland had won it was too late to prepare another cartoon, so Gillam set to work making the necessary changes in the plate, capping his labour with a likeness of himself in the form of a monkey turning an uncomfortable somersault. Two outstanding cartoons of the later '90s, "Don Quixote Bryan Meets Disaster in his Encounter with the Full Dinner Pail," and "Be Careful: It's Loaded!" a warning to Spain just before the outbreak of the Spanish-American War, were the work of Victor Gillam.

American caricature of the present century is abundant and of a high order. Syndicate service has brought the work of the most efficient and highly paid cartoonists to the readers of the most rural communities. There is a Pulitzer prize annually awarded for the cartoon deemed the most effective. Conspicuous among these awards for recent years have been (1921) to Rollin Kirby for "On the Road to Mandalay," in the New York *World*; (1924) to J. N. Darling for "In the Good Old U.S.A.," in New York *Tribune*; and (1926) to Nelson Harding for "Toppling the Idol," in the Brooklyn *Daily Eagle*.

POSTER

A POSTER is a printed, written or illustrated announcement publicly exhibited. Its usual function is to call attention to goods or service; but, to fulfil that object, it has not merely to arouse attention; it must provoke interest and create a desire. However attractive pictorially or textually a modern poster may be, commerce, the chief patron of poster art, finally judges a design by its value as a link in the chain of salesmanship.

The poster is seldom given entire responsibility for influencing the public; rather is it regarded as a form of "reminder" advertising—an ally of the press advertisement, the creator of a favourable atmosphere. The average "commercial" poster is intended to influence two groups—the retailer, who, it is hoped will stock the advertiser's goods, and the public who will purchase

FROM THE ORIGINALS BY (1) ERIC HARDEY, (2) R. T. COOPER, (3) F. C. HERRICK, (4) ADOLPHE TREIDLER

MODERN POSTER ADVERTISEMENTS

Four examples of modern British and American poster design, illustrating the adaptation of artistic principles to the uses of publicity

them. Posters have a very wide range of duties to perform in addition to selling goods. They deliver every kind of message, to every type of "audience," in an infinite variety of styles. Actually, the poster or placard can trace its ancestry back almost to the dawn of civilization.

History.—Egyptian wall-paintings, mural decorations and inscriptions, produced over 3,000 years B.C., have been discovered by archaeologists, much of this work, together with that of the early-Babylonian, Assyrian, Greek and Roman craftsmen, displaying a precision of line and a decorative beauty which are the envy and despair of the modern poster-designer. Tablets of wood, papyrus and parchment were also used, in ancient Egypt, Greece or Rome, for the purpose of issuing announcements, while it is the lettering of the Trajan column which has inspired the finest types of poster lettering of to-day.

Later Developments.—In later days, the sign-board was adopted as a form of advertisement, the hanging sign being a picturesque feature of mediaeval architecture throughout Europe. Written handbills were an additional means of enabling the shopkeeper to bring his goods and service to the notice of the public, and vast possibilities were suddenly presented to him by the invention of printing, by Gutenberg, before 1450, and by its introduction into England by Caxton in 1476.

The first letterpress poster soon made its appearance in England; and shortly afterwards, in France, a royal proclamation was issued in poster form. During the 17th century, the general use of posters was forbidden, but in time their value to the community was recognized, official restrictions were removed, and the first pictorial posters made their appearance. These were illustrated by wood-cuts. Pedlars and packmen, hucksters and showmen, strolling players and proprietors of booths, also used handbills and miniature posters, decorated by wood-cuts; and these simple, primitive illustrations have formed part of the artistic inspiration of the leading poster designers of to-day.

The wood-cut was, however, destined to be superseded by lithography (*q.v.*) as a medium for the designing and printing of posters. Invented in 1796, and developed for printing purposes by Senefelder, the new art of drawing and engraving on stone, metal plates and "transfer" papers, opened up possibilities almost as vast as those which followed the invention of the printing press.

The first lithographed posters are interesting as historical curiosities

103

only, the earlier wood-cuts possessing infinitely more character. Lithography was seized upon as a means of producing a more elaborate, "highly-finished" form of illustration, and it is to France that we have to turn for the earliest lithographed posters of quality.

The modern poster began with Jules Chéret, a Frenchman, born in Paris in 1836, self taught as a draughtsman. He served his apprenticeship as a lithographer in England, and when 30 years old became interested in announcements of theatrical managers and placards put out about that time urging recruiting for armies. In 1867 the world saw the first modern poster of Chéret's, an announcement of a play enacted by a young woman, then 22 years old, who was to make her name immortal—Sarah Bernhardt. The poster announced a fairy play, entitled: *La Biche au Bois.*

The first Chéret posters, with their filmy female figures seemingly floating in space and flaming colours, excited interest, held attention, and caused favourable comment. Orders for Chéret's posters came from music halls, dealers in cigarettes, drinks, toilet articles, newspapers, circuses, charity fêtes, and the streets were gladdened with merrily dancing figures. Chéret designed more than 1,000 posters, the best of which can be found in books devoted to the art.

The poster spread from France to Germany. Later it travelled across the Pyrenees to Spain, and from France to Switzerland, and over the Alps into Italy, from France to Belgium, and across the English Channel to England, across the North Sea to Holland, and from Germany it found its way to Austria-Hungary, the poster invasion finally reaching Russia and travelling across the Baltic Sea to Norway and Sweden. From the British Isles and the Continent of Europe, the poster went to the United States, and later to Canada, thence to Australia.

In England the first to attract attention by his posters was Frederick Walker, who in 1871 made a poster for the dramatized version of *The Woman in White*. Members of the Royal Academy were attracted to the newly discovered medium, and Sir John Millais exhibited "Bubbles," advertising a soap. This poster pleased England immensely. Then followed Aubrey Beardsley, with his weird posters, Walter Crane, R. Anning Bell, the "Beggarstaff Brothers" (James Pryde and William Nicholson), J. W. Simpson, Gordon Craig, Dudley Hardy, Maurice Greiffenhagen, J. Hassall, Will Owen and others.

In Germany Ludwig Hohlwein won not only a national, but an international reputation, and books of his posters are sold throughout Europe and America; his posters are so compelling that he is regarded as a master of his craft. Other German poster artists whose work reached the highest standards include Otto Fischer, Sattler, Speyer, T. T. Heine, Max Klinger, Dasio, Hofmann, Franz Stück and L. Zumbrusch.

Leon Bakst, the Russian genius, and H. Cassiers, Belgian, have done much to bring renown to their native lands by their posters of distinction. Japan's greatest poster artist is Toyókuni.

The poster, as it is known to-day, did not exist in the United States previous to 1889, except for the theatrical and circus posters made by Matt Morgan. Posters began in the United States in the '90s, when Louis Rhead and Will H. Bradley began to produce their decorative placards. These were used principally for the announcements of magazines and the books of publishers. Later business and commerce saw the great value of poster advertising, and enlisted the services of Maxfield Parrish, Ethel Reed, Will Carqueville, J. J. Gould, Howard Chandler Christy, J. C. Leyendecker, Frank Hazenpflug, James Montgomery Flagg, Charles Dana Gibson, and others.

On the poster panels of to-day, in the United States, may be seen the work of Harrison Fisher, Linn Ball, G. C. Beall, Norman Rockwell, Fred Stanley, William Oberhardt, Fred Mizen, Clarence F. Underwood, Karl Johnson, F. Nelson Abbott, Arthur von Frankenberg, John E. Sheridan, Harry Morse Mayers, Hadon Sundblum, John O. Brubaker, Charles E. Chambers, McClelland Barclay, Lucille P. Marsh and other noted artists.

With the outbreak of the World War posters took on a new significance in all nations actively engaged in the struggle. In countries where there was not conscription, posters were most effectively used to stimulate recruiting. Before conscription in England (during the first stages of the war), more than 2,500,000 posters were posted in the British Isles alone to get men to enlist, the posters representing the work of about 100 artists. Taking a lesson from Great Britain, the Governments of the countries actively engaged in the war spoke to their nationals through the medium of the poster, appealing to the civilian population in behalf of subscriptions to the war loans, the conservation of food, aid for the organizations engaged in war work, such as hospitals, milk funds, destitute dependents, the Red Cross, the Y.M.C.A. and other activities that war entails.

Brangwyn and Spencer Pryse produced work for Britain and Belgium which was full of dignity and nobility. In France, Steinlen, Faivre, Willette,

Poulbot and Fouqueray appealed to the patriotism of their countrymen. In Germany the belief in force and might was hammered into pictures by Engelhard, Louis Oppenheim, Puchinger, Otto Leonard and Wohlfeld. Austria's actions were justified or defended and her causes championed by Krafter, Arpellus, Buo and Kurthy.

Standards.—In the half century or more since the poster became a popular means of outdoor publicity, women have been predominant in many of the posters displayed. The irresistible charm of childhood illumines many posters. Birds and animals are also favourites with poster designers. But whatever is pictured on a poster, this courier of commerce must have these important features: it must be new and interesting, have attention-value, simplicity of design, brevity of text, good composition, pleasing colours, and "selling power"—the latter usually achieved through expression of a basic link of interest between the product and the public.

Great strides have been made in the development of the poster as an organized advertising medium. Modern business in America has discarded the old-fashioned and unkempt "billboard," and posters of various sizes are no longer made. Due to the Outdoor Advertising Association of America, there has come the standard structure in two sizes surrounded by a green moulding as a frame for the poster. These standard panels are found in over 16,000 cities and towns in the United States. Many of these structures are illuminated.

In Great Britain, hoardings, though not standardized, have greatly improved in character and design, under the influence of the British Poster Advertising Association. In Germany a poster hoarding is practically unknown, the design being shown on special advertising kiosques or pillars. France uses both kiosques and hoardings.

BOOKS

ART OF THE BOOK

THOUGH THE BOOK has tended to become more and more a personal possession, until it is now a necessary adjunct to the ordinary man's life instead of

A REPRINT OF THE BIBLE ACCORDING TO THE AUTHORISED VERSION OF 1611

1. Binding of the Bible. This volume, comprising the books Genesis to Ruth, is bound in orange decorated with gold
2. Illustrated title page of the same edition of the Bible
3. A page from the Book of Exodus
4. The final page of the first volume of the Bible. The page design illustrates the Book of Ruth

PLATE IV   BOOKS

Jean François de GALAUP comte de LA PÉROUSE 1741-1788

est dans les appartements du Roi, au château de Versailles. Une pièce sobre. Au mur, des cartes. Sur les tables, des livres, des manuscrits. Sur une des mappe-mondes, le Roi trace du doigt l'itinéraire d'un long voyage. L'épée au côté, encore jeune dans son uniforme de capitaine de la marine, un homme se tient près de lui et regarde. Le doigt royal va toujours plus loin. Il contourne l'Amérique, remonte vers l'Asie, redescend vers la Chine, erre dans un grand espace bleu : l'Océan. Là sont des terres inconnues. Le doigt s'arrête, comme pour dire : " Vous irez là ". Le capitaine fait signe qu'il a compris.

■ Le roi, c'est Louis XVI ; le capitaine : La Pérouse. Jean-François de Galaup comte de La Pérouse, était né au Gua, près d'Albi, en 1741. Entré à quinze ans dans la marine, La Pérouse conquiert ses grades, à la pointe de l'épée. La France vient de déclarer la guerre à l'Angleterre. Elle veut soutenir les Américains qui ont proclamé leur indépendance. Avec ses soldats, Lafayette se bat sur le sol même des Etats-Unis. Pendant ce temps, nos marins sous les ordres d'Orvilliers, d'Estaing, de Suffren, de Lamotte-Piquet, affrontent résolument les flottes anglaises sur toutes les mers. Le jeune La Pérouse prend une part active à ces batailles. A 18 ans, il est blessé et fait prisonnier dans le combat de Belle-Isle. Remis en liberté, ses actions d'éclat lui

1

And ek I knowe, of longe tyme agon,
His thewes goode, and that he is nat nyce.
Nauauntour, seith men, certein, he is noon ;
To wis is he to doon so gret a vice ;
Ne als I nyl hym neuere so cherice
That he may make a vaunt by iuste cause ;
He shal me neuere bynde in swich a clause.

Now sette a cas, the hardest is, ywis :
Men myghten demen that he loueth me.
What dishonour to myn estat is this ?
May ich hym lette of that ? Why nay, parde !
I knowe also, and alday here and se,
Men louen wommen al biside hire leue ;
And whan hem list no more, lat hem leue !

Ek wot I wel he worthy is to haue
Of wommen in this world the thriftyeste,
As ferforth as she may hire honour saue ;
For out and out he is the worthieste,
Saue only Ector, which that is the beste ;
And yit his lif lith al now in my cure ;
But swich is loue, and ek myn auenture !

Ne me to loue, a wonder is it nought ;
For wel wot I my self, so god me spede,
Al wolde I that no man wiste of my thought,
I am oon of the faireste out of drede
And goodlieste, who so taketh hede ;
And so men seyn in al the town of Troie.
What wonder is, though he of me, haue Ioye.

2   7¹

men när hon ej blev tvingad att ge, fast hon ville så gärna,
    låtsar hon väl med sin blick glädje, men ledsen hon är.
Våld led Phoebe en gång, och med våld togs ock Hilaira ;
    bägge de rövade strax fingo sin rövare kär.

Känd är sägnen ju väl, men förtjänt av att åter förtäljas,
    huru den scyriska mön brud åt haemoniern blev.
Ren var skönhetens olyckspris av gudinnan betålat,
    vilken på Ida de två andra besegrat med fog ;
ren sonhustrun till Priamus förts från landet i fjärran,
    och uti Ilions borg satt hon där nu som gemål ;
samtliga svuro en ed den förnärmade maken att hämna ;
    skymfen, som drabbade en, gällde för alla som skäl ;

3

Auf ein ächtes Wort der Weisheit muß alles (scheinbar) beim Alten bleiben ; ist aber alles (scheinbar) sogleich geändert oder änderungswert, so war das Wort nicht vom rechten Geist.

❋❋❋

Wer nicht weiß, wie tief vergeblich ein großer Mann ist, der weiß nicht, was ein großer Mann ist ; für den war er — vergeblich.

❋❋❋

Der freie Mensch ist einem Volke wenig nütze, wohl aber der sich befreiende, — der sich nicht ganz befreiende.

❋❋❋

Wer an der Welt mitzutun wahrhaft berufen ist ; der gerät nicht in ein Übermaß von Leiden, wenn es

4

ZEITSCHRIFT
FÜR
BÜCHERFREUNDE
HERAUSGEGEBEN
VON
GEORG WITKOWSKI

1918/19 HEFT 3
NEUE FOLGE 10. JAHRGANG
VERLAG E. A. SEEMANN. LEIPZIG.

5

USE OF ILLUSTRATION AND DECORATION IN MODERN EUROPEAN BOOK PRODUCTION

1. French. Page, with colour illustration, from *Voyages et Glorieuses Découvertes des grands Navigateurs et Explorateurs Français*

2. English. Page from *Troilus and Criseyde*. Illustration by Eric Gill, wood engraving

3. Scandinavian. Page from a translation of Ovid's *Ars Amatoria*. Illustration by Yugve Berg

4. German. Page from *Aphorismen* by Moritz Heimann

5. German. Facsimile of a title-page reproduced in "Die neue deutsche Buchkunst," by Hans Loubier

the semi-magical weapon of the few who read, it depends, as a thing of beauty, on the fact that it is an inscription, a thought written down. From the Babylonian clay amulet with its charm in writing, as old as civilization, to the modern "book oath" of the law-courts, we find this reverence for "frozen thought" persisting in men's minds. From the impulse of reverence sprang religion, and from religion art, which grew at first in order to make sacred objects more potent. The craftsman of older days took his inspiration directly from the fundamental human emotions of awe and curiosity instead of from the theories of professors, and by directing his reason upon an emotional state of mind was able to explore the technique of his craft, and, quite incidentally, to achieve beauty independent of the whims of aesthetic fashion-mongers. No art is the worse for being criticized with an eye to the purpose and state of mind in which it was produced; but in considering the book we are forced into such an attitude, because we are dealing first and foremost with an instrument of thought, and only secondarily with an object of art. We must keep in mind not only the fact that every rule for the beautiful book arises from some practical need for lucid exposition, but, more important still, we must remember the almost superstitious reverence with which the craftsman regarded man's unique gift of ciphering and deciphering thought. The modern "fine book" is the direct descendant of the sacred book of the past, but any inscription at all has a peculiar relation to the intellect. The gramophone record is not an inscription, because it is deciphered not by the intellect but by merely mechanical devices; hence no embellishment will ever be lavished upon it. But when a message directly enters the mind through the eye, it must be clothed in relation to its importance.

Ancient Books.—The hieratic books of ancient Egypt furnish an early example. The famous surviving ms. of the "Book of the Dead" has called on the utmost resources of calligrapher and illuminator. It is a long roll of papyrus, the early equivalent of paper (*q.v.*). Although this was made of the inner bark of Nile reeds, beaten flat, it seems to have been produced in qualities of extreme fineness and flexibility. Pliny mentions a roll containing the entire Iliad, which could be enclosed in a nut-shell. This may be a myth, but at least it was not considered beyond belief. Parchment was introduced as an expensive substitute in the 2nd century B.C.; but despite its more enduring qualities not a single complete parchment book from the golden age of Roman or Greek literature has survived to our day. Our earliest Latin ms. is possibly of 4th-century origin. The roll form of book, whether of parchment or

107

papyrus, measured often 16 ft. and sometimes far more in length, and was well adapted to the needs of important texts, sacred or profane. In its original form, reading down (or up) from one scroll rod to the other, it keeps nearest to its parent, the inscribed stone tablet, and may have been hung banner-wise in Egyptian temples. An interesting survival of this use of books for exhibition is found in the "Exsultet" rolls of the mediaeval church. The deacon read or sang the tract *Exsultet iam angelica turba* at the Easter vigil, unrolling as he did so a long scroll which hung down from over his lectern. This was painted with illustrative miniatures, upside down from the text he read, so that they were revealed to the congregation as he proceeded.

When, however, the writing was arranged long-wise on the roll it had to be broken up into blocks or sections, the length of the line being governed by ease in reading. These blocks of text then took the familiar rectangular form of our own book page. Merely folding the roll back on itself would convert it into a modern book of leaves as long as the edges were not cut. But the roll was regarded, because of its solemn uses, as a single object rather than as a collection of pages for easy reference; hence it was generally wound, not folded, from one end-rod to another—whence our word volume (from *volvere*, to roll). The end-rods were furnished with bosses and the rolls were enclosed in *scrinia*, cases. Both of these were elaborately worked by craftsmen when the value of the book demanded it, so that Seneca could accuse certain wealthy bibliophiles of paying more attention to their elaborate titlings and cases than to the literary worth of the contents of their libraries. This satire still has point.

As the book grew away from its original function in the temple and became the property of private owners, the needs of convenience altered its appearance. The book of leaves or pages existed as an informal contemporary of the roll, not only in the primitive *diptychs*, or wax-coated folding tablets, which formed the ancient note-book, but by the first century, in genuine published works. Possibly the difficulty of binding papyrus by piercing it through with threads hindered the development of such books. Certainly parchment, better for this purpose, was more costly; but already in the 1st century Martial was unconsciously sounding the knell of the roll in his line (Epigr. I., ii.) "Let the great folk have their *scrinia;* my book can be held in one hand." Martial also mentions (I., lxvi.) "virgin sheet" (*charta*) being soiled by rough chins; which gives us a picture of the difficulty with which a long roll was held open while the reader searched for a particular passage.

He also tells of a friend who returned one of his books unrolled to the end rod (*explicitum . . . ad sua cornua librum*) as a proof that it had been read. These *cornua* would seem to have been fashioned of bone or ivory, perhaps for greater flexibility. The roll was held in the left hand and unrolled with the right; many grave-monuments show sculptures of readers holding rolls so that the final page hangs down: "the book is ended." Parchment, which was less brittle at the edges than papyrus, seems to have been specially destined for the *codex* or leaf book, which has three free edges instead of two, and these three multiplied by the number of pages in the book. It also withstood corrections and expunging better than papyrus, and gave a freer surface to the illuminator. Magnificent Greek mss. from mediaeval times were sometimes written in gold upon purple-stained skins. What illumination there was in ancient books would seem to have been more like the modern, straightforward illustration of our own books than like the work of the mediaeval artists, who made decoration spring naturally from the writing of the text. Surviving mss. of Terence, for example, which seem to have been copied from late classic books, show that the pictures were really needed to illustrate the positions of the actors on the stage. Massive initial letters were known, and a rudimentary title-page appears in the inscription of the first leaf of some early Greek manuscripts.

Although the *codex* was dependent on parchment for its development, the latter material was used for writing in Greece from the earliest times. The *codex* originated, it would seem, in Greece or Asia Minor as a form specially suited to books of law (whence our word "code"), in that pages could be excised or added after statutory changes without destroying the continuity of the volume. It may also have perpetuated (for law is conservative) the primitive tables of stone or wood on which decrees were first inscribed. The single pages could, like these tables, be first exhibited and then piled together. But works of literature were soon issued in *codices*, although the fine book as we are considering it was not affected at once by the innovation. As late as the 3rd century of our era the jurist Ulpian defined "books" as rolls to the seeming exclusion of *codices*, although this definition was soon extended to the humbler form.

Though Christianity did not noticeably stay the destruction of ancient books inevitable after the barbarian invasions of Rome, the church of the 3rd to 5th centuries rendered a distinct service to the physical arts of the book by sharply reviving the idea that only sacred writings are worthy of preservation in a beautiful form. A secular author, however great, is at the mercy of the mere literary tastes of subsequent generations; but revealed or pious writings depend on no such whims. Hence a tradition of copied texts was possible. Had there been no church, the fine book might have disappeared entirely in the West; as it was, the *codex*, which gradually superseded the roll, became a far more reasoned and workable thing in daily use in the churches than it could have become on the shelves of rich amateurs in imperial Rome, who— like ourselves—had lost sight of the motives that inspire true craftsmanship. The Gospels were often bound in jewelled cases *because* they were used in public rituals.

The Early Mediaeval Book.—When Charlemagne sent to Rome for a copy of the Gregorian sacramentary, with an idea of establishing a standard of worship as well as of language, the fine book profited by the new script invented for this purpose no less than by the added vigour and realism of decorations inspired by the tastes of the imperial court. Under CALLIGRAPHY, page 164, there is noted the discrepancy between national styles of writing which made this standardization so necessary; but whereas the hands of early mediaeval France, Italy and Spain were degenerate growths from the writing in capital letters of the classic period, there existed a very important school of fine book-making in Ireland from the 6th century which continued the finest style of Roman 4th-century writing and added to it an original and powerful system of decoration. One of the most pretentious and successful books of all time is the "Book of Kells," a book of the Gospels produced in Ireland in the 7th century. On seeing the curiously sophisticated and intricate embellishments of this ms. one realizes that the "spark of civilization," almost extinguished in Western Europe at this time, was well guarded in the Irish monasteries. The Irish sacred book, with its somehow rigid perfection, influenced English work from 664 on, but became more fluid and casual in Saxon hands. Alcuin of York, who was one of the greatest figures of Hiberno-Saxon book work, was called in by Charlemagne to direct the deliberate revival of book production at the end of the 8th century. The so-called *carolingian minuscule* thus evolved allowed a page of great lightness and crispness, due to the simplicity of the letters used; this in turn produced a freer style of illumination. The bold, outstanding initial letter (which, brightly painted, served as a useful "pointer" in finding passages) comes into a closer relation to the text; vines descend from it until they cover the margin, and finally a whole illustrative scene is incorporated within a large initial.

From the middle of the 13th century we are able to see what magnificent unity was achieved by the mediaeval book, not through any self-conscious canons of "taste," but because the craftsmen concerned were all imbued with the same set of ideas, indeed the same pictorial traditions. The binding of the kind of book we are considering, i.e., the "fine" book, was often of gold or silver set with the unfaceted precious stones of the day, each one of which had a spiritual and medicinal value to the mediaeval mind. There are crucifixion scenes in *repoussé* metal or ivory. Occasionally an older ivory *diptych* would be mounted to serve as a binding; but in general the pages themselves (in such copies as remain unaltered) show the same grouping of figures and stylish treatment as do the covers. Respect for older texts made the miniaturists conservative, and many illustrative scenes can be traced back, by their grouping and costumes, through a chain of earlier mss. to a presumptive original, now lost, such as the copy of the Vulgate written for St. Jerome, which would itself have been an object of reverence.

The Late Mediaeval Book.—The increased sprightliness of decoration, approaching sheer naturalism, was counterbalanced as time went on by the formalizing of script. The final formalization was the angular letter which, at the dawn of the Renaissance, was contemptuously nicknamed "gothic" (much as we said "hunnish" in the World War). The "gothic" page is as near as we have come to an abstract form of beauty in writing, because it is rigidly consistent and links each letter into a rich, massive text-page. But "abstract" beauty will not do for the book, however little it be meant for reading and however much for a display of magnificence: and the scholars who revived the Carolingian letter in the 15th century rightly forsook optical consistency for practical legibility, which is a very different thing. Still, whatever its demerits as a readable text, the formal letter attributed to Gutenberg (the supposed perfector if not the inventor of printing, *c.* 1454) is aesthetically as much a monument to the age that was passing as it was historically a presage of the future. Before dealing with the changes brought about by the printing press it would be well to note how books were affected, during the middle ages, by the purpose for which they were made. Liturgical, legal and other books differed widely and imposed definite rules on the craftsman. Just as portability distinguishes the book itself from the inscription, so the small book became roughly differentiated from the large one. The latter, comprising the volumes regularly used in churches as well as most of the secular romances which delighted the nobility, were kept on shelves and transferred for reading purposes to a lectern; in some libraries books were even chained down to baffle thieves. Of the many liturgical books of this character the most important is the *missale* or mass-book. Such reverence was felt for this rite that craftsmen soon evolved special rules for its written text. The Canon, for example, was in larger letters than the rest of the text, and was placed in the middle of the book, a necessary thing in days when end-leaves were often in danger. The music-books of the liturgy had to be large in order that a choir might read from one page; books of lections could be propped up and read to a community. But with the practice of reciting the hours arose the *breviarium*, a book definitely intended to be carried about. Indeed, in England it was known as a *portiforium*. The book of hours plays a long and important part in the history of the book arts. It was the intimate companion of lay folk as well as of the clergy, and its comparatively small size admitted of its being lavishly decorated by wealthy owners. The *Little Hours of the Virgin*, in particular, offered the scribe a relatively short text and the illuminator a charming series of subjects. Books of hours made for important personages show more and more response to the layman's desire for show and splendour; and it is difficult to think how this desire could be better gratified than by the glowing blue of powdered lapis that shone on the Virgin's cloak in painted miniatures; by the glint of gold-leaf in the marginal vines, raised by sizing, the better to catch the light; by the rubrications of pure vermilion (now become so rare) interspersed among the lines of text, or the binding, often worked in embroidery by pious hands or intricately tooled. A book like this might well be treasured by queens: it was a unique and intensely personal work of art.

The Printed Book.—After contemplating such a masterpiece one is tempted to wonder whether the printed book should strictly be considered as a work of art at all. However beautiful a piece of typography is (and it has unique and subtle beauties of its own), it is in its very nature a replica, a thing produced by a machine. The earliest printed books, by imitating closely every artistic rule of the calligrapher, profited by 14 centuries of previous experiment; type-founders, while they could not equal the nervous fineness of the best writing, certainly attained a new consistency and clarity of letter design; and yet the lover of written books, fine hand-tooled bindings and original painted illustrations may quite rightly maintain that such original pieces alone deserve the title of works of art, not of reproduction. Collectors and rich patrons, however, could still add a hand-tooled or inlaid binding and make it an individual work of art to that extent; binding, until the introduction of machine stamping and mass production, remained the most personal handicraft connected with typography. Illuminators, too, continued for a while to work on the printed page.

But as soon as printing was generally introduced (after 1456) it became obvious that no mere imitation of ms. style would serve the printed book. The artist's hand, the hand of the creative craftsman, had been transferred from direct writing to the work of designing and engraving the steel punch from which type-matrices were made, and to cutting the wood or metal used for illustrations. The printed page is quite literally, the "proof" of the unseen labours of the punch-cutter and engraver. This gives us, inevitably, a new set of artistic rules. An example is found in the "block books" which were sheets of paper "rubbed off" like proofs from engraved planks of wood inked with liquid, not greasy, ink. Whether these "block books" antedated printing or not, they were closely allied to the single xylographic print which certainly did so; and like the latter, they show how the mechanical problems of the cutter on wood forced him to "buttress" one set of lines with another, executing the lettering with the same rugged freedom as the cut and acquiring perfect homogeneity. When the colourist had added the faint glaze of his pigments, the result was of naïve and almost touching beauty—although the *Biblia pauperum* and the rest were the very opposite of "luxurious" books. The Chinese and Japanese block book could not, on account of the intricacies of the alphabet, be swept away almost at once by type printing, so that we are able to see, in oriental books of this character, what the block book can attain in technical sophistication, when the lettering is done by experts and the colour wood-cuts by masters.

The popularization of mechanically produced books was aided, and their appearance greatly affected, by the use of paper. While this substance was being made in France as early as 1189 it was never popular with calligraphers; the slightly acid ink from the scribe's pen was made so as to "bite" into the smooth surface of vellum without any pressure. But printers, with their oil-and-varnish ink, found that the absorbent surface of paper was the perfect medium for receiving pressure, by which ink was actually driven into the substance of the sheet.

Effect of Illustration.—Illustration was seldom used "for art's sake" in the 15th century; but there were many kinds of books that demanded the use of explanatory pictures. The new interest in natural science and the outer

113

world produced herbals, geographies and books of travel like Breydenbach's celebrated *Pilgrimage* (Mainz, 1486). The 16th century added the modern text-book, and with the *Hypnerotomachia* printed by Aldus in 1499 began a long line of "emblem books," collections of symbolic pictures dear to the Renaissance mind, which had an influence upon decorative printing. Each of these kinds of books affected the type-page in some way. The "pocket edition" invented by Aldus for the convenience of scholars, offered little opportunity for lavish decoration; but the book of hours continued, until the 1540s, to call on the resources of the book artist. Music part-books appeared at the beginning of the 16th century, in a distinctive oblong shape.

Engraved illustration was attempted in books as early as 1477 but it was not until the printer-publisher had tired of the many possibilities of wood-cutting that the copper plate came into general use (*post* 1550). By that time types of almost fragile delicacy were being cut; with proper inking and press-work they would have rendered discreet typographic support to the engraved title-pages and frontispieces which added a magnificent and not too alien touch to the book. Christophe Plantin of Antwerp, in the mid-16th century, was one of the last of his period to attempt unity in fine books. But he naturally gave much attention to engravings, and these had the effect of making patrons think of "fine books" as "fine picture-books" so that the punch-cutter, the ultimate typographic craftsman, lost prestige, save in such exotic efforts as polyglots. The first entirely successful attempt to restore all-round beauty to the book was made at the behest of Louis XIV., when the French national printing office produced its famous folio *Médailles* (*see* TYPOGRAPHY, page 219) with the newly-cut "King's types" of Grandjean. By this time the printer had learned how to deal with engraved and etched illustration, and the French 18th century produced the brilliant phenomenon of those octavos and duodecimos illustrated by Gravelot, Cochin and other masters, which were made for the eternal joy of collectors. Wood engravers began to imitate the delicate strokes of the *burin*. There was a general effort toward refinement of the printed page.

But it was John Baskerville of Birmingham who, by experimenting in 1757 not only with type design but with paper, ink and the press, revived the idea of the book as a technical whole, something more important than the sum of fine parts. A Baskerville book in a contemporary English black binding is a thing of the happiest consistency from beginning to end, and shows how little need the intelligent printer has for decoration or plates. Baskerville's followers could hardly improve on this serene style without evolving (as they eventually did) a hard and icy perfection of page, which is not so much tiring to the eye as to the mind. The post-Baskerville style in England was open, serene and friendly; the late 19th century Didot style in France was crisp and magnificently logical; but the books influenced by Bodoni of Italy (d. 1812) had an arbitrary perfection which was ill interpreted by his followers. The reaction, when it came in the 19th century, was two-fold. Decoration followed the whimsicalities of the romantic-gothic style with the new technical freedom of lithography and white-line wood engraving; typefounders and printers began to "revive" ancient type faces, so that the more pretentiously designed books took on the self-conscious archaisms of museum replicas. But this piracy of the past had at least an educative value, and prepared the way for the labours of William Morris and the "private presses" at the end of the century. The so-called "crafts" movement was once more to bring instructed reverence to the task of revising the outworn rules for the making of beautiful books. Our own modern typographic achievements are good inasmuch as we realize that all standards of craftsmanship depend on knowing, not only how things should be done, but why they are worth doing.

MODERN ENGLISH AND CONTINENTAL BOOKS

The Private Presses.—William Morris brought back dignity to the printed book in a time of its abject abasement. Indeed, he brought it too much dignity. His books were designed not for the common usage of his day, but, as it were, for the private pomps of mediaeval princes. They were beautiful, but they were not true. Yet they have served a noble purpose, conceived and executed as they were with the passionate faith of a protestant against the ugliness and tawdriness of the industrial 19th century. Morris sought to overthrow the machine. Hand-made paper, hand-cut punches for his types, hand composition, hand press-work: these were the articles of faith in the war against the machine. The result was that there were from 1892 to 1910 a few books printed superbly, almost arrogantly, and a multitude of books monstrous in their ignorance and ugliness. There was nothing between. There was no contact between the two classes.

The second and third decades of the 20th century have seen this contact made. That is their contribution to the art of book printing. The machine has not been tamed—it was never wild; the machine has been *saved*. It has been saved from the corrupt use of its nature. Its nature is to make—to make beautifully. It may make ugly things beautifully, or beautiful things beautifully. But the hand of man cutting letters and printing them painfully on a primitive press upon hand-made paper may make ugliness beautifully just as the machine may. If it is forcing the issue to say that the hand is part of the human machine, it is strictly and relevantly the truth that every type, be it never so hand-designed, hand-cut, hand-cast and hand-set, is a mechanical unit, and that every tool used by Morris in the making of his type, and in his use of it, was essentially a simple form of machine. The whole purpose of printing is to make cheap mechanical reproductions of certain symbols conveying sound and sense. The process of writing and illuminating a ms. in the 12th century is as far removed from the process of hand composition of type as it is from mechanical composition. The wheel, the lever, the wedge, the screw, the pulley—these and these only in less or greater complication make the handpress of Gutenberg and the greatest and latest rotary machine.

The significance of Morris's Kelmscott Press and the other private presses which it inspired (the Doves Press of Cobden-Sanderson and Emery Walker, Hornby's Ashendene Press and Rickett's Vale Press are the most notable) was, therefore, essentially not that they were "hand" presses, but that they were controlled by artists and designers of high competence and honourable enthusiasm. These artists and designers were expert amateurs. Their output was so small and expensive and "precious" as to justify the slightly derogatory sense which the word "amateur" carries; and though it was also conceived lovingly enough to justify the literal sense of the word "precious," it is the fact that the first importance of the private presses lies not in their own productions, but in the effect of their work upon fully mechanical book production. The effect was not first or directly upon the large printing houses. They were very slow to learn. Between them and the lesson were the prejudice of the professional against the amateur, and, even more, many acres and thousands of tons of preposterous type equipment. The first was overcome when it was realized that it was "good business" to be in the typographic movement; the second was disposed of even more completely when type-setting machines replaced the hand compositor in book work—for vast quantities of type became useless, and fetched during the World War a high price as scrap metal.

Modern Methods.—The principal type-setting machines for book work are the monotype and the linotype, of which the former has at present by far the greater variety of good type-faces. The monotype machine produces single types—separate "characters," whereas the linotype machine casts the type in lines, or "slugs." The common virtues of the type-setting machines are that they reduce the cost of composition; that they provide new type for each book; that, as they cast their own letters from matrices, the printer never runs short of a particular type, as he was apt to do in the days of hand composition; and that type after use is not laboriously "distributed," but put into the melting-pot. The particular merit of the monotype machine is that it possesses at least a score of admirable type-faces, as compared with no more than perhaps a dozen really good book types available at great expense to the hand compositor; and that these can be set with a nicety and flexibility of spacing (half the secret of good composition) actually beyond the power of the hand compositor. In short, compared with the old hand processes, the type-setting machine gives a wider range of type-faces with always new types; *can* set these types with greater subtlety; and *does* set them more cheaply. The type-setting machines used with as much skill as hand-set type will give a better result, and, in alliance with fast but very perfect cylinder printing presses, will give this result not to a few but to a multitude. It has taken us from the day of "the book beautiful" and given us the day of the beautiful book. The machine has fulfilled the democratic purpose of printing.

Function of the Typographer.—A new character in the printing industry has appeared to make use of this opportunity. He is the *typographer*. As is the architect to the builder, so is he to the printing house. He may be independent of both publisher and printer, and be called in by one or other as need demands. He may be in the permanent employ of the publisher. He is seldom in the permanent employ of the printer. His is a new profession, a new industrial function. The printer has become the executant. He receives his instructions and obeys them with all his technical skill. He is part of the machine, and his function is that proper to the machine. The machine, let it be repeated, has its own standard of beauty, which we call efficiency. A good printer is an efficient printer. A good typographer is a designer capable of using the mechanical equipment of the printer, the paper-maker and the binder, as tools in the production of a beautiful book. If the printer protests against this delimitation of his power, it must be said that he has in general only himself to blame. The few printers who add typographers to their staff maintain a reputation as something besides executants.

117

GRAPHIC ARTS

The Cambridge University Press, the Curwen Press and the Westminster Press in England are of this class.

Several important English publishing houses—William Heinemann, Jonathan Cape and Chatto and Windus, for example—pay very careful attention to the production of their books. They give to their printer precise instructions as to the size of the page, the "face" or character of type to be used, the closeness or openness of setting, the proportions of type to margin, and their relative positions on the page, the lay-out of the title-page and so on. The results of this initial care and thoroughness are apt of course, to become quickly established as formulae; but they are good formulae, and have assisted materially in the education of public taste in the matter of good book production. It is now a common thing to see the good (or bad) style and printing of a book with no "artistic" pretensions commented on in reviews. This is a distinctly new and encouraging departure for the average commercial book.

The most definite move in the direction of the full and considered use of modern printing equipment has, however, come from certain "semi-private" presses which specialize in the production of "limited editions." The limited edition appeals to three publics: the book collector, who does not read a book so much as fondle it; the speculator, who sees in it an article of commercial profit if the demand much exceeds the supply; and the people who "use books for reading" but still like to have them in a dress appropriate to their subject, and made of pleasant and enduring materials. These three classes in combination make a considerable public. The pre-machine limited edition was very narrowly limited; perhaps 2 or 3 or, rarely, 500 copies might be struck off the hand-press. In 1923 the writer began the publication of fine editions in the making of which the machine was exploited for economy at every point where machine processes were as good as hand processes. The "limit" of the editions was raised to about 1,500 copies, and prices much lower than had before been asked for "fine books" were thus made possible. It was quickly found that a very large public existed in England and America for books made on this plan, and many other undertakings of somewhat similar style have contributed admirably-made and moderately-priced books to the shelves of the book lover. Traditional style, in this the most significant development of current book production in England, has not been ignored, nor has it been slavishly imitated. There has been a sort of honourable understanding, for instance, that old illustrations and decorations should wherever possible give way to new. Inventiveness in the variations on old typographical themes is recognized and rewarded by a public becoming more and more familiar (chiefly by means of the writings of Stanley Morison and D. B. Updike) with the history of printing and with examples of its most illustrious styles. Thus, things work at present in a virtuous circle. The semi-private presses, which combine the functions of typographer and publisher but not necessarily that of actual printer, have learned from the handpress a true style which is adaptable to the more fully mechanical processes of an up-to-date printing house, paper mill and bindery. Their support makes economically possible the inventiveness (on the printing side) of the type-setting machine companies, who in their turn are able to offer to the commercial printer excellent characters of types which otherwise he could not possess. Thus contact is made with a great and "untypeconscious" public, which begins to take notice of the physical appearance of its books. From this uninstructed sense of comfort and propriety develops an interest in these books which are made expressly with an eye to beauty, either by well-controlled hand or by well-controlled machine methods.

Modern Typographic Style.—The books of the typographer-publisher presses, most of them reprints, are in general dressed in a format and printed in a type and style created, developed or mitigated for the special requirements of each particular work. If one word can summarize the whole art of the book, it is *suitability*. The modern typographer, unlike the designer of the private press books, has all the equipment of all the printing houses at his disposal in his search after this highly elaborated quality of suitability. Many considerations—the "atmosphere" or the actual date of the text, the nature of the illustrations, with such factors as the desired size of a page, or the extent of the contents—will in conjunction suggest the typographer's choice. If all the lessons which the private or precious presses taught, perhaps the most significant was this: a well-made book is a unity. Subject, paper, type, pictures, binding—all these are to be judged not independently for a self-possessed merit, but each item in relation to the next, and all to the whole. True, Morris and Cobden-Sanderson, in building up a book as a unity, put too much stress upon physical processes. No illustration seemed to them appropriate, for instance, which was not itself printed as a letter-press—a typographical surface of which the raised parts take ink from the roller and impress the paper. But flat surfaces, like the lithographic stone, or intaglio surfaces, such as copper-plates, which require a different printing

119

process, may very well afford entirely suitable results to the eye which is not blinded by pedantry. The great *Daphnis et Chloé* of the Imprimerie Nationale used Garamond's types and lithographic illustrations. And its success or failure is not to be judged by the consideration that in the 16th century lithography had not been invented. There is no limit, except his own inventiveness, to the range of the modern typographer's designs. Such a press as the Doves, on the other hand, maintained a general uniformity of design throughout its publications, because it possessed only its one strongly characteristic type-face, which virtually imposed its own will on the typographer, being capable of but little variety in its disposition on the page.

Book Printing on the Continent.—On the Continent, Germany shows the most interesting recent developments in printing. Just before and after the World War, a number of private presses stimulated the demand for good printing, and provided a training ground for typographic artists. The collapse of the mark spelt ruin to many of these private undertakings; but the typographers, thus released, have turned their attention (with greater benefit to the general reader) to the designing of books for the commercial publishers. The Morris revival in England had a great though over-appreciated effect upon Germany typography at the end of the 19th century. The German derivatives of Morris's types and Burne-Jones's illustrations are definitely unpleasant—a kind of mediaeval "art nouveau." The true inspiration of the notable book work done by both private, semi-private and commercial presses in Germany is none the less English. Edward Johnston, the English calligrapher, sent German typographers and type-designers back to the written letter. Upon pen-forms the new German typography is surely founded. Moreover, Rudolph Koch and others experimented with the making of "block books," and learned thereby a pictorial style of letter-making.

The Insel Verlag of Leipzig, one of the many German firms familiar to English collectors of limited editions, has, like other similar firms, turned its attention to the production of unlimited editions at low prices, with marked success. The Propyläen Verlag of Berlin, which has also made many fine limited editions, is issuing a pleasantly printed series of excellent modern editions and reprints at only 2s. each. Both of these concerns have maintained the function of typographer with those of printer and publisher.

The printing of novels by some of the leading German firms has been improved out of all recognition. In spite of the fact that the paper used has to be of inferior quality in order that the books can be produced at the prices current in Germany, the efforts made to secure a good impression by means of suitable inking have been so successful that the appearance of the novels published by such firms as Fischer, Ernst Rowholt of Berlin and Kiepenheuer of Potsdam, is highly agreeable. A striking thing about present-day book production in Germany is the use made of patterned papers to give distinction to the covers of cheap books. German typographers also make very excellent use of printers' "flowers" in the decoration of their book covers. Their expert handling of the collotype process of pictorial reproduction means that German books on the fine arts are incomparably better produced than similar books in England. They are also very much cheaper. Germany owes a great deal of her technical expertness in printing, as in other applied arts, to the excellence of her technical schools and institutes, which are supported by the State and served by the best artists and technicians of the day. Switzerland shared in this excellence of instruction, and her standard of book production is also high, following in the main the trend of German development.

In France, the general level of printing is not nearly so high, though certain rather expensive volumes well printed on fine paper have recently appeared, and the standard of the ordinary paper-bound book has risen considerably in the case of the publications of certain houses, among which the *Nouvelle Revue Française* ranks high. The standard of illustration in France is much higher than that of printing; indeed, the value of the expensive French book has hitherto lain almost exclusively in the excellence of its illustrations, with the printing a secondary and unimportant affair. In particular, illustrations coloured by the *pochoir* or stencil process have been brought to a high state of perfection. The pre-War *Gazette du Bon Ton* deserves much credit for this development. The Couluma Press of Argenteuil is responsible for much of the good printing to be found among French books of the day. It is now making a significant addition to its plant of a monotype composing machine. Its handling of monotype material is certain to prove most interesting. What should be a help to the wide dissemination of well-printed books is the custom of certain French publishers of re-publishing their limited editions subsequently in un-numbered editions on cheaper paper. In some instances, there are as many as six editions, ranging downwards according to the paper used and the number of the impression to a final edition costing but a few francs. Unfortunately it often happens that the "imposition," i.e., the setting of the page of type in relation to the margin of the page, goes awry in these reprints, and that the press-work is very poorly done.

Belgian printing is strongly under the influence of France. Belgian books, like French ones, are bound only in paper, and consequently the finest examples of book production in both France and Belgium are, compared with English books of similar standard, very inexpensive. In Holland there are a number of private presses which have produced good work, but the general level of book production is low. The only strong influence in the direction of improved printing comes from the Enschedé foundry, which is not only producing good types, but also printing them very effectively.

Sweden, which formerly followed the lead of Germany in printing matters, has of recent years broken away from this influence, and is developing along her own lines in this as in other branches of applied art. She now favours a much lighter style of printing than that common to Germany, and makes considerable use of "old-face" types rather than of the newer, heavier type faces popular in Germany. But her books maintain a simple sturdiness in their general style as well as in the details of ornamentation, and the "peasant art" motif is clearly discernible.

The contribution of Spain to fine contemporary printing is not large. The monastery of Montserrat is responsible for some strikingly good books. Apart from that, there is a school of competent book printers, whose interest seems to be chiefly in the Didot style in France since the late 18th century.

Italy is not happy in her printers. The average commercial book is very poor, although the Scuola del Libro at Milan is exerting a good influence on the printing trade, and the printing house of Bertieri and Vanzetti has done some good work. But the book as a work of art owes more to, and has more to expect from, the Milan publisher Mondadori, who has recently established his own press at Verona, and has associated with him there Herr Hans Madersteig, whose small editions set in the Bodoni types were unexcelled for their technical skill in all printing history. The State-sponsored editions of D'Annunzio's works have been entrusted to him.

Soviet Russia has contributed some very interesting examples of an aggressive and telling style in printing. The illustrations, in the form of strong and vigorous wood-cuts, are often striking, and the type and style of printing in conjunction with these wood-cuts is provocative and stimulating. The best of these Russian publications have been in the cheaper ranges of book production. No doubt the fact that so many adults in Russia are only now learning to read has had a considerable influence on the very direct and blunt and almost poster-like style of Russian printing.

Czechoslovakia shows a well-informed but definitely conservative taste in printing. Method Kalab of Prague and the national printing office may be mentioned as sources of satisfactory books, employing mainly English monotype faces in their production.

MODERN AMERICAN

THE RENAISSANCE of fine book-making, due in England to the unbounded enthusiasm and ability of William Morris and continued in a more restrained style by his disciples, Cobden-Sanderson of the Doves press and others, has had a marked influence on book design and printing in America. The leaders in this revival of the art of the book in the United States were D. B. Updike and Bruce Rogers. But an excellent foundation was laid for them in the closing years of the 19th century and the early part of the 20th by two outstanding printers of a preceding generation: Theodore L. De Vinne and Walter Gilliss.

De Vinne and Gilliss.—The work of De Vinne (1828–1914) fell mostly within the 19th century but continued into the 20th and set a fine example of high standards in the art of printing for the emulation of the younger generation. De Vinne was one of the founders of the Grolier Club, the most distinguished among American book clubs, and he planned and printed the majority of its early publications. The De Vinne press not only printed limited editions of fine books for wealthy amateurs, but also established high standards on work which involved, for that period, large scale production; such for instance as the *Century Dictionary*, the *Century Magazine*, and *St. Nicholas*. De Vinne strove constantly to benefit the printing craft, artistically, socially and economically. He was an ardent student of the history of typography and was the author of a number of books on this subject and on the practice of printing. In book printing his composition was well planned and carefully executed, and the quality of his press-work was unexceptionable. He produced many fine books, the simplest of which are the best, at a time when the printing art in the United States had fallen to deplorable levels. Though not a great artist when compared with some who were to follow him in the next generation, he must be credited with a great accomplishment in the period in which he worked.

Walter Gilliss (1855–1925) was the other distinguished book printer of

De Vinne's generation who did much fine work during the first quarter of the 20th century.   During most of this period he did not himself manufacture his printing but he planned it in every detail of typography, paper, printing and binding, and supervised its production with meticulous care.   His judgment in visualizing the typography of a book before it was set in type was unerring, a rare faculty among book designers.   His original lay-outs, marked with the most minute instructions, were seldom departed from.   Most of his work was classical in its simplicity; when he indulged in ornament he appeared to be under 18th century French influence.   He was secretary of the Grolier Club from its earliest days, and through this and other like connections enjoyed the warm friendship of the leading amateurs of fine books, for many of whom he produced privately printed volumes of great charm—notably the series of dainty volumes for the discriminating bibliophile, William Loring Andrews.   He planned much of the printing of the Metropolitan Museum of Art, which has set new standards in institutional printing.   His most important book was undoubtedly the *Iconography of Manhattan Island* executed for I. N. Phelps Stokes.   At one time in his career, he was concerned also with printing of larger volume, producing *Life* and *Vogue* during the infancy of those periodicals.   In the field of type faces, Gilliss was very partial to Elzevir and Caslon and he played a not inconsequential rôle in the revival of the latter face.

The Merrymount Press.—Daniel Berkeley Updike (b. 1860) entered the printing business in 1893 with a very definite ideal; the practice of printing as an art.   Yet he aimed to make the enterprise a success financially as well, and has proved that these two ends are not, in every case, mutually exclusive. The first equipment consisted of a composing room only, but later presses were added so that the standards of press-work—too often faulty in well-designed books—might be worthy of the typography.   He named his plant the Merrymount press.   The first book of importance to be executed was the *Altar Book*, printed in 1896 in the "Merrymount" type, a new face designed for Updike by Bertram Grosvenor Goodhue, the distinguished American architect.   The illustrations were by Robert Anning Bell and the borders were designed by Goodhue.   A glance at the pages from this book (Plate V. fig. 1) will show to what extent Updike was at this time under the influence of William Morris.   The type was black, the borders heavy and the tone of the illustrations in keeping.   A pioneer in introducing the Morris style—then a novelty in book-making—in the United States, Updike did not practice it long. Following—and also to a large extent leading—the taste in book design, his printing soon became much lighter in tone. Herbert Horne designed for him a lighter type face, the Montallegro, the punches for which were cut by the celebrated English punch-cutter, Edward P. Prince. It was used first in 1905 in Condivi's *Life of Michelangelo Buonarroti* and later in the various volumes of the *Humanists' Library*. Types, in addition to Caslon, which Updike has used most extensively, and with great success, are Montjoye and Oxford, a typefoundry face of earlier years which he has had cast for his own use; also in recent years he has made a limited use of several of the newer types of European origin: Poliphilus, Naudin and Champlevé. Hitherto all his composition has been done in foundry-cast type, set by hand, often by women compositors.

The field of printing in which Updike stands alone is the making of beautiful books by the capable and tasteful use of type alone, without embellishment of any sort, gaining all desired effects of display or emphasis by the use of italic, small capitals, letter spacing, a well-chosen initial here and there, a right relation of sizes, sound spacing between elements on the page and correctly proportioned margins. All this is done in any one book with the use of one simple face of type in a full range of sizes. The fine artistry he attains by the simplest of means is represented, for example, in a number of college catalogues and reports of institutions, notably in the catalogue of the John Carter Brown library. Updike, however, does not disdain the use of type ornament or other embellishment in proper places, but it is always an incident in the plan of a book rather than the dominating feature of the design. The standards of workmanship at the Merrymount press are exigent, so that well-designed books shall not suffer from blemishes of execution. Updike indulges no fetish regarding hand-work where the results he wishes to achieve can be obtained by more effective means. Thus his presswork is done on power-driven cylinder presses of modern type.

In the judgment of many discerning critics, Updike is the best American printer of the current generation. His primacy is due, according to these critics, to the fact that he does not exaggerate in the effort to make beautiful books; he is not restlessly seeking some new device to make a book different from other books for no reason better than a desire for difference. He works on a positive rather than a negative principle, that each book shall be perfectly fit in design to its purpose and subject. If this rule leads him into new fields, he does not hesitate to enter them; should it lead along the paths of tradition he will follow obediently. According to the Merrymount Press's own statement, "an economy of means and a sort of disciplined sobriety mark its product; and this comes about, probably, through aiming at suitability—a quality which involves discarding whatever does not organically belong to the particular work in hand." Updike has rendered a great service to typography in his two-volume work, *Printing Types* (1922), which was awarded the gold medal of the American Institute of Graphic Arts. This book gives a review of the historical development of type design, with a running critique of the aesthetic merits or demerits of the better faces of each period. He is also the author of a series of essays on the work of the printer, *In the Day's Work* (1924), which state many of the principles on which he works. He likewise edited for the Grolier Club a reprint of Mores' *A Dissertation Upon English Typographical Founders and Founderies* (1924).

Bruce Rogers.—Bruce Rogers is the most celebrated of the fine printers in America, and his books are now the vogue among collectors, a situation which has led to a sharp appreciation in the market value of the best which he has designed. He has the advantage of being himself an artist of ability and has thus been able to design some of the type faces and almost all the decorations which have gone into the making of his books. Rogers is a traditionalist at heart but he is also endowed with a sprightly inventiveness which has leavened the style of all his work. His first interest in book production was concerned with illustration. He drew for undergraduate publications at Purdue University and after his graduation in 1890 he worked on the art staff of the Indianapolis *News*. Soon after he became acquainted with Joseph M. Bowles who had established an American organ of the "Arts and Crafts" movement called *Modern Art*. Bowles showed Rogers some of the Kelmscott press books which had just begun to appear. They were a revelation to the young artist and, his interest began to widen from illustration alone to embrace the art of the book as an integral whole. In 1895 he designed a few decorations for Thomas B. Mosher, the idealistic publisher of Portland, Me., these being used in an edition of A. E.'s *Homeward Songs by the Way*, in the colophon of which the name Bruce Rogers appears for the first time. In search of financial support Bowles moved *Modern Art* to Boston, and Rogers soon followed to that city—an excellent field for the budding talent of a young book designer. In 1900 Rogers cemented closer a relation already established with the Riverside press of Cambridge, Mass., a special department for the production of fine books in limited editions being set up

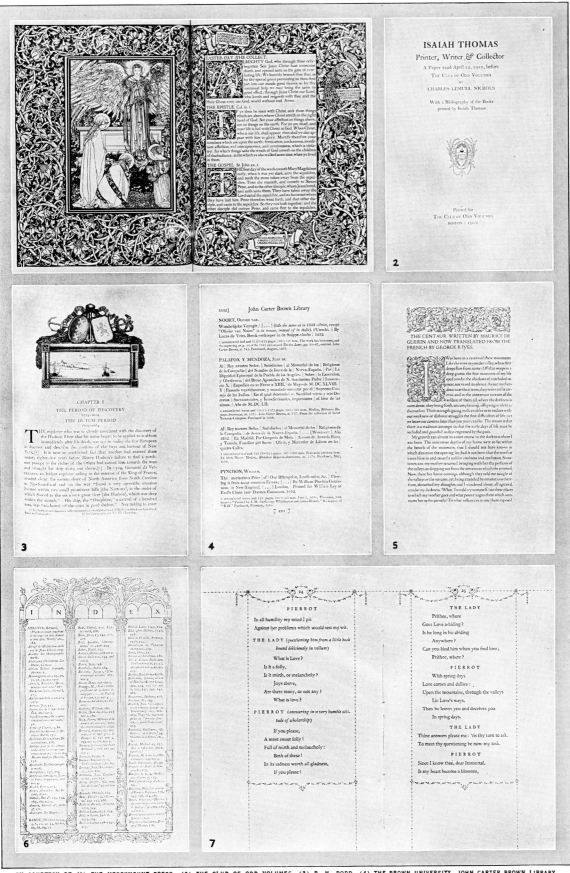

PAGE DESIGNS OF MODERN AMERICAN BOOKS FROM 1896 TO 1923

1. *The Altar Book*, designed by D. B. Updike. 1896. 2. *Isaiah Thomas, Printer, Writer and Collector*, by C. L. Nichols, designed by D. B. Updike. 1912. 3. *Iconography of Manhattan Island* by I. N. P. Stokes, designed by Walter Gillis. 1915. 4. *Catalogue* of the John Carter Brown Library, designed by D. B. Updike. 1919. 5. *The Centaur*, by Maurice de Guérin, designed by Bruce Rogers. 1916. 6. *Geoffroy Tory, Painter and Engraver*, by Auguste Bernard, translated by G. B. Ives and designed by Bruce Rogers. 1909. 7. *The Pierrot of the Minute*, by Ernest Dowson, designed by Bruce Rogers. 1923

PLATE VI   BOOKS

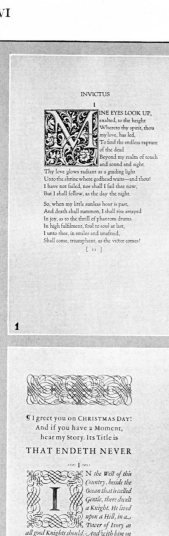

PAGE DESIGNS FROM MODERN AMERICAN BOOKS

1. *Songs of the Love Unending*, by Kendall Banning, designed by Frederick and Bertha Goudy. 2. *Anchors of Tradition*, by Caroline Hazard, designed by C. P. Rollins. 3. *Reminiscences of Leonid Andreyev*, by Maxim Gorki, translated by Katharine Mansfield and S. S. Koteliansky and designed by Frederick Warde. 4. *That Endeth Never*, by Hildegarde Flanner, designed by Porter Garnett. 5. Plantin's *Index Characterum*, edited by Douglas C. McMurtrie, designed by Elmer Adler. 6. *The Book of Ruth*, designed by Edwin and Robert Grabhorn. 7. *The Letter of Christopher Columbus*, designed by Edwin Grabhorn. 8. *The Silverado Squatters*, by R. L. Stevenson, designed by John Henry Nash. 9. *Jean Guttemberg*, translated and designed by Douglas C. McMurtrie

at that plant under his supervision. From this department issued a succession of charming volumes which promptly won favour with bibliophiles and collectors, many of whom entered subscriptions for all books which might be issued. Time has justified their confidence.

The most attractive feature of the Riverside books was their variety. With the celebrated English presses, to have seen three of their books was to have seen all. With Rogers's work each volume was different, in typography, in decoration (where decoration was used), in format, in binding. And the style of each volume was related, as only a master of book-making could relate it, to the subject of the text it embodied in printed form. Among the more important books produced at Cambridge were the folio Montaigne (1902–04), *Franklin and his Press at Passy* (1914), executed for the Grolier Club, and a translation of Auguste Bernard's *Geofroy Tory* (1909), for which latter volume Rogers redrew with an exquisite touch the crudely printed but exceedingly beautiful borders engraved on wood by Tory, with the result that they were printed as the great French master would have wished them to appear. (*See* Plate V., fig. 6.)

The relation between Bruce Rogers and the Riverside press terminated in 1912 and the designer went abroad for a year. On his return he fell in with Carl Purington Rollins who was operating a small printing office in an old mill, the Dyke mill, at Montague, Mass. Here Rogers printed his perhaps most celebrated book, a slim volume—little more than a leaflet—bound in boards, *The Centaur* by Maurice de Guérin, translated by George B. Ives, a page of which is here reproduced (Plate V., fig. 5). This was set in the Centaur type, a very skilful recreation of the great Roman type of Nicolas Jenson, the design and decoration of the book being modelled after the style of Robert Estienne, the French printer of the early 16th century. Only 135 copies were printed, most of these being presented by the designer to his friends. The auction price of this leaflet has gone above $300.

After a period of work as adviser to the University Press in Cambridge, England, Rogers returned to America and became consulting designer of books for William Edwin Rudge who moved to Mt. Vernon, N. Y., a printing plant which had already, in New York City, earned a reputation for printing far above the average. He also became adviser to the Harvard University Press. Since his association with Rudge, Rogers' work has shown a new verve. He became enamoured of type ornament—i.e., decorative units cast like single types—and he has used this material in many whimsical and astounding ways. The finest example of its use may be seen in the borders, printed in rose, framing the pages of *Pierrot of the Minute*, by Ernest Dowson, produced in 1923 as one item in the printers' series of the Grolier Club. Specimen pages of this book are here shown (Plate V., fig. 7 d.). This volume must always be considered among Rogers' finest achievements in creative design. He has also carried the use of type ornament to even more fanciful extremes in several notable pieces of advertisement.

Other Eastern Typographers.—Carl Purington Rollins, who operated at Montague, Mass., the press at the Dyke mill already referred to, has been for a number of years typographic adviser to the Yale University Press. In this capacity he has put the impress of beauty upon many trade publications issued at moderate prices. He also operates in his home a private press, performing all the processes of manufacture with his own hands. As a book designer Rollins ranks with the best. His period typography is authentic and ably conceived, and all his work gives evidence of a sure and discriminating taste.

The Village press, whose address has been successively Oak Park, Ill., Hingham, Mass., Forest Hills, L.I., and Marlborough-on-Hudson, N.Y., is a personal enterprise of Frederic W. Goudy and his wife. Village, Kennerley, Forum, Italian old style, and many other fine type faces have been designed by Goudy. The issues of his press, always extremely limited in number, are set in the types he designs, and the decoration used is also a product of Goudy's brush or pen. The pieces are usually small, no large book having issued from the Village press, but they all give evidence of the unquestioned artistry in matters typographic of the master of the press. Being published through no regular channel, their fugitive character makes them the despair of amateurs seeking to acquire a reasonably complete collection.

Elmer Adler is one of the latest entrants into the guild of fine bookmaking, working in New York under the name of the Pynson Printers. His press is operated as a business enterprise which makes no concessions to commercialism in the quality of its work. Well grounded in the classic traditions of typography, Adler has been willing to use new types and follow new modes, if they are sound ones, with the result that much of his work is refreshingly original in style without being freakish. As to type faces he has relied principally on Garamond and Bodoni Book, but has also used effectively some of the more modern types, particularly those designed by the German artist, Lucian Bernhard. He has rendered another service to good book-making in having designed, for Alfred A. Knopf, numerous books of general circulation which have exceeded his own manufacturing facilities, and laid out, also for Knopf, the typography of the *American Mercury*.

Frederic Warde, who was doing interesting work as typographic adviser to the Princeton University Press, left that institution for extensive travel in Europe, in order to become familiar with Continental book arts and to do work of an experimental character on his own account. While abroad he revived, in collaboration with Stanley Morison, one of the most interesting of the 16th century Italian cursive types, Arrighi, the punches for which were cut by hand. Warde has now returned to America and can be depended upon for some distinguished work in the field of book design.

San Francisco Printers.—From New York and New England it is a long jump to the next centre of fine book printing, San Francisco. The initiative here must be credited to John Henry Nash, a typographer of distinction with personal attributes which have enabled him to make a business success of fine printing, which must often be a hobby, subsidized in one way or another. His way was made the easier by the patronage of a distinguished American collector and he has received other important commissions for the execution of fine books. Nash is an enthusiast for close spacing and his typography is well planned and set. His press-work, which is done outside under his close supervision, is excellent. In style Nash's printing is more flamboyant than that of the other fine printers; he makes generous use of colour, rules and decoration. The possible criticism is that he sometimes strains a little after effect. But he has, on the other hand, the very distinct merit of having established an individual style. He has printed numerous books for the California Book Club in addition to those commissioned by private collectors, and has also published several handsome volumes on his own account.

Edwin Grabhorn, in association with his brother Robert, has established an enviable reputation within a very few years for doing as fine printing as is done anywhere to-day. He plans his work with exquisite taste in a truly original style. The Grabhorns do all branches of their work in their own small office; hand composition, presswork, illumination and binding. They print their hand-made paper wet, which is becoming a lost art, and attain a uniformity of colour and perfection of impression almost beyond criticism. Both are still young men and much brilliant work may confidently be expected of them.

Taylor and Taylor, also in San Francisco, have done much creditable book printing, and two young men, the Johnson brothers, who work under the name of the Windsor press, show signs of real virtuosity as book typographers.

Recent Contributors.—At the Laboratory press at Pittsburgh, Porter Garnett has not only done some fine printing himself—notably his privately printed volume *That Endeth Never*, a page of which is shown in Plate VI., fig. 4—but has also made a substantial contribution to the cause of fine printing in America, by training talented students in its principles and artistry. Among the other men who have done or are doing fine work in the book printing field during the 20th century are Spencer Kellogg, Jr., at the Aries press, Eden, N.Y.; Clark Conwell at the Elston press, New Rochelle, N.Y.; William A. Kittredge at the Lakeside press, Chicago; Will Ransom at Chicago; A. B. McCallister at Los Angeles; and Douglas C. McMurtrie at Greenwich, Conn.

Two commercial publishing enterprises deserve consideration in any review of fine book printing in America. The first of these, the Roycroft press at East Aurora, N.Y. founded by Elbert Hubbard, was directly inspired by the work of the Kelmscott press. Its earliest work, done in the spirit of idealism, was good, but as commercial success became the paramount consideration its standards were lowered. In Portland, Me., Thomas B. Mosher, a publisher with a love for less known items of good literature and excellent taste as to format, produced many lovely volumes which became widely known.

Modern Facilities.—The modern fine printer interested in doing work of the highest quality is fairly well provided with facilities. Modern press equipment, either of the platen or cylinder variety, when properly operated, will deliver impression as perfect as can be obtained on a hand press and with a much greater uniformity in ink distribution. Almost all the finely printed books being produced to-day are printed on power presses. As to type supply, the foundry offerings have improved greatly during the 20th century; the companies making type composing and casting machinery have shown an interest in fine types which they lacked in earlier years, European sources have been tapped for supplies of good types, and a number of the designers have had special faces cut for their own use. As regards paper, a few American mills have been making better and better grades of stock for book printing, though it has been necessary to import the large amounts of hand-made paper which have been required. The quality of ink is reasonably satisfactory though there is still room, in this field, for much improvement. Fine

CRAYON

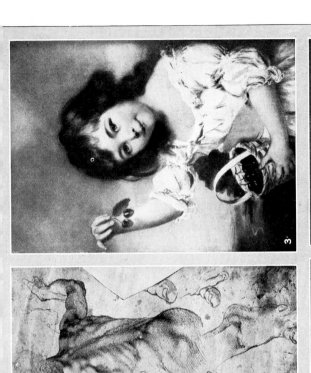

CRAYONS AND PASTELS, 16TH–19TH CENTURIES

1. Pierre Bouguer, crayon portrait by Jean Baptiste Perronneau (1731–83). The original is in the Louvre

2. Crayon studies for the Libyan Sybil, by Michelangelo (1475–1564), for the ceiling of the Sistine Chapel, in the Vatican, Rome

3. Girl with cherries, pastel by John Russell (1745–1806). The Louvre

4. Crayon studies for a mural, by Pierre C. Puvis de Chavannes (1824–98)

5. Landscape in crayon by Thomas Gainsborough (1727–88)

6. Girl with a monkey, pastel by Rosalba Carriera of Venice (1675–1757)

THE CAISSONS, BY JOSEPH PENNELL (1860–1926)

One of a series of etchings by Pennell on American industrial subjects

binding is to be had in several centres, the good work being done for the most part by English artisans who have settled in America, but there are also a number of women binders who have taken up this craft in the amateur spirit and have produced highly creditable work.

The cause of fine book-making has received great impetus from the "fifty books" exhibition held annually under the auspices of the American Institute of Graphic Arts. It was difficult to find 50 good books, produced during the current year, worthy of inclusion in the first exhibition in 1923, but with the growth in prestige of this annual show, publishers have displayed a keen rivalry to have their books included among the 50 honoured by the choice of the jury. The exhibition has thus undoubtedly exercised a beneficial influence on the artistry of American book-making, an influence which seems destined to continue.

CRAYON

CRAYON, a black or coloured material for drawing, generally in the form of pencils, but sometimes in powdered form. Obtainable, to some extent, from native earthy and other compact and friable mineral substances, crayons are, for the most part, artificially prepared mixtures of a base of pipe or china clay with Prussian blue, chrome yellow, vermilion, ochres, umbers and other pigments cemented together by the introduction of some weak adhesive, usually gum tragacanth. Calcined gypsum, talc and compounds of magnesium, bismuth and lead are occasionally used as bases. The required shades of tints are obtained by adding varying amounts of colouring matter to a given quantity of the base. The use of chalks, especially red earth, is of ancient origin as testified by surviving examples, and Horace's *rubrica picta aut carbone* would show that the conflicts of the famous gladiators were delineated in red chalk as well as charcoal. It is, however, with the use of the medium in more modern ages that we are now mainly concerned, especially when, in the 16th century, the artists used black chalk on white paper, and when, as the century advanced, they began more and more to employ it together with other mediums for the purpose of suggesting colour.

131

GRAPHIC ARTS

First black chalk heightened with white, on a tinted paper, then black and red crayon, heightened with white, on papers of various tonality. With the specific use, however, of red crayon, in *sanguine*, as the French call it, draughtsmanship seemed to extend its scope and capacity, as we see particularly in the exquisite drawings of Watteau, done in infinite numbers, not only as notes and studies for pictures, but for the sheer joy of drawing, with all their inexpressible sense of grace and vitality inherent in the just emphasis of the accents of every figure, and the rhythmic significance of every line, and a general expression of animation. "*C'est de la sanguine qui contient de la pourpre*" wrote Edmond de Goncourt *à propos* the incomparable Watteau, "*c'est du crayon noir qui a un velouté à nul autre pareil; et cela mélangé de craie avec la pratique savante et spirituelle de l'artiste, devient, sur du papier chamois, de la chair blonde et rose.*" There is little in the use of crayon that we could not learn from the inimitable drawings of Watteau if only we had the wit to divine the magic of his art. How to commingle the red, black and white strokes with the tone of the paper so as to suggest the illusion of a natural garment of colour, how to rub the vermilion chalk on the black with the finger or a stump or a rag, so that a lovely tone shall evolve, how to draw those expressive lines that positively sparkle with the living accent, how to judge the exact tones of white that shall lighten the contours and the shadows, which the paper always shows between as a half tone; in all these is the secret of Watteau's pre-eminence. This secret was never quite shared, for all their talent and charm, with Boucher, Greuze, Lagonard, Lancret, Baudouin or Chardin, who put their touch in *sanguine* to the test of unconscious rivalry.

Most of the old masters used chalk for their drawings at one time or another, giving it preference in many instances to pencil, or reed, pen and ink, or sepia wash, as for instance in the 15th century Gentile Bellini did a self-portrait in black chalk, and Francesco Morone a "Virgin enthroned with Saints" in red. There were, however, certain outstanding masters whose expressive lines in red and black chalk reflected a clear vision of character inherent in the contours. There were the Clouets, Jean and François, successively court painters to Francis I. whose crayon drawings, almost in outline, were so peculiarly distinguished for their psychological truth, and there was Holbein, whose series of portrait drawings at Windsor, is one of our glorious possessions. To obtain a full effect of colour he would variously tint the paper, and rub the tint away where light was wanted, or he would

132

add white, the drawing being done with red or black chalk, the essential character of the face and head being exactly defined, and the chalk then rubbed to soften the tone suggestively, and a supplementary line or so of silver point being introduced for accent. The magnificently rich drawings of Rubens were done with black chalk heightened with white, or with the red crayon, while Van Dyck used chalk on a blue or brown paper, the choice of paper, by the way, influencing very much the effect of the chalks in the drawing. Titian and Tintoretto drew in black and white on blue paper, and Fra Bartolommeo on salmon pink or yellowish paper, while Correggio used red chalk with washes of red bistre heightened with white, Leonardo caressed the toned paper, so to speak, with his exquisite enfolding lines in red, and Piero di Cosimo, among others, reflected his influence. The black or red crayon was used characteristically with individual powers and finesse by Michelangelo, Raphael, Andrea del Sarto, Pontorno, Carpaccio, Lorenzo de Credi, Dürer and Lucas van Leyden, Rembrandt, Ruisdael, Esias van de Velde, Claude Lorrain, Callot, Gravelot. Of English artists, Richard Wilson used chalk for classic landscape studies with beautiful effect, but the supreme master of the crayon in English art was Gainsborough, who, with the softening influence of the stump, made nature speak pictorially with grace, beauty and vivacity as well in landscape as in the human figure. A notable series of drawings in red chalk is that by Alfred Stevens, the famous sculptor, but among the moderns Whistler's manner of using coloured chalks was most lovely and distinguished. A new invention of oil colours in crayon form, purporting to be used as a substitute for brush painting, was invented at the beginning of the century by I. F. Raffaelli, the French painter and etcher, who painted many pictures with the new medium. The colours, however, are said to have soon lost their brilliancy.

ETCHING

ETCHING is the process of biting lines or areas by means of acid or some other chemical. By etching generally we mean the process of biting these lines in a metal plate with a view to its being printed from, and by an etching, the print taken from a plate so etched. Lines may indeed be etched on a metal plate which is itself intended to serve some decorative purpose, with no idea of prints being taken from it, but etching of this sort should more properly be treated in connection with decorative metal work and has no significance here. Etching, as above defined, has this important point in common with line engraving, that the lines which are to appear black on the print are incised as opposed to those in wood engraving which are in relief. The process of printing from an etched plate is, therefore, identical with that of printing from an engraved plate. Etching only differs from line engraving in the process by which the lines are incised; in the latter case, by an instrument of triangular section which scoops a shaving out of the metal; in the former, by chemical action. A print from an etched plate may generally be distinguished from a print from an engraved plate, by the fact that in the former the lines do not diminish or increase gradually in thickness but do so in more or less abrupt stages; that the endings of the lines are square, whereas in the latter they taper gradually to an end. These differences are inherent in the different processes. It is obviously impossible to end a line abruptly by means of a triangular gouging instrument, such as a burin; if the burin were stopped suddenly the shaving it forms in its course would be left. In etching, on the other hand, the thickness or thinness of the lines being obtained by successive bitings and each successive biting being comparatively uniform over the plate, a line, which is intended to gradually diminish in size, has (microscopically perhaps) a form like that of an extended telescope. Engraving has, of course, been constantly used in combination with etching and it is often a matter of difficulty to distinguish between the parts which are purely etched, those which have been first etched and later strengthened by the engraving tool and those which have been directly engraved. A further word should be added on the subject of dry-point. This is merely the process of scratching with the etching needle direct on the plate. In its passage the needle leaves an irregular ridge on either side of the line which it makes (burr) to which the ink adheres, so that a dry-point line when printed has at first a slightly blurred, but rich effect: this burr wears away quickly and the scratched line by itself, when printed, is then faint and meagre. Dry-point, though it is independent of the use of mordants, is generally employed in conjunction with etching for the richness of its effect.

The number of satisfactory prints which may be taken from an etched plate varies according to the hardness of the metal and the depth to which

134

the lines have been etched. A fine line on a copper plate may be almost obliterated after 200 or 300 impressions: a dry-point line will, as has been indicated, lose its characteristic effect very much sooner. Some of the prints taken from Rembrandt's plates 50 years ago are almost, though not quite, as good as those taken during his lifetime.

HISTORY

ETCHING, like engraving, was probably invented north of the Alps, and it is in Germany, France and England, and above all the Netherlands, that the greatest triumphs of the process have been achieved. It will be most convenient in a brief summary of its history to deal with its progress in the Teutonic countries from its beginning to the end of the 17th century, and then to return to Italy, France and Spain. As a means of decorating metal, particularly armour, etching was practised at least as early as the middle of the 15th century. It seems probable that, as the earliest engraving was the work of goldsmiths, so the earliest etching is to be credited to the armourers. The idea of printing from such a plate they no doubt borrowed from the goldsmiths. The first etching, to which an approximate date can be given, is a portrait of Kunz van der Rosen by Daniel Hopfer (working 1493-1536), which a rather complicated line of reasoning assigns to the year 1504 or earlier. Daniel Hopfer was one of a family of armourers working in Augsburg, but was an artist of much originality. Hans Burgkmair the elder (1473-1531), the dominating personality of the Augsburg school, and on whom the Hopfers largely depended, executed a single etching, no doubt learning the process from the lesser artists. The earliest etching which actually bears a date is one by the Swiss goldsmith, soldier and draughtsman, Urs Graf (d. 1529), of the year 1513, most probably done at Basle. Albrecht Dürer (1471-1528), with the eagerness for experiment which characterized him, tried etching, but apparently found it an unsympathetic medium and after a few experiments gave it up in favour of engraving. His half dozen etchings dated between 1515 and 1519, impressed though they are with that great artist's personality, are among the least satisfactory of his reproductive work. Iron, the metal used in all these first attempts, did not allow of much delicacy, and the result, compared with line engraving on copper, for which it was regarded as merely a less laborious substitute, unsatisfactory. However, it was a new process which everyone must try out for himself. In Holland Lucas van Leyden (1494-1533), who probably

135

learnt the process from Dürer during the German's visit to the Netherlands in 1520–21, etched a few plates. These are technically superior to Dürer's, and of importance as probably the first examples of the use of copper for etching, which made it possible for line engraving to be used in combination with it. The fine portrait of Maximilian which Lucas van Leyden made in 1521 is an example of this combined use of etching and engraving, the whole of the emperor's face being finished with the burin. Dirick Vellert at Antwerp (working 1517–44), an artist of delicate accomplishment, uses a technique much resembling Lucas's, though the majority of his works are engraved. Nicolas Hogenberg of Munich (working 1523–37), whose artistic career was passed at Malines in the service of Margaret of Austria, was one of the first northern artists to use etching with rapidity and freedom, and his frieze of the entry of Charles V. into Bologna in 1530, in a number of plates, is important from its size as well as from its subject. Frans Crabbe (the Master of the Crayfish; d. 1553), who was associated with Hogenberg, also followed his example in etching, but his work is unequal in quality.

Dürer's followers in Nuremberg, Hans Sebald Beham (1500–50) and Georg Pencz (1500–50) etched only a few plates, for the most part in the years immediately following Dürer's experiments. Albrecht Altdorfer (about 1480–1538) of Ratisbon, also no doubt impelled by Dürer's example, tried his hand at etching as early as 1519, and later used it for the first pure landscapes produced. Augustin Hirschvogel (1503–53?) and Hans Sebald Lautensack (working 1524–63) in Vienna followed Altdorfer's example in landscape, but without quite the freshness and charm of its originator. The only succeeding etcher of importance in Germany is Jost Amman (1539–91), who worked at Nuremberg.

In the Netherlands, line engraving usurped the field in the latter half of the 16th century and comparatively little etching was done. Jan Cornelisz Vermeyen (1500–59), the court painter of the Emperor Charles V., had etched a number of plates. He is probably the earliest example in the Netherlands of the painter, with no training as an engraver, turning his hand to etching. His plates, some of them of large size, are still executed in rather a formal style but are extraordinarily fresh and effective. Marcus Gheeraerts the Elder (c. 1521–1604), of Bruges, was the author of a charming series of small plates illustrating Aesop (1567), which are etched with a delicacy and sensitiveness hardly equalled by Adrian van Ostade or Hollar. Gheeraerts spent the latter part of his life in England, where he issued further etchings,

136

the first to be published in that country. Hieronymus Cock (1510?–70), the publisher, did some admirable landscapes of the conventional type, and the great Pieter Brueghel (1525?–69) and Frans Floris (*c.* 1517–70), the fashionable painter of the time in Antwerp, each etched one plate, while Hans Bol, the landscape painter and draughtsman of Malines (1534–1593), within rather narrow limits, was an etcher of considerable charm. Paul Bril of Antwerp (1554–1626), who passed practically the whole of his life in Italy, is chiefly interesting as a link between the conventional Italian landscapes evolved in the Venetian school and the native style of the Netherlands. Hercules Seghers (*c.* 1590–1645), an artist of real originality, is dependent on Bril's theatrical conventions, while still in contact with Rembrandt. Seghers's curious experiments in printing and colouring by hand, though they cannot be actually classed as colour prints, as he never attempted to print with more than one colour at a time, are interesting and unique. Esaias van de Velde (*c.* 1590–1630) and his brother Jan (*c.* 1596–1641) are the earliest of the Dutch etchers who looked to Holland for the subjects of their landscapes. Simple, almost meagre in technique as their etchings are, they render with a naïve charm and directness the views in their native land. Willem Buytewech (*c.* 1585–1625), from whose drawings the Van de Veldes worked, is well known as a painter of individuality, which appears in his few etchings.

The enumeration of the names of these few etchers who worked in the Netherlands at the end of the 16th and beginning of the 17th century, leads up to, but does not explain the importance, which, with surprising suddenness, the medium attained in the hands of Rembrandt Van Rijn (1606–69), and Anthony Van Dyck (1599–1641). The latter's achievement, remarkable as it is, is limited in scope and quantity, but as it precedes Rembrandt's in point of time will be dealt with first. The famous "Iconography" was planned by Van Dyck as a series of engraved portraits of contemporaries eminent in the arts. Etching was to play only a subsidiary and preliminary part in it, and, in fact, it was only for 18 of the 100 plates issued that Van Dyck himself executed preliminary etchings. The rest were engraved in line by the professional engravers trained in the school of Rubens. These 18 etchings, too, were subsequently finished by these same engravers, and it is only in the very rare impressions taken from these plates, before the additions were made, that Van Dyck can be appreciated as an etcher. His methods are quite independent of previous practice and of the conventions of line engraving. No doubt, the fact that he regarded the etching as merely preparatory, was partly responsible for their freedom from preconception. His natural instinct for form, aided to a certain extent by the example of Barocci and Italian etchers, led him straight to the secret of etching which we have since come to recognize is the essential one. His methods seem so obvious, that it is difficult as well as superfluous to try to describe them. Economy of line and contrast between this and the whiteness of the paper is the main secret. The heads stand out realized with quite extraordinary force and precision. There is no use of dry-point or of tone on the surface of the plate: the effect is gained by clean draughtsmanship.

Van Dyck's example as an etcher had comparatively little immediate effect; it is in modern times that his influence is most apparent. The great influence which he excited during his lifetime and for the rest of the 17th century was on portrait *engraving*, through the "Iconography" in its completed, engraved state.

Rembrandt's importance as an etcher is greater than Van Dyck's in proportion to the superiority and greater versatility of his genius. The number of his etchings, varying indeed with the trend of criticism from the 140 accepted by Prof. H. W. Singer to the 300 allowed by Prof. A. M. Hind, is at all events considerable, and comprises every variety of subject, scenes from the Old and New Testament, *genre*, portrait, still life, landscape. In his treatment of each subject in turn, his method is as fresh and untrammelled as was Van Dyck's in relation to portrait. But unlike Van Dyck's, Rembrandt's approach was gradual, and final and complete as each successive achievement appears to us, to him nothing was satisfying or final. The earliest dated etching, the small portrait head of his mother of 1628, is a masterly achievement, reflecting with great exactness the style of portraiture of his early Leyden period. Between this date and about 1632, his style undergoes no material change, though his etchings vary enormously in quality and elaboration. About 1636 the influence of Rubens, apparent in his painting, is correspondingly seen in his etching in a different and lighter chiaroscuro, with a tendency to sharper contrasts in light and shadow. The so-called "100 guilder print" of 1649 (Christ blessing little children) marks the apogee of his next period, in which dry-point plays an important part, and where the whole plate is covered with a network of fine lines, giving almost the appearance of mezzotint. To 1653 belong two of his largest and perhaps

PLATE II

ETCHING

ON THE ROAD TO BESSEMER, BY JOSEPH PENNELL (1860–1926)

One of a series of etchings by Pennell on American industrial subjects

19TH AND 20TH CENTURY ETCHINGS

1. Going North, by Frank W. Benson, contemporary
2. Wild Fowler, by Frank W. Benson
3. A Sultan, by Marius A. J. Bauer, contemporary
4. Spanish Dancer, No. 1, by Laura Knight, contemporary
5. Black Lion Wharf, London, by James McNeill Whistler (1834–1903); second state

his most wonderful plates the "Ecce Homo" and the "Three Crosses," in the latter of which his feeling for the dramatic moment, his tremendous power of expressing emotion in terms of chiaroscuro, are triumphantly exhibited. The technique has become slightly less elaborate; heavy individual lines are more apparent, there is less use of cross hatching and a tendency to model in vertical parallels and a masterly use of the effects of tone left on the surface and of dry-point. In the etchings which follow up to the last-dated one of 1661, there is a further tendency towards the still broader and more drastic treatment visible in his latest paintings, and a more complete reliance on heavily etched line without dry-point. The landscape etchings, most of which belong to the years about 1640 and 1650, stand somewhat apart in the comparative simplicity of their aim as studies from nature, with the exception of the most famous, the "Three Trees" of 1643, which is as dramatic as any of his subject etchings. The portraits are, for the most part, in the more careful and elaborate technique of his earlier period, and perhaps insisted on by his sitters. The greatest are among the numerous portraits he etched from the mirror in every variety of costume and character.

Rembrandt's contemporaries in Holland, except for his immediate associates and followers Jan Livens (1607–74), Ferdinand Bol (1618–80), Jacob (c. 1616–1708) and Philips Koninck (1619–88) and J. G. van Vliet, remain comparatively uninfluenced. Anthonis Waterloo (1609?–1677?), who enjoyed in the 18th century an enormous and exaggerated vogue, has indeed some claims to importance as a landscape etcher, and Alart van Everdingen (1621–75), in his small plates, mostly of Norwegian scenes, shows a delicate and observant talent. Jacob Ruysdael (c. 1628–82) may claim a place next to, though indeed far below, Rembrandt's as a landscape etcher. His delicate and exquisitely finished etchings are in the nature of detail studies of particular woodland scenes, diversified by still water reflecting the trees. Of the Dutch painters who looked for their theme to Italy, Nicholas Berchem (1620–83) and Karel du Jardin (1622–78) are the best known. Their landscapes included as important parts of the composition human figures and animals, and they serve as a link connecting the landscape with the animal and *genre* painters. Of the animal painters Paul Potter (1625–54) is the most famous; of the *genre* painters Adrian van Ostade (1610–85). Ostade uses etching with a painter's eye, and knows equally well how to render with extraordinary subtlety the subdued light of the squalid interior, and the glow of sunlight on a scene of rustic festivity.

GRAPHIC ARTS

The only etcher of note to work in England during the 17th century is Wenceslaus Hollar (1607–77), who was born at Prague but spent the greater part of his life in the British Isles. Of the very large number of etchings which he executed the majority was intended to serve merely utilitarian and topographical purposes, but in spite of this nearly everything that he did shows at least a touch of real artistic feeling.

Though etching, as we have seen, was probably invented north of the Alps, it is in Italy that its potentialities as an independent graphic medium were first realized. Francesco Mazzuoli (Parmegiano) (c. 1503–40) in his few plates uses the etching needle not as a substitute for the burin, but with the freedom of the pen. His etchings are obvious reproductions of his masterly but rather facile drawings, which enjoyed a very great contemporary popularity, and he most probably employed etching as a method of satisfying the demand for his drawings. Following his example, most of the great Italian painters thought it incumbent on them to make at least a few etchings. Of Parmegiano's immediate following the Venetian painter, Andrea Meldolla (Schiavone) (d. 1582), is the only etcher of importance, and his work in this direction is almost entirely derivative from that of his prototype. Battista Franco (1498?–1561), the Venetian follower of Michelangelo, did a certain amount of etching, but in a lighter and more formal style, and the work of the other Venetians like Battista and Marco' Angelo del Moro, G. B. and Giulio Fontana and Paolo Farinati, show rather a reaction against the freedom of Parmegiano's style, to which, however, Jacopo Palma the Younger (1544–1628) returns with some measure of success. Federico Baroccio of Urbino (1528–1612), in his two or three etchings, works out quite a new and striking method of his own, detailed and careful, but at the same time quite different from the conventional engraver's style, and a masterly rendering of the peculiar effects of chiaroscuro at which he aimed in his paintings. Annibale Carracci (1560–1609), the most brilliant exponent of the so-called eclectic school of Bologna, in his few etchings is less original, but they still have the stamp of a real artistic personality.

In etching, as in painting, the artists of Italy are roughly divided into two schools during the 17th century: the one following the orthodox teaching of the Bolognese Carracci, the other deriving from Michaelangelo da Caravaggio. The division is no longer a territorial one and the eclectics worked side by side with the "tenebristi" or followers of Caravaggio. This close contact led by degrees to a mutual influence by one school on the other and

140

the original line of demarcation becomes gradually obscured. Guido Reni (1575–1642), an actual pupil in the Carracci school at Bologna, is the most eminent of the eclectic etchers, and his well balanced, delicately sentimental style became the classic type for most of the etchers in France and Italy during the century. Simone Cantarini and Giovanni Antonio and Elisabetta Sirani are agreeable echoes of Guido. G. F. Barbieri (Guercino) (1591–1666) in his few etchings is more original and shows some Caravaggiesque influence as does Giuseppe Caletti (*c.* 1600–60). G. F. Grimaldi (1606–80?) the chief landscape etcher of the school, is conventional and dull. Carlo Maratta (1625–1713) carries on the Carracci style into the 18th century. The greatest etcher working in Italy in the 17th century is undoubtedly the Spaniard José de Ribera (1588–1652). His style, in so far as it is not to be classed as Spanish, is definitely Caravaggiesque, but his technique as an etcher is partly derived from the Bolognese. The sensitiveness of his outline, which plays an important part in his work, and the sureness with which he knows how to render the changes from brilliant light to darkest shadow, are extraordinary. Ribera's pupil, the Neapolitan Salvator Rosa (1615–1673), the painter of romantic bandit-infested landscapes, in his etchings, the less pretentious ones particularly, shows some of the charm which we associate with his fantastic world. In Genoa, Benedetto Castiglione (1616–70), whose talent has something in common with Salvator's, is attractive from the grace which characterizes his etchings and interesting from the fact that he was influenced by Rembrandt's work. In Venice, Giulio Carpioni (1611–74) etches with vividness and grace romantic scenes in a technique derived from the Carracci. Pietro Testa (1611–50), who worked in Rome, is an unequal but not uninteresting artist, with a curiously Venetian feeling for light which anticipates Tiepolo.

Little etching was done in France in the 16th century. The frescoes decorating the palace at Fontainebleau executed by Rosso Fiorentino, Primaticcio and their followers, were reproduced in etching by Antonio Fantuzzi, Leonard Thiry and other artists engaged in the work, but these are crude and hasty works. Jean Cousin (d. 1590) is credited with two or three etchings of more merit, and the architect and designer, Jacques Androuet Ducerceau (*c.* 1510–80), used etching for his delightful architectural compositions with a truly French grace. But with the 17th century and the names of Jacques Callot (1592–1635) and Claude Lorrain (1600–82), France attains a position of real importance in the history of etching. Callot, unlike most of his contemporaries and successors who depended almost entirely for their inspiration on Italian classicism, is essentially and originally French. Technically, his innovations consist in his handling of the individual line, by the thinning and thickening of which exclusively his effects are obtained, but he is also the inventor of a new world of minute fantastic figures, a sort of French stage fairyland. Besides their extraordinary elegance, such series as the *grandes* and the *petites misères de la guerre*, have a point and an emphasis in their narrative which is surprising on so minute a scale. The technique of subsequent etching could not and did not remain uninfluenced by Callot's practice, but his only close follower is an Italian, Stefano della Bella (1610–64). The French academicians of the *grand siècle*, Le Sueur, Le Brun and the rest with their ready-made classical formulae had no chance of success in a medium as personal as etching should be, and it remained for Claude Lorrain with his direct reactions to the landscape which he saw around him to produce the only great etchings of the period besides those of Callot. Though his conception of landscape painting was bound by certain theatrical conventions, in his drawings and etchings he approaches his subject directly and at the same time with the true landscape painter's instinct for selection. He is not a good etcher technically; there is something fumbling and amateurish in his work, but in spite of these disadvantages, he somehow succeeds in producing landscape etchings of an extraordinarily moving quality.

The 18th century did not find in etching its most characteristic means of expression. In France, whose artistic preponderance in Europe during the period was undisputed, line engraving was more extensively and more successfully practised. Etching was to a large extent employed, it is true, but mostly as a preliminary to or in conjunction with engraving, and such mixed productions may more legitimately be classed as engravings (*q.v.*). Antoine Watteau (1684–1721), François Boucher (1703–70), Honoré Fragonard (1732–1806) and the brothers Augustin (1736–1807) and Gabriel de St. Aubin (1724–80), all practised etching to a limited extent. Jean Duplessi-Bertaux (1747–1813) etched historical scenes largely of republican and Napoleonic times with a spirit and delicacy quite in the tradition of Callot.

It is, however, in Italy and Spain that the great etchers of the century flourished. Giovanni Battista Tiepolo of Venice (1696–1770), whose brilliant decorative painting is the culmination of rococo art, showed as an etcher

THE TECHNIQUE OF ETCHING

1. First trial-proof of the *first published state* of an etching by E. S. Lumsden. Nitric acid has been used throughout

2. Seventh trial-proof of the *second published state* of this etching. Additional work was done on the sky and the boats were re-bitten

PLATE V   ETCHING

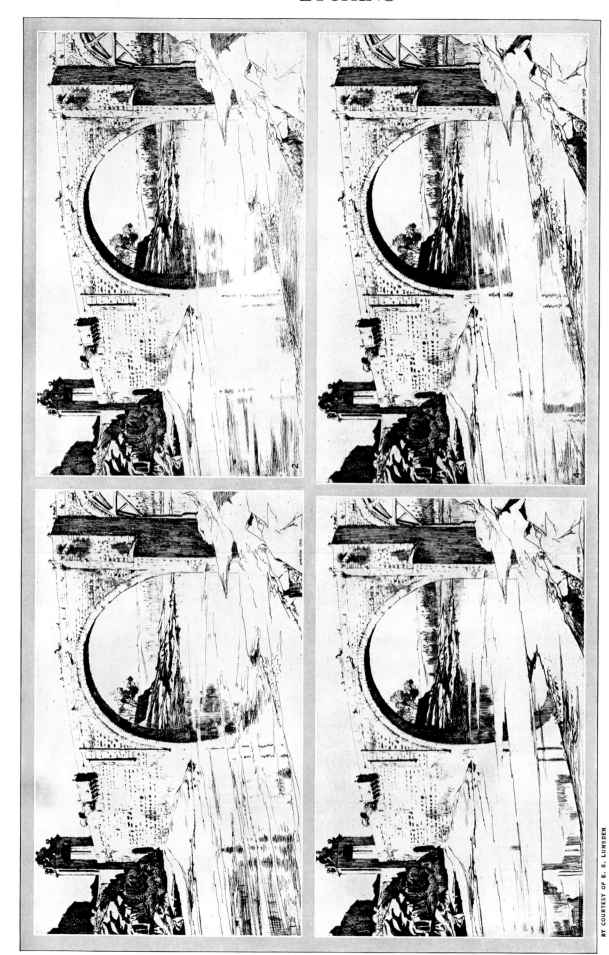

STAGES IN THE TECHNIQUE OF ETCHING

1. Alcantara Bridge, Toledo. The first trial state of an etching by E. S. Lumsden, showing alterations on the copper
2. Second state. The distance and water have been scraped out and re-drawn
3. Third state. The lines of the water have been removed once more, and replaced by vertical strokes
4. Final (published) state. The lines of the water have been re-drawn a third time, once more horizontally. The bridge remains untouched throughout, the difference in strength being due to printing only

equal brilliance. His technique, recalling that of José Ribera and G. B. Castiglione, is yet entirely original in its almost complete avoidance of heavy defining shadow and his method of rendering the broad, grey shadows by systems of herring bone and irregularly arranged short lines. His scenes, laid in a brilliant and all-enveloping sunlight, comprise some of the stock 18th century sylvan and Arcadian *genre*, as well as more imaginative subjects, but treated alike with a peculiar point and irony. Antonio Canale (Canaletto) (1697–1768), Tiepolo's contemporary in Venice, distinguished as the most brilliant portrayer of his native city, was an etcher of almost equal distinction. His 31 etchings of Venice and the neighbourhood reproduce faithfully the quality of his painting. It is, indeed, remarkable in him and in Tiepolo how their etching is directly dependent on their painting. They seem each independently to have discovered that method of etching extraordinarily complicated and original, which would most exactly correspond to the essential quality of their painting. In each case the result is not, as might have been anticipated, a lifeless reproductive technique, but a brilliant addition to the repertoire of etching. Giovanni Battista Piranesi (1720–78), the third great Italian etcher of the century, though also a Venetian by birth, worked nearly all his life in Rome. The bulk of his very extensive etched work is archaeological, but his feeling for architectural composition and for the quality of the etched line entitle this work to be regarded from the artistic point of view.

Francisco Goya y Lucientes (1746–1828) inevitably finds a place at the beginning of any account of modern art, and indeed his work looks forward into the 19th rather than backward into the 18th century, so extraordinarily fresh and original it is and so free from any of the typically rococo elements which mark 18th century art. Yet technically, Goya derives from Tiepolo (he visited Italy during his youth) and his earliest work in etching, though it reproduces paintings by Velázquez, is very much in Tiepolo's style. But his original compositions, the series of the *Caprichos*, the *Proverbios*, the *Desastres de la Guerra* and last of all the *Tauromaquia*, show the evolution of an original technique with the use of aquatint for the backgrounds. The mysterious satirical works, the *Caprichos* and *Proverbios*, although the exact target at which their shafts are aimed is uncertain, are overwhelming in the bitterness and intensity of their satire and the horror of the imagination which they show.

With the notable exception of Goya's work there is comparatively little

143

of interest to record in the field of etching during the first half of the 19th century. It is one of those periods of stagnation which occur before a revival. In England, work of distinction, based on that of Rembrandt's contemporaries such as Ruysdael, was done by John Crome (1768–1821) of Norwich, as well as by John Sell Cotman (1782–1842), most of the latter in the process, invented at the end of the 18th century, called soft-ground etching. The names of Thomas Girtin (1775–1802) and J. M. W. Turner (1775–1851), can hardly be omitted in view of their pre-eminence as landscape painters, but their work in etching, masterly as it is, was in neither case intended to be final. Girtin's etchings were preparatory to aquatints and Turner's to mezzotints. Andrew Geddes of Edinburgh (1783–1844) is the author of a number of plates of real distinction, marked by a considerable and intelligent use of dry-point, and Samuel Palmer (1805–81) is a landscape etcher of individuality.

The painters of the "Barbizon" school of landscape in France, Théodore Rousseau (1812–1867), Charles Jacque (1813–1894), C. F. Daubigny (1817–78), J. F. Millet (1814–75) and Camille Corot (1796–1875), all etched. The most prolific and important for his influence on the etchers of the next generation was Jacque, whose style shows the influence of Ostade and the Dutch etchers of the 17th century, while C. F. Daubigny, as an etcher, shows great power and originality. Millet in his plates, executed in a style which resembles that of Ostade's etchings magnified to about four times their original size, portrays those subjects of peasants at work familiar in his paintings, with the same instinctive understanding. Corot used the etching needle only occasionally, but in a manner which, for all its seeming scratchy incompetence, vividly reproduces the atmospheric effects of his paintings. The greatest figure in French etching of the century, that of Charles Meryon (1821–68), stands rather curiously aloof from that of his contemporaries. Precluded by colour blindness from the practise of painting, he is that rather rare phenomenon—an etcher who is not a painter. Influenced by a study of the work of the admirable, but comparatively little known Dutch 17th century topographical and marine etcher, Reynier Zeeman, and obviously, to a certain extent, by Piranesi rather than by contemporaries, Meryon evolved for himself a system of line which, in its clarity and incisiveness, is unrivalled for the rendering of architectural subjects. His reputation, resting, as it does, on a small number of plates of the streets and churches of Paris, might, on the face of it, seem exaggerated, but the extraordinary perfection and inevitability of design which these show seem to create out of a restricted subject matter a formula of universal application.

The revival of etching in England in the 19th century was due, in large measure, to the influence of three men of whom undoubtedly the greatest was James McNeill Whistler (1834–1903). American by birth, but thoroughly cosmopolitan, a large part of his life was passed in England and it was here that his influence was perhaps most pronounced. His conception of etching, as of art in general, even more than his practise, has had the profoundest effect. Rembrandt was undoubtedly the chief influence on his etched work. His idea of an etching as an exact and inevitable composition from which no single one of the innumerable lines which go to make it up could be removed or displaced by a hairbreadth, is almost justified by the perfection of some of his exquisite plates. Sir Francis Seymour Haden (1818–1910), Whistler's brother-in-law, though an amateur, exercised a direct influence on English etching even greater than Whistler's, who had little immediate following. Haden was by no means an echo of Whistler: though inspired by him in the first instance, his was too independent a character to allow of anything in the way of imitation. He also went back to Rembrandt for inspiration and etched with an incisive strength and clarity which are admirable, though his work can hardly compare with the greatest. The third important influence on English etching was that of Alphonse Legros (1837–1911), a Frenchman and first Slade professor of art in London, where most of his life was spent. His was not a talent of extreme originality, but he had a great feeling for, and understanding of, etching and an extraordinary power of assimilating the methods and thoughts of the great masters.

Whistler had in Théodore Roussel (1847–1926) another Frenchman settled in England, a follower as fastidious as himself who later evolved an original method of colour etching; and in Walter Sickert (b. 1860), an artist of real originality who has since developed along his own lines and founded an important school. In the tradition of Seymour Haden may be counted Sir D. Y. Cameron (b. 1865), whose landscape etchings and dry-points are marked by faultless taste and distinction, and Muirhead Bone (b. 1876), who has specially developed the architectural theme. The most distinguished pupil of Alphonse Legros was William Strang, whose portrait etching in particular is admirable, but who perhaps fails by a lack of concentration in his powers to convince as a great etcher. The etched work of Augustus John (b. 1879) is the characteristic occasional work of an important painter, in the tradition of the great masters, while that of Franck Brangwyn (b. 1867) is distinguished by its impressive size and feeling for composition in landscape and architecture. Sir Frank Short (b. 1857), for many years director of the school of engraving at South Kensington, exercised, after Haden and Legros, the greatest influence on etching, and was himself an etcher of great technical ability, though perhaps better known as the reviver of the process of mezzotint.

The succeeding generation has been extraordinarily prolific in etchers of real distinction, and the first quarter of the 20th century may well come to be regarded as one of the important epochs in the history of etching. It is a matter of difficulty to class and arrange contemporary achievements, and it will suffice to name a few of the more prominent. As an etcher of landscape as well as of subject, largely Eastern, James McBey (b. 1883) has certainly attained an important position by the originality and strength of his work. Henry Rushbury (b. 1889), in a style something akin to Muirhead Bone's, is doing extremely fine work in landscape, while Sir George Clausen (b. 1852), E. S. Lumsden (b. 1883) and many others have a merited reputation in the same *genre*. F. L. Griggs (b. 1876) has revived the imaginary architectural composition originated by Piranesi, and made of it a delicate and original means of expression. In portraiture, Francis Dodd (b. 1874), Gerald Brockhurst (b. 1890) and Malcolm Osborne (b. 1880) have done admirable work.

In Holland, as might well be expected, much work of importance was done in the second half of the 19th century. J. B. Jongkind (1819–91), Josef Israels (1824–1911) and Mathijs Maris (1839–1917), though the work of the latter is the occasional essay of a painter, are artists of the first rank, while C. Storm van's Gravesande (b. 1841) and Marius Bauer (b. 1867), of whom the latter is still in the plenitude of his power, have contributed something considerable to etching. Scandinavia has produced one etcher of astonishing virtuosity in the person of Anders Zorn (1860–1920), and in Germany and Austria, while no artist of the very first rank has, so far as one can judge, appeared, much etching of real distinction has been and is still being done. Since Whistler the interest in etching in America has been very intense and a great deal of work has been done, largely, it is true, by artists working abroad, of whom Joseph Pennell, D. S. Maclaughlan (a Canadian by birth), Frank W. Benson, Herman J. Webster and Arthur W. Heintzelman are perhaps the most notable.

TECHNIQUE

Materials.—The essentials for producing an etching are: (1) A metal plate; (2) a mordant resist or "ground"; (3) a point which will cut through the ground; (4) a mordant; (5) ink, paper and press. For fine work artists generally prefer copper, for coarser, simpler designs zinc is equally capable of yielding the best results. But from the closer-textured copper a greater range in light and shade is possible.

Before applying the "ground" the plate's surface must be cleaned thoroughly, to allow as perfect contact as possible. This may be done by means of any solvent—turpentine, benzine, petrol or ammonia—with whitening and a soft rag. Tarnish may be removed with vinegar (or acetic acid) and common salt.

The Ground.—Rembrandt's is said to have been: (*a*) Virgin wax, 1 oz.; mastic, $\frac{1}{2}$ oz.; asphaltum or amber, $\frac{1}{2}$ oz.; or (*b*) wax, 2 oz.; Burgundy pitch, $\frac{1}{2}$ oz.; common pitch, $\frac{1}{2}$ oz.; asphaltum, 2 ounces. A similar recipe is in use to-day. The ingredients are melted together carefully—first the asphaltum, then the wax, and last the pitch or mastic. The mixture should be allowed to boil up two or three times and then poured into warm water to set, being formed into suitable balls while in the water.

A transparent ground may be manufactured with five parts of wax and three parts of gum-mastic by weight. The ground is applied by melting on the heated plate and spreading as finely and evenly as possible by means of a so-called "dabber" or leather-covered roller. To make the dabber, a circular card about 2 in. in diameter is cut, a wad of cotton-wool placed upon it, and the whole covered with fine kid or silk. Before the ground cools the usual though by no means universal practice is to smoke it by passing the inverted plate backwards and forwards—taking care never to rest at one spot —over wax tapers or an oil lamp. This dark surface shows the line and strengthens the ground as a resist.

In place of smoking Rembrandt is said to have used a white lead powder. This has the advantage of causing the line-work to appear dark on a light surface, like drawing with a grey pencil on paper. Quite recently a Scottish etcher, Henry Daniel, has discovered that, for this purpose, oxichloride of bismuth has admirable qualities. It is spread over the still slightly-warm ground with a very soft, full brush. Not being really incorporated with the ground it is attacked and removed by the acid when biting

147

begins, but this is no great disadvantage. Many etchers prefer a liquid made by dissolving ordinary ground in ether or chloroform. This is poured very quickly over the plate (in a tray) and the residue returned to its bottle.

Points.—Every etcher has a favourite point. A most satisfactory and easily made one is a long gramophone needle pushed butt-foremost into a pen-holder and secured with sealing-wax. This is an ideal, not too sharp yet fine tool. Another, which serves equally for additional dry-point work, is the engineer's pricker, the points of which can be changed and reversed while in the pocket. The object of the needle is to remove the *ground* without scratching too much into the *metal*. A very sharp point destroys freedom, and causes irregularity in the attack of the mordant.

Biting.—When the drawing has been made upon the prepared wax surface with as steady and equal pressure as possible, comes the *biting* or fixing of the design. If the plate is to be entirely submerged the back also must be first coated with a resist. For such a purpose a liquid varnish is necessary, as to re-heat the plate would destroy the lines drawn. The best ingredients are methylated spirit and shellac (in proportion two to one) to which some black pigment has been added to cause less fluidity and allow the varnish to be visible when dry.

Three mordants are commonly employed at the present day. The first, and most used by artists, is nitric or nitrous acid mixed with an equal quantity of water. The second, the so-called "Dutch mordant" is prepared by dissolving $\frac{1}{5}$ oz. potassium chlorate in 5 oz. of hot water, and adding 1 oz. of hydrochloric acid. The third is iron perchloride, most used by process-etchers. Artists probably prefer nitric because it is much the most rapid in action, and because the constant and obvious ebullition makes easy the detection of any over-looked line or dust-hole in the ground. The other mordants attack more gently without bubbles, consequently "foul-biting," as it is called, may easily go on unnoticed until too late. On the other hand, iron perchloride, while reasonably fast, bites more deeply in proportion to the width of line, as the edges are not broken away and the ground undermined as happens with strong nitric. The iron also darkens copper, permitting the lines to be more easily watched if used with an unsmoked ground. Its only drawback is the formation of sediment, which retards the action at the bottom of the lines, but can be dispersed by keeping the bath in motion. If rocking is not sufficient, the plate must be bitten inverted—resting upon slips of wood or other material not affected by the mordant—after which the deposit can be distinctly seen at the bottom of the dish. Full (saturated solution) strength is too thick for fine etching, and half that or a little more is far quicker than the cold "Dutch" bath. In many ways iron perchloride is the most reliable of the three mordants.

Before beginning the biting it is well to place the plate in a bath of commercial acetic acid for a few minutes, in order to remove impurities which may otherwise clog the lines—perspiration from the hand while drawing, for instance. This is particularly needful when one portion of the drawing has been made considerably prior to another. It allows all parts to be attacked simultaneously, which in the case of a delicate distance, for instance, needing but a very short biting, is of the utmost importance.

Various Methods.—In working the more orthodox plan is to complete the drawing entirely before beginning to use the acid. Then the plate, placed bodily in the bath, is left sufficiently long for the most delicate lines to be etched. The determining of the exact moment for removal is largely a matter of experience. The plate is then washed with water, carefully dried by means of blotting-paper, and those lines which are deemed of sufficient depth "stopped out" with a fine brush and the shellac varnish. Allowing this to dry, the process is then repeated until those lines which are required to be deepest of all are bitten when the plate is, for the time at least, finished. In the earliest days of etching no stopping out was reverted to, Dürer and Hopfer biting their lines to one depth only; and, generally speaking, the fewer stoppings the simpler and better the result.

Then there is the method employed by Haden. It is the reverse of the preceding. With the grounded plate placed in the bath, the artist begins by drawing those passages which he desires to be the strongest of all. As the lines are drawn the acid attacks them and the etcher passes on to the next darkest parts, ending by drawing the faintest lines immediately before removing the plate from the bath. This obviously requires great speed and certain judgment, allowing of no mistakes or hesitation. It is the resulting spontaneity which so charms in Haden's work.

Lastly, there is the compromise between the above processes resorted to by Whistler in his later manner. The drawing is more or less completed —in Whistler's case out of doors—then a little acid is poured upon it and (controlled by a feather) moved about here and there, being permitted to stand longer on some lines, less long on others, until the whole is bitten without recourse to stopping out. At the same time new lines are added where required to give strength or closer texture, light lines often crossing stronger ones (as also in Haden's method) and yielding less formality in the result than is easily obtainable by the older way of working.

But the etcher is by no means compelled to do the whole of the work upon a single ground. It is often expedient to do part only, remove the wax by means of turpentine or other solvent, pull a proof as a guide, re-ground the plate and continue. In re-grounding (which cannot safely be done with the roller) care must be taken to fill in the already bitten lines, as their edges are very liable to be attacked in renewed biting. Insufficiently bitten work can also be rebitten by carefully laying a ground on the surface only (here the roller is perhaps safer than the dabber) while leaving the lines open. It is a hazardous undertaking, except where already deep lines are concerned, and generally results in loss of definition.

Proving.—When biting has been accomplished by one method or another and ground and backing removed, the plate is ready for "proving." The result will be the *first state* of the plate. *Any* additional work constitutes a new state, without relation to the number of proofs printed. There may be one only or 500 of each state; but the removal of a single line or adding of, say, a date creates technically a further state. Even where the artist, realizing that his alterations were a mistake, returns as nearly as possible to his original, the last will still be the third state, if proofs of the two previous ones are preserved. For instance, the eighth state of Whistler's "Bridge" is only distinguishable from the first by careful examination of both, though intermediate proofs are easily recognized. These working states are known as trial-proofs, as when an edition of more than one state is published the tentative trials are ignored—only those issued receiving the titles of first, second or third *published states*, e.g., Haden's "Agamemnon." Few etchings are left untouched after the first ground is removed, and it is as often necessary to cut out lines as to add them. For this a "scraper" is required. It is a tool difficult to handle and to sharpen. To remove the marks left by the scraper, snakestone is used with water, and to regain the polished surface charcoal and water and finally oil or plate-polish. Another useful etching tool is the polished steel "burnisher." With this light scratches may be rubbed out or over-heavy lines reduced. With these implements and soft rag almost anything is possible in the way of alteration. The pulling of the proof itself is one of the most fascinating of the processes which together go to the making of an etching. And yet quite a number of etchers delegate this—the real birth of the final work—to a professional printer!

PRINTING AND PAPER

Printing.—The expense of a really good roller press is perhaps partly responsible, but a good printing press is an essential. Small machines which have little power are worse than none at all, as their results are apt to discourage the beginner. The more delicate the line in the plate the more pressure—"pinch"—is necessary. The best modern presses are geared, and the large double-geared ones can be run with little physical exertion. The old machines were built with wooden rollers and travelling-bed, the modern entirely of iron and steel. The printing-ink is formed by grinding Frankfürt or French black powder (mixed usually with umber or burnt sienna to add warmth) with burnt linseed-oil. The burning of the oil thickens it and makes it more adhesive. Several strengths are used, which yield very different results. When mixed and well ground the ink should be sufficiently stiff not to fall quickly from the palette knife, and it is spread solidly over the surface of the heated plate by a roller or the older dabber.

The roller is made of gelatine, covered by some material to prevent adhesion when the warmth from the plate softens its composition. Stockinette is excellent for the purpose, but great care is needed to avoid any scratching edge at the seam. The roller's length should be about 3 in. and its diameter $2\frac{1}{2}$ inches. The ink, after being well worked into the lines and spread evenly all over the plate, is wiped off gradually by means of pads of stiff book-muslin or Swiss-tarlatan. The hand presses firmly and equally—avoiding a scooping action—as if polishing the metal. A firm pressure forces the ink into the lines while removing it from the surface—all but a very fine film. A "clean-wiped" proof is finally polished by the base of the palm.

To soften and enrich the clean-wiped plate a piece of clinging muslin may be dragged lightly over the surface, pulling the ink a little out of the lines. This is called *retroussage*, "dragging" or "bringing up." It can also be done by going over the plate once more with the fully charged printing muslin, but this leaves a slightly granular effect upon the surface as well. Wiping is capable of great variation and the strength of oil plays an important part in the way in which the ink comes off the surface. An etching is never wiped so that no film of oil remains. A good printer will consider what colour, of ink and paper, will produce the best result; whether the plate shall be clean or only rag wiped, etc.

Paper.—Many etchers prefer old paper because the decay of its size renders it soft and pliable, and consequently more readily forced into the lines in passing between the rollers. Its colour is also more beautiful and often it is made of better material—that is, linen rags unspoilt by modern bleaching with dangerous chemicals, or adulterated with dressings.

The paper is well damped before use but should have no excess moisture on its face. This may refuse the surface film of oil on the plate and white granulations appear on the proof. Very thin oil is specially liable to this. Before beginning to print, the edges of the plate should be examined and filed smooth, to prevent the paper being cut. When the inking and wiping has been accomplished, the warm plate is laid upon the travelling-bed of the press, a sheet of paper is taken from its damp pile, examined for hairs or dust, and placed face down upon the plate, one or two sheets of new soft blotting-paper laid over it and five or six thicknesses of printing blanket over all. The blanket is of two qualities—the two nearest the plate being fine "fronting" and the rest of coarser thicker material. When everything is in place the whole is pulled between the rollers, once only. Removing the blankets, the printing and blotting papers are peeled off the plate in one solid piece. When dried, the proof can be removed and flattened.

FURTHER METHODS

Soft-ground.—This method—the French *vernis mou*—is much less practised than it was in the early 19th century. The line somewhat resembles a chalk drawing. Its granulated texture renders it very suitable as a basis for aquatint, but its own qualities were fully exploited by that great master, Cotman. Everything depends upon the addition to the ordinary etching ground of tallow, usually an equal quantity, in hot weather less. This makes a very clinging compound, with which the plate is covered in the normal manner; but instead of being directly drawn upon, a sheet of grained paper is placed over the surface and the drawing executed upon this with a pencil, care being taken to avoid contact with the paper otherwise than with the point. When the design is complete the paper is peeled off, taking with it those portions of the ground corresponding to the lines drawn. The stronger the pressure the more ground will stick to the paper and the wider the line exposed ready to be bitten by the acid. The grain of the paper will show in the character of the bitten line.   Except that stopping-out is hardly required, the biting is carried out exactly as described above.   The line relies upon breadth rather than depth for variation.   A smooth paper will hardly produce any result, but tissue is excellent.   Tissue paper is also serviceable for re-working, as it is semi-transparent.

Aquatint.—Instead of with line aquatint deals with tone in broad masses.   In most of his plates Goya, the greatest exponent of the medium, employed an etched line as guide and basis for the tonal work, but not in all.   (*See* Aquatint.)

A variant of aquatint is to form the porous ground by passing an ordinary wax ground through the press several times in contact with sand-paper; this is known as "sand-grain."   Its fineness depends upon the quality of the paper and the number of passages through the rollers.   Joseph Pennell produced some good plates in this manner.

Pen-method.—This has recently been revived in London.   It was used by Gainsborough in conjunction with aquatint, and though hardly possible to employ for fine work, its quality blends better than that of the needle line with tone work.   The drawing is made upon the bare plate—good results have been obtained on steel in recent times—with a pen or brush and ordinary ink or a soluble gum—gamboge and water is excellent.   When dry (but not more than a day old, or it will harden), an etching ground is laid over it, not too thickly.   When this is hard the plate is submerged in water for half an hour or so, whereupon the ground above the lines will come away as the ink dissolves.   The lines can then be bitten in the usual manner.

MEZZOTINT

Mezzotint or Mezzo tinto, as it was first called, is a process of engraving whereby a copper, or steel, plate is first prepared to produce uniformly black impressions on paper.   This is done by pricking the plate with innumerable small holes which will hold ink.   In connection with mezzotint, as with all other forms of engraving, the ink used is a thick ink which does not run.   After the surface of the mezzotint plate has been prepared, the high lights in the portrait or picture to be produced are obtained by scraping away and burnishing parts of the plate, thus reducing, or obliterating, the small holes according to the effect desired. The pricking of the plate, originally done with a roulette or small wheel covered with sharp points, was later done with an instrument called a *cradle*, or *rocker*. The process not only punctures the plate to hold ink, but, at the same time, produces a burr on the surface of the metal, which, cutting into the paper when in the press, causes a deeper absorption of ink, and produces that velvety effect so characteristic of the fine mezzotint engraving in an early impression. The surface of the punctured and roughened plate is left undisturbed where the deepest black is required, and by a graduated scraping of the plate, which removes both burrs and punctures so that ink is held in lesser degrees, middle and light tones are obtained when an impression is taken from it. Dots made with a sharp point on a polished metal surface were long used as an adjunct to engravings. They show on silver plates engraved for Niello (*q.v.*) in the 14th century. Prints on paper from line engravings cut on metal plates, probably copper, were first made about the middle of the 15th century, but dotted, or pointille work does not seem to have been much used for some time after that.

The 17th Century Dutch School.—About the middle of the 17th century, Ludwig von Siegen, a Dutch officer in the Hessian army, who was also an amateur artist, applied the old device of dotted work to a metal plate, by means of a small roulette, and succeeded in producing an excellent print entirely by its use. In 1654, von Siegen met Prince Rupert, count palatine of the Rhine and grandson of James I., at Brussels. Prince Rupert was a skilled amateur artist, and he became deeply interested in von Siegen's invention, which he at once tried. In a short time he produced a very fine piece of rouletting in a print of *The Large Executioner*, after Spagnoletto, a Spanish painter. The curving lines, made by unskilful use of a large roulette, show clearly in the background. William Sherwin was a native of Hertfordshire, and a well known line engraver. He was also a friend of Prince Rupert, who is said to have taught him the new art and presented him with a roulette. Sherwin made mezzotint portraits of Charles II. and of his queen in 1669, both of which were dedicated to Prince Rupert.

The early mezzotinters were mostly Dutchmen, and they did not succeed particularly well. Curiously enough, most of their work was done in England. But eventually, a great Dutch artist, Abraham Blooteling, arrived in England in 1673, and was much attracted by the new art. Blooteling did much splendid work, particularly after Van Dyck, Kneller and Lely. But he did much more for the art of the mezzotint than produce beautiful prints, because he radically changed and improved the technical part of the process. Instead of using only a roulette to produce dark space, he began by roughening the plate all over, so that if printed from, it would show simply a black space, and then he cut away the roughness with a scraper to make the light places as required. This plan produced most brilliant effects. Blooteling also invented a tool, now called a rocker, which is like a very small spade with a toothed edge, and with this powerful instrument a copper or soft steel plate can quickly be roughened all over, rendering the use of the old roulette obsolete. The early users of the rocker roughened their own plates, but now this can be professionally done by the dealers.

The 18th Century English School.—After Blooteling, and during the 18th century, a remarkable school of English mezzotinters became prominent, and did such distinguished work that abroad the process became known as *La manière anglaise.* This pre-eminence was due, not only to their remarkable skill and the great beauty of their work, but also to the fact that there were in England at that time, several portrait painters of the very first rank for them to interpret. We owe the existence of the finest mezzotints ever done to the inspiration of men like Lely, Reynolds, Lawrence, Romney, Hoppner, Constable and several others of lesser reputations.

Early in the 18th century an Irishman, T. Frye, tried several byways of art before he specialized in mezzotint, but he ended by "scraping" a series of large portrait heads after drawings of his own. When in good condition, heads by Frye are extremely decorative. Another Irishman, J. MacArdell, became one of our greatest mezzotinters. Sir Joshua Reynolds had so high an estimation of MacArdell's work that he once declared he would be immortalized by his engravings. This is now beginning to prove true, because Sir Joshua's paintings are in many cases deteriorating badly, whereas a mezzotint, carefully kept under a sunk mount, is extremely long-lived. Richard Earlom (1743–1822) used only the roulette where he wanted shadow. He engraved the *Liber Veritatis* of Claude Lorrain, and by doing so he suggested the *Liber Studiorum* of J. M. W. Turner.

The numerous mezzotints made by Valentine Green (1739–1813) are all of the highest order of excellence. He was especially successful in his rendering of the beautiful full length figures of ladies, painted by Sir Joshua Reynolds, and he frequently printed his engravings in brown ink.

GRAPHIC ARTS

John Raphael Smith began his artistic career as a miniature painter, but eventually became one of the foremost mezzotint engravers. He worked mainly after Sir Joshua Reynolds, but was very happy in his interpretation of Romney's graceful work. Smith made several engravings after his own drawings.

S. W. Reynolds made a series of 357 small mezzotints of portraits by Sir Joshua Reynolds. Mezzotints, however, are not satisfactory when done on a small scale. S. W. Reynolds was, in larger subjects, a highly skilful artist, and engraved many excellent plates after his own work. He did mezzotinting on some of the plates in Turner's *Liber Studiorum*.

William Say used etching as an adjunct to most of his fine mezzotints, but he was never satisfied with the small number of prints that could properly be made from a copper plate. He was the first mezzotinter to experiment with the use of steel instead, but he did not carry his ideas out successfully. Shortly afterwards, however, T. G. Lupton carried farther the experiments, with the use of steel instead of copper. Say seems to have tried with hard steel and Lupton used soft steel very successfully. Instead of being able to print only about 50 proofs of the highest excellence from copper, it was found possible to print about 1,500 from steel, without any appearance of deterioration. The dark places on a mezzotint are those to be looked for in worn prints. They ought to look like black or brown velvet. Steel engravings on mezzotint are often very delicate and charming, but they have a tendency to hardness. The method was also carried out by D. Lucas, but not so successfully as by Lupton. Now copper engravings can be steeled over several times and prints from such plates can never become rare.

Samuel Cousins was an apprentice to S. W. Reynolds, and used etching and line engraving freely with his mezzotint, so much, indeed, that his method is known as the "mixed" style. But his work is effective and very popular. Cousins killed the art of line engraving in England by reason of his fine plate of Bolton Abbey, after Sir Edwin Landseer, published in 1837. This plate proved that such a picture could be produced much more easily and effectively by mezzotint than it could by line engraving.

Among modern mezzotint engravers many are highly skilled, and most of them have chosen particular artists for their especial study. Sir Frank Short has been particularly successful in his interpretation of G. F. Watt's powerful work; C. W. Campbell with the delicate fancies of Sir E. Burne-Jones; J. D. Miller follows Lord Leighton; G. P. Robinson, Sir Frank Dicksee; Norman Hirst, W. Draper, and now the process of photogravure has reached such a high state of excellence that little room is left for the earlier art.

TECHNIQUE IN ART

TECHNIQUE is the manner of artistic execution, the performance or method of manipulation in any art, but as to just how inclusive this definition should be regarded is a question. Certain authorities claim that technique is distinct from any consideration of general effect or expression, while others assign to it the meaning of the doctrine of the arts in general. The first conception might be called "Mechanical technique" and the latter "Technique principle."

In this work the mechanical technique in each art is treated under each individual heading as the mechanical techniques vary considerably in detail —that of the sculptor being different from that of the wood-engraver, and that of the painter differing from that of the etcher. This article will therefore deal only with the broader conception of the definition—the technique principle, or those underlying rules which are found to be true in the practice of all of the arts.

It may be said that such a discussion falls within the field of aesthetics, but the difference lies in the fact that while aesthetics is a metaphysical discussion of man's conception of beauty, the technique principle is a discussion of how to obtain beauty or human appeal in a work of art. The one is philosophy and the other is a practical science based upon observation and reason. The one has to do with a discussion of the result, while the other shows how this result, indescribable as it sometimes may seem, can be obtained. The means whereby man can appeal to man in the creation of beauty, modern science has analyzed to a remarkable degree, and just as Henri Bergson in *L'Evolution Créatrice* destroyed the old philosophical conception of negation by the application of modern psychology, so have many of the old principles of philosophic aesthetics been destroyed by like methods. The modern artist must not only have mastered rules of anatomy and perspective through study such as that of many of the old masters over the dissection tables, and of mathematics, but must inquire into the psychological reactions caused by light or by various colours, the chemical action of his paints, the analyses of movement as revealed by the motion picture camera and many other phases of modern scientific development, and therefore the old conception of the artist as an intuitive being dreaming his way through life and seizing now and then with the aid of a divine fire a dream which he in some inexplicable way makes tangible and durable for his fellowmen, must be cast aside. The artist may dream, as the man of science or the inventor dreams of the creation of some remarkable work, but the work itself is a painstaking process of reason and the result may often be quite different from the cloudy original blur which was the first conception. The study of the subconscious has done much to explain intuition, and the modern man has learned to place less faith in the vision of glory which used to move his forefathers, for he realizes that these immediate apprehensions of "truth" are topsy-turvy mirages of what may or may not be proved true by the searchlight of modern scientific reason. The modern artist is first of all a modern man in every sense abreast of the times, and, as an indispensable prerequisite, every artist must first learn to appeal to his fellowmen.

Although the modern artist is perhaps more awake to the necessity of adopting this viewpoint, because of the recent marvelous developments of science, nevertheless many of the great masters of the past have also expressed themselves clearly along the same lines. Leonardo da Vinci has said "Thou, O God dost sell unto us all good things at the price of labour" and throughout all of his writings Da Vinci has laid stress upon reasonable labour rather than trust to inspiration. Rodin said, "Nothing will take the place of persevering study—to it alone the secret of life delivers itself." Turner stated that he had no secret but hard work, and Pliny relates that the secret of Apelles was due to constant practice. Hundreds of other examples might be quoted, but it is sufficient to say that throughout the ages both in the Far East, where a great painter has been quoted as saying, "Man cannot call himself an artist until he has painted 10,000 pictures," to the western schools represented by such quotations as above, artists in writing of their own work have laid great stress upon the labours of pure reason involved, while critics in writing of art (that field in which they have as a rule never practised) explain it on the grounds of a mysteriously intuitive and God-sent passion. Due to the critics, art has too long been considered a gift of the gods and artists who are usually contented to let the results of their labours speak for themselves have too long been misunderstood. Let us therefore examine a few of the processes of thought of which they make use.

Conception.—The original conception of a work of art or of an invention of any sort is usually largely intuitive, in that it may be said to reach out beyond the regular step by step procedure of pure reason. The possibility of such and such a thing often occurs suddenly after a long and arduous searching of the facts which may be more or less involved. The mind grasping the trend in which the assembled facts seem to be leading will reason ahead of the yet unproved result and the inventor or artist may say to himself that if such and such could only be done the result would be desirable, and he then sets himself to obtain this result as he conceives it. Thomas Edison must have said something of the sort to himself when he first made an electric wire glow in a vacuum and suddenly perhaps imagined the possibility of stringing these glowing bulbs along a street so that it might be illuminated by a current of electricity. The artist's conception is similar. He suddenly realizes that a certain grouping of figures under an illumination of a certain sort producing certain highlights and shades would give a magnificent effect for some cathedral mural decoration. For years this general idea may be kept in the back of his mind until the opportunity offers itself and certain other relative conditions fall into line and make it possible for him to attempt its development.

His first step is often a preliminary sketch which is rough and undetailed and which is only a sort of notation aiding him to keep his general scheme in mind. He may then proceed to work out the details just as does an inventor. "Will such an arm if lifted procure a more rhythmical line in the composition?" "Would such a raising of the arm be natural to the figure?" "Is this shadow to be darker than that or would it be too much of a spot and should it glow with a diffused light reflected from some nearby surface?" "What surface could be brought to use in the reflecting of this light?" and similar questions occur in his mind and must be solved logically and reasonably.

During the solution of these questions he may make innumerable sketches or notes just as the scientist takes notes during the various steps of experimentation in his laboratory, and it is through the assembling of the more important of these various considerations that finally the work of art is actually conceived and constructed.

GRAPHIC ARTS

Expression of Material.—Among the fundamental considerations of every great artist is that of the appropriate expression of the material in which his work is to be executed. Watercolours should not be handled in such a way as to resemble oil; brass should not be finished to imitate bronze; and the reason for this is that people who may never have consciously thought about art have learned to associate certain characteristics with each substance they find about them. There is a feeling of disconcerting surprise when these characteristics are not evidenced, like the sensation when one touches one of the metal desks made to appear so perfectly like wood. One may never have considered consciously the warmth of wood though subconsciously one's mind has taken note of it. This surprise whether to the sense of touch or sight is always misleading and is usually ruinous to the effect of what might otherwise be an excellent work of art. We know for instance that iron is so strong that man cannot bend a slender rod of it and if we are confronted therefore with an iron garden gate made of thick and uselessly heavy pieces of metal we mistrust that it is iron and suspect that it may be lead or some other substance. Tapestry lends itself to a certain sort of design which can be better expressed in its weave than it can in a mosaic or fresco.

The faculty for properly expressing the medium, avoiding its limitations and taking advantage of its possibilities, is one not arrived at by intuition but by careful research and practice, so that the artist sometimes learns almost *to think* in the medium which he has studied. Thus a painter may actually learn to see a landscape in brush strokes, or a composer of music associate at once a certain section of the score with the tone quality of a certain instrument or group of instruments.

The Expression of the Tool.—Fully as important as the consideration of material is that of the characteristics of the various tools with which it is to be worked. The brush of sable, the tjantjing, the etching point, the chisel, the wheel of the gem cutter or even the fingers of the sculptor modelling in clay, will each make a certain cut, mark or impression which must be studied in relationship to the material. It is unpleasant to see clay carved with a sharp instrument as though it were wood, or stone, or to behold what appears to be a woodblock print and find that it has been painted with the brush.

Not only must the mark of the tool be considered in relationship to the material but it is capable if properly handled of a beauty in itself comparable to the single note drawn by a master hand from a fine violin. Look at the line drawn upon a piece of paper by a master draughtsman. Is it not similar to the violin note with its gradations of shade and its sweeping curve? The expression of beauty in a masterful handling of the tool so that each note is pleasing was a joy to the ancient artist and he would often spend years acquiring this deftness which many modern artists have been fooled into thinking is unnecessary because of the stressing of originality and spontaneity in art training.

But even this carelessness, deplorable as it is, is more forgivable than the custom of the last century of deliberately faking tool marks. Wood cut by machines to give the appearance of being hand-hewn and iron artistically dented to appear hand-forged had come to be almost universally accepted though nothing could show greater evidence of dishonesty of technique and bad taste.

Style.—No two artists can paint the same face or the same landscape in the same way any more than two business men can sign their names in the same way. Neither the style nor the personality of the artist need be thought about and certainly should not be artificially cultivated. However, if one is to permit his style to grow he must not hamper it by the slavish copy of some other artist's personal style. He may to advantage copy works of art again and again, but should do so simply to broaden his outlook, as a writer may read the books of many other writers.

The present day stressing of originality in art teaching is responsible for much of the worst of our modern art. Technique is all that can be taught. Style and originality of real value can only come after the artist's experiences both in life and in art have broadened and enriched his personality, for the artist cannot express a personality until he has one and, if he has one, he cannot help but express it.

Suitability.—Suitability to surroundings is an element often lacking in the art of to-day due to a strange occurrence which took place during the decadence of the Renaissance. It is interesting to know that during the best periods of art the distinction between fine arts and applied art was not clear. In Egypt it was unknown. In Greece sculptors did as masterful work for the pediment of a building as for a pedestal. In the Orient the distinction has not existed for thousands of years and a porcelain vase or a piece of lacquer may be regarded just as highly as a painting or a piece of sculpture.

Michelangelo and Cellini did not recognize the distinction and were as proud of what might be called their craftsmanship or works of applied art as they were of those which could be labelled "fine art." Both were craftsmen at heart and unspoiled by what occurred immediately following their times.

"Fine Arts" as a term came into use meaning painting, sculpture, music and poetry, with sometimes the inclusion of architecture or those arts which exist for the pleasurable qualities alone and apart from any utilitarian consideration, but "fine arts" came to be thought of as of greater importance than applied arts for, if some of the arts are termed fine, the implication is that the other arts are less fine, and the result of this usage was that people came to consider art which had no application superior to art which was applied. They argued "Yes, that is beautiful for its purpose, but this is finer for the very reason that it has no purpose other than that of being beautiful."

The result was a tendency toward less and less consideration of the principles of application of art. Sculptors preferred to work in their studios than to co-operate with architects. Great painters ceased to do murals and worked upon easel pictures. Recently, however, there has occurred a happy revolt against this attitude, more especially in America because it was found there that applied art paid better than fine art. In other words the public had judged, and with the disappearance of the marble pedestal and whatnot from the Victorian interior, there was also a disappearance of bibelots and the old time easel paintings so that the artist is now confronted with the necessity of studying the antique as did the great masters and the principles of proper spacing, and must adopt the more modest attitude that his work, in order to be successful, must be considered as only part of an ensemble.

Time Consideration.—Works of art differ from works of nature in that they cannot reproduce themselves and should therefore express in some way their vulnerability before the onslaughts of time. Part of the appeal of the antique is due to the fact that it is bowing with such grace and such pathetic dignity and beautiful spirit before the inevitable. The patina of an old bronze or the iridescence of an ancient glass vase is the touch of great Nature bidding it return to its original state.

Structure.—Structure itself may be considered but an admission of the necessity for fortification against time and when proper structure is not observed one can foresee at a glance the indignity of the final defeat. Some works of art like some people grow more beautiful with age, for the scars of

162

MEZZOTINT

ENGLISH MEZZOTINTS OF THE 18TH CENTURY

1. "Mrs. Carnac." After Sir Joshua Reynolds by John Raphael Smith (1752–1812)

2. "Mary Amelia, Countess of Salisbury." After Sir Joshua Reynolds by Valentine Green (1739–1813)

3. "Lady Hamilton" ("Nature"). After George Romney by John Raphael Smith (1752–1812)

4. "Georgiana, Duchess of Bedford." After John Hoppner by Samuel William Reynolds (1794–1872)

THE HANDWRITING OF THE DOMESDAY BOOK

Excerpts from the Domesday Book, a census of lands in England, prepared by command of William the Conqueror in the 11th century: xii. Itemisation of the lands of Wm. de Scohies in Carlion Castle and Tornelaus hundred xv. Itemisation of the land held by Wm. Son of Baderen in Bremesese hundred. xvi. Itemisation of the land held by Wm. Son of Norman in Radelau hundred. xvii. Itemisation of the land held by Thurstin Son of Rolf in Bremesese hundred

years serve only the more clearly to prove the sturdiness within. It is wise therefore for the artist to think of the final conditions of ruin of his work and build it in such a manner that it will be beautiful as long as it is recognizable.

Fragility.—If structure appeals to us because of its intelligent defence against time, fragility undoubtedly appeals because of its pitiful bravery, for just as we have regard for some men for their reasonable sanity we like others for their careless daring. It is this appeal which has undoubtedly been responsible for the preservance of some of the delicate glass which has been passed from hand to hand down through the ages. Each hand though perhaps calloused by the sword or plough, though made careless by wine and laughter has touched it with a certain amount of care because of the realization of its brave stand against time.

A most strange and interesting study is this element, time, and our accounting for it, for though we realize that in it lies ultimate destruction we anxiously look for its touch on many works of art, feeling a mistrust for those things which have not proven themselves against it. Sculptors finish their bronzes with artificially applied patina not for the purpose of faking antiquity but simply to satisfy the eye as the boy with a new pair of shoes will scuff them in the dirt to take off the newness. A round corner is more beautiful than a sharp new one. Old polished wood is more beautiful than new and a painting, a statue or a piece of furniture finds a pleasing richness as the years impose a modification of the exact statements of the artist's brush or chisel.

Such considerations as those few outlined above will give the reader an idea of what the artist is thinking about as his work proceeds, and an understanding as to why and how it is made to appeal to the mind of his public. Abstract beauty may exist, though the philosophers seem to have some difficulty in defining it, but some of the elements of beauty which appeal to man in a work of art can thus be analyzed, weighed and combined by the artist into a worthy result.

CALLIGRAPHY

CALLIGRAPHY is the art of fine writing. Writing is a means of communication by agreed signs; if these signs or symbols are painted or engraved on wood or stone we have that extension and application of writing known as *lettering, i.e.*, a large script generally formed with mechanical aids such as the rule, compass and square. But it is the essence of handwriting that it be free from such, though not from all, government; and of beautiful handwriting that it possess style. When the agreed forms, passing through a mind sensitive to symmetry, are expressed upon vellum, paper or other suitable material by an instructed hand with an appropriate tool, the result may be a handwriting possessing style. Calligraphy may be defined as freehand in which the freedom is so nicely reconciled with order that the understanding eye is pleased to contemplate it. Hence we immediately recognize the beauty resulting from right proportion of the components to the whole of a letter, and between the parts to the whole of a word. Many scripts of the remote or recent past, such as the Rustic Capitals, Uncial, Half-Uncial, Quarter-Uncial, the Caroline Minuscule and the later Gothics, demonstrate that handwriting, though an elementary craft, is capable of infinite variations. Changes of fashion so affect the form, the cutting of the tool and the manner of holding it, that a collection of the hands employed in pre-Renaissance Europe exhibits a series of almost bewildering variations. The necessity for speed is the first great cause of variation; a second equally potent occasion lay in the use of special hands for certain purposes. In the mediaeval period, outside the monastic scriptoria where the most formal upright and deliberate text hands were written, there were several recognized classes occupied with writing such as clerks, public scriveners, public notaries and in addition certain others who were ancestors of the later professional writing-masters. Finally, there were writers of the special hands used in documents issued from the papal and other chanceries. Most of these classes, in the hope of preventing forgery, wrote hands of deliberate complexity.

The Renaissance, by its reaction from the complicated late Gothic and reversion to the simpler Caroline hands, indeed changed the writing tradition of all Europe, but not all the cisalpine countries adopted the new hands simultaneously—the tenacity, in fact, of Gothic is only in our own day being broken in its chief stronghold, Germany. Though the humanists deliberately reverted to the Caroline hand, theirs was not a barren facsimile of the 9th century letter for, since they laboured for a return to classical traditions, many scribes broke completely with the Caroline exemplars in the matter of majuscules, so that adaptations of the old Roman geometrically formed inscription letters appear upon the vellum pages of humanistic codices equally with majuscules based upon the fine Tours forms.

The Renaissance did more than merely revert to the art styles of antiquity. In its early phase it was a movement in which a limitless curiosity of the mind—the mark of the true humanist—predominated and had not yet aroused the jealousy of the church. Indeed in the early 15th century, ecclesiastics vied with secular scholars in the task of renewing art and science. To record our least legacy of that age, we make acknowledgement to the secular humanistic scribes for the fine round book letter which is the foundation of our "roman" printing; to the scriveners of the papal chancery for our running hand. In an age in which science, religion and art were the chief, and commerce a subordinate interest, these novel scripts were introduced and propagated by artists and ecclesiastics, while merchants, bankers and lawyers kept accounts and indited conveyances in a tortuous Gothic. The development of handwriting owes nothing to commerce until the next century, and then everything.

In mediaeval society it depended upon the officials of Church and State. Hands were invented and books written in accordance with liturgical, administrative and judicial requirements. Like other courts, the Roman *Curia* maintained (and maintains) a group of canon lawyers and scriveners known as the Apostolic Chancery from which were issued papal bulls, and later a more modest class of document. A small easily formed hand was[1] reserved by order of Pope Eugenius IV. (1431–47) for the engrossing of these minor documents written fast (*brevi manu*) and known as "briefs." The script itself became famous as "*cancelleresca corsiva*," chancery cursive, and in the next century printed and engraved models of it abounded.

The first works on letter formation deal with capital letters and were compiled by enthusiastic admirers of the old Latin inscriptions, like Ciriaco of Ancona, who transcribed, collated and copied all the memorials, grave-

[1]Mas Latrie (*Trésor de Chronologie*).

stones and tablets they could discover. Andrea Mantegna introduced into his famous frescoes at the Eremitani in Padua careful renderings of certain inscriptions (since destroyed). Feliciano of Verona compiled a collection of inscriptions and dedicated it to Mantegna; and from the same scholar's hand we have (Cod. Vaticanus 538) a codex which represents the earliest extant treatise on the shapes of inscription letters. The ms. is dated 1463 and is the first to give diagrams and instructions for the geometrical formation of Roman capitals.

The earliest printed work of the kind is a modest anonymous work with an undated colophon: "*impressum Parme per Damianum Moyllum, Parmensem.*" As there are extant several mss. signed by Damiano Moille we may guess that he had a share in the authorship as well as in the printing of the alphabet. There is bibliographical evidence for concluding the date of publication to lie between 1480–83.

At about the same time the friar and mathematician Pacioli, notable as a friend of Leonardo, was busy on his *De Divina Proportione*, a treatise which included an appendix on the geometry of letter-making. The Padre's book was not printed until 1509, but existed in a finely illuminated manuscript copy much earlier, having been presented to Ludovico Sforza (*Il Moro*) of Milan.

Fanti of Ferrara brought out in 1514 the first extension of the geometrical method to the rounded Gothic letter then greatly used for large choirbooks: *Theorica et practica Perspicassimi Sigromundi de Fantis . . . De Modo Scribendi Fabricandique omnes Litterarum species* (Venice, Rubeus, 1514). The title is fuller than the contents, for Fanti gives no more than the Roman capitals in the method of Feliciano, Moille and Pacioli, plus a set of round semi-Gothic letters similarly made, which designs were roughly cut on wood by da Carpi. Whereas the models of capitals already published had been useful to architects and antiquarians and a few scribes, Fanti's small Gothic letters (lower case) of the kind then known as "modern letter" (*lettera moderna*) were serviceable to the numerous clerks in monasteries and elsewhere. Arrighi, a calligrapher from Vicenza and subsequently an assistant in the Apostolic Chancery, published in 1522 a book of models of a current correspondence hand based upon the *lettere de brevi*. This, the first of all copybooks, was entitled *Il Modo et Regola da Imparare di scriuere littera corsiuà ouer cancellerescha nouamente composto per Ludovico Vicentino*. The script in this first publication of Arrighi, *scrittore de breui apostolici in*

Roma, as he styles himself, is a singularly effective and beautiful combination of the neo-Caroline minuscule, slightly inclined by speed, with perpendicular majuscules reminiscent of the inscriptions, whose austerity is relieved with additional characters of a decorative form, *BCDEPRN*. There are also to be found flourishes, ligatures, initial and terminal letters of grace and freedom. Arrighi's fine professional hand is ornamental in comparison with the somewhat angular and pinched version of the same hand as it was officially used 50 years before. The popularity gained by the chancery script during the half-century 1470–1520 exposed it to great risks. Writers of diplomatic documents practised it with a discretion foreign to the temper of Mantegna, Cellini, da Vinci and scores of other artists, nobles and scholars who adopted it. The habit of writing "private" letters with a view to their being handed about as specimens of true Latinity developed interest in calligraphy, and with this powerful support the new cursive rapidly became the favourite correspondence script of the fashionable classes, absorbing a multitude of mannerisms which corrupted it until its original simplicity was scarcely recognizable. While in Vicentino's specimens flourished forms were offered as an occasional pleasant alternative to the rigid capital and both were modestly proportioned to the height of the ascending letters *d*, *h* and *l*, later models exhibit an irritating superfluity of display. The burin of the copper engraver produced an excessively brilliant line which tempted pupils to employ a correspondingly fine pen, so that the later writing of the century was dominated rather by the technique of the engraver's burin than that of the scribe's pen. The first book in copper-plate is the handsome and ornate, though practical, *Libro* of Hercolani, a notary of Bologna (1571).

His book is valuable as a good specimen of the late chancery hand distinguished by its decorative treatment of the ascending and descending letters. In the pure Vatican style these forms terminated in an angular serif, which existed side by side with a variety which terminated in a short blunt curve from right to left. The angular serif went out of use before 1520 and thereafter no models of the chancery hand for secular or official Vatican use recommend it.

Gradually, by means of a fine pen and a supple wrist, the originally unassuming serif was turned into the most conspicuous feature in the word—and in the page—so that a late Italian 16th century letter is almost a network of deliberately formed blots. This development may be conveniently watched in the books of Palatino, a first-rate scribe who gained great renown in Spain where he was copied by Ycia. Pens then became finer and enabled Periccioli (Siena 1610) not only to execute very delicate calligraphical *entrelac* borders but exceedingly subtle script which gained a seductive sparkle when reproduced from intaglio plates. All the Italian scripts found their way abroad; the fine early hands and their bulbous successors may be met in various parts of Europe. The Italian artists transplanted to Fontainebleau by Francis I. included a humbler rank of decorators, craftsmen and calligraphers. These found Gothic, formal and cursive, generally practised. Tory wrote an Italian hand and his *Champfleury* a plea for beautiful lettering and an elaboration of the geometrical method of making Roman capitals he had learned from Pacioli and Dürer. Gothic book hands are also given, but we have to wait a generation for a French pattern book of correspondence hands. In the books of Hamon and de la Rue we find good chancery models and a number of *Lettres de Fantaisie* (alphabets of wavy, crooked, club-footed and other similarly treated latins). *Cursive françoyse*, as current Gothic was called, always appears in the early French books. This was the letter from which the *Civilité* type was made, and which in the next generation was to be amalgamated with the Italian hand producing the elegant compromise known as "Ronde." It has a vigorous character and may rank as the French national hand, still employed to-day, but with its Gothicisms heavily diluted. Early fine Rondes are to be found in the book of Louis Barbedor (1628).

In the middle of the 17th century, Colbert, when Louis XIV.'s financial secretary, took in hand the revision of French official scripts and, in consequence, the clerks in the offices of State were instructed to abandon the old Gothic cursives and to confine themselves to the upright Ronde known as *financière*, inclined *bâtarde*, and a running form known as *coulée*.

Such changes gained effect gradually: generations of masters recommended almost non-Gothic as the "Italian hand," so great was the prestige of that name. The rise of the fine French school of portrait engraving influenced the use of Roman scripts and the opposition of Colbert left Gothic scarcely a vestigial existence by the end of the century.

To Colbert, the eminent master Senault dedicated his fine book—*Livre d'ecriture representant la beauté de tous les caractères financiers maintenant à la mode* (1660). Other French models of calligraphy circulated also in England and in Holland; French influence in England being more direct than the Italian, though there were such Italians as Petruccio Ubaldini who taught

168

calligraphy to the English Court (*c.* 1580). Jean de Beauchesne and John Baildon's *A Booke containing divers sortes of hands*, also a "*True and just proportiō of the capitall Romae*" (London, Thomas Vautrouillier, 1571) is the first English manual of calligraphy. Beauchesne is the same who had brought out *Le Thresor d'Escripture* in Paris (1550). Both contained admirable models; the English book having handsome forms of current Gothic and secretary hands as well as fine italics.

Billingsley's *The Pen's Excellency* (London) still has many more secretary, court and other Gothic hands than Roman. Billingsley's is one of the few English books independent of the designs of Barbedor and Materot which powerfully affected London masters of the 17th century. But though England learned much from France, specimens of the work of Van der Velde, Boissens, Perlingh and other conspicuous Dutch exponents of the art were highly esteemed when the London writing-masters found their services demanded by youths training for clerkships in the growing English commercial houses. The Dutch possessed at that time most of the carrying trade and were for that reason directly imitated in England. The Dutch naturally copied the Frenchmen since French literature was not only read but, owing to the repressive legislation against Paris printers, also printed in the Low Countries.

The difference between the late Italian 16th, early French and Dutch 17th century hands was not considerable—mainly a matter of width of letter. The Italians had a habit of angularizing the letter, the Dutch of widening and giving it greater inclination. What French, Dutch and English writers commonly called the "Italian" hand is a free, flowing and obviously inclined hand in which the ascenders are looped and the majuscules entirely cursive—wholly different from the Chancery of Vicentino. This was the result of the demand for speed, itself the concomitant of commercial development.

English writing gained in currency as commerce expanded. When in 1658, Oliver Cromwell broke the Dutch commercial power and, by his Mercantile Act, secured that every cargo shipped to England was carried in English bottoms, there resulted a vast increase in the nation's shipping. Commercial clerkships became desirable positions, bringing a fine opportunity for such professors as Snell (1693), Seddon (1695) and others who all learned from the Dutch masters, but whose hands drew away from their models and finally expressed those characteristics which came in another generation to be regarded by the rest of the world, if not by Englishmen, as thoroughly English and admirable for the purposes of salesmanship. Thus the commercial success of England drew hearty foreign respect for the script in which English Bills of Lading and Notes of Exchange were made out; named *Anglaise* in France, *letra Inglesa* in Spain, it dominated in Italy itself at the end of the 19th century as "*Lettere Inglese*." Gothic now persists only with the greatest difficulty—where once it had been used for the text of deeds it fights for existence as a script for titles, and to-day 𝖂𝖍𝖊𝖗𝖊𝖆𝖘 and 𝕿𝖍𝖎𝖘 𝕴𝖓𝖉𝖊𝖓𝖙𝖚𝖗𝖊 witnesseth its sole traces.

In contemporary France the *ronde* is being hard pressed by *anglaise*. The *Cours d'Inscription Calligraphique*, published by École des Travaux Publics has a very extensive circulation, and though treating of *bâtarde* and *ronde* gives primary place to *anglaise*.

The situation is not very different in present-day Spain. The magnificent 16th century specimens of Iciar (1550) and Brun (1583) were adaptations of the hand of Palatino and Vicentino, but these writers succeeded neither in acclimatizing these nor inventing any new, living, national hands. This was achieved by Lucas, who created a characteristic Spanish upright round-hand and companion inclined *bâtarde* which with astonishingly trifling variations remained in possession for two centuries, giving way only before *anglaise*. The hands of many English writing-masters were familiar to the leading Spanish calligraphers of the 18th century. It would be an exaggeration to claim that the script, which we are accustomed to term "copperplate," possesses an attractive personality. It is colourless, thoroughly unromantic and dull. These, however, were precisely the qualities which commended it to those who wrote out invoices. Above all it was expeditious, and the writing-masters of London knew better than to teach them to tricking out of ascenders with solid blacks or capitals with meandering loops which a generation of earlier masters thought would endear their own calligraphy to present and future. The simple and practical nature of English business hand did not exactly serve the material interests of the English writing-master. Plain round-hand is not so difficult to acquire as to need either perpetual practice at home or continual resort to a master. The early American colonists followed the calligraphical styles of the home country and Benjamin Franklin practised a fine *anglaise* from which a printing type was subsequently engraved. The first American copybook (Jenkins, 1791) continued the mid-18th century English script. In 1809 Joseph Carstairs of

170

CALLIGRAPHY FROM THE 15TH TO THE 17TH CENTURY

BY COURTESY OF (1, 6) THE PEGASUS PRESS, "A NEWLY DISCOVERED TREATISE ON CLASSICAL LETTER DESIGN" (FACSIMILE BY STANLEY MORISON)

1. Excerpt from "Damianus Moyllus, Alphabetum," the first known printed work on letter-formation, Parma, 1480. Facsimile by Stanley Morison from "A Newly Discovered Treatise on Classical Letter Design"

2. From a writing-book by Giovanniantonio Tagliente, Italian. 1525

3. Specimen from the first copybook of script, written by Ludovico degli Arreghi, surnamed Vicentino, and published 1522. Facsimile by Stanley Morison

4. Excerpt from Lodovico Curione, "Il teatro delle cancelleresche corsine." Rome, 1594

5. Eustachio Cellebrino; specimen of Italian semi-gothic hand used by legal and commercial classes. Very rare. One copy in a private library in New York and one in Berlin

6. Excerpt from John Ayres, "Tutor to Penmanship." London, 1698. Facsimile by Stanley Morison, from "Caractères de l'Ecriture dans la Typographie"

EXAMPLES OF EUROPEAN CALLIGRAPHY DURING THE 16TH AND 17TH CENTURIES

1. Excerpt from "Arte de Escrivir" by Lucas (Madrid, 1608)
2. Excerpt from "L'Ecriture Nationale Française se développant de la Civilité à l'Ecriture Financière"
3. Page from "Recopilación Subtilíssima," by Yciar (Saragossa, 1548)
4. Excerpt from "Expédiée Bâtarde, Anglaise coulée," by Bourgoin
5. Page from "Arte de Escrivir" by Casanova (Madrid, 1650)
6. Page from Pierre Hamon's, "Alphabet de l'invention des Lettres en diverses écritures" (1651)

7. De Louis Barbedor: L'Ecriture financière dans sa naisueté auec les autres Escritures françoises propres. Paris (1628)

CALLIGRAPHY

London championed a theory of handwriting in which the forearm and not the fingers controlled the script. His book was translated into French and Spanish and was introduced into the United States by Foster in 1830. It was employed overseas with such success that it even became known as the American System. The American hand,[1] however, did in fact develop from a continuation of this movement of the forearm and a condensation of the running hand exemplified in Jenkins. Dayton copyrighted in 1855 the first specimen of what developed into a style which now may fairly claim to rank as the national American hand. It is a style which requires a very fine pen as the down strokes taper from top to bottom. There is a slightly increased slope, a tendency to flourished terminations and a noticeable degree of condensation. It had little success at first and it is possible that it would have made no progress but for the plagiarization by the very active "Professor" Spencer, who, in spite of the protests of Dayton, claimed the design as his own and taught it throughout a chain of business colleges established in 44 cities by the time of his death in 1861. The style which is known to this day as the Spencerian system is by no means without its exponents. It is not a particularly unpleasant letter except when written carelessly.

Nineteenth-century England learned to write from the copybooks of Vere Foster, whose lithographed models expressed edifying admonitions in a flawless current hand of the plainest style. The "Civil Service" hand also, an upright version of the same design, was and is commonly practised. Both scripts are declining, for one thing because when written with great speed they become illegible. The pressure of life to-day tells heavily against decent handwriting. Writing too much and therefore too quickly we corrupt the shape and become accustomed to low standards. We may find a way out by practising two hands, a rough scribble and a ceremonial script. Twentieth-century mechanics ensure a future for correspondence calligraphy if the desk equipment of every schoolboy and girl could include a typewriter.

To inculcate a good modern current hand Mr. Hewitt's *Oxford Copy Books* are to be recommended.

So much for the epistolary department of post-Renaissance calligraphy (the early fine formal book hands may be studied in the article on PALAEOGRAPHY: *Latin*). Calligraphical book hands settled the forms of the earliest printing types, but were themselves affected when the type forms acquired a momentum of their own. It is not true that typography killed calligraphy

---

[1] "La Méthode de J. Carstairs faussement appelée Méthode *Américaine*," Paris, 1839.

outright—some of the finest calligraphy in the history of book production was executed within the memory of the generation which witnessed the invention of printing, as may be seen from the work of Antonio Sinibaldi of Florence and Mennius of Naples, to name only two famous scribes of the Italian school. The anonymous calligrapher whose splendid "Chantilly" *Caesar* is fit to rank with the finest of mediaeval manuscripts, heads a not less brilliant French school. The art died for lack of patrons, not for lack of calligraphers. These eked out a penurious existence as rubricators attached to printing houses, or as engrossers of choir-books which required larger characters than type founders were willing to cast.

The age of Louis XIV. witnessed an abortive revival of calligraphy to which the manuscripts by Jarry, Gilbert, Damoiselet and Rousselot remain a pathetic testimony. This school so formalized their book hands and cursives as to deceive the eye into thinking that they were types. Scribes like Eclabart were in fact able to write whole books in a letter indistinguishable from printing type.

Gothic remained here and there in occasional use and, even in our own day, it not infrequently garnishes a presentation address. Col. Lindbergh's reception by the City of New York in 1927 was signalized by the presentation of a gorgeous address of welcome in which the regard of the American nation was tendered in a text comprising four or five cacophonous Gothics, semi-Gothics and Romans. If in any English address the calligraphy has been handsome and noble or even sober and dignified, it will have been due entirely to the teaching and practice of Mr. Edward Johnston whose *Writing* and *Illuminating and Lettering* (London, 1906) created a new interest in calligraphy among wealthy amateurs and collectors and a new school of excellent scribes. To Mr. Johnston's teaching therefore we owe that revival of fine calligraphy in which England may well take great pride. Mr. Johnston did what the Renaissance had done before him: he went back to the Caroline Minuscule and though he learned, and learned well, from certain fine English mediaeval hands his own beautiful book-hand is individual and underived. As the Exhibition of the Society of Scribes and Illuminators (London) proves, he has created a body of skilful English calligraphers, whose fine scripts give us no excuse for using the debased Gothics and pinchbeck Romans laboriously confected by the hack employees of the west-end heraldic-artist, the court stationer and the Fifth-Avenue bookseller.

Johnston's influence has not been merely national; it has perhaps been greatest in Germany. The works of Neff, Dürer and of Baurenfeind were succeeded by an indifferent posterity and until our own generation Germany used a mean informal Gothic for commemorative and other purposes where a ceremonial writing was required. In 1910 Mr. Edward Johnston's pupil Fräulein Simons introduced his teaching into Germany with great success and the printing revival due to William Morris which had already made rapid progress rallied to its support. In 1928 Germany has a school of calligraphers second to none in inventiveness and skill. The Gothic letter does not lack champions: the Austrian Professor Larisch and Herr Otto Hupp, two of the generation who were writing before Mr. Johnston's movement assumed its present importance, both practised Gothic. Prof. Koch of Offenbach is a representative of the present lively generation and for a variety of national and other reasons prefers to work in Gothic, though he learned from Johnston the handsome Roman and italic hands. F. H. Ehmcke, though skilled in Gothic, specializes in Roman. There are not wanting certain influences in Germany which while seeking inspiration from the new movement would be happier if the old Gothic hands could be revived. Thus the *Bund für Deutsche Schrift* exists to encourage the Gothic hands. It remains to be seen whether this reaction will be successful.

There is perhaps a tendency on the part of the Johnstonian school to narrow its interest and practice to formal book-hands and to ignore the need for a simple, easy, running cursive. The layman fears that if he writes with a modicum of care his script will be confounded with his office boy's, and it is even claimed that "character" in handwriting is more important than legibility. This is a *reductio ad absurdum* and it may be replied that a self-respecting person employing the inevitable and natural movement of his pen to make modest capitals and a lower-case script in which the angles shall be regular, the characters symmetrically rounded, the descenders and ascenders proportionate to their bodies will there and then have the elements of legibility, style and character.

PENCIL DRAWING

A PENCIL DRAWING is one made by a piece of graphite sharpened into a fine point, and held in a porte-crayon, and the term is usually applied to a drawing made with this material upon vellum or parchment. The greatest masters of this particular art were Dutchmen, and the best productions were those of the 17th century. In a great many instances it is quite certain that the extremely elaborate plumbago (graphite) drawings done by Dutch artists were intended for the purpose of engravings, and of several of them, this can be proved by putting the finished engraving by the side of the elaborate plumbago drawing. Considering the clumsiness of the material, it is amazing that the artists elaborated such exceedingly delicate and beautiful work as many of these plumbago drawings exhibit. It seems almost certain that they must have been drawn under a lens, and it is clear that the artist possessed a steady hand to a very unusual degree.

One of the earliest workers in plumbago was Simon van de Pass (1595?–1647) whose pencil drawings were almost certainly either for reproduction on silver tablets or counters or for engraved plates. Abraham Blooteling, the Dutch engraver, executed a very few portraits, but they appear to have been only first sketches, from which eventually he made larger ones, and from these engraved his plates. He was followed by the man who is perhaps the greatest exponent of the art of drawing in plumbago, David Loggan (1635–1700), a pupil of Van de Pass, and a man well known for his long series of engravings representing the colleges of Oxford and Cambridge. He executed portraits with the utmost dexterity, and with marvellous minuteness, the lines representing the intricacies of a lace ruffle, or the curls of a wig, being unusually perfect. Better known is William Faithorne (q.v.).

Next in eminence and skill comes Thomas Forster (fl. 1695–1712). He was one of the greatest draughtsmen in this particular form of portraiture. Forster was responsible for a few prints, but examples of them are of the utmost rarity. His work can be studied with advantage in the Holburne Museum at Bath, at Welbeck Abbey, or at the Victoria and Albert Museum, London.

There are two other Englishmen who should be mentioned, Robert and

174

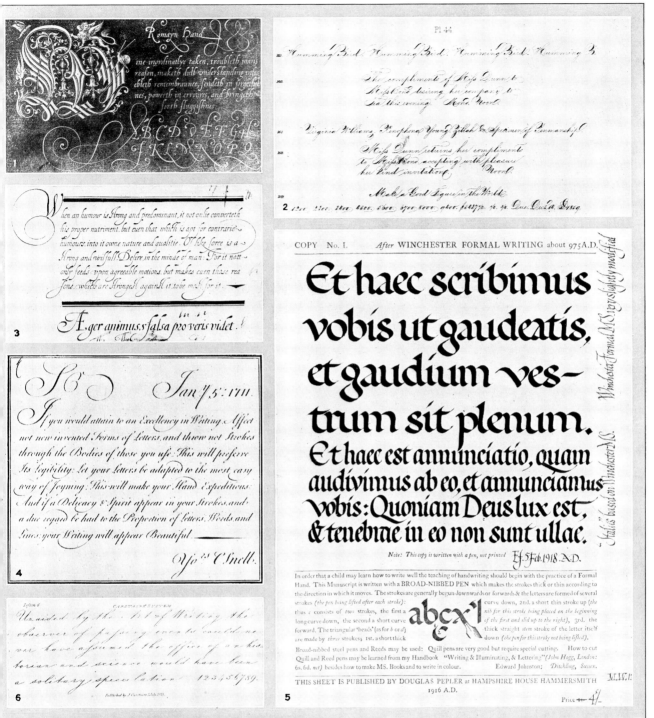

EXAMPLES OF CALLIGRAPHY FROM THE 16TH TO 20TH CENTURY

1. Excerpt from "A Book Containing Divers Sorts of Hands," the first English manual of calligraphy, written in 1571 by John **Baildon** and Jean de Beauchesne, showing the influence of early French script

2. Spencerian or semi-angular penmanship engraved about 1857 by Gerlack, and published by Plunney and Company, Buffalo, N. Y.

3. Specimen of penmanship from Martin Billingsley's *The Pen's Excellencies or the Secretaries Delight*, 1618, showing Gothic influence

4. A copy of an engraving by Charles Snell in *The art of writing in its Theory and Practice*, published in London in 1712

5. Copy sheet from Edward Johnston's manuscript illustrating his particularly handsome type of calligraphy, a blend of roman and italic hands introduced at the beginning of the twentieth century

6. Illustration from *The Fashionable Penman*, showing the method of handwriting advocated by Joseph Carstairs. According to this system, the forearm, not the fingers, controlled the script

PENCIL DRAWING

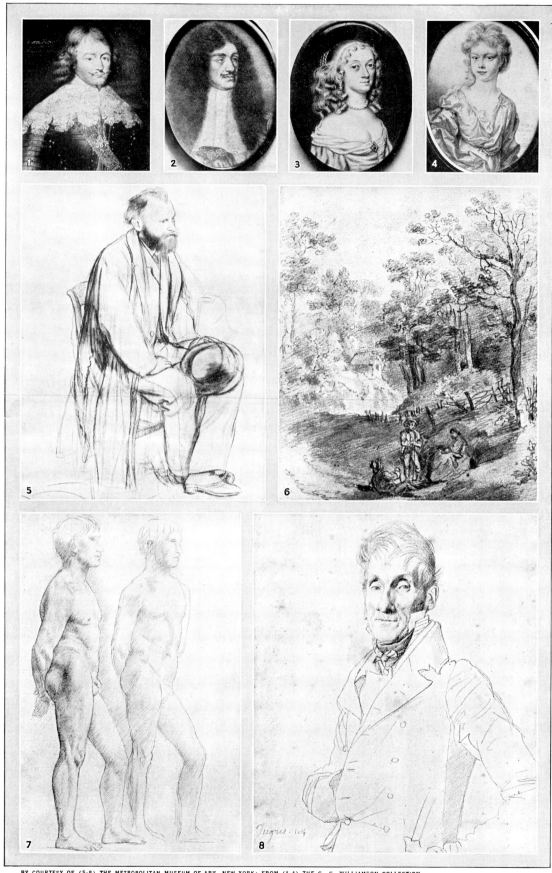

FRENCH AND ENGLISH PENCIL DRAWINGS

1. Drawing in "plumbago," with some wash work, of Sir Bevil Grenville, dated 1636, by Peter Oliver (1594–1648), English. 2. Drawing in "plumbago" of Charles II., by David Loggan (1635–1700). 3. Drawing of Mary, daughter of the 1st Marquis of Lothian, by David Paton (fl. 1650–1700), English. 4. Drawing in "plumbago" on vellum of Elizabeth, Viscountess Tracy, by Thomas Forster (fl. 1695–1712), English. 5. Portrait of Edouard Manet, by Edgar Degas (1834–1917), French. 6. Landscape by Thomas Gainsborough (1727–88), English. 7. Study by Alphonse Legros (1837–1911), French. 8. Portrait of an Unknown Man, by J. A. D. Ingres (1780–1867), French

George White, father and son. The former (1645–1704) was a pupil of David Loggan (who originally came from Danzig); he was a prolific engraver, most of whose drawings in plumbago on vellum were evidently executed for the purpose of engraving. George White, his son (1684–1732) was taught by his father, and finished some of his father's plates.

Reference must also be made to the use of plumbago by the painters of miniatures in colour. Hilliard used plumbago for preparing designs for jewels and for seals, Isaac and Peter Oliver for sketches in portraiture. A draughtsman in plumbago whose works are exceedingly scarce was David Paton, who worked in 1670. Then there were early engravers, such as George Glover (d. 1618) and Thomas Cecill (*fl.* 1630), who executed plumbago drawings, evidently studies for engravings. Of Glover's work the only known signed example is in the writer's collection. The work of Jonathan Richardson (1665–1745) and also the work of his son must be alluded to, but it is believed that, by their time, the graphite had been enclosed in a wooden rod, and that therefore the drawings may more naturally be called pencil drawings.

Draughtsmen in Indian ink have prepared portraits on very much the same lines. Among them were the two Fabers (1660?–1721 and 1695?–1756) in Holland, the elder having been born at The Hague, as he himself stated on his portrait which was in Vertue's collection. Of the two the son was the greater artist, although both of them were responsible for many very fine portraits drawn in Indian ink, as a rule circular, often set within lined borders and frequently adorned with coats of arms and inscriptions, equally minute and wonderful. Another able worker in Indian ink was a Swede, Charles Bancks (*c.* 1748), and another, a Swiss, Joseph Werner, born 1637, who made his drawings upon brown paper, and in some cases heightened the work with touches of white paint. Amongst other exponents of this art are the following: Thomas Worlidge (1700–1766), F. Steele (*c.* 1714), W. Robins (*c.* 1730), G. A. Wolfgang (1692–1775).

PENCILS IN ART

ARCHITECTURAL DRAUGHTSMEN, renderers, engineering draughtsmen and artists find lead pencils indispensable in their work. Hard, medium and soft pencils are necessary with every pencil artist, and he must make his own selection to fit his own needs. The uses of the various degrees of hardness are shown in the following table:—

175

GRAPHIC ARTS

Perspective and Object Drawing . . . . Grades 3B to HB
Nature Drawing . . . . Grades 3B to H
Pose Drawing . . . . Grades 3B to B
Scientific Drawings . . . . Grades HB to 9H
Mechanical and Architectural Drawing . . . . . . Grades HB to 3H
Lettering . . . . Grades 2B to H
Commercial Art . . . . Grades 3B to HB
Artists' Sketching . . . . Grades 6B to 3H
Architectural Renderings . . . . Grades 4B to 3H
Engineering Drawings . . . . Grades HB to 9H
Commercial Draughting and Design . . . . Grades HB to 9H

Broadly speaking, a soft pencil is used for dark tones and a hard pencil is used for light tones. A very soft pencil will produce a light tone, but the quality is not as fine, and a fuzzy appearance is likely to occur instead of the easy, flowing quality of a hard lead. The pressure can be determined only by constant practice, and both hard and soft pencils, as well as various qualities of paper, should be used by the young artist.

LINE ENGRAVING

Line Engraving, the process of incising lines in a metal plate from which it is intended to take an impression or print. It differs from other reproductive process in that: (1) the engraved line is that part which is printed, *i.e.*, it is intaglio as opposed to surface printing (employed in woodcut, *q.v.*); (2) the line is incised without the use of chemical action (employed in etching, *q.v.*); (3) the line is incised with a burin or graver (fig. 43), a sharp chisel-like tool of

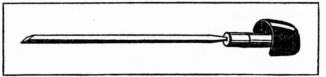

Fig. 43.—THE BURIN OR GRAVER USED FOR INCISING LINES INTO THE
METAL PLATE

quadrangular section, which is pushed *forward* and removes a small shaving, leaving the edges at the furrow comparatively clean (as opposed to drypoint [*q.v.*], where the line is scratched by a needle drawn towards the operator,

176

which in its passage leaves minute ridges on either side of the line, called burr). In line engraving the infinitesimal burr which is left by the graver (shown enlarged in fig. 44) is removed (as in fig. 45) by a sharp instrument called a scraper (fig. 46), whereas the effect produced by the burr is of the essense of drypoint.

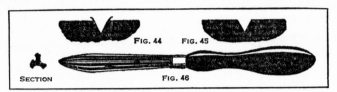

FIG. 44.—ENLARGEMENT SHOWING BURR LEFT BY THE GRAVER
FIG. 45.—ENLARGEMENT SHOWING ENGRAVED LINE AFTER BURR HAS
BEEN REMOVED BY A SCRAPER
FIG. 46.—THE SCRAPER

The method of printing from an engraved plate is the same as from an etched plate. (*See* ETCHING.)

HISTORY AND TECHNIQUE

THERE IS very little doubt that engraving was first practised north of the Alps, but at what place or at what exact time must remain a matter of uncertain conjecture. That it was evolved in the workshops of the goldsmiths, subsequently to the more obvious process of woodcut, is generally admitted; a date somewhere between 1410 and 1430, and a place somewhere between the Alps and the North Sea, in the basin of the Rhine, may be regarded as probable. The earliest engravings have generally been considered to be those of an artist named, from the subject of his most striking work, the Master of the Playing Cards. The place where this engraver, who was almost certainly a goldsmith, worked was probably South Germany or Switzerland. Engraving, in his hands, was already an elaborate medium, presupposing a previous development of some years. The Master of the Flagellation of 1446, the first engraving to bear a date, worked in a very similar style and may be assumed to be the pupil of the Master of the Playing Cards. Contemporary with the latter, or possibly even earlier, is an engraver who worked in the Netherlands or Burgundy, known as the Master of the Death of Mary. His ideas of distance and perspective were less advanced than those of his German contemporary, but this may have been an individual weakness not necessarily implying an earlier date. There were other engravers working about the same time or a little later whose work can be distinguished and localized in Burgundy or Flanders.

177

GRAPHIC ARTS

With the Master who signed with the initials E.S., and some of whose works are dated 1466 and 1467, engraving in Germany had reached a further stage of development. The dates on his engravings mark the end of what was probably a long career, and his earlier works show his derivation from the Master of the Playing Cards. The number of his surviving engravings, something over 300, implies that he was, at any rate, primarily an engraver by profession, and the influence of his style and technique on all subsequent engraving north of the Alps and even in Italy, can hardly be exaggerated. Martin Schongauer of Colmar (d. 1491) clearly derives from the Master E.S., and may even have been his pupil. He has developed from E.S.'s still rather tentative technique a regular system of cross hatchings admirably suited to his purposes, and the precision and delicacy of his technical equipment, combined with the distinction and real power of his design, go to make his engravings among the most beautiful achievements of the 15th century. Contemporary with Schongauer, and the only engraver of the period at all comparable to him in importance, is the anonymous artist known as the Master of the Hausbuch (or of the Amsterdam cabinet), who probably worked somewhere in the neighbourhood of Mainz and is known as a painter and draughtsman; he was presumably, unlike Schongauer, only secondarily an engraver. His work has almost the freedom and some of the character of drypoint and is very different in style from Schongauer's.

The last quarter of the 15th century in Germany is a period prolific in engravers. Schongauer's immediate scholars and imitators, whose names or initials it is not necessary to enumerate here, are numerous. The course of engraving in the Netherlands after the middle of the 15th century runs more or less parallel with that in Germany, though there are no artists of equal importance with E.S. and Schongauer.

Albrecht Dürer of Nuremberg (1471–1528) who, though not actually Schongauer's pupil as an engraver, is his virtual successor, carries on the Gothic tradition and later develops it, in contact with the Italian renaissance and by the power of his own fantastic and thoughtful temperament, into that grand and most significant expression of the Teutonic genius which we recognize in such engravings as the "Knight, Death and the Devil," the "Melancolia" and the "St. Jerome." Dürer was more than an engraver, but it was in this medium, perhaps, that his genius found the most perfect expression; he must be considered in view of this absolute fitness of means to expression as one of the greatest, if not the greatest, of the world's engravers.

178

Lucas van Leyden (1494–1533) in Holland, was in his own time placed on a level with Dürer, but posterity will hardly endorse this contemporary view, though his earlier engravings, beginning with the "Mahomet and the Monk Sergius" dated 1508 in his 15th year, have a naïve directness and lucidity of expression which are admirable. His engraving further marks an increase in the delicacy of tone values, which even Dürer had not attained. His later work shows a surrender, first to the influence of his great German contemporary, then to that of Raphael's works as interpreted by Marcantonio Raimondi.

Italy.—Vasari's statement that the art of engraving was invented by Maso Finiguerra about the year 1460 has long been disproved. Not only, as we have seen, was engraving known and practised north of the Alps some decades earlier, but even in Italy itself examples dating from at least ten years before Finiguerra's alleged discovery, can be found. These earliest Italian engravings, which emanate most probably from the workshops of Florentine goldsmiths, are in marked contrast to contemporary German productions, showing a much lower level of technical skill both in the actual engraving and in the printing. A first small group of Florentine engravings dating from about 1450 was succeeded by another group which may with very great probability be associated with the name of Maso Finiguerra (1426–1464). There is every reason to credit the tradition that he was an engraver, and the style of this second group is closely related to that of works in intarsia authenticated as his, and to that of a large group of works in niello (*q.v.*), an art of which he was reputed to be the greatest master. Closely connected with, and probably executed in Finiguerra's workshop after the master's death, are a number of other engravings, such as the series of the "Prophets and Sibyls." These, with the engravings actually attributed to Finiguerra, are usually grouped together as Florentine engravings in the Fine Manner as opposed to a more important group distinguished as in the Broad Manner. These, which are mostly later in date than the fine manner prints, some being copies from the latter, aim at reproducing the effect of pen drawings and derive their inspiration in part from Botticelli. Baccio Baldini who, Vasari states, engraved Botticelli's designs, may be the engraver of some of them.

The first great Florentine painter actually to use the graver himself was Antonio Pollaiuolo; his only engraving, the "Battle of the Nudes," is stylistically to be included in the group of prints in the broad manner. In Andrea

Mantegna (1431–1506), Italy produces her first really great engraver, great rather as an artist than as a craftsman. The "Virgin and Child," probably one of his earlier works, the great Entombment and the frieze of the "Battle of the Sea Gods" are as noble expressions of the great painter's genius as any of his pictures. A whole group of engravers was inspired by Mantegna and worked after his designs. Their work owes most of its worth to Mantegna, though they are competent workmen in the same manner. No greater contrast could be found with Mantegna's style than that of Jacopo de' Barbari (d. after 1512), a Venetian, who assimilated the northern technique of engraving and used it to express a rather charming vein of his own.

By the beginning of the 16th century we find quite a number of known engravers working in the north of Italy, such as Benedetto Montagna of Vicenza (about 1470 to after 1540), who continues the style of his more important father, the painter Bartolommeo, the gifted Giulio Campagnola in Venice (about 1482 to after 1514), whose work, executed in a curious dot manner akin to the later stipple, shows the nearest approach in engraving to the effects Giorgione was aiming at in painting, and others.

But it is to Rome by way of Bologna that we must now turn. Marcantonio Raimondi (c. 1480–c. 1530), trained in the workshop of the goldsmith-painter, Francia, in the latter city, at first engraved solely after drawings by or in the style of his master. Marcantonio's powers and his technique gradually improved with study and by copying Dürer and Lucas van Leyden, and after a stay in Florence and Venice he betook himself about 1510 to Rome. Here he came into contact with Raphael, who supplied the engraver with sketches from which to work. It is this contact which has given to Marcantonio his enormous, perhaps exaggerated reputation. We possess Raphael's drawings for "The Massacre of the Innocents," Marcantonio's most famous engraving, and can consequently judge of it not only on its merits, but in relation to Raphael's conception, and it stands the test triumphantly. With Raphael's death, in 1520, the life went out of Marcantonio's work; he continued to engrave after his paintings, but there is an obvious deterioration.

Sixteenth Century Engraving.—The influence exercised by Raphael, especially through the engravings made by Marcantonio and his followers, over European art south and north of the Alps, can hardly be exaggerated, though, in Germany, the victory of the Raphaelesque was not so overwhelming or so sudden. The so-called Little Masters, the two Behams,

180

Bartel (1502–1540) and Hans Sebald (1500–1550) and George Pencz (*c.* 1500–1550) of Nuremberg, together with Jacob Binck (d. about 1569) and Heinrich Aldegrever (1502–after 1555) continued the tradition of original engraving, along the lines which Dürer had inaugurated, and added something to the sum of the engraver's achievement, and in Ratisbon Albrecht Altdorfer (*c.* 1480–1538), of a previous generation, was the chief exponent of a quite individual style. But with about the year 1550, engraving, as well as the other arts in Germany, has passed its prime and the second half of the century is a decline, redeemed by fewer and fewer works of originality.

With the middle of the century engraving in the Netherlands has become commercialized. Engravers are employed by publishing firms, like that of Jerome Cock at Antwerp, to reproduce works, Netherlandish and Italian alike, for which there appears to be a demand. Even works engraved by Italians are published in the Netherlands, while Netherlandish engravers at the same time work in Italy, so that the sharp lines formerly delimiting the national styles are blurred. The tendency is for the technique of Italian engraving, which from the first owed something to northern models, to assume an even more northern character, while the influence of Italy is a general one on all northern art and only incidentally on engraving. The output of engraving in what is now Belgium, especially in Antwerp, during the two middle quarters of the century is enormous, but its character uninteresting; after about 1570 the centre shifts to Holland and it is the school of Hendrik Goltzius, Jacob Matham and Jan Saenredam, who continue and exaggerate the mannerisms of Lucas van Leyden's later style, which is most characteristic of the period and has the most influence on the subsequent development of engraving.

In Italy the school which Marcantonio had founded comprised a number of skilful engravers who continued the work of popularizing the paintings of Raphael and his pupils. But it was the Marcantonio in his latest and least satisfactory phase, who was their model, and the pupils rather than Raphael himself their inspiration. By about 1560 the art is mainly represented in the persons of foreign engravers like Cornelius Cort, and it is in this school that Lodovico Carracci and other Italian artists were trained.

In France, the 16th century produced one outstanding artist of small accomplishment as an engraver, but a remarkable genius, Jean Duvet (1485–*c.* 1561), and a group of engravers working at Lyons in the first half of the 16th century produced work of some decorative charm, while the portrait engravers foreshadow the great school of portrait engraving that followed in the 17th century.

The Seventeenth Century.—By the beginning of the 17th century engraving has come definitely to be regarded as a reproductive medium. Original engraving is now an exceptional phenomenon. Generally speaking, however, during this and the succeeding centuries the engravers are either independent or employed by publishing firms to engrave after miscellaneous artists, some living and some deceased. A feature of the 17th century is the increasing popularity of portrait engraving, which now became practically the most important branch of the art.

The engravers formed in the school of Rubens derive technically from Goltzius and his successors. Their brilliant but formal and inelastic technique, though sponsored by the master himself, was, it must be admitted, unsuited for the rendering of the spontaneity and exuberance of Rubens. The engravings are, in fact, dull, certainly the one fault of which Rubens himself could not be accused. But the best of these engravers, Pieter Soutman (1580–1657), Lucas Vorsterman the elder (1595–*c.* 1675), and his pupil, Paul Pontius (1603–1658), and the brothers Boëtius (*c.* 1580–1634) and Schelte (*c.* 1586–1659), a Bolswert, are admirable engravers in their way. Some of these also contributed to the famous series of engravings known as Van Dyck's *Iconography*. Eighteen of these plates were in the first place etched by Van Dyck himself, to be finished in some examples but not improved by the regular engravers. These elaborated plates suffer in contrast to Van Dyck's masterly etchings, but they are, in fact, sound examples of engraving, and exercised a considerable influence on subsequent engravers of portrait. In Holland, at the same time, an interesting and important school of portrait engraving came into existence, which was not without influence on the French school of engravers.

It was in France, and mainly in the special branch of portrait, that engraving in the 17th century attained its greatest perfection. The 16th century Netherlandish style of portrait engraving practised by T. de Leu, Leonard Gaultier and others, survived into the beginning of the 17th century. It was the influence of painting as practised by Rubens, Van Dyck and Philippe de Champaigne, which altered the conception of portrait painting, and consequently of portrait engraving. The earliest engravers to show the new influences at their fullest extent were Jean Morin (d. 1650) and

Claude Mellan (1598–1688), though the former's work is mainly etched. Mellan, in particular, founding his technique on that of the engravers of the Italian school, evolved a very distinctive and effective style from which cross-hatching was entirely eliminated, and which depended on the variation in the breadth of the individual parallel lines. Robert Nanteuil (1623?–1678), unlike Morin and Mellan, not only engraved, but himself drew the vast majority of his portraits, which adds greatly to their liveliness and life-likeness. His style, deriving from that of Mellan and the engravers of the school of Rubens in the first place, was later improved by the addition of elements borrowed from engravers like Morin. He models his faces in a series of small wedge shaped strokes, cunningly contrived to reproduce the desired texture. Gerard Edelinck (1640–1707), though lacking Nanteuil's extraordinary sincerity, is an engraver of great ability, and his interpretation of pictures by Lebrun and portraits by Rigaud and Largillière are typical examples of the art of the *grand siècle* at its *apogée*, while Antoine Masson (1636–1700) may be regarded as the third great portrait engraver of the century.

The 17th century in England produced one engraver of a merit, not comparable to that of Nanteuil, but still considerable, William Faithorne the elder (about 1616–1691), whose models are Claude Mellan, and later Nanteuil. But line-engraving in England was superseded in popularity towards the end of the century by the newly-invented process of mezzotint (*q.v.*), and Faithorne formed no school and had few successors of lasting influence.

The Eighteenth Century.—The pre-eminence of French engraving in the 17th is still more marked in the succeeding century. France has now become the artistic centre of Europe. The technique developed by Gerard Edelinck and Gerard Audran is continued and, if possible, further refined by the Drevet family, their scholars and successors, until engraving has been reduced to an almost mechanical formula, perfect in its way, but without life or individuality.

Portrait painting is not considered, however, as the most important product of the 18th century. It is in the engraving of society *genre* that we have to seek what is newest and most typical of the century. Watteau's elegant world of society, its most characteristic creation, is faithfully reflected in contemporary engraving. A number of skilful engravers were employed by Watteau's friend, Julienne, to engrave the master's complete works after his

183

death. These engravers succeed in rendering in line the shimmer and the grace of Watteau's painting, as far as this was translatable.

The style of engraving which was formed in the interpretation of Watteau's works was obviously well adapted for illustration, which now begins to have an importance which it had not enjoyed since the 16th century. There arose at the same time, in cultivated and fashionable society, a new desire to possess beautifully illustrated volumes, and new editions of standard works illustrated by the leading engravers of the day found a ready sale. It was the professional engravers in the Watteau tradition who were employed not only to engrave but also to design these illustrations. In many, if not in most cases, indeed, pressure of work made it impossible for them actually to engrave what they had designed, and they were necessarily forced to employ others to do this. But even in the latter case so close is the connection between the designer, who is an engraver himself, and the executant engraver, that engraving has ceased to be merely reproductive and has again become a medium of direct and original expression. A characteristic of reproductive line-engraving from the beginning of the 18th century onward (it is especially important in the case of the French illustrators and of the engravers of the Turner school) is the use of etching for the preliminary laying in of the design subsequently gone over and completed with the graver. The number of able illustrators who worked in France during the latter part of the century is very large and their excellence extremely uniform. Two artists may be singled out for especial mention, J. M. Moreau the younger (1741–1814), and Augustin de St. Aubin (1736–1807).

Italy, in the 18th century, has nothing to show in engraving at all comparable. The most original work was that produced in Venice by Giovan Marco Pitteri (1703–1786), in a style resembling that of Mellan. The work of Giovanni Volpato (1733–1803), and his famous pupil, Raphael Morghen (1758–1833), with all its prodigious skill, is decidedly devoid of life and character.

In England excellent work was done in engraving by Sir Robert Strange (1721–1792), who learnt his art in Paris, by William Woollett (1735–1785), whose landscapes after Richard Wilson especially form a real contribution to engraving, and by William Sharp (1749–1824), whose works after English portrait painters are of particular excellence.

Nineteenth Century.—Illustration in England, though it had never attained the distinction which had marked it in France, was not brought to a sudden end, as it was on the other side of the Channel, by the Revolution. A great deal of work, much of it, however, wholly or in part in stipple, was produced in this line in England at the end of the 18th and beginning of the 19th century.

The name which stands out at the period is that of William Blake (1757–1827), who, trained as a regular engraver, still executed his most characteristic and distinguished work in other mediums. The illustrations to the *Book of Job* and Young's *Night Thoughts*, wonderful as their conception is and worthy of Blake's genius, are carried out with much of the monotonous accomplishment of contemporary work, and lose, rather than gain, by the skill which Blake had acquired as a professional engraver. The popularity of Turner is reflected in the very numerous landscape engravings which were made by such engravers as W. B. and G. Cooke, John Pye, R. Brandard, E. Goodall and others, after his water colour drawings. They are usually in the form of illustrations and on a small scale, but engraving seems hardly suited to the rendering of the peculiar qualities of the great landscape painter, and, amazing as is the skill with which Turner's obviously untranslatable creations are interpreted, the dullness of entire efficiency engrosses them. This blight, and the beginning of the use of mechanical means such as machine ruling, lies over all the work produced in England, and indeed, in Europe and America, in the middle of the century. Merely reproductive as its purpose was, engraving obviously had no future in competition with the rapidly perfected photographic processes, and by the end of the century had died out almost completely.

Engraving of a less elaborate form, its technique deriving from that of the age of Dürer, had pursued its humble course almost uninterrupted through the 17th, 18th and 19th centuries in the hands of engravers of heraldic bookplates. Craftsmen like C. D. Sherborn (1831–1912) in England, did sound work in this field, and form a link which connects the recent revival of engraving since the World War within the great tradition. It is too early yet to speak of the permanence or importance of this movement, which, if partly archaistic in tendency, still derives its chief strength from the realization that the engraved line has a particular incisive beauty and character of its own, a character more circumscribed and more exacting than that which the etched line possesses. Engravers like Pieter Dupont (1870–1911) in Holland, who was perhaps the earliest rather isolated resuscitator of the medium, E. Laboureur in France, whose work in line, however, differs singularly little from his etched work, and in England younger men like Stephen Gooden, R. S. Austin and Job Nixon are doing work of originality and character. (*See* Engraving, page 188.)

BARK–CLOTH

Bark-Cloth, cloth made of the inner bark of trees, soaked, and beaten out with a club to the required thickness, is essentially both in origin and in use a tropical and sub-tropical material, its manufacture and use being found from the Congo across Africa (including Madagascar); from the Malay peninsula through Indonesia and Melanesia to Easter Island, reaching its highest perfection in Polynesia; and in the tropical regions of Central and South America. It is being ousted everywhere by the introduction of native or imported cloth, and among many tribes the art of making it is already lost. There is evidence of a far wider distribution in former times. In India the Laws of Manu ordained that a Brahman purposing to end his life in religious meditation in the forests should clothe himself in skins or bark-cloth; it is still made in the Garo hills and before the introduction of imported cotton clothes it was the usual dress of the Vedda of Ceylon. A Kayan of Borneo reverts to a strip of bark-cloth when in mourning; and in the Belgian Congo, if a Bushongo woman has lost several children, she puts on a mourning robe of bark-cloth. Folk tales of the Bushongo fix the traditional date (about 780) when bark-cloth garments superseded complete nudity. Among the Yao of Nyassaland the girls are dressed in bark-cloth during their initiation ceremonies. It was once made in New Zealand where the paper mulberry, not being indigenous, was cultivated, but both trees and industry are now dead.

The making of bark-cloth depends on several factors—the need of clothing, the existence of trees with suitable fibrous inner bark, and the discovery that this could be beaten out into "cloth." In Central America bark-cloth is common on the Mosquito coast; it provides loin-cloths for the men, skirts for the women and long sleeveless mantles for both sexes as waterproofs. In Brazil the "shirt tree" (a *Lecythis* allied to the "monkey-pot") provides a bark which needs little or no preparation. A length of the stem four or five

186

feet long is cut off, the bark is peeled off in one piece, soaked, and with two holes cut for the arms, the shirt is made. But the typical bark-cloth trees are absent from the South American forests; the less civilized natives wear no clothing, while among the more civilized cotton weaving is universal. In Africa there are numerous kinds of *Ficus* which have suitably fibrous bark. Bark-cloth was the natural clothing and an important industry in Uganda up to the middle of the 19th century. It was man's work to plant and cultivate the bark-cloth trees and make the cloth, which was used both for their ample garments and for draping the house walls, and for fines. A thick kind was also used for bed-clothes; several layers one on the top of the other two or three feet high made excellently springy beds for kings and chiefs. The "paper mulberry" (*Broussonetia papyrifera*), which is extensively cultivated in the East for paper making, grows wild in Burma, China and most of Oceania, and various kinds of *Ficus* (*F. prolixa*, *F. tinctoria*, *F. bengalensis*, the banyan tree, and *F. religiosa*, the "sacred fig tree") as well as the bread-fruit tree (*Artocarpus incisa*) are used for making bark-cloth in the islands of the Indian and Pacific oceans.

The method of making bark-cloth differed very little in the various islands. A suitable length of branch or sapling was cut, the outer bark was scraped with a shell, and the inner strips, several feet long and an inch to a few inches wide, were left to soak in water. When thoroughly soaked the strips were beaten out on a flat, hollow log with a grooved wooden mallet, frequent wetting and continuous beating felting the fibres together (occasionally gum was used) until a piece of the required size was made. In Tahiti a bale was often 200 yd. long, and a yard wide, and the wealth of a chief was estimated by the number of bales hanging from his palace roof. In Fiji a man would wind 200 yd. round and round his body as a display of wealth. The cloth was variously coloured according to the bark used, *Ficus* becoming dark brown, breadfruit lighter brown, and paper mulberry beautifully white when dried and bleached. The common cloth was often dyed with casuarina bark, but the better kinds were decorated with patterns, either sketched out and painted on by the artist, impressed by pressing leaves or flowers in the dye (Tahiti), or (in Samoa and Fiji) printed with printing boards, or by blocks made of strips of cane or midribs of palm leaves stitched on to the piece of leaf. Stencilling was found in Fiji alone. The making of *tapa* was woman's work, from princess to peasant.

In Uganda, the bark was peeled off the living tree, the third or fourth barks being usually the best, though a tree would continue to provide fresh barks for 30 or 40 peelings. . . . Different trees yielded differently coloured cloth, the common kind, when exposed to the sun, colouring light brown and better kinds terra cotta. A special tree was grown to provide pure white bark-cloths to be used at the king's coronation.

ENGRAVING

IN ITS WIDEST SIGNIFICATION, engraving is the art of cutting lines or furrows on plates, blocks or other shapes of metal, wood or other material. In this sense the craft has been used for decorative purposes from remote antiquity. In the narrower connotation with which this article is concerned, *i.e.*, engraving for the sake of printing impressions on paper or allied fabrics, the art cannot be traced back before the Christian era. By a transference of terminology, illogical but stereotyped by usage, these impressions or prints are also called engravings. In the still more limited signification of line-engraving, the art does not go back before the first half of the 15th century.

The term is used, however, in a looser sense to include all the methods of engraving, cutting or treating plates, or blocks of metal, wood or stone, for printing impressions. These methods can be classed most conveniently as: (1) *Relief prints*; (2) *Intaglio prints*; (3) *Surface prints*, according as to whether the black line of the design (*i.e.*, the part inked for printing) on the original block, plate or stone is (1) in relief, (2) in intaglio (*i.e.*, cut into the surface), (3) on the surface (*i.e.*, on a level with the rest of the surface).

These divisions correspond roughly to (1) *Woodcut and wood-engraving;* (2) *Engraving and etching on metal;* (3) *Lithography;* each class requiring a different kind of printing.

Woodcut, the earliest of the methods used for making prints, as far as records are known, whether in the East or in Europe; the furrows on the block are cut by a knife, and it is only in its later development that the graver replaces the knife, being used on sections of box-wood instead of a softer wood in the plank.

188

ENGRAVING

In the East the earliest certain date of a picture printed on paper from a wood-block occurs in a Chinese work, the *Diamond Sutra* Roll of A.D. 868 (Stein collection, British Museum), but this shows an art already in considerable development. In Europe the printing of wood-blocks on textiles was a frequent practice in the middle ages, but impressions on paper hardly date before about 1400.

The earliest *line-engravings* were probably printed a few decades later; the first dated example belongs to 1446. Line-engraving was certainly developed by the goldsmiths, having a particularly close relationship to niello work, though Vasari errs in referring the actual discovery to the Florentine niello-engraver, Finiguerra.

Etching, in which the furrow is not cut, but bitten (etched, eaten) by acid, was not practised until about 1500, the earliest dated etching belonging to 1513.

Dry-point, in which the plate is scratched with a steel point like a pencil; used occasionally from the end of the 15th century, but not to any large extent until Rembrandt's time; it has constantly been used since by etchers, either purely or in combination with etching.

Mezzotint, the earliest of the processes to aim at purely tonal effects, was discovered by Ludwig von Siegen about 1642, and practised with the greatest brilliance in the later 18th century for the reproduction of Reynolds and contemporary portrait painters.

Aquatint, another tone process, wherein the grain is achieved by etching through a porous ground, is generally supposed to have been introduced by J. B. Le Prince about 1768, though occasional examples of a similar grain may be quoted at an even earlier period than that.

Stipple, another method introduced about the middle of the 18th century, is obtained by a system of dots, first etched and then finished with the point of a curved stipple graver. A system of dots, obtained by various means such as roulettes, is also the basis of *crayon-engraving*, which imitates the character of a crayon drawing. It was the immediate forerunner and constant companion of stipple.

Many of the intaglio methods already described are occasionally found in combination on the same plate: such as line-engraving on the basis of an etched foundation (particularly in the 18th and 19th centuries); etching touched with dry-point; aquatint combined with various forms of crayon-engraving, especially by the colour engravers of the 18th century. Line-engraving, etching and other intaglio methods are sometimes found combined with woodcut or wood-engraving, notably in certain 17th and 18th century chiaroscuro engravings, and in Baxter's colour-prints in the 19th century.

Lithography was introduced by Aloys Senefelder about 1798. It may be regarded as the most direct method of imitating the character of original chalk drawing, but it possesses qualities of its own which justify its position apart from the multiplication of designs.

The following notes deal with general matters relating to engraving and prints:—

Original Engraving (etching, etc.) does not imply the original plate (block, etc.), but any print of which the engraver is his own designer.

Impression is the term applied to any print from block, plate or stone.

State signifies a stage of development in an engraving. An artist often takes impressions (or proofs) of his work at various *states* of an engraving.

Counterproof is a proof taken, not from the original plate, but from a wet impression, with the purpose of obtaining a picture in the same direction as the original plate, generally to aid the engraver in making corrections or additions to his copper.

In view of the common misconception that engraving invariably implies reproduction (for the multiplication of an original design by engraving must be clearly distinguished from an engraving which reproduces the work of another artist), it is necessary to emphasize the importance of engraving in its various manifestations as a medium of original expression, constantly appreciated and used for the sake of its own inherent and varied qualities by many of the greatest artists from the 15th century onwards.

FINE ARTS

IN A GENERAL SENSE the fine arts are those among the arts and industries which man cultivates for his necessities or conveniences, and which minister also to his *love of beauty*. Architecture, for example, providing shelter and accommodation, offers in its use and mechanic perfection visions of the

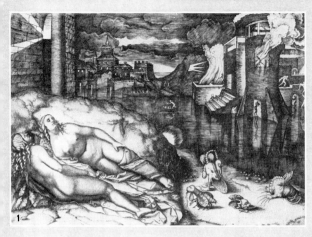

EARLY ENGRAVINGS FROM ITALY AND THE COUNTRIES NORTH OF THE ALPS

1. "Raphael's Dream" by Marcantonio Raimondi (*c.* 1480–*c.* 1530), an Italian artist who did much of his best work in association with Raphael between 1510 and 1520

2. "Battle of the Nudes," the only engraving by the Florentine painter and sculptor, Antonio Pollaiuolo (1429–98)

3. Study by the artist known as "The Master of the Playing Cards," generally considered to be the first engraver. He probably worked in South Germany or Switzerland between 1410 and 1430

4. Landscape after Rubens by *Schelte a Bolswert* (*c.* 1586–1659), one of the best of the engravers in the Rubens school

5. "St. Jerome in his Study," engraved in 1514 by Albrecht Dürer of Nuremberg (1471–1528)

6. "Joseph in Prison" by Lucas van Leyden (1494–1533), a Netherlander whose work is marked by naïve directness and delicacy of tone value

7. The right portion of the frieze, "The Battle of the Sea Gods," by Andrea Mantegna (1431–1506), Italian engraver and painter

PLATE II

LINE ENGRAVING

LINE ENGRAVINGS OF THE 15TH TO THE 20TH CENTURY

1. Illustration by William Blake (1757–1827) for the book of Job. 2. "Les Adieux" engraved (1777) by N. de Launay, the younger, after a design by J. M. Moreau, the younger (1741–1814). 3. One of the 300 engravings by the Master E. S., 15th century, German. 4. "A Woman of Scanno" by Robert Austin. Contemporary English. 5. "Mercury and Argus" engraved by J. T. Willmore (1800–63) after J. M. W. Turner (1775–1851). 6. "The Nativity" by Martin Schongauer (c. 1446–1488), German. 7. "Frockas, Count de Feria" one of the series known as Van Dyck's "Iconography." Engraved by Paul Pontius (1603–58). 8. "The Cumaean Sybil" by Andrea Mantegna (1431–1506), Italian. 9. "Louis II., Prince de Conde" Aug. 1662, engraved by Robert Nanteuil (1623–28), French

strength, fitness, harmony and proportion of parts; but also by its dispositions and contrasts of light and shade; by colour and enrichments; and by variety and relation of contours, surfaces and intervals, has decorative competence and so is accounted a fine art.   In the graphic arts we observe that love of beauty can cover the interest of visual excitement such as caricature and the grotesque.   The terrible, the painful, the squalid, the degraded,—in a word every variety of the significant,—may be brought within the province of fine art on the ground that the art of man springs from his impulse to create, and thereby associates with creation the kindred pleasure, that of witnessing and appreciating what is made to attract that interest.   In common usage there is often confusion between art-making and art-seeing as measures of art-values.   But the word *fine* has a special signification for aesthetic creation, as conditioning its power over material.

"God saw creation that it was good," and "in the image of God," we read, "man was created."   The word *image* admits the power of the artist to fine art vision and in this connection *design* has a cognate association.   On the other hand when the spectator of art finds pleasure or satisfaction in an executed work of craft, his mental exaltation comes in seeing what the creator imaged and recognizing its *fineness*.   Such recognition may come in mutual co-ordination with the spirit of the age—acting as a mass instinct in the broad sense of the designer and his clients being of one mind.   But it may go on to the schooling of temperament, and so become the conscious *taste*, acting as a gauge or rule upon the *images* of craft.   Such alternating relations and the constant varieties in human *design* and *taste* have given rise to a formidable body of speculation and discussion.   The present article, dealing with con-crete processes and the material results of the creative activities of man, de-fines them as fine art in general; classifies the fine arts in their main distinc-tions and discusses their historical aspects in various phases of image-design and taste-association.

A popular and established theory distinguishes *art* from *nature*, in that man is deliberately the fabricator of art, while nature functions outside him. Design itself is a dexterity of which one of the essential qualities is the will and premeditation of the artist.   We reckon the songs of birds as *instinctive*, and this "epithet colours the skylark's outpourings as of a different order from the poet's."   The distinction is, however, modified as we realize that the power of *imaging* has grown by natural instinct in evolution out of the desire to make.   The earliest workers in sculpture or painting were the cave-dwellers of the prehistoric ages who scratched the outlines of animals of the chase on implements or who made models of them upon their cave walls. Children can be seen still as innocent artists making for themselves, just for the pleasure of seeing what they make. So the original or rudimentary type of the architect-artists was evolved when a savage found his satisfaction in tidiness and developed an instinct of fitness in his ordering of the skins or the tree branches that covered his tent or hut. So the first artificer was a maker of club or spear to his pleasure in its handling—the primitive art-monger having small reason for pleasing anybody but himself.

As early in history the primitive dancer and singer were seeking their audiences, so the artificer wrought, with an eye to please others too. The historical sequences of art pass from *craft* to *style;* and it will be shown that as long as these were in full accord, the current association was working for an instinctive satisfaction and it has its *images* in the balanced economy of craft and taste; but when *taste* or some imported association of style began to lecture workmanship, art lost its creative will, and craft decayed.

There is accounted also a disinterested sphere for the art instinct in that the spectator has a share in the designer's ideal and a sympathetic, indirect satisfaction for himself therefrom. But the first-hand pleasure of design is that of the creative imagination; and in its spontaneous working we have engaged "incalculably complex groups of faculties, reminiscences, preferences, emotions," that constitute the *vision* of the artist. The product is a finished work of craft, and so has its power to please, graded by craft capacity. But skill in any useful art means a practised conduct of the hand, fashioning material to a particular end. The artist differs from the mechanical workman in the nature of his *images* of beauty arising in the material associations of his craft, and so he is consciously solving aesthetic problems according to the excitation of an ordering as well as a creating instinct in himself.

The conclusion is that images of beauty make the substance of the fine arts and create the several qualifications of architecture, sculpture and painting. Architecture, for example, is a *mistress art* in that its occasions demand the full substance of aesthetic vision. "The architect has liberty for the disposition of his masses, lines, colours, alternations of light and shadow, of plain and ornamented surface, and the rest." In him *material* association formulates his images, because in supplying definite accommodations, he has mechanical necessities to meet in laws of weight, thrust, support, resistance and other properties of solid matter. The sculptor and the painter, too, have

192

their spheres of action in physical appearance. But the sculptor is creating surface aspects by a mechanical tooling. He materializes his *images* by cutting them into stone, marble or wood, or by shaping them in metal, plaster, etc. The painter finds to his hand a more extended range of natural facts and appearances, because his pictorial images are flat on a plane surface, as worked in terms of his painting tools. In all three fine arts, however, the artist's operation has its every bloom and virtue, in the nature of a material regulation. The rank of artistry may be gauged by the spectator, but the working test has been the artist's power to grasp and realize his vision in the terms of his craft. It is claimed for the fine arts that their ideality of form and colour is a sort of "play—a free vent for an energy over and above what is needed to be spent upon the conservation, perpetuation or protection of life." However, the superfluous or optional character of art is that it comes in the instinctive gratification of a free creative choice and by such transmitted pleasure, public taste is gratified.

We are following in general terms R. G. Collingwood's *Outlines of the Philosophy of Art* in that he defines art (1) as the creation of objects, or the pursuit of activities called works of art by people called artists—works distinguished as products intended to be beautiful; (2) as the creation of objects or the pursuit of activities called artificial as opposed to natural—that is objects created or activities pursued by human beings consciously free to control their natural impulses and to organize their life on plan; (3) as creating that frame of mind which we call artistic, the frame of mind in which we are aware of beauty. While the mechanical pleasure of tool-using bridges the distinction between art and industry—so the spiritual sense of the *image* brings fine art into line with literature and music—which are not arts of objective completion, but of powers of interpretation.

The systematists of the 19th century thought themselves competent to grade the fine arts in terms of philosophical analysis. Hegel ranged architecture, sculpture and painting as coming in a natural order of evolution—ancient architecture the expression of obscure symbolic ideas; sculpture the classic passage into clear-cut, lucid thought; painting the modern sum of romantic ideality. Herbert Spencer seems to track out the passage from ancient to modern—as one from the hieratic simplicity of the architectural monument to the decorative complexity of the sculptural and pictorial uses of advanced city life, and finally in our civilization, the elaborate and emotional complex which moderns account as the art of the picture. Such analysis can be seen to rank the painter's genius as the ultimate crystallization. And in this sense art history is read nowadays as character analysis, and written up as a sublimation of temperament. Criticism was initiated when Vasari wrote the lives of the Renaissance painters in 1550, and to this day we have his successors, decorating the story of art with literary values. The temperamental factor in the development of painting has been well studied by D.S. MacColl, who distinguishes three outstanding varieties: "The Olympian painter," he says, "is king and master in a world made for his use; he is on the gods' side and his art mirrors their perfection of form, their happiness in majesty of calm possession. The Titan is rebel against the Powers, his spirit is of passion and strife"; and his art develops as a social revolution. A third temperament is of the mystic who "seeks in humility and meekness values outside things visible," and recognizing the nothingness of assertion, surrenders his perception of reality to an inner sense of second-sight. With increasing distinctness in the last 300 years the temperamental conditions of fine art have marbled the basal colouring of the picture habit in associations of schools and cliques. Olympians, Titans and mystics appear master individualities, linking up the Renaissance with our painting. Olympian graces appear in pictorial procession from Raphael's allegories to the flattered portraits of humanity and circumstance which have in the 16th, 17th and 18th centuries made the staple of fashionable master craft. In idyllic atmospheres have been stayed the contentments of the Dutch and French *genre*, its domestic atmosphere and homely landscape; and similarly the poetry and pleasantry of the English academicians has been steeped in a mild-mannered geniality. Titan mentality must be allowed to the painter scientist, such as Leonardo da Vinci; to Rembrandt adventuring into untrodden paths of chiaroscuro; to Salvator Rosa brigand hunting in the wild; to Breughel sidling away to the fair-booth and *kermesse* dance. So too were the high-handed despisers of convention, Hogarth and Goya, handing on the torch to the rebellious anarchists of the French painting cliques. Yet there was the line of mystics too—Giorgione painting he knew not what; Velázquez finding a new wonder in the focus of the eye; El Greco imagining a chaos of line and colour; Blake making his mystery of ghostly hope and fear; Turner adventuring flights into the glory of the air; or Corot painting a fairy light for spring-time willows.

Temperament and circumstance have had to make literary standard values of fine art. Taine has laid stress on the vicissitudes of racial and

194

political development for initiating or repressing pictorial genius. Fromentin, however, questions such deduction, observing how the Dutch innocence and simplicity were no reflection of the stirring life and dramatic heroism of the Netherlands revolt from Spain: whereas French painting in the 19th century was moulded continually to the trend of revolutionary politics. Latterly our experts are laying less stress on philosophical analysis and we may summarize the 20th century appraisement of art as, seeking practical definition, Sir C. J. Holmes in his *Notes on the Science of Picture-Making* gives the present-day conditions that govern picture practice.

"All great art, being emphatically personal, is accompanied by variation from previously existing standards of excellence. This personal variation is marked by a new intensity of feeling, by a new sense of vitality and by a new rhythm of pattern. All great artists are pioneers possessing these characteristics. In their followers, the second-rate artists, we find less intensity of feeling, less vitality and a feebler rhythmical sense. Emotion is the keystone of painting as it is of poetry. What is not strongly felt is no material for the artist. The painter's emotion sums up and concentrates his experiences (imaginative or visual) in terms of rhythmical paint as the poet does in terms of rhythmical words. Theory is not a substitute for talent, but its necessary teacher. Principles of design are not rigid moulds into which the subject-matter of a work has to be squeezed. Their task is to suggest to the artist the particular means, by which each given subject can be perfectly expressed. Tradition is no more than the body of principles, which secure conformity between art and its contemporary environment. What is a perfect tradition for one period or climate may thus be a fatal influence in another period or climate, because it does not fit the changed conditions. Hence the danger of revivals of old methods. Systems of art teaching have commonly failed from not recognizing the necessity of progress, from enslavement to a fixed canon of ideal beauty. No such fixed canon of ideal beauty can be set up as a standard for future achievement. We cannot do again what has already been done by a great artist; we must do something different. Each field of artistic activity is exhausted by the first great artist who gathers a full harvest from it."

Art history in successions of style and in appraisement of art value has no verdict to offer as to what is *great art* in definition of greatness. We may say that fine artistry is figuration, yet also transfiguration; but to be proficient in his craft is the artist's necessity for himself; to be ideal is his instinct, for so he assures partnership with the spectator. Art history has been a serial evolution of art instincts crystallizing into styles. Their succession in world history may be indexed as ancient, classic, mediaeval and modern, but this is just to link up art manifestations with phases of human progress.

PROGRESSIVE ASPECT OF ARTS AND CRAFTS

The Magic or Attributive.—The primitive instincts of fine art can be taken as promotions of physical advantage, in handling a weapon, say, or as required for the successful covering of a hut. Then secondly, as adding to these instinctive joys the design-value of *taste*. The imitative representation of deer and mammoth upon weapons, the modelling and painting of animals in cave interiors were purposed "power" in magic sense:—the aesthetic capacity was insurance to the "devotee" of success in the chase—or such a control over the quarry as would, by creating its image to the hunter's mind, bring it to his hand. The visioned reality was started in the sense of a religious exercise, as setting up profitable commerce with the unseen. Prehistoric art in Europe had millenniums of evolution, and in the height of its accomplishment toned form and colour into "images," that sophisticated art calls primary elements of design. Then in later cave paintings graphic sense loses touch with reality, passes into symbol and pattern, and so originates the alphabet—mind usurping the domain of craft.

The Hieratic and Palatial.—Political and religious intention evolved art aspects for both palaces and temples in many eras of earliest Asian arts. The cycles of Sumerian, Chaldean and Babylonian dominion illustrate the successions of conquering civilizations in the delta of the great rivers; on the back lands came the sinister aspects of Assyrian dominion; in central Asia Minor the Hittite; and later at Persepolis the Persian art. In the Nile basin were mounting to artistic fruition and dying away five dynastic periods of Egyptian style—succeeding one another in eras of 800 years or so. Priest and Pharaoh in long tradition controlled architecture, painting and sculpture, up to and even past the Hellenistic development of Greek style. The linking up of Egyptian craft design with magic is illustrated in the tomb-tablet of the Egyptian Mertissen where we read—*c.* 2200 B.C. "I was an artificer skilled in my art. I knew my art, how to represent the forms of going forth and returning—so that each limb was in its proper place. I knew how the figure of a man should go—the poising of the arm to bring the hippopotamus low—the carriage of a woman. I knew to make amulets against fire burning or floods

196

drowning. No man could do this but I and the son of my body. Him has the God decreed to excel in art and I have seen his perfection in every sort of precious stone—in gold, in silver, in ivory and in ebony."

However, in the discovery of the Akhenatan cult and the Tutankhamen tomb there is record of a curious but short-lived break away from the craft formality of the Egyptian tradition. There came a generation of freer mentality and naturalistic observation before hieratic sway returned. The Egyptian connection has not been made clear with what excavation has revealed in Crete and other parts of the eastern Mediterranean basin. But a highly developed architecture of city building and palace decoration has been unearthed, showing *fresco* of high accomplishment, and works of relief modelling, that are of ordered and well-schooled taste. The successive periods are dated beside the later Egyptian eras, and in domestic and graphic expressions there were anticipated the furnishing and decorative crafts of the Italian Renaissance. The pottery, especially, was remarkable for a free rendering of flowers; the modelled animals in metal are distinct from the hieratic conventions of Egypt and Assyria. But to its art era came the dissipation of craft interest following on the commercial distribution of art products. There came, too, a razing of the Minoan palace-cities that had been the centres of this Mediterranean culture, and it passed away with small contribution to the genius of the "classic" style that was to register the next cycle of civilization.

The Classic Aspect.—Ancient art in Babylonia and Egypt was of local cult; its eras rose and fell with the dynastic empires and religions of the Near East. A wider area than the Mediterranean basin was due to the European era of style that came in the Greek and Roman developments of Hellenic civilization. A local nucleus of Dorian immigration and culture had descended from mid-Europe into a Mediterranean expansion in the 6th and 5th centuries B.C., strong enough to displace kindred evolutions, Ionian, Phoenician and Etruscan. After the Hellenic prime at Athens, there followed in Alexander's conquests the wide Hellenistic diffusion in displacement of Oriental survivals. Then in the 1st century B.C. the Roman empire-making founded a world-art, under the tutorship of Alexandrian craft, but under the aegis of Greek literature also. For 500 years the classic educations of society were controlling craft, and in them the classic arts flourished, declined and fell with the decay of the Roman empire of the west. In descent from it a decorative, aniconic graft of Greek craftsmanship remained to bear fruit in the

Christian empire of Byzantium; so that in due course arch and dome with concrete surfacing of structure were propagated in the Arab overflow of the Moslem faith. But neither Byzantine, nor Moslem art could secrete the *ethos* of Greek construction, nor the *images* of Greek humanism. The sculptural and pictorial arts of west Europe may claim to be Byzantinesque, but never, till the modern revivals, could architecture as a fine art think itself Greekesque.

The evolution, dispersion and decline of the Hellenic cult are a well-documented instance of a cycle with dominance for some centuries of culture. The essential national creation had been that of settlers in Greece, Dorian and Ionian stocks whose issue was expressed in the marble temple that had a human beauty enshrined in the material of its exercise. In humanity and simplicity Hellenic culture had an outlook on life that freed religion from the monster-godships which Minoan, Assyrian and Egyptian art had imaged. Greek sense dethroned the witch-doctor, and in the national piety of a citizen priesthood achieved its marble Parthenon. Hellenic sculpture was humanity in being, with the athlete as its model of manhood, and the maid as that of womanhood. The painting crafts resolved line and tone into an intellectual analysis of light, which in the Greek vase was shaped and figured as a ritual music. But the architect as chief craftsman, and the sculptor as priest of art came to be exploited abroad in literary translation of Hellenistic phrasing. Commercial associations of artists were engaged to found new cities and to set up Hellenistic types and standards of human beauty. In the grouping and arrangement of decorative themes the craftsman became a man of artistic choice: his dexterities were specialities in the sophisms of academic direction. The sculptor set portraiture of emotion and dress by the side of traditional representations of the gods and heroes. So the curve of Greek art passed on from Hellenic simplicity into Hellenistic elaboration and obtained the patronage of Roman culture; illustrating how craft associations first image style and then find their energy sapped by the extraneous association of learning. Hellenic art made its temple the crown and centre of a city's devotion; but the city of Athens lost its art when the idealisms of the Greek worship obtained cultured and political currency. Men and women had been deified in Greek sculpture—in Roman the imperial power was immortal, and for an emperor's divinity art formalized an imperial priesthood of fine art from Britain to Mesopotamia. Greece had been content with a simple constructive system of columns and horizontal entablatures; and in marble unity had invented and perfected her three successive modes, or orders of architecture—Doric, Ionic and Corinthian (*qq.v.*). But the genius of Rome found her imperial destiny in the dome and the triumphal arch. Her conglomerate creed covered Europe even as the Pantheon ceiled the lounge of her public bath. Her cosmos was graded as her amphitheatres were graded for her public shows. Indeed the triumphal arch, not the pediment, was symbol of her sovereignty: a vast constructiveness—temple, palace, bath, amphitheatre, forum and aqueduct, ordered and levelled her proletarian empire to be uniform in its imperial arts as in its legionary garrison. In the Roman house memorial sculpture was its ancestral cult, and filled the atrium with portrait statutes and busts, and dilettante scholarship had a corresponding piety to the past in copies or studies of the ancient masterpieces in wall paintings of classic subject and perspective fancy. In the crafts of ancient Rome was consummated a decorating capacity that passed on to Byzantium, in turn bequeathing its *récipés* to mediaeval church-building.

Mediaeval Aspects.—The break up of west European civilization was completed in the barbarian over-runnings. For one year (A.D. 410) the great Rome is said to have been without a single inhabitant. Free painting and free sculpture ceased to exist and Italy lost or discontinued the crafts of building. For 500 years Christian churches took derelict columns and architraves from pagan pillar avenues, using for their halls of religious service, arcades and apses from the market places of deserted cities. It was for the Byzantinesque Christians to use the big square bays of the Roman bath, and with dome construction to attach to its rubble surfaces mosaic pictures. But the free statue, in the religious cult of the East had come under interdict, and for 600 years the sculptural arts were degraded to rudimentary and subordinate uses, to a graphic pettiness of ivory-carving and metal-chasing. Painting assumed a rigid hieratic imagery for the mosaic pictures of apses and vaults of churches, or was practiced in manuscripts and service-books according to the recipes of a cloistered monkish craft. The Carlovingian clergy of Gaul and Germany had service-books and ivories as school text-books; but specially in earliest advance were the English crafts of sculpture and painting, appearing foremost in recovery of a religious freedom.

In Celtic-Nordic genius there matured the new aspects of fine art, but for them Romanesque and Gothic had as trainers and instructors the monastic institutions, which in or about the year 1000 under the patronage of the papal hierarchy were dominating European culture. Under the Cluniac expansion of abbey-building was propagated a gospel of craft practice for all the arts and sciences of life. As Dorian stock and Ionian schooling established the marble accomplishment of Greece, so the fine art of stone found in the mixture of race and church culture the cradle of an era. Stone was the preciosity wrought, masoned, sculptured and lifted to the sky. The built church was the service-book of Christian civilization in which all the philosophy of four centuries wrote itself as art. In Cluniac sculpture the figure grew out of the stone, and the statue out of the pillar; in the Cistercian abbey fine art was the mason's refinement of structural economy; in the secular and episcopal schooling of religious pomp and circumstance came the towering majesty of the Gothic cathedral. In the 13th century the mason had taken fine art to the summit of craft execution. But in France before the end of it the vitality of cathedral structure was ceasing to animate masonry and the tool of the carver became specious for the accomplishment of the ivory image or the enamelled casket. The master-masonry of French architecture traversed Europe, but as inventive of style there had succeeded the decorated creation of the English 14th century to which associations of chivalry lent an aesthetic life. This was especially distinguished in memorial tombs, and in the sculpture of recumbent effigies worked by the English masons. In mid-14th century came the Black Death pestilences contributing such a set-back to the association of art and chivalry. There succeeded commerces of art furniture, and shop-use dictating the architectural enrichments of sculpture and painting. For two centuries Burgundian sculpture and Flemish painting acted as sponsors to a northern Renaissance, in which French Flamboyant with its veneers of decorative tracing made a last stand for continuance of Gothic style in architecture.

The phases of fine art practice ran their course with little distinctions of individuality in the artist. One mason or another made good in the quality of his work in association with the spirit of his time. Sculpture as *imaging* thought was still work of a *coementarius* or builder. After 1300 his capacity as king's mason, or goldsmith or as painter might take him into special appointment. But it was *c.* 1400 that the Sluters were sculptors, and the Van Eycks painters under the patronage of the dukes of Burgundy in formulating a new accomplishment for personal artistry. In Italy Pisani, Siennese and Florentines, painters and sculptors, emerging from the body of church furnishers, claimed fine art consciousness among their fellow craftsmen, and established cities as centres of special craft. For Italy had never taken Gothic

200

style to its heart as the economic realization of stone construction, with enthusiasm for covering the greatest area and lifting the highest vault. By 1400 there had come to Italian art another quest, that of regathering the threads of the Byzantine arts of form and colour, to reweave the tapestry of classic scholarship.

Following the migration westward of Greek scholars, the classic forms of architecture became the study of Roman architects such as Brunelleschi and Alberti. But a more subtle sense of renewal attended the achievements of sculpture and painting, as Donatello and Masaccio took study of nature as a joy of life. For this renaissance was the ascetic ideal giving place to the physical. In power, beauty and grace the personages of the Christian faith and story were put into visible kindred with the heroes of ancient paganism. Not as pedantry merely, but in the experiment of craft was fine art the heir of both antiquity and Christianity. The 15th century set Florence in the high place of art, in that she had become mistress of a culture at once scientific and religious, that had fine art and fine industry in united fellowship and competence to express the stirring life of republics, prince despots and church potentates, military captains and merchant princes vying with one another as patrons of the artist. There came a wealth of occasions for sculpturing and picturing, for monuments of civic and personal commemoration, for representations of pageantry and battle, for the allegoric conception of sacred and profane story. The Italian accomplishment of the *cinquecento* practised the heroic painting of fresco for the walls of council halls, for princes' palaces and popes' churches; classic loggias were furnished with marble and bronze statues; churches had pillared screens and monuments; while every city square showed its shrine or fountain; and every chapel its painted altar-piece. We may speak of this as a rebirth of artistic crafts but it was also the discovery of the *artist* as a man. A well patronized painter of illuminations, visiting Rome in 1536, has recorded himself as meeting Michelangelo and saying, "You Italians give the greatest honour, the greatest nobility and power to be more, to a man who is a splendid painter and sculptor, not as other nations do to generals and statesmen. With you as compared with great princes it is a painter alone that is called divine."

In this golden age came the use by painters of oil prepared as a drying pigment. With brighter and more facile brush technique than tempera-decorations, or the plasterer's art of wet fresco, studio or work-shop pictures became portable chattels in detachment from architectural structure. Thus were lost the intimate religious connections of fine art with altar use, as well as its broad treatments on chapel wall-surfaces. The brush attuned to new capacities of illustration and sensation, equipped the picture artist in Italy and northern Europe alike, for fresh fields of adventure, in which moral and aesthetic sensations had place. In a new capacity Italian purveyors of accomplished design were brought into the service of German emperors and French and English kings. The new art arrived for Europe in a succession of schools as Italian, Flemish, Dutch, Spanish, French and English "national" interpretations of a faculty that enriched the special fineness of the painter's art. But when Leonardo da Vinci as the honoured artist passed into the service of the dukes of Milan, when Raphael at Rome was the accepted decorator of the papal court, the artist-painter was no longer of one city, or of one ideal. Venetian colour had its commission as well as Florentine science and Titian was educated for a world-wide currency, as had been Michelangelo. They had become the representative European artists when subject-painting discovered that technical facility could replace religious idealization. With Raphael, Titian and Coreggio, art made terms with classic allegory, and, in the discovery of the palette sense, Titian and Rubens founded the dynasties of temperamental artistry. They were painters, courtiers and diplomats, as purveyors of authorized masterpieces. Rubens with his pupils and assistants, Van Dyck, Snyders, Teniers, etc., at work on courtly portraiture, on fleshly allegory, on boars and tigers, on tavern scenes, landscapes and village fêtes was in all just the Renaissance expert, commissioned to furnish art pieces for princely and private galleries and alike for church, palace or civic hall. His great work was a canvas fitted into the allotted space in wall surface; an exhibition entity in honour of the great art of painting.

Portraiture beyond the Alps, however, long kept to its mediaeval economics, and serious workmanship. Painters and engravers such as Dürer and Holbein were vowed to associations of design in craft essentially Gothic. The trades of the furniture arts in Brussels, Bruges or Antwerp, were scarcely touched by scholarship. But by 1600 the painter had been to Rome and Venice for his authorized education, and Rubens in the fire of his prodigious temperament, with true fusion of Flemish and Venetian qualities, in closing the Renaissance period was handing on an *art nouveau*. His Olympian creed, *Catholic* in its association with the Roman Church, and *Classic* in the doctrines of Roman virtuosity ruled taste for half the world. The gilded luxury of it became an accepted tradition for all the craft interests of civilization and, for some two hundred years, the fine arts in all European countries were accepting the Italian pedantries of design. The Palladian orders, popularized as patterns, or examples of ancient scholarship, and their materializing in stone, were propaganda for that new vision of art which established correctness to pattern that became the stock in trade of accomplished architectures in France and the Low Countries, in mid Europe and Spain, and at last in England, each country conforming its style to its assimilation of book knowledge, but still by means of material needs, instincts and traditions, capable of giving to classic uniformity a national economy of style.

The 17th, 18th and 19th Centuries.—In Italy the outstanding figure of the 17th century was that of the architect and sculptor Bernini. In works of fountain and monument he visioned a new sensibility for masonry, that has acquired the name of Baroque. The Palladian conventions were endowed with a specious virtuosity of curved and flowing rhythm that remained in the Latin countries for long the accepted trade-mark of classic decoration. Its free modelling and clear colour scale was specially the birthright of Jesuit Rococo, which, born of the counter Reformation was carried round the world in the Catholic churches of the Spanish and Portuguese Indies. In Baroque and Rococo was the era of fine workmanship that for two centuries adorned Italian, Flemish and French styles. Art-workers grouped for the production of what is useful and fine in its degree—who deserved the place and name that the ancient Greek gave them in the word Τέκτων (artificers)—initiated a style of salon decoration and furniture, for which Louis XIV.'s minister Colbert organized a system of State factories and academies of art. The architectural stylist had at his beck figure sculptors, picture painters, potters, weavers, smiths, gold workers, glass and china makers. In forms of rococo artificiality every natural form was translated with no restraint of either structural or religious conscience. The variety and exuberance of craft device, with its perfect finish, made the Louis periods text-books for decorative magnificence in Europe.

Fashion and the grand sentiment of gala were ruling the technique of the art of painting, by the side of devotional and classical association. The sentiment of parlour and tavern was translated by Fleming and Hollander into picture truth. In the wide stretches of the Netherlands were shore and sea, and specially air vision indoor and outdoor. In portraiture and landscape the Flemish-Dutch school of realists were painters of air from 1600 to 1670. The great magician was Rembrandt, able to conjure with the textures of light and darkness and to figure thereby not merely natural aspects but the problems of human individuality. The shadow mystery of his world was progenitor of much that in modern painter's art has become orthodoxy.

A painter too of air and light contemporary in the Spaniard Velázquez, whom the Renaissance had bred with the Flemish sense of adventure. Sensitive to the visual and subtle perspective of mutual values, he staged figures and objects in space—accepting the eye-focus as the interpreter of visible relations and reactions. Another outstanding master of the aerial scholarship was the French painter Claude Lorrain, who avowedly went to Rome to found his radiant vision on the landscape of the Roman campagna and the adjacent hills and coasts. The Poussin brothers beside him added to classical composition an impressionist figuring of sacred and profane images. Such were new scholarships of art outside the Rococo currency of the Colbert workshops. Then came the art engraver of the latter part of the 18th century with his golden age on the skirts of the traditions of the cinquecento. At first the great masters of Italian and then of Dutch painting were circulated in black and white in a way their original work had not contemplated. Soon in many industrious crafts, draughtsmen of the 17th and 18th centuries discovered tone qualities and rendered black and white in the full body of mezzotint or in refinements of line texture such as copper engraving achieves. The vast widening of the picture field for domestic walls or for illustrative connoisseurship made the dawning of the modern period; but there was a setting, too, of much of that sense of dedication that belonged to themes that had been those of religious and classic scholarship. It was symptomatic of the cycle of art, that in breaking through its banks the fine art of painting ran afield into shallows.

The 18th century era for English painting was to mature in the new horizons of pictorial adventure. The aristocratic portraitures of Reynolds and Gainsborough had been those of close allegiance to the tradition of the Fleming Van Dyck, who, the immediate pupil of Rubens, had himself drawn from the Venetians. Gainsborough and Wilson, too, English pastoral landscapists, were of the Claude school. But Hogarth proclaimed himself a rebel spirit, with the petulant assertion that the English world was to his hand to give him picture sense uncommitted to classic prescriptions—with no Olympian serenity to gloss a "Cheapside" medley or a "Shrimp Girl's" portrait. Then, too, in humble guise the typographical illustrator, for the pride of country gentlemen's seats, drew and coloured landscape settings to architectural views. But from this low estate the English water colourist was to rise to esteem; and though his place in the English academy was denied him, yet by the end of the 18th century great masters, like Crome and Constable, were oil and water painters both and it was water-colour artistry that carried Turner into acknowledged pre-eminence as a great modern master of fine art.

In Europe, eclectics of the 17th and 18th centuries had arisen outside the main Italian traditions; Carpaccio, Tiepolo, Canale and Longhi, errant stars rising and setting in the twilight of the Venetian decadence; Piranesi, a Roman etcher had a mystic sense of horror; his contemporary Blake in England toned visions of sanctified joy, toned to meek expressions of line and colour. In Spain the forerunner, initiate to the mystic significance of the modern cult was Goya, at once impressionist and hypnotic, "smearing his canvas with paint as a mason plasters his wall," a composer of the "Caprices" and "Misères de la Guerre" with the protesting energy of a French Revolutionist.

The antique graces of the old tradition still haunted the shrine of art, and in the latest years of the century we see a symptomatic return to severer principles and purer lines of scholarship from the Baroque and the Rococo. The pure and rhythmic grace of the English Flaxman in its sense of classic design was scarcely sculpture. In Italy came the over-honeyed accomplishments of Canova and his school; and with scarcely robuster fibre were the statue works of the Norwegian, Thorwaldsen, practising in Rome; in France were graphic appreciations of classic virtue as read in Livy; in England the 19th century opened with a mild classicality and much pastoral and idyllic work of agreeable but shallow elegance; and the Nazarene school of German painting expended itself in a religious expression of singular insipidity. For French painting, however, the classic movement with roots in the associations of the French Revolution and attitudinizing as Roman virtue obtained a technical reality of picture force in David. There were, too, an accomplished purity and sweetness in Prud'hon's "nude" idylls. But the last and truest classic of France, Ingres, who was at the same time in portraiture a modern realist, painted on into the romantic era. With Géricault and Delacroix, romance had its literary associations rampant for two generations; but by side of them, French landscape painting had got inspiration from the English Constable. Thus in the second quarter of the 19th century the curtain was being lifted for the drama of creative progress that was to be staged for French and English art.

Modern Aspects of Art and Craft.—The 19th century was seeking its *vision* of fine art in the association of painting quality with representative mimicry. The title artist had become the monopoly of the picture-making class committed to the figuring of nature; the architect was accounted just a draughtsman of style—and sculptors might shape and carve as nude model reproducers. In literary use the word "art" came to be accepted for what is put into a frame or hung in an exhibition. As a prophet of imitative reality the art critic established his reputation. Europe recovered its power to breed artists in academies when word-power stocked studios; in architecture the battle of style was fought between the religious and the pagan; scientifically the Greek revival read itself into porticoed churches and pillared railway stations; garden landscapes were primed with pepper-box "Parthenons"; *national* taste protested itself romantic in the Elizabethan lodge and the castellated *picturesque*—and Christian faith materialized in sham Gothic and in clearing out 18th century galleries and pews from historic churches. In literature England and the Continent were founding the "romantic" of history and the "wild" of nature, and for two generations Victorian picture habit sought pictorial success in tags of sentiment and took poetic description as accredited art material. In period furniture, arts and crafts revived an auctioneer's aptitude for descriptive title, and found credit in affected reproduction of the antique. The popularity of the Gothic movement of church revival may be said to have baptized the pre-Raphaelite coterie of painters. But with Ruskin's benison came the rejection of much time-honoured science of academic composition and brush handling; and there was new confirmation of the painter's colour-sense in the pictorial *vision* reforming itself. Victorian art had an era of creative abundance with the slick summaries of Millais, and the stark realism of Ford Madox Brown; in the over-studied archaeology of Holman Hunt as in the poetry and impassioned mediaevalism of Rossetti and Burne-Jones; equally in Orchardson's historical and social occasions and in Whistler's "Nocturnes" or Albert Moore's mannequins—in fact, picture poetry stormed art as it had literature. There was novelette absorption, too, of both sculpture and painting in France; in the *Salon* exhibitions, and the *place* and *boulevard* pieces of Carpaux and Dalon. We have Bartholemé in his procession of the dead entering the tomb staged as a Dantesque masterpiece; Rodin working stone or bronze into textured poems—as psychical occasions rendered, with the metre and terseness of a quatrain. Though an ugly philosophy has distorted art in some continental schools we have had French caricature and English humour in *black and white* playing its part in social morality. Daumier, and the woodcut illustrators of the English '60s and their successors cannot all be accused of Freudian tenets.

Still the French experimenters were shifting all the practical tenets that had been gospel for the painting arts. The craft vision of modern art-workers promulgated as science plays for the literary stage. Writing in the 11th edition of the *Encyclopaedia Britannica*, Sir Sidney Colvin said: "The movements of the Impressionists, the Luminists, the Neo-Impressionists, the Post Impressionists and Cubists, initiated in Paris, have been eagerly adopted and absorbed, or angrily controverted and denounced, or simply neglected and ignored according to the literary equipment of groups of artists and fashions of critics; there has been a vast amount of heterogeneous, hurried, confident and clamant innovating activity in this direction and in that, much of it perhaps doomed to futility in the ages of posterity but at any rate there has not been stagnation."

Written 25 years ago this should be supplemented by a further analysis of the 20th century aspects of art and craft. Much of the hope that Morris and his coadjutors introduced into craft has been drowned in the increasing industrial flood. Are we marking time for some new values of fine art to take their place in the social system? Perhaps so! But the associations of education are at present confining capacity to commercial specialities of knowledge, and as they have done so vocation and profession have grown neglectful of the universal issues. Learning has become fitted into grooves, running in which, craft—whether as labour or commerce is regardless of common appreciations, and only half educated for the practical purposes of life. If in such words, also, we rank the present output of all the fine arts, we necessarily accept as sponsor for it the social revolution of the 20th century which is rapidly bringing the whole world into a single community, and making fine art an individual pursuit, ceasing with the artist.

WOODCUTS AND WOOD-ENGRAVING

TO-DAY THE WOODCUT is used as a direct expression of artists who themselves cut and print the block. During the greater part of its history the medium has been used quite differently. It has been a reproductive process; a craft rather than an art. Craftsmen have cut out of the block drawings made for the purpose by artists and then passed the block to other craftsmen for printing. This is comparable to our photo-engraving reproductive process—the difference being that the older method was done by hand whereas the present one is mechanical. In both cases the method was merely a means to an end and quite detached from the original conceptions of the artists involved. In making drawings for reproduction, either by woodcut or photo-engraving, artists are thinking in terms of ink or pencil lines on paper—not of lines which their hands are carving out of wood. A work so detached from its medium does not exploit the peculiar quality of that medium. It lacks unity and completeness. It loses force. For some ten centuries of its known history the woodcut, as a process, has been so handicapped. Only during the last thirty or forty years has it arrived at what might be called its full functioning maturity.

TECHNICAL PROCESSES

TECHNICALLY SPEAKING the woodcut is pictorial type. It prints pictures as type prints letters of the alphabet, by raised lines or areas that catch ink from a roller and deposit it on paper under moderate and more or less even pressure. This analogy roots in history as well as fact. The first printed letters were woodcut type carved into pictorial woodcut blocks in explanation of the picture. The first movable type was a cutting up of this block type in order to save labour by rearrangement and re-using. The woodcut raised line is the opposite of the intaglio, or sunken line, which is etched or engraved on copper. In the print etched or engraved lines catch the light and cast minute shadows, thus giving a life or sparkle to the work that is impossible with any other mediums. The woodcut gives a flat surface print, with an

208

interplay of solid black and white, and a slightly varying texture and intensity that is quite unique.

The raised line of the woodcut is simply a part of the original untouched surface of a block or plank of wood; if no cutting away were done the print from this block would be solid black. Each stroke of the tool removes a section of the ink-holding surface, thus preventing its printing and letting of the white of the unprinted paper into the black of the printed. Like the world at dawn, the woodcut-picture actually emerges from blackness into light.

There are two kinds of woodcuts, the black line and the white line. The black line, or woodcut proper, is one for which a drawing is made on the block and all spaces between lines gouged out or cut away. In other words a black line drawing is reproduced in approximate (but never complete) facsimile. The black lines are conscious lines. The white lines or spaces are left-overs which receive either secondary or no consideration *per se*. In the white line cut, or engraving, the reverse holds; the white line that is gouged out will receive first attention, the black lines and spaces between, second. In the first case the artist conceives his drawing as starting with white paper and growing towards black; in the second as emerging from black into light, as in actual fact it does. Both systems have their advantages but the second, or white line, being the natural method, because it makes a positive instead of a negative use of each gouge or cut, would seem to be the most logical.

Cutting the Block.—The black line cut is ordinarily made on a plank or block of soft wood like beech, apple, pear, cherry, sycamore or whitewood cut parallel to the grain as in ordinary lumber. Preferably it is of type height (about $\frac{7}{8}$ in. as shown in fig. 48), planed and sanded to a perfectly smooth and level surface, and cut with a sharp knife. An ordinary pen knife will serve as a makeshift, but the carver (fig. 47) set in a cord-wrapped handle is better. The knife makes a sloping cut which tapers upward along each side of each line, thus supporting the line on a widened base (as shown in fig. 48).

When two lines are close together and parallel the sloping cuts on adjacent sides of each would remove a V-section between them. This V-cut can be made with one stroke instead of two by using the "V" or parting tool shown in fig. 47. Larger areas are removed with gouges of varying widths and depths (fig. 47). The method requires, as is readily seen, two or more cuts to release a single black line—two if the lines are in a parallel and close-together series, four if a line is segregated, and anywhere up to eight if the lines are cross-hatched. (*See* A, B, and C, respectively, fig. 48.) Laborious, round-about, forced—such is the reproductive black-line method.

The white line is engraved, rather than cut, into the end-grain of very fine hard wood, usually box-wood. The box-wood blocks are about $\frac{7}{8}$ in. high

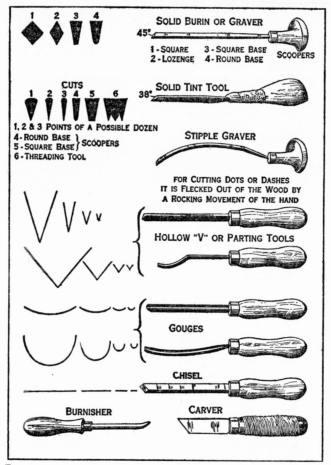

FIG. 47.—TYPES OF TOOLS USED IN WOOD ENGRAVING, AND SHAPES OF CUTS

and across the grain. Into this hard fine grain lines are gouged out with hollow V- or U-shaped parting tools or gouges, or with solid metal burins or scoopers. All these tools are shown in their varying widths, depths and shapes in fig. 47. The burins, tint-tools and scoopers are held in the palm of the hand (Plate I.), and pushed forward; the threading tool cuts several lines at once. The knife in cutting is pulled toward the body and may be held as shown in Plate I., fig. 3 or grasped as one would grasp a dagger. Chisels may be pushed by the hand or hit with a wooden mallet. In the process of cutting, the block is held on a leather bag filled with sand. The left

DESIGNS OF BARK CLOTH MADE IN THE TROPICAL REGIONS

1. A Fiji Island design
2. A Samoan pattern which was apparently suggested by imported calico

3. A Tapa pattern beaten out in the Hawaiian Islands
4. A Tapa pattern from the Fiji Islands
5. A Tapa pattern from the Island of Samoa

PLATE II

BARK–CLOTH

NATIVE WOMEN MAKING BARK CLOTH OR TAPA AND IMPLEMENTS USED IN DOING SO

1. Native woman outlining designs for painting on a strip of tapa, which is spread out on the grass in front of their houses

2. Sections of tapa showing it in its finished and decorated state and the implements used in making tapa

3. A wooden beater used by the natives of the Uganda region, in Africa, in making their bark cloth, a section of which is shown behind the beater

4. Tongan women, of the Samoan region, beating the strips of tapa on a log with rude implements

5. A native of New Guinea preparing a strip of bark cloth for a belt

hand holds and turns the block easily against the pressure of the cutting tool in the right. (Plate I., fig. 2.)

Fundamentally, the methods of the white and the black line woodcuts are the same in the actual technical process and the ultimate end achieved. In the black line cut the cutter is conscious only of the black lines he is reproducing; in the white line engraving he is exploiting the white lines, at the same time being fully conscious of the blacks by which he must obtain the whites. Xylography is a general title that covers both methods.

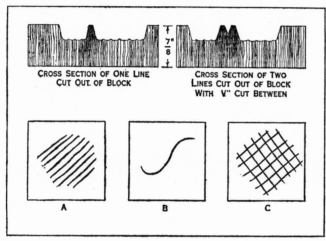

FIG. 48

In etching and pencil drawing (*qq.v.*) the point glides easily over a smooth surface, flexibility and freedom being the consequent result. In copper-plate and wood-engraving there is resistance to a cutting tool which must be forced through resisting material. This tends to give a certain directness and rigidity to all lines, straight and curved. A slow uniformly changing curve would be more natural than a jerky, hectic, quickly curving one. The medium, therefore, lends itself to an abstract quality peculiarly adapted to contemporary creative expression. This adaptability, no doubt, explains the preponderance of woodcuts among the so-called "modern" works in print.

Artists of Western civilization, it is interesting to note, have never made use of the potentially different characteristics inherent in lines of different types as have the artists of Japan and China. In Japanese art, for instance, there are the eighteen types of lines varying from stiff wiry ones expressing the starched garments of court nobles to the jagged ones expressing the rags of beggars. Among Western woodcutters, John J. A. Murphy has probably canvassed such possibilities more thoroughly than any other artist.

GRAPHIC ARTS

Drawing on Block.—There are a number of ways of drawing on the block. For a black line cut the drawing to be reproduced can be made with India ink, or Chinese black, with corrections in Chinese white. For a white line-cut the simplest and most flexible method, in that it allows erasing as easily as on paper, is with a lead pencil. The pencil drawing can be fully developed and then translated into white lines as the cutting proceeds. When mechanical exactness is required the subject can be photographed directly on a block prepared by the proper sensitizing of its surface. Photographs or wash drawings on the block have been commonly used during the latter part of the reproductive period—*i.e.*, up to the end of the last century. Timothy Cole, for instance, so photographed his subjects onto his block and then proceeded to interpret the photograph into white lines.

Printing.—Woodcut printing is of two kinds, black and colour, and may be done either by hand or on a regular type-printing press. For black printing the finest obtainable quality of proving ink ground in oil is used. The ink is spread on a glass or marble slab with a special composition hand-roller (of the same type as used in printing presses). After a thorough working onto the roller in a uniform and exceedingly thin layer the ink is transferred to the surface of the block by several movements of the roller across the block in different directions. The paper may be India in several textures or soft hand-made Japanese such as the Gifu. Or it can be the less enduring machine-made domestic in many varieties. The India is adapted to the white line engraving, the harder textures to the finer lined blocks; the Japanese and domestic to the coarser lined blocks.

In the case of a hand print, the right sized sheet is laid over the inked block and pressed down with a sheet of cardboard. A second cardboard coated with beeswax to make it slide easily, a steel burnisher, as in fig. 47, or a Japanese baren, is then rubbed over the first with considerable pressure which will vary in different sections of the block as the nature of the work demands. Less pressure means greyer and less even blacks, more means blacker blacks. This flexible control of pressure by the printer allows a quality of varied tone and texture in the hand-made print that can never be rivalled by any other method. In distinguished printing of this character a single print will take from 15 minutes to 3 hours of printing time. Corners of the print may be lifted to test results during this hand process.

In the case of a machine print the block is mounted in a printing press like any type form and the print made with uniform pressure. This pressure,

212

however, can be varied artificially by the same overlay and underlay system used in type printing. When darker blacks are required thin sheets of paper are cut to proper size and pasted to the proper spot under the block itself or on the tympan against which the paper lies, in a registered position. The thicker these are the heavier the pressure in that spot, the darker the resulting black and the greyer the surrounding blacks.

Colour Printing.—Colour printing may be done from one block or a series of blocks. When printed from one block the colours are painted with a brush into the desired section of the uncut surface as in the case of a monotype. Each print thus becomes an original painting which is transferred by pressure to paper. If the colour is to be in spots no lines are necessary except guide lines. It facilitates the process of painting the block if these guide lines are white lines gouged out of the block around separate patches of colour. In the print the white unprinted line becomes part of the decorative pattern, giving a hint of mosaic effect. This process could never be used for a realistic picture. A regular line block could of course be printed in colour instead of black, thus getting a different effect. When many blocks are used for one print we have the Japanese colour printing process undoubtedly the highest developed art of colour printing the world has so far produced.

In this process there is a key line block to be printed in black or any desired colour. Each succeeding block, then, prints one, or sometimes two or three well-separated (so they do not overlap in painting on the black) colours onto the same key-block print. The number of blocks so printed may run all the way from two or three to a dozen or fifteen, gaining in range and subtlety as the number increases. The blocks are larger than the actual print thus including an unprinted margin in which two sunken notches are cut into the block to take one corner and one edge of the paper and thus provide accurate registration. All the blocks, of course, are printed in succession on the same piece of paper.

Colour printing ink is made of any kind of finely ground dry ink colour mixed with water instead of oil. It is applied with brushes of varying widths, a separate one for each colour, which paint over the entire block high and low sections alike. The brush charged with colour is dipped into a paste made of finely ground rice flour either before it is applied to the block or immediately after, the paste and the water-paint being thoroughly mixed by a sufficient brushing on the block. This paste changes the character of the colour from a mat finish to a more brilliant one. Also it gives adhesive quality which under

213

the pressure of printing incorporates it thoroughly with the paper. Carefully dampened paper is laid on the block and rubbed directly on the paper with a Japanese bamboo-covered, stiff, slightly convex pad called a baren. (Plate I.) The amount of pressure determines the intensity of the colour of the print.

Chiaroscuro (clear-obscure).—In Europe during the 16th century another type of colour printing developed called chiaroscuro. The method comprised two prints from two blocks on one paper. One was a usual black line print, which as a line picture was complete in itself. The other was a tone block to be printed as one solid ground-colour in sepia, soft warm grey or other colours from which certain spots were gouged out to leave significant white highlights in the print. The final result resembled the wash-drawings of the masters and undoubtedly came into use as a means of approximating their effect.

The method is said to have been invented by Jobst de Negker at Augsburg. In Germany Hans Baldung Grien (1475–1552), Lucas Cranach (1472–1553) and Burgkmair (1473–1531) were among the first to practice it. In Italy Ugo da Carpi who worked in Venice and whose first print was dated 1518 was its foremost exponent. After dying out it was revived in Germany at the end of the 18th century and has persisted to the present. In the United States Rudolph Ruzika, A. Allen Lewis and others are practising the method today.

Uses.—"The possibilities of the wood block," says Frank Weitenkampf in his *How to Appreciate Prints*, "have been exploited to a remarkable degree. It has rendered line and tone, given the precision of the pen and ink sketch or the etching, and the free, granular irregularity of the charcoal smudge, translated paintings with the set regularity of the line engraving on copper or, abandoning the line *per se*, with an attention to tone and colour and texture, which often gave even the illusion of brush marks. It has been used for the rudest handbills and for the most elaborate reproductions of famous works of art; it has served as an original art, as a direct means of expression, and, crossing the bounds of black and white, it has imitated wash-drawings in two or three tints, and has entered the domain of colour printing in elaborate reproductions, as well as in the highly sensitive form of art exemplified in the Japanese chromo-xylograph. It has been employed to illustrate in the rudest form the songs and ballads hawked about the streets, and in perfection of craftsmanship works such as the Doré Bible; it has been put to the practical use of reproducing wallpaper, and it has brought forth works treasured by the collector, though so different in style as the engravings of Dürer or Holbein, and those which are the work of some of the modern disciples of art in the United States."

HISTORY OF THE WOODCUT

THE PRINCIPLE of cutting relief characters in metal, wood or stone has been practised far back toward the dawn of history. Cut metal plates were used in Egypt, India, Greece and Rome. Carved stamps or dyes were used for pressing letters into the moist clay of bricks in Egypt and for branding slaves in Rome. Both intaglio and relief carvings were known and used for these various purposes. Woodcuts were used in the Middle Ages to stamp monograms and to print colour designs on textiles, a custom practised in the Orient from time immemorial.

The earliest prints on paper so far found come from China of the T'ang dynasty (A.D. 618–905) when woodcuts in one colour were produced in great quantities as cheap substitutes for religious paintings. The oldest of such cuts now known is dated A.D. 868 and was found by Sir Aurel Stein in 1907 in the Caves of a Thousand Buddhas at Tun-huang in Chinese Turkistan. Throughout their history in China no artist of any note designed expressly for the woodcut. Even when the complex colour printing from many blocks came into use, beginning, so far as is known, about the time that colour printing began in the Chiaroscuro prints of Europe, *i.e.*, in the 17th century, this medium was used by craftsmen for the reproduction of paintings. The earliest known Chinese colour print is from a book called "Shih chu chai Shu hua p'u" and is dated 1625.

The method spread to Japan in the 8th century and for a long time was confined to reproducing popular religious figures. In Japan, however, there arose a whole school of artists who, though like the Chinese, still valuing painting as the supreme medium, did design expressly for the woodcut, thus conceiving their designs in terms of the carved line and colour block. The best of these were masters of the first rank.

For the greater part of their entire history, then, particularly as a reproductive process, woodcuts have been a widely used pictorial medium. Cheap in price, printed in quantity, close to the hearts and minds of common people in their choice of subject and story, they were used not as the collectors' items they have become today, but in every home as part of the furniture of actual life. They were looked at, studied, talked about, absorbed. They took the part of picture books when books were still the hand-lettered creations of monks, chained to the "library" tables of churches and kings. They were books in embryo, in fact.

In the religious cuts (and in the beginning practically all were religious) the people could see the characters of the Christian drama intimately in a form different from but related to the great paintings in the churches. Brief printed captions began to appear beneath the pictures telling the story of their heroes. These cut into the block were the first type. Later, about 1436, when Gutenberg invented printing, cut into separate letters, they became the first movable type. When the printing of books began the woodcut inevitably became the means of illustration. Being pictorial type it went with letter-press type. In fact the harmony between text and illustration of the 15th and 16th centuries has never since been equalled in general practice. So right was the combination that even when, in the 18th century, taste ran to the greater elegance of copper plate engraving and the almost total abandonment of the woodcut, the latter still kept alive in incredibly rude form in chap books and other popular literature. It carried over in fact to the revival in the 19th century when again it became the main medium of illustration in press and books. Memory in this country can easily go back to its general use in magazines and elsewhere. The form was decadent as it gradually died out before the advance of the cheaper photo-engraving process, but it was still the medium of the people as it had always been. Taking its history as a whole through its great period in the 16th century, decline in the 17th, decay in the 18th and revival in the weakened form of the white line toned picture in the 19th, the woodcut is undoubtedly a close second to the book in the role of entertainer, instructor and guide to the human race in the last 500 years of its struggle toward its present civilization.

In Europe the earliest known woodcuts were playing-cards dating back to the beginning of the 15th century. Pictorial prints go back as far as 1410. The earliest dated pictorial print is generally (but not always) admitted to be the St. Christopher of 1423. It is simple, crude, and naïve. It was done with single lines, almost an outline drawing, for its full effect it, and practically all prints of its time, depended upon hand-colouring after the print was made.

From 1423 to 1490 the black line woodcut developed from a crude beginning through the block-books that immediately preceded type printing to a mastering of the medium that has not been surpassed in that department to this day. The block books originated in Germany and the Netherlands— the oldest ones being *Biblia Pauperum* (*c.* 1450) of German origin, and the *Apocalypse*, the *Canticum Canticorem* and *Biblia Pauperum* (*c.* 1470) of the Netherlands. Dürer's drawings on the block made from 1492 to 1526 and cut laboriously by craftsmen woodcarvers, were complex, sophisticated, varied in quality of line and texture, yet they attained this complexity with lines that were most natural to the medium, that avoided, except in the darkest shadows, the forced (in this medium) cross hatching of pen and ink drawings. Here, then, at the time that America was being discovered was a mature art in mediaeval Germany, which set the pace for other nations. The subjects were mostly religious.

Dürer (*q.v.*) was the first great master to use the woodcut extensively as a way of reproducing drawings made for it. Without attaining the unity of means and expression typical of today he refined and widened the process. He had many followers, among them the little masters Altdorfer, the Behams, Pencz and others who forgot the usual religious subjects to record, with a touch of un-German decorative quality learned from Italy, the labours, merriment or debauchery of the everyday life of their time. Influence flowed back and forth between Italy and Germany, Dürer influencing leading Italians like Marcantonio Raimondi (1480–1530), and vice versa. By 1490 in the north countries individual blocks were giving way to blocks cut for such newspapers of the day as the Nuremberg Chronicle of 1493 and for book illustrations. In Italy the art centred in book illustrations from the beginning. Lippmann, in his *Art of Wood Engraving in Italy in the Fifteenth Century*, notes this difference between the North and the South by saying, "In Germany the proper function of book illustration was instruction; in Italy, ornament."[2] In thus stating the case he must have meant obvious ornament for there is a decorative design quality in the German work that goes far beyond "instruction."

Holbein (*q.v.*) was the next great artist to design particularly for the woodcut. Working through the woodcutter, Hans Lützelburger, the greatest master of the knife the craft has produced, he achieved what is probably as complete a synthesis between the means and the expression as is possible with the black line method. His *Dance of Death* series of blocks is one of the outstanding attainments of the medium.

In France the woodcut started in Paris with the cutting of blocks for the popular and frequently published *Books of the Hours*. Its chief masters in the 16th century were Jean Cousin and Bernard Salomon who worked around 1550. In the 17th and 18th it gradually declined. In 1766 Jean Michel Papillon wrote his famous *Treatise on Engraving* and showed in his work the minuteness of technique that was typical of the decline.

Thomas Bewick (1753–1828) did not invent the white line pictorial wood-engraving, there being evidence in his work that he was influenced by Croxall's cuts in his *Aesop* of 1722. He was, however, the first to give it popularity. The woodcut during the 18th and 19th century decline rivalled the cameras as a recording instrument. By adapting itself to the mirroring of a dozen mediums it had been forced into a sphere not its own. Bewick furnished the mechanism for this decline as well as that for the revival from it. The illustration of one of his blocks in Plate II. fig. 7. shows the nature of his work. His finest productions are the illustrations to *British Quadrupeds* (1790) and *British Birds* (1797).

William Blake (1757–1827) made only a few small woodcuts. He used the white line method. Technically they were not particularly skillful. But pre-eminently they are *wood*-engravings. They emerge from blackness into light. They are plastic. They exploit the inherent quality of the medium. In doing these things they are the forerunners in character as well as technic of the significant work of today.

At the end of the century we find Felix Vallotton in Paris playing with solid areas of blacks and whites—one of the first to pick up the thread begun in Florence 500 years ago (*see* the early Florentine woodcut shown in Pl. II. fig. 6.) the thread that in the 20th century is to develop into the dominant means of the modern expression.

MODERN TENDENCIES

THE WRITER'S CONTENTION that the present is the most fertile period in the history of the woodcut, in actual, contemporary achievement and in future possibilities is supported by two main reasons. The revolution in the mental approach to the making of pictures, which is the contribution of the first quarter of our 20th century to art history, and which involves a change from thinking of pictures as imitations or reports of nature to a conception of them as creatively reorganized interpretations, has brought the woodcut (which has been more sensitive to the new vitality than any other print medium) back into the fold of the *grand tradition*. Next in importance to this exceed-

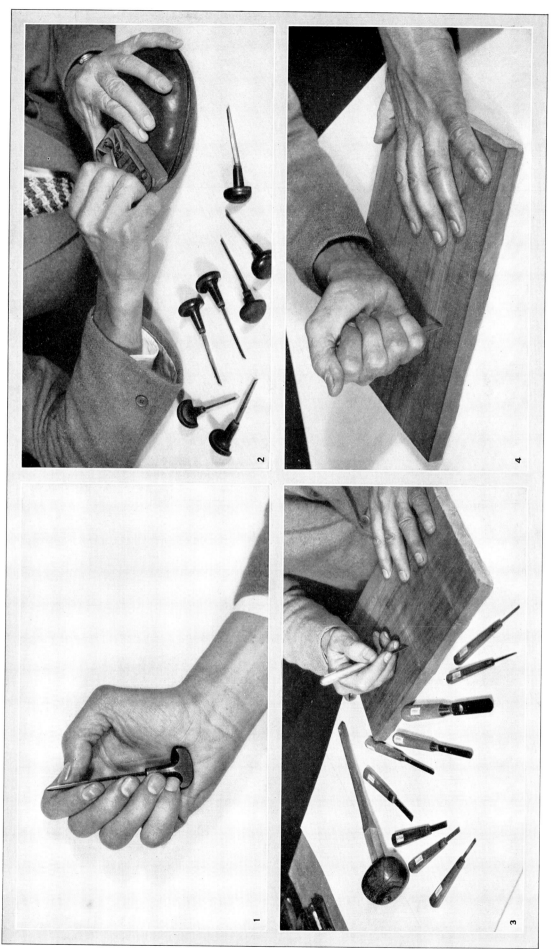

THE PROCESS OF WOOD-ENGRAVING

1. Correct position of the burin for engraving on wood. The knuckles of the hand should rest on the block. Tool should be pushed forward or backward by a contracting of the palm

2. Engraving into the hard end grain of a box-wood block with the burin. Various shaped burins and tools are on the table. Note leather cushion for holding block steady

3. Holding knife for cutting on the flat side of a plank block. On the table are various shaped gouges and flat chisels used for removing large or small areas of wood

4. Cutting a block of wood with the knife held in the sloping position. This gives a widened base to each black line left raised above the cut away portion

PLATE II   WOODCUTS AND WOOD-ENGRAVING

EARLY WOODCUTS

1. "The Buxheim St. Christopher," from a facsimile reproduced by the American Institute of Graphic Arts; earliest dated woodcut in Europe, made 1423. 2. Early Florentine woodcut. 3. Woodcut from Hans Holbein's "Dance of Death Series." 4. "Crucifixion" by Albrecht Dürer. 5. Frontispiece to Breydenbach's "Pilgrimage to Jerusalem," 1486. First known woodcut in which cross-hatching was used. 6. Print made about 1560, typical of the decorative Italian style. 7. A woodcut of an owl from an illustration in Thomas Bewick's "History of British Birds," published in 1825. 8. White line woodcut by William Blake, one of the first woodcuts to have the qualities of the art today

ingly significant event, the woodcut has found itself technically. That is, it has, in the last thirty or forty years, ceased forced service as proxy for another medium, the line drawing, and blossomed into a self-expression based on its inherent qualities. Its usefulness, however, has passed from the multitude who now find their pictorial entertainment in the photo and the pen and ink "funnies," to the few who care to seek out and pay the higher costs of what has become an aristocratic art—aristocratic, yet the lowest priced of all original pictorial works of art. (Prints made and signed by the artist are counted originals.)

This *grand tradition* includes work that is universal rather than particular in conception, creative rather than reportorial; it is older than the woodcut medium by many centuries. Work of today is rooted in fertile soil only when it belongs in both of these classifications. From the one it gains time-*less*ness, from the other, time*li*ness.

TYPOGRAPHY

TYPOGRAPHY is the art of printing. It has as its first object not ornament, but utility. The printer must never distract, even with beauty, the reader from his text. In the printing of books there is less room for individuality of style than in the typography of propaganda. The laws of typography in books intended for general circulation are based upon (a) the essential nature of alphabetical writing; (b) the force of tradition. But strict as the conventions are, there is not, and can never be, a rigid character of typography applicable to all books produced in a given geographic or ethnic area; or a universal formula acceptable to all books printed in Roman types. The strength of tradition expresses itself in the details of book arrangement and these vary widely. Certain laws of linear composition are, however, obeyed by all printers who use the Roman letter.

A fount of Roman type consists of (1) Roman: CAPITALS, SMALL CAPITALS, lower case, : ."; 1 2 3 4 5 etc. (); and (2) *Italic: CAPITALS, lower case.* In addition to these, as necessary adjuncts, the printer possesses (3) spaces,

(4) leads, (5) straight lines of metal known as *rules,* and (6) a collection of mobile ornaments, head- and tail-pieces, flowers, decorated initial letters, vignettes and flourishes, wood blocks of borders, etc. Another decorative medium at his command lies in his use of (7) colour (red being the most widely used). For emphasis he possesses (8) special types of notably heavy face, and may use colour for the same purpose. (9) Space is another valuable element, margins, blanks, etc. being filled in with what are known as "quotations." Finally (10) there is the nature (colour, weight and texture) of the paper.

Composition is the selection and arrangement of all these elements; *Imposition* is the due placing of the composition upon the sheet; *Printing* comprises the press-work, securing a perfection of register (backing up), the quality and crispness of inking. Typography, therefore, controls composition, imposition and paper. The paper must be of a character capable of expressing the value of the composition. The margins must be proportionate to the area of the text, allowing convenient space for thumbs and fingers at the side and bottom of the page. The mediaeval margins as adopted by the Kelmscott Press, are handsome and agreeable in certain books, but, are neither agreeable nor convenient in other books, *e.g.,* where the page dimension is necessarily small or narrow, and the book is to be carried in the pocket. For this and other books, the type may well be centred on the measure of the page, and slightly raised above ocular centre.

Composition.—The fundamental principles of page-composition are deducible from the ocular facts of alphabetical printing in the Roman letter. The eye cannot, with ease, read pages of words composed of letters designed with sharply contrasting thicks and thins. Nor can the eye agreeably read a mass of words composed even in a rightly constructed letter, unless the line is kept to a certain maximum length; that is to say, the reader's eye cannot comfortably seize more than a certain number of words in any given size except in a proportionate length of line. Nor can a reader comfortably seize a letter, a word or a line, unless the printer's setting is related to the reader's normal habit of vision when holding a book for reading. The typographer's respect for these principles will generally protect the reader from the risk of "doubling" (that is, reading the same line twice), or from being given a book in a large and "staring" type.

The average number of words which the reader's eye can conveniently seize is between 10 and 12 (some 48 characters). The typographer, while exerting himself to the utmost to respect this ocular limitation, may often be confronted with certain conditions which make it impossible for him to secure a type of the right related size. He is often forced to the use of a small type, and in order to obviate the risk of "doubling," he inserts leads between the lines of type and thus increases the space between them.

The practice of leading, denounced in certain quarters, is an essential necessity. The typographer, therefore, in making the best use of his material, must make legitimate use of leads. It may be added, too, that in certain compositions, leads produce a happy effect; and in not a few cases, their absence may ruin a composition set even in a relatively large type.

The typographer should know how to extract the utmost from the use of a type which is narrow in relation to its height—leading and spacing play a decisive part here. A round, open, wide letter may, for certain purposes, be set "loose"; *i.e.*, the space between the letters will be greater (or appear greater by reason of the curves of the c, o, e, g, in the lower case), than in a relatively condensed letter. Consistency will here insert a satisfactory lead between the lines.

The space between words composed in a condensed letter is less than that between words in a round, wide form. A lead should always precede and follow quoted matter. Where there is no leading between the lines, and the composition is necessarily tight, it may be an advantage to set leads between the paragraphs.

Indention is a most important detail. The opening sentence of every work should automatically manifest itself as such. This may be contrived by using a large initial letter, by printing the first word in CAPITALS, or SMALL CAPITALS, or CAPITALS AND SMALL CAPITALS. The first word may be set into the margin; but it should *not* be indented. Indention marks paragraphs—the subsequent sections of the text. Where for any reason it may be necessary to avoid indention in paragraphs, a lead is plainly desirable. Absence of indention and of lead means the virtual extinction of the paragraph.

The depth of the page will be related to the length of line. The measure must be symmetrical, displaying a form pleasing to the eye. A rectangle is more pleasing than a square.

A rectangular page composed of lines of 10–11–12 words long will generally be satisfactory. It remains to add the running page-heading, and the folio. The page-heading may either range to the left and right in the opening (fixing the two pages as a unity); or range to the right and left; or it may be centred. The folio may be centred at the foot, or range either way at the top or bottom; but it cannot be centred at the top without abolishing the running page headline. This may be done, but it is an undesirable practice. The running headlines may be set in capitals of the text, in upper- and lower-case of the text, or in any combination of capitals. The use of full-sized capitals renders over-conspicuous a repetitive feature inserted for extrinsic convenience—that is, the identification of loose leaves. By reason of its position, the headline looks ragged if set in upper-and lower-case. It seems best, therefore, to employ small capitals; all capitals are best separated by hair spaces as their rectangular structure and preponderance of perpendiculars tend to solidify the composition.

Full-sized capitals may well be used for chapter headings, the number of the chapter being kept in small capitals, and both indications being hair spaced. The practice of dropping the chapter opening is justified by the fact that the eye, in travelling from the generally occasional blank at the end of a chapter to the beginning of the next, finds a companion blank an agreeable consistency. It has also the psychological advantage of saving the reader from feeling overpowered by the text. The rectangle of type is so imposed upon the edge as to allow centre, head, fore-edge and tail margins of a dimension proportionate, first, to the length of line and, secondly, to the disposition of space at points where the text is cut into chapters, and where the body joins the prefatory and other pages known as "preliminaries." These last, less strictly governed by convention than the text pages, offer the maximum opportunity of design to be found in the volume.

The history of printing is in large measure the history of the title-page. The title when fully developed occupied a recto page, either partially or wholly; and the title-phrase, or a catchword of it, has generally been set in a conspicuous size of type. Sixteenth century Italian printers generally used large capitals, copied from inscriptions, or more exceptionally, from caroline manuscripts; while English use followed the French in employing a leading line of large upper- and lower-case, followed by a few lines of pica capitals. Next came the printer's device, and at the foot of the page, his name and address. The large sizes of upper- and lower-case, being an inheritance from printers who were accustomed to black-letter (never set in solid capitals), have gone. The device also has vanished, except from the University Presses.

CONTEMPORARY WOODCUTS

1. "Frauenkopf" by Karl Schmidt-Rottluff (1884–   ), German
2. From a series of "Ten Pictures Behind the Front" by J. E. Laboureur (1877–   ), French
3. A woodcut by John Nash (1893–   ), English
4. "Memories" by John J. A. Murphy (1888–   ), American
5. "Weib vom Manne begehrt" by Max Pechstein (1880–   ), German

6. "The Dance" by Cecil Buller, American, contemporary
7. "Lovers Surprised by Storm" by Douglas Percy Bliss (1900–   ), English
8. "Dunes—Pheasants" by B. Essers, Dutch, Contemporary
9. "Franklin Stove" by Wanda Gág. American

STIPPLE AND CRAYON ENGRAVING

ENGLISH STIPPLE ENGRAVINGS OF THE 18TH CENTURY

Stipple engraving consists of a design drawn in a series or group of dots through an etching ground on a copper plate, and bitten with acid, then completed with dots made directly in the copper by a curved stipple-graver and perhaps a toothed wheel called a roulette

1. "Countess Spencer," engraved by Francesco Bartolozzi (1727–1813) after the painting by Sir Joshua Reynolds (1723–92). 2. "Dressing for the Masquerade," engraved by John Raphael Smith (1752–1812) after the painting by George Morland (1763–1804). 3. "Constancy," engraved by William Ward (1766–1826) after the painting by George Morland. 4. "Emma," engraved by John Jones (1745–97) after the painting by George Romney (1734–1802)

The contemporary title-page is a bleak affair; in nine out of ten cases the blank between the title and the imprint of the printer-publisher tends to be the most outstanding feature. When the device was first abandoned, the author, printer or publisher took advantage of the leisure of the reader and the blank at their disposal to draft a tediously long title, sub-title and indications of the author's qualifications, designed to fill the entire page. The present day publisher goes to the other extreme, reducing the title to as few short words as possible, followed with "by" and the author's name. A professional writer may insert, *e.g.*, "Author of *The Deluge*" under his name, but three and sometimes four inches of space separate this from the first line of the imprint. Consequently unless the title be deliberately set in a size of type out of all relation to that of the remainder of the book, this space is over-conspicuous. It is clear that a volume in 12-point does not require a 48-point title unless it be a 300-page folio in double-column.

Care for the typography of a book means care for its unity. There is no reason for a title-page to bear any line in a type larger than twice the size of the text-letter. If the book be set in 12-point, the title need be no larger than 24-point—or even slightly smaller. It should be set in spaced capitals as a rule. The author's name, like all displayed proper names, should also be in capitals. The headings to the preface, table of contents, introduction, etc., should be in the same size and fount as the chapter heads; and should be dropped if they are dropped. The order of these pages remains unsettled, except that all begin on a recto page. The logical order of the preliminary pages is half-title, title, dedication, contents, introduction, preface. This rule is applicable to most categories of books. Novels need neither table of contents nor list of chapters, though one or the other is generally printed. If it is decided to retain either, it would be reasonable to print it on the back of the half-title and facing the title page, so that the entire nature of the book will be indicated to the reader at a single opening. Where the volume is made up of a few short stories, their titles can be listed in the blank centre of the title-page.

Book Sizes.—In addition to fiction, belles-lettres and educational books are habitually published in portable, if not in pocketable formats, crown octavo $7\frac{1}{2}'' \times 5''$ (in America known as 12mo) being an invariable rule for English novels published as such. The novel in the form of biography will be published as a biography, $6'' \times 8\frac{1}{2}''$, the size also for history, archaeology, science, art, and almost everything but fiction. Novels are only promoted to this format when they have become "standard." Size, therefore, is the most manifest difference between books.

Another obvious difference is bulk, calculated in accordance with the publisher's notion, first, of the general sense of trade expectation, and, secondly, of the purchasing psychology of a public habituated to certain selling prices vaguely related to number of pages and thickness of the proffered volume. Inconsistently enough, weight does not enter into these expectations. These habits of mind affect the choice of fount and size of type, and may necessitate the adoption of devices for "driving out," *i.e.*, making the setting take up as much room as possible. By putting the running headline between rules or rows of ornaments; introducing unnecessary blanks between chapters; contracting the measure; exaggerating the spaces between the words and the lines; excessively indenting paragraphs; isolating quoted matter with picas of white space; inserting wholly unnecessary sectional titles in the text and surrounding them with space; contriving to drive a chapter ending to the top of a recto page so that the rest of it and its verso may be blank; using thick but not heavy paper; increasing the depth of chapter beginnings and inserting very large capitals thereto; the volume can be inflated to an extra 16 pages—a feat which the able typographer accomplishes without showing his hand to the reader.

Limited editions of standard authors, or of authors who desire to rank as such, are commonly given a rubricated title. Under no circumstances, however, should red appear anywhere else in the work. Hand-made paper is generally used for editions-de-luxe, and none but the brave among typographers will disregard the superstitious love of the book-buying classes for its untrimmed, ugly and dirt-gathering rough edges. There is another category of limited edition produced by typographers working freely, without the handicap of trade conditions. These books are rapidly increasing in number, and use a wide variety of format, of type, of illustration and of binding.

Because, rather than in spite of, mechanical methods and standardization, printing is more various to-day than ever before. Whereas English books of whatever category of 20 years ago were printed in only three designs of type, no fewer than eight founts are employed to-day. It has been necessary that most of these are reproductions of classic old-faces, but it may well be that the near future will witness a real renaissance of type design based upon a sensitiveness to rightly-controlled type forms, and not animated by an uninformed curiosity for the original and the bizarre.

STIPPLE AND CRAYON ENGRAVING

STIPPLE-ENGRAVING was a little art of prettiness and daintiness, particularly well adapted to the translation of anecdotic pictures of a sentimental, mildly romantic, or domestic character, such as were turned out in great numbers, to supply a vogue in the English market during the reign of George III., many of which, popular in their day, survive only in the colour-prints and, though rarely of much artistic value, are yet now highly valued for their merit in survival. Nevertheless there were in the brief hey-day of the art a few among the multitude of designers and engravers who, realizing its limitations, made the most of its qualities, and these, such as J. R. Smith, William Ward and John Jones, the great mezzotinters, Charles Wilkin, Thomas Burke, and whenever he chose to do so, Francesco Bartolozzi, with Peltro William Tomkins, Knight, Cheeseman, Schiavonetti, and others used the medium with individuality, undeniable charm and some artistic effect.

As a separate method, stipple-engraving came to England from France probably about 1764, by way of the crayon manner and the pastel, and these had evolved originally from the dotted manner, to which Ludvig von Siegen refers, in announcing the wonders of his own invention of mezzotint in 1642, as one of the modes of engraving which it was not. The dotted manner, a process of punching the plate with awl and mallet, called *opus mallei*, was used for its own sake with pictorial effect by Jan Lutma, an Amsterdam goldsmith, and the son of Rembrandt's sitter; but graven dots had been used earlier as accessory to line-engraving by Giulio Campagnola, Ottavio Leoni, and others, while in England the earliest important engraver of portraits, William Rogers, in Elizabeth's reign, had stippled the face of the Queen, while Lucas Vorsterman used dots also to suggest the flesh in his Charles I.

But in the 18th century, when the crayon and pastel drawings of Boucher and others were popular in France, the aim of the engravers was to reproduce their texture on the copper-plate. The idea was in the air, so to speak, and several were engaged in the attempt to materialize it. Thus, the invention of the crayon manner was claimed separately by Jean Charles François, Gilles Demarteau, who used his own version of it with artistic feeling, and Louis Marin Bonnet, an ingenious engraver to whom we owe at least the "pastel manner." This was a subtle development of the crayon mode admitting colour variety from a series of plates, as we may see in Bonnet's really fine print, *La Tête de Flore*, after Boucher, but François seems to have been actually the first in the field. The means used to imitate crayon drawing resembled soft-ground etching, though to produce the appearance of the chalk lines the etching-ground was perforated by tools of the roulette order, and various kinds of needles, while, after the usual biting by the acid, the finishing touches were given by graver, dry-point and roulette, though one often fancies the methods of soft-ground had been employed. François taught this crayon engraving, and with it the application of colour in printing *à la poupée*, to William Wynn Ryland, a young English line-engraver, who had been studying with Le Bas in Paris, and who, when funds were lacking after his return to London, bethought him of the new manner of engraving he had learnt. Then having called Bartolozzi into collaboration, they both modified and developed it as stipple-engraving.

The new method proved very easy of accomplishment, simple and rapid. The outline was etched in a series of dots, and all the shadows were put in with large or closer dots, or tiny groups of dots. When all the biting was over, the ground was removed, and the finishing was done with dry-point and stipple-graver, a curved tool. Then the printing was done with black, red, or several coloured inks, a rag-stump, or *poupée*, being used, and the plate freshly cleaned for each impression. Beginning by translating the pretty pseudo-classical designs of Angelica Kauffman and Cipriani, which acquired a very popular vogue, Ryland and Bartolozzi found the new method exceedingly profitable. To the ready hand of Bartolozzi it came almost as a fairy gift, with the facilities of the medium linking themselves to his sweet caressing sense of beauty. Indeed, he developed it with richer character in its fine shades than the unfortunate Ryland could do, as we may see in many notable prints after Reynolds and other distinguished painters. All the painters of the day were anxious to share in the profits so readily made by the stipple-prints which were filling the print-sellers' windows, and few native engravers could resist the easy attraction of the new method, while it brought also Italian and French engravers to learn it, and work here for the English market. There was also, up to the war with revolutionary France in 1793, a great trade in English prints on the continent, and Bonnet and other French engravers, adopting the stipple method, tried to get a share in this trade by issuing prints with titles often in misspelt English. Sir Robert Strange, the eminent line-engraver, launched an indignant tirade against stipple, and even denied its claim to be regarded as engraving at all, though there was no denying its efficacy as a medium for colour-printing, the white of the paper, showing between the tinted dots, affording a peculiarly luminous quality, and thus giving it a superiority over the coloured mezzotint, though it must be admitted that rarely was the stipple or the mezzotint of old time completely printed in colours, some portions invariably being left to be coloured by hand. Nevertheless, the popularity of stipple continued as long as the special subjects for which it was used remained in fashion, and as long as the leading 18th century painters and engravers survived the period of their comparatively short though successful collaboration, but it really waned with the advent of colour-lithography. Stipple-engraving is rarely practised nowadays as a separate art, though a recent attempt has been made to revive it for original expression by Dorothy Woollard. As a medium for original colour-printing it has completely given place to aquatint, woodcut or wood engraving, lithography, or relief-etching from several plates.

PEN DRAWING

THE ART OF LINE DRAWING is perhaps the oldest of the graphic arts. The Greeks seem to have considered drawing and writing as essentially the same process, since they used the same word for both. This points to the early identity of the two arts when drawing was a kind of writing and when such writing as men had learned to practise was essentially what we should call drawing, though of a crude and simple kind.

Materials.—The earliest pens were made of the bamboo reed, the hollow stalk of the calamus, or other wood with the end frayed or pulped. Greek and Roman scribes at a later time used reeds cut to a point and slit like the modern pen; copper pens of the same type, of Roman manufacture, are to be found in museums to-day. This pen possibly antedated the common use of the quill pen made from the wing feather of the goose. Ink, in its earliest form, was made from soot and charcoal mixed with gum; there were also vegetable stains and berry juices. In China the invention of ink is credited to Tien-Tcheu who lived between 2697 B.C. and 2597 B.C. One of the oldest books known, the maxims of that ancient Egyptian ruler Ptah-hotep, dating from beyond the 25th century B.C., shows the use of red and black inks. The development of these mediums, however, was not toward a graphic art, but rather toward the written word, of history and literature, devoid of design or pictorial embellishment.

For paper, the barks of trees (especially lime trees), papyrus, linen and the prepared skins of calf or sheep, as well as vellum and parchment, were used. Finally the use of parchment replaced that of papyrus because of its susceptibility to ready erasures, its two usable sides and its thinness. The old scroll and the triptych of wax gave way to the codex with its leaves of vellum. With this convenient form under his hand the scribe for once became the artist and his pen found a facility which brought forth some of the most treasured contributions to the graphic arts; these are the hand-lettered, illuminated books which began to appear a little later than the 4th century and reached their greatest beauty during the following two or three centuries.

The basis of the many beautiful designs in these books is the pen line, with flat tones of colour and applications of burnished gold. With the invention of printing, which began with Gutenberg, with the first printed date of 1454, and the development of means of reproducing the line drawing, the art of the book continued. This was, in fact, the beginning of pen and ink art and, incidentally, of illustration, which is that art that accompanies the written word and adorns the printed page.

Development.—The art of pen and ink, as we know it, began with outline drawing as practised by Villard de Honnecourt and others in the Gothic period. The Florentine masters of the early Renaissance such as Pollaiuolo and Botticelli excelled in the rendering of form; shapes were well defined by means of a continuous and rhythmic outline, and Leonardo da Vinci combined the well defined outline with delicate shading in parallel lines. Michelangelo modelled the muscles in detail by numerous little crosslines and his outline is not continuous; Raphael excelled in sureness of line and in the suggestion of form by the simplest means; in north Italy Pisanello, by delicate pen strokes, rendered the texture of things such as the hairy furs of animals; the Caraccis and the Bolognese school developed a pictorial style by the close study of nature and the practice of engraving; Guercino's and Barocci's brilliant studies were highly prized though not free from mannerism. This pictorial style reached its height in the drawings of two Flemings, Rubens and Vandyck, who were deeply impressed with Italian art. Their drawings are inspired by a very robust reality in which the visible surface of things is observed in detail; their style is curiously informal. The deliberate calligraphy of the earlier northern engravers, of Dürer, Schongauer, Lucas and Leyden, is replaced by a fluent literal draughtsmanship where colour and tone are suggested by cross-hatching or washes.

Rembrandt is the greatest exponent of the pen and wash technique. He relied mainly on delicately toned washes for the rendering of light and shade. Other followers of this method were Claude de Lorraine with his fine pen-drawings of Italian landscapes, Nicolas Poussin with his careful preliminary studies for composition, and Tiepolo with his sketchy technique. Many more draughtsmen might be mentioned, their drawings pretended no detached place as works of art, and no strict adherence to the limitations of the pen was observed. It was with the development of process reproduction at the beginning of the 19th century that pen and ink art as a separate art came into being.

Technique.—Three main divisions appear in the method of the pen and ink drawing, which have been vaguely mentioned in speaking of the drawings of Rembrandt, da Vinci and Rubens. The first of these deals with sheer line or draughtsmanship with slight or strong allowance toward tone; the second deals with tone conception, as of the colourist, with much or little allowance toward line; and the third deals with line and tone or colour equally estimated and treated consciously as in design. Upon closer study, however, these general methods fall into six more specific divisions: (1) The outline or open drawing, in which much or little may be included. The range of this method may run from the fragmentary or the compact line, of the manner of Holbein, to the manner of Heinrich Kley, who plays so continuously upon outline, even upon the outlines of the inner bones of animals and men, that tone finally appears. (2) Outline with shadow massings in slow or fast line tone, as in the case of much of Vierge's work and that of Charles Keene and of Griggs. In this method much is made of the two-tone effect with white the strong value; it may reach the other extreme, wherein the low tone becomes a brush black, dominating the whole drawing with the white high-lights arising out of it constituting the structure of the picture, as in the work of Sartorio, the Italian.   (3) Outline, freely or otherwise done, with the introduction of local colour, arbitrarily and more or less flatly applied.   This typifies much of the work of Phil May and of Charles Dana Gibson.   (4) An approach to form and colour with or without outline, suggested by loose and delicate strokes of the pen, wherein form and colour emerge delicately from the white paper.   This is well seen in the work of Abbey and of Norman Lindsay of Australia.   (5) The same method as the above with a more positive introduction of local colour and textures and, by reason of more general or background tone, a decided localization of white with touches of flat black.   This is seen in the pen work of Fortuny and of Casanova.   (6) The method that belongs to the decorator or ornamentist, of men like Crane and Beardsley.   It is the flat presentation with a main viewpoint not toward reality and truth but toward romance and formalism, with the slow conscious line and tone laid in with intent for surface design and beauty.

All pen and ink drawing will be found to touch upon these few methods, with variations in effect and technique.   Technique is like handwriting; while it may be cultivated, it soon becomes the sign of an inner sense and feeling back of the hand.   The artist with the pen, observing objective life, whether it be primarily structural or tonal, or both, and with pen to paper, interpreting the feel of the contact there, comes naturally to the line that is his own; and in his tones, where the artist with the brush might escape confession or lose expression, the artist with pen and ink puts on expression and meaning over and above the main content of his work.   Thus in the work of Thomas Fogarty, in the touch and play of his pen, may be perceived a fine gentility and a sense of relationships that are rich and subtle; while in the drawings of J. Coll, one feels the strong dramatic gesture and sees the subjective qualities.   In like manner, in the pen drawings of Marold and Meissonier, neither of whom seemed to feel or to stress the line greatly but strove for full tone by fine cross-hatchings, lightly stroked surfaces and values semi-stippled with whites apparently scratched with a knife, is observed a sureness determined, it seems, by an allegiance to things academic.   The decorative drawings of Garth Jones have a classic and mural bigness, with a free and bold yet conscious line, while the decorative works of T. M. Cleland are executed as if by a master craftsman with a hand expert at the laying in of ebony and gold.

The work of the author of this article is characterized by partial or full tone with line made use of not so much for the presentation of form in drawing as to designate the movement and stir of things not seen but felt, as of the wind and the movements in sensation of distances and height. The line and its direction are employed also to present, through the effect of broken colour, the qualities of depth and solidity and a visual activity in tone or a compositional treatment of tone areas.

Present-day Uses.—Considerably less pen and ink art is found in the weekly and monthly popular periodicals of the United States and Great Britain since the advent of the half-tone process reproduction. Behind this, of course, is the aim of editors to meet only the desires of the readers who seek only a photographic presentation of fact; the half-tone printed on coated paper suggests this reality. However, many of the high-class magazines continue the use of the pen and ink drawing, seeking always to improve the quality of illustration, and laying special emphasis on decorative values. In England the most distinguished pen and ink artists are often associated with *Punch*. Outside the periodical field, where they are used for both illustrative and decorative purposes, pen and ink drawings are widely used in textbooks and encyclopaedias.

BOOK-PLATES

THE BOOK-PLATE, or *ex-libris*, a printed label intended to indicate ownership in books, is nearly as old as the printed book. According to Friedrich Warnecke, of Berlin, the oldest movable *ex-libris* are certain woodcuts representing a shield of arms supported by an angel (fig. 49), which were pasted in books presented to the Carthusian monastery of Buxheim by Brother Hildebrand Brandenburg of Biberach, about the year 1480. The woodcut, in imitation of similar devices in old mss., is handpainted. Many other authorities claim that there is another which antedates the Brandenburg. It is that of Johannes Knabensberg (Hans Igler). It is a woodcut found in an old Latin vocabulary. Some authorities date it *c.* 1450, others *c.* 1470–80. In France the most ancient *ex-libris* as yet discovered is that of one Jean

Bertaud de la Tour-Blanche, dated 1529; and in England that of Cardinal Wolsey, 1515–34. Holland comes next with the plate of a certain Anna van der Aa, in 1597; then Italy with one attributed to the year 1622. The earliest known American example is the plain printed label of John Cotton, 1674.

A sketch of the history of the book-plate must obviously begin in Germany, not only because the earliest examples known are German, but also because they are found in great numbers—often of the highest artistic interest—long before the fashion spread to other countries. Albrecht Dürer

FIG. 49.—15TH AND 16TH CENTURY BOOK-PLATES

The plate, left, believed to be the earliest movable book-plate, was pasted in books presented to the monastery of Buxheim, Germany, by Brother Hildebrand Brandenburg c. 1480. That at right was made for Sir Nicholas Bacon in 1574 for the books presented by him to the University of Cambridge

is known to have actually engraved at least six plates (some of very important size) between 1503 and 1516 (fig. 50), and to have supplied designs for many others. Several notable plates are ascribed to Lucas Cranach and to Hans Holbein, and to that bevy of so-called Little Masters, the Behams, Virgil Solis, Matthias, Zundt, Jost Amman, Saldörfer, Georg Hüpschmann and others. The influence of these draughtsmen over the decorative styles of Germany has been felt through subsequent centuries down to the present day, notwithstanding the invasion of successive Italian and French fashions during the 17th and 18th centuries, and the marked effort at originality of composition observable among modern designers. The heavy, over-elaborated German style never seems to have affected neighbouring countries; but since it was undoubtedly from Germany that was spread the fashion of ornamental book-plates as marks of possession, the history of German *ex-libris* remains on that account one of high interest to all who are curious in the matter.

It was not before the 17th century that the *movable ex-libris* became tolerably common in France. Up to that time the more luxurious habit of

FIG. 50.—BOOK-PLATE OF LAZARUS SPENGLER, ENGRAVED IN 1515 BY THE GERMAN PAINTER AND ENGRAVER, ALBRECHT DÜRER

stamping the cover with a personal device had been in such general favour with book-owners as to render the use of labels superfluous. From the middle of the century, however, the *ex-libris* proper became quite naturalized; examples of that period are very numerous, and, as a rule, are very handsome. It may be here pointed out that the expression *ex-libris*, used as a substantive, which is now the recognized term for book-plate everywhere on the Continent, found its origin in France. The words only occur in the

233

personal tokens of other nationalities long after they had become a recognized inscription on French labels.

English Styles.—In many ways the consideration of the English bookplate, in its numerous styles, from the late Elizabethan to the late Victorian period, is peculiarly interesting. In all its varieties it reflects with great fidelity the prevailing taste in decorative art at different epochs. Until the last quarter of the 17th century the number of authentic English plates is very limited. Their composition is always remarkably simple, and displays nothing of the German elaborateness. They are as a rule very plainly armorial, and the decoration is usually limited to a symmetrical arrangement of mantling, with an occasional display of palms or wreaths. Soon after the Restoration, however, a book-plate seems to have suddenly become an established accessory to most well-ordered libraries. Book-plates of that period offer very distinctive characteristics. In the simplicity of their heraldic arrangements they recall those of the previous age; but their physiognomy is totally different. In the first place, they invariably display the tincture lines and dots, after the method originally devised in the middle of the century by Petra Sancta, the author of *Tesserae Gentilitiae*, which by this time had become adopted throughout Europe. In the second, the mantling assumes a much more elaborate appearance—one that irresistibly recalls that of the periwig of the period—surrounding the face of the shield. This style was undoubtedly imported from France, but it assumed a character of its own in England. As a matter of fact, thenceforth until the dawn of the French Revolution, English modes of decoration in book-plates, as in most other chattels, follow at some years' distance the ruling French taste. The main characteristics of the style which prevailed during the Queen Anne and early Georgian periods are:—ornamental frames suggestive of carved oak, a frequent use of fish-scales, trellis or diapered patterns, for the decoration of plain surfaces; and, in the armorial display, a marked reduction in the importance of the mantling. The introduction of the scallop-shell as an almost constant element of ornamentation gives already a foretaste of the *Rocaille-Coquille*, the so-called Chippendale fashions of the next reign. As a matter of fact, during the middle third of the century this rococo style (of which the Convers plate [fig. 51] gives a typical sample) affects the book-plate as universally as all other decorative objects. During the early part of George III.'s reign there is a return to greater sobriety of ornamentation, and a style more truly national, which may be called *the urn style*, makes its appearance.

Book-plates of this period have invariably a physiognomy which at once re-calls the decorative manner made popular by architects and designers such as Chambers, the Adams, Josiah Wedgwood, Hepplewhite and Sheraton. The shield shows a plain spade-like outline, manifestly based upon that of the pseudo-classic urn then so much to the fore. The ornamental accessories are symmetrical palms and sprays, wreaths and ribands. The architectural boss is also an important factor. In many plates, indeed, the shield of arms takes quite a subsidiary position by the side of the predominantly architec-tural urn. From the beginning of the 19th century, until comparatively re-cent days, no special style of decoration seems to have established itself.

FIG. 51.—ENGLISH BOOK-PLATES OF THE 17TH AND 18TH CENTURIES
The plate on the left is that of P. A. Convers, 1762, and is representa-tive of the rococo style that affected decorative art during this period. That on the right, the book-pile model, was made for W. Hewer, Samuel Pepys's secretary, in 1699

The immense majority of examples display a plain shield of arms with motto on a scroll below, and crest on a fillet above. Of late years, however, a rapid impetus appears to have been given to the designing of *ex-libris*; a new era, in fact, has begun for the book-plate, one of great interest.

The main styles of decoration (and these, other data being absent, must always in the case of old examples remain the criteria of date) have already been noticed. It is, however, necessary to point out that certain styles of composition were also prevalent at certain periods. Many of the older plates (like the majority of the most modern ones) were essentially pictorial. Of this kind the best-defined English genus may be recalled: *the library interior—* a term which explains itself—and *book-piles*, exemplified by the *ex-libris* (fig. 51) of W. Hewer, Samuel Pepys's secretary. We have also many *portrait-*

plates, of which, perhaps, the most notable are those of Samuel Pepys himself and of John Gibbs, the architect; *allegories*, such as were engraved by Hogarth, Bartolozzi, John Pine and George Vertue; *landscape-plates*, by wood engravers of the Bewick school, etc. In most of these the armorial element plays but a secondary part.

The value attached to book-plates, otherwise than as an object of purely personal interest, is comparatively modern. The study of and the taste for collecting these private tokens of book-ownership hardly date farther back than the year 1875. The first real impetus was given by the appearance of the *Guide to the Study of Book-Plates*, by Lord de Tabley (then the Hon. Leicester Warren) in 1880. This work, highly interesting from many points of view, established what is now accepted as the general classification of styles: *early armorial* (*i.e.*, previous to Restoration, exemplified by the Nicholas Bacon plate); *Jacobean*, a somewhat misleading term, but distinctly understood to include the heavy decorative manner of the Restoration, Queen Anne and early Georgian days (the Lansanor plate, fig. 51, is typically Jacobean); *Chippendale* (the style above described as *rococo*, represented by the French plate of Convers); *wreath and ribbon*, belonging to the period described as that of the urn, etc. Since then the literature on the subject has grown considerably. Societies of collectors have been founded, first in England, then in Germany and France, and in the United States, most of them issuing a journal or archives: *The Journal of the Ex-libris Society* (London), the *Archives de la société française de collectionneurs d'ex-libris* (Paris), both of these monthlies; the *Ex-libris Zeitschrift* (Berlin), a quarterly.

Until the advent of the new taste the devising of book-plates was almost invariably left to the routine skill of the heraldic stationer. Of late years the composition of personal book-tokens has become recognized as a minor branch of a higher art, and there has come into fashion an entirely new class of designs which, for all their wonderful variety, bear as unmistakable a character as that of the most definite styles of bygone days. Broadly speaking, it may be said that the purely heraldic element tends to become subsidiary and the allegorical or symbolic to assert itself more strongly. Among modern English artists who have more specially paid attention to the devising of book-plates, and have produced admirable designs, may be mentioned C. W. Sherborn, G. W. Eve, Robert Anning Bell, J. D. Batten, Erat Harrison, J. Forbes Nixon, Charles Ricketts, John Vinycomb, John Leighton and Warrington Hogg. The development in various directions of process work, by facilitating and cheapening the reproduction of beautiful and elaborate designs, has no doubt helped much to popularize the book-plate—a thing which in older days was almost invariably restricted to ancestral libraries or to collections otherwise important. Thus the great majority of modern plates are reproduced by process. There are, however, a few artists left who devote to book-plates their skill with the graver. Some of the work they produce challenges comparison with the finest productions of bygone engravers. Of these the best-known are C. W. Sherborn and G. W. Eve in England, and in America, J. W. Spenceley of Boston, Mass., K. W. F. Hopson of New Haven, Conn., and E. D. French of New York City.

DRY-POINT

THOUGH GENERALLY CLASSED as a variety of etching, and in practice often combined with that process, dry-point is, strictly speaking, a kind of engraving.

In etching the needle scratches only through the etching ground and exposes the surface of the plate; the latter is then placed in a bath of acid, and it is the chemical action of the acid that eats out in the copper a line of sufficient depth to hold printing ink. In dry-point, on the contrary, as in line-engraving, the lines are hollowed out by the tool itself in direct contact with the copper, as directed by the engraver's hand, without the intervention of any chemical action. Zinc can be used instead of copper, but this metal wears out quickly.

Methods.—The "dry" point, so called because no bath of acid supplements its use, is a tapering pointed instrument of steel, of stronger build than the point or needle used by the etcher and sometimes sharpened at both ends; but many modern engravers have substituted for steel a diamond point, or more rarely a ruby, fixed in a vectal handle. With one of these instruments the engraver works directly upon a plate of hard and polished copper, either shiny or blackened, ploughing up a line, shallow or deep, according to the amount of pressure used. Along one edge of this line, if the

237

point is slanting, or along both edges if it is held upright, a raised edge of copper is turned up by the tool, and this ridge is termed the "burr." The burr, when the plate is inked for printing, becomes clothed with ink and produces in the impression the rich, soft and velvety effect which constitutes the peculiar charm of a dry-point proof. If the burr is removed (as it easily can be, should the engraver desire it with a scraper) the somewhat thin line thus produced is less easily distinguished except by a practised eye, from the characteristic lines produced by the burin or the etching point. The burr is delicate and is easily worn out, either by too vigorous wiping when the plate is inked (experienced printers of dry-point use the palm of the hand for wiping the plate in preference to rag or muslin) or by too great pressure in the printing press. In any case the burr does not last long and the "bloom" of the early proofs of a dry-point soon wears off. The first two or three proofs, though they may be rough and uneven, often have a charm which can never be replaced by the more even printing of the bulk of the edition, and at some stage, it may be after a dozen proofs, or 20 or 50, according to the manipulation of the plate and the depth to which the lines have been sunk, deterioration inevitably becomes noticeable, unless the plate has been protected from wear by steel-facing. Some engravers assert that this precaution in no way affects the beauty of the proofs, and of some dry-point plates this may be true. But most engravers and most collectors are of opinion that there is an appreciable difference and that, according to Prof. H. W. Singer, "a trained eye can distinguish between the good, warm impressions taken from the copper and the hard, cold ones, taken from the plate after it has been steeled."

There can be no doubt that dry-points printed from the steel-faced plate for book illustration, such as André Dunozer de Segouzac's illustrations to *Les Croix de Bois* by R. Dorgelès (1921), can ill sustain comparison with the few artist's proofs taken before the steel-facing. In fact the process is thoroughly unsuitable for any purpose that requires the production of a large edition printed with mechanical regularity, and the dry-point only yields its essential charm in the hands of a sensitive and conscientious printer—none is better than the artist himself, if he understands the art of printing also —who knows when to stop, at the moment when the plate begins to show signs of wear, and does not feel bound to fulfil a contract by delivering a certain number of proofs, whether the plate will bear it or not. The dry-point, more than any other process of engraving, needs to be under the direct con-

PEN DRAWING

BY COURTESY OF (2, 3, 5, 7) THE METROPOLITAN MUSEUM OF ART, NEW YORK, (10) MRS. E. A. ABBEY; PHOTOGRAPHS, (1) JOHN P. NEWMAN "THRONES AND PALACES OF NINEVEH" (HARPER AND BROTHERS), (4) JOSEPH PENNELL, "PEN DRAWING AND PEN DRAUGHTSMEN" (MACMILLAN), (6) CERVANTES, "DON QUIXOTE" (E. BENN, LONDON, AND CHARLES SCRIBNER, NEW YORK); FROM (8) "GLI ADORNATORI DEL LIBRO IN ITALIA" (CESARE RATTA), (9) C. D. GIBSON, "EDUCATION OF MR. PIP" (LIFE PUBLISHING COMPANY)

EXAMPLES OF PEN DRAWING AND ITS PROTOTYPES

1. "Jewish Captives," a bas-relief in simple outline on the palace wall of Sardanapalus in ancient Nineveh (c. 668–628 B.C.)

2. Page from a 14th century Italian manuscript with border; combined pen and brush lettering

3. "St. Catherine" by Albrecht Dürer (1471–1528), German painter and etcher

4. "The Unfaithful Servant" by Rembrandt van Rijn (1606–74). Dutch

5. Title page of Old Testament from the Luther Bible, 1524, drawn and designed by Erhard Schoen, printed at Nürnberg by Friedrich Peypus

6. "Don Quixote Tied to the Window," an illustration drawn by Daniel Vierge for Thomas Shelton's translation of Cervantes' "Don Quixote," 1906

7. "Venus Lamenting the death of Adonis" by Luca Cambiasi (1527–85), signed with his monogram, L. C. Italian

8. "The Crucifixion" by G. Aristide Sartorio (1861–   ). Contemporary. Italian

9. "Mr. Pip loses his way." From the "Education of Mr. Pip," 1898, by Charles Dana Gibson, American

10. "Enter Mistress Ann Page with wine," from the "Comedies of Shakespeare" series, 1896, by Edwin Austin Abbey (1852–1911). American

11. "The House of Rimmon" by Franklin Booth, American, contemporary

EXAMPLES OF EARLY BOOK-PLATES

1. Earliest known English book-plate, 1515–30, that of Cardinal Wolsey. Not printed, but drawn and coloured by hand

2. Heraldic. Fifteenth century woodcut. One of the three earliest German book-plates known to-day. It was found fastened to the cover of an old Latin vocabulary and is thought to antedate the Brandenburg book-plate

3. German. Earliest portrait book-plate. A copper plate engraving by Albrecht Dürer, 1524, of Bilibald Pirckheimer, a Nuremberg jurist and councillor to the Emperors Maximilian and Charles V.

4. Earliest known Italian dated book-plate, 1622. Anonymous

5. Eighteenth century English book-plate in Chippendale armorial style. This Nicholas Bacon is not to be confused with the Sir Nicholas Bacon of the 1574 book-plate (Fig. 1. Page 867)

6. Early American book-plate, that of Paul Revere, unsigned but undoubtedly engraved by Revere about 1775

7. Earliest known American book-plate, bearing the date 1674 and belonging to John Cotton

8. George Washington's book-plate. Armorial engraving in the Chippendale style, probably between 1765 and 1775

9. Earliest known Dutch book-plate, that of Anna Vander Aa. It bears the date 1597

trol, at every stage, of the artist who has invented the design to which he feels this process, rather than another, to be appropriate.

Corrections.—Two advantages which the dry-point process offers to the original etcher are the power which he possesses when using it of seeing exactly what he is doing with his tool upon the plate, and the comparative ease with which he can make alterations if he changes his mind or requires to correct a fault. Lines already made can be almost entirely obliterated with the burnisher or worked over with other lines, whereas in etching such alterations can only be effected by the much more difficult operation of laying a new ground. To quote E. S. Lumsden, "Corrections are very easily made in dry-point, because so little metal is *removed* from the surface, the strength depending principally upon the upturned ridges. This means that the sides of the lines are comparatively easily closed up by pushing them together with the burnisher. If the passage is to be reworked with heavy strokes, there is no difficulty at all; but if the original surface has to be recovered in order to print a clean tone from it, there is often considerable labour to erase the scratches altogether, as under heavy pressure the faintest indications of a line will show up in the proof. With care and patience anything can be done, and the freshness of the surface kept intact."

The comparative ease with which changes can be made results, in the case of some modern original artists whose work is done in dry-point, in a multiplicity of states. Of a celebrated recent dry-point by Muirhead Bone "A Spanish Good Friday," there are no less than 39 states, the engraver having repeatedly changed his mind about some detail, or thought of a fresh improvement that he could introduce, after he had begun to take proofs.

Dry-point and Etching.—Dry-point has sometimes been used by line-engravers, instead of etching to which they far more frequently resort, in the first preparatory stage (outline) of plates which are subsequently to be finished with the burin. Much more usual is the combination of dry-point with etching. Such a combination may be made either for the purpose of the general enrichment of an etched plate, in a second or subsequent state, by the addition of the dry-point burr, or for the sake of introducing small corrections, which can be made far more easily, though less permanently, by the addition of a few touches or lines with the dry-point than by an additional biting of the etched plate, which involves stopping out or the laying of a fresh ground. Dry-point additions to an etched plate can be readily distinguished by a trained eye in early impressions, but they wear away gradually till all trace of them is lost, and it is the presence of a clearly visible dry-point work, with all the richness that it was intended to impart, that confers value on early impressions of such an etching as the "Hundred Guilder Print" of Rembrandt, in its second state, or on the single state of "Christ Healing the Sick" by the same artist, though both the rich early impressions and the bare late ones from the worn plate which has lost its burr have to be described as belonging to the same state.

HISTORY

IN A RETROSPECT of the use of pure dry-point during the centuries which have elapsed since the invention of engraving, it will appear that its popularity has been intermittent, and that there have been prolonged periods during which, in one country or another, if not in all countries, it has quite fallen out of favour.

Earliest Work.—Its first appearance is earlier than that of etching, for there can be no doubt that the scarce and valuable prints of the "Master of the Hausbuch," a painter-engraver who worked in western Germany (probably on the middle Rhine) about 1480, were produced with the dry-point or possibly with the burin used in the same way, so as to scratch the surface of the copper and throw up a burr, which was not scraped away. This engraver is also called the "Master of the Amsterdam Cabinet" from the fact that the largest collection of his prints, numbering about 80 in all, is in that collection, but the name is to be deprecated, as it suggests that he was a Dutchman. He was a very original artist, and a keen observer of nature, with a technique quite unlike that of any other 15th century engraver.

Dürer.—The next engraver whom we find employing dry-point is Albrecht Dürer, who resorted to this process only in or about the year 1512, and probably abandoned the experiment when he discovered how few good proofs a plate engraved in this manner could yield. There are only three dry-points by Dürer, "The Man of Sorrows" 1512 (Bartsch 21, Dodgson 65), "St. Jerome seated near a Pollard Willow," 1512 (Bartsch 59, Dodgson 66), and its companion print, the undated "Holy Family" of similar dimensions (Bartsch 43, Dodgson 67). Of the two latter dry-points very few good impressions are extant, for the burr wore off rapidly and the majority of extant specimens have been taken from the worn-out plates. Of Dürer's first work in this technique, "St. Jerome," two proofs only exist of a first state before the monogram (in the British Museum, and the Albertina, Vienna). These are of superior quality; the Albertina impression of the second plate is also very fine indeed. A fourth dry-point, "St. Veronica" (Bartsch 64), dated 1510, which figures in the older catalogues as one of the great rarities in Dürer's work, for only two impressions are known, is now discredited, for it has been proved to be a copy of an unsigned woodcut published at Nüremberg in a *Salve Animae* of 1503. Hans Sebald Beham alone of the followers of Dürer used dry-point, and that but sparingly. It is hardly found again in the history of German engraving until a much later date.

Italy.—In Italy also the process was used in early times, chiefly by Andrea Schiavone, or Meldolla (1522?–82), an engraver who worked at Venice, and perhaps also by the monograminist H.E., for early impressions of his prints show signs of burr which in the usual later prints would not be suspected.

Rembrandt.—In the Netherlands dry-point was hardly used, if at all, before the 17th century. Its varied uses, as described above, for the enrichment of the etched plate by the addition of burr to the etched line as well as for the production of pure dry-points, were first discovered and exploited by the greatest of all painter-etchers, Rembrandt, who in his middle period, from about 1639 onwards, used this technique increasingly, in a thoroughly personal manner, for the sake of substituting "colour" and warmth for the drier effect of the pure etchings of his earlier period. From 1640–50 Rembrandt used dry-point extensively for retouching his etched plates—"The Death of the Virgin" and the "Hundred Guilder Print" are examples taken from the beginning and close of this period—while in his last period (1650–61), plates wrought wholly in dry-point became more and more frequent. Among the finest of these must be reckoned "The Goldweigher's Field" (1651); "The Vista" (1652); the two large plates, "The Three Crosses" and "Christ Presented to the People," of 1653 and 1655 respectively and the "Portrait of Arnold Iboliux," 1656. An impression of the exceedingly rare first state of this portrait, in the Rudge collection, sold at auction in Dec. 1924, realized the large sum of 3,600 guineas, the highest price hitherto paid at an auction for an etching, if not for a print of any kind.

The 18th Century.—After Rembrandt, no very considerable use of the dry-point was made by any of the great engravers for a lengthy period. The 17th century was in all countries an age of line-engraving and etching, while in the Low Countries, Germany and England, the invention and development of mezzotint were claiming attention. In the 18th century dry-point was used here and there by a number of painter-etchers, amateurs in their technique as compared with the professional engravers, who found the medium congenial and probably took hints in their use of it from their study of Rembrandt. A beautiful example of such an 18th century dry-point is the portrait of himself, dated 1739, by Arthur Pond (reproduced, *Print Collectors' Quarterly*, 1922, ix. 324). One of the little subjects illustrating the destruction by fire of the Foire de Saint Germain in 1762, by Gabriel de St. Aubin, is a dry-point which seems in its modernity a precursor of the 19th century. In the period which preceded what is known as "the revival of etching," that is to say, during the first half of the 19th century, several English and Scottish etchers produced dry-points of remarkable merit. Among these were D. C. Read, of Salisbury (1790–1821), E. T. Daniell, of Norwich (1804–42), and especially the two Scottish painter-etchers Andrew Geddes (1783–1844) and Sir David Wilkie (1785–1841). Of the last two, catalogues describing all the states of their plates with reproductions of five specimens, will be found in the fifth and eleventh publications of the Walpole Society, 1917 and 1923. Geddes' "Portrait of the Artist's Mother," his "Peckham Rye" and some other landscapes, and Wilkin's one pure dry-point, "The Lost Receipt" are of conspicuous merit if compared with the dry-points of any period. The French etcher, Charles Jacque, also produced, long before 1850 a number of dry-point landscapes, with figures or horses, of great beauty.

Modern Work.—The etchers of the "revival," both in France and England soon brought the dry-point, as well as etching, into renewed favour. In the hands of Haden it yielded masterpieces like "Windmill Hill" and "Sunset in Ireland"; in those of Whistler "Finette," the "Portrait of Axenfield," "Weary" and many more. Legros, soon after 1860, produced "La Promenade du Convalescents," "Femme se baignant les pieds," "Pêcheurs d'écrevisses," and many beautiful landscapes. His pupil, Strang, half a century later, did much fine work in dry-point; so has Sir D. Y. Cameron, especially in his later work since 1903, and especially after 1910. Another master of the technique was Theodore Roussel (1847–1926). Of outstanding excellence among French dry-points of the late 19th century are those of the sculptor Auguste Rodin, whose portraits of Victor Hugo, of Henri Becque, of A. Proust, and "Allégorie du Printemps" and "La Ronde," are among

Plate II   BOOK-PLATES

BOOK–PLATES BY MODERN DESIGNERS

1. By J. W. Spenceley
2. By F. Charles Blank
3. By Sidney L. Smith
4. By Arthur N. Macdonald
5. By Dugald S. Walker
6. By Albert Daniel Rutherston for H. C. Coleman
7. By C. F. A. Voysey
8. Book-plate by Sherborn
9. By J. J. Lankes
10. By Sidney James Hunt
11. Design by Paul Woodroffe
12. By Sidney James Hunt
13. By J. J. Lankes
14. By E. D. French
15. By Franz von Bayros
16. By George W. Eve

DRY-POINTS BY ENGRAVERS AND ETCHERS FROM THE 16TH TO THE 19TH CENTURY

1. "St. Jerome seated near a Pollard Willow" (1512) by Albrecht Dürer, the first of three dry-points. From the impression of the second plate in the Albertina Museum, Vienna

2. "Holy Family" by Albrecht Dürer. Undated, probably about 1512

3. "The Man of Sorrows" (1512) by Albrecht Dürer. This plate and the two preceding were the only dry-points made by Dürer

4. "Portrait of Himself" (1739) by Arthur Pond, one of the English painter-etchers of the 18th century who used the dry-point technique with success

5. "Spectacle des Tuileries" (1760) by Gabriel de St. Aubin. Touched up in dry-point in 1763

6. "Paysage, O'Orage" (1848) by Charles Jacque, a French etcher who produced a number of dry-point landscapes with figures of horses

7. "Portrait of the Artist's Mother" (1822) by Andrew Geddes

8. Trial proof (Oct. 7, 1877) of "Windmill Hill," dry-point by Seymour Haden, one of the leading English etchers of the 19th century

9. "Sunset in Ireland" (from a very rich imprint) by Seymour Haden, 1863

the masterpieces of the medium. The French painter and etcher, J. L. Forain, produced some superb dry-points about 1909–10 and later. Among modern British engravers, Muirhead Bone is pre-eminent as a master of dry-point, in which medium almost the whole of his very numerous plates since 1898 have been wrought. His brother-in-law, Francis Dodd, since 1907, has done much good work in dry-point, and among later followers Henry Rushbury has come into the front rank. Another excellent engraver in dry-point is Edmund Blampied; C. W. R. Nevinson produced work of great merit in this medium during the World War.

ADVANCED TECHNIQUE

SOME DRY-POINT ARTISTS use a plate prepared or blackened as for etching, taking care to cut through the varnish to the metal surface underneath, and using the varying emphasis required by their design; for in dry-point everything must be drawn delicately or strongly by the artist himself as in ordinary drawing. The difficulty of working on the blackened plate is that it is not easy to judge exactly what emphasis has been used in making the lines, so the bare plate is more often used and a little weak black paint rubbed into the lines to mark their progress. Great care should be taken to do such inking of the lines as gently and as sparingly as possible, as the burr is easily injured during the progress of an elaborate plate with the result that the earlier portions of the work may look quite different from the later. Another difficulty will be found in the varying degrees of *sharpness* of the point used. A steel point requires resharpening frequently and the sharpening may not be exactly the same each time and this difference will be found reflected in the work. To obviate this, a diamond or ruby point is frequently used and works very smoothly when in good condition. It is, however, somewhat brittle and apt to flake away in strong cross-hatching or by striking the edge of the plate.

Dry-point has several striking advantages over etching: (*a*) The work can be more easily judged on the bare plate, being positive in character, *i.e.*, the lines appearing black (if filled in with black paint) exactly as in the print. (*b*) Corrections are more easily made as the lines are shallower and the metal being thrown up in furrows and not removed from the plate, can be forced back into the groove with a burnisher. Additions to the work can be easily made since the plate requires no regrounding and rebiting as in etching. (*c*) A trial print can be easily taken at any stage of the work,

243

though it should be remembered that the fewer trial proofs that are taken the better, as a dry-point may easily be worn out in the course of a protracted series of trial proofs.

The point, the burnisher and the scraper are the three instruments used in dry-point: the use of the scraper is of much more importance than it is in etching, as the burr can be wholly or partly removed by it and the whole significance of the line altered. Some artists even remove the burr altogether and depend on the "nervous" character of the dry-point line for their effect.

One great disadvantage of dry-point is the difficulty of obtaining a large number of prints of equal excellence, owing to the delicate character of the work compared with etching or line-engraving. This has been largely overcome by the practice of steel-facing the plate before printing. It has led (especially in recent years) to the mixed plate, where dry-point is strengthened and stiffened by engraved lines done with the burin. The result is work obviously clearer and firmer in character than many pure dry-points, but lacking the particular charm of the best dry-point prints where spontaneity and vivacity (not characteristics of the burin) are most important assets. The best qualities of the two mediums are really incompatible. We cannot imagine a burin line introduced into the masterpieces of dry-point without fatal results. Dry-point is also used to lend to etched plates a "warmth" or "accent," or simply as the easiest method of making necessary additions. The difficulty then is that the dry-point lines wear out under the pressure of printing much earlier than the etched lines, and it becomes necessary to renew the dry-point work from time to time. From the pictorial point of view dry-point has the disadvantage of producing a picture too often "out of tone" and "spotty," owing to the somewhat accidental emphasis of the burr. From the point of view of style the dry-point needle is capable of too many different kinds of strokes; yet these difficulties only add to the fascination of trying to overcome them as they have been overcome by the great masters of the art.

Steel-facing and Printing Dry-points.—The question of steel-facing is surrounded by a prejudice in the eyes of collectors because it allows of larger editions being printed. The old steel-facing was heavy and clumsy compared with what is used to-day, and must have injured the dry-point on its application. Then, too, editions used to be printed from the copper and only after that steel-faced for a commoner kind of print. And the steel-faced plate being considered "fool-proof" was handed over to unintelligent printing—the fact not being recognized that a steel-faced plate really requires more and not less care in printing. For the delicate tones of the printing ink are more difficult to estimate with nicety on the less "sympathetic" surface of the steel. Still, it is true that for certain plates requiring delicate tones of printing-ink to supplement the line work steel-facing is not appropriate. If steel-facing is determined on, this should be done immediately the plate is completed and it should be remembered that the cleaner the plate and its lines have been kept during working the better, as the plate has to be made chemically clean before the electro-steeling and the smaller the amount of cleaning required the better for the preservation of the burr and the delicate lines.

Printing dry-points is a difficult art for the line and its burr lends itself to many different styles of printing. Care should be taken to give a clearness and purity to lines which so easily become clogged and heavy. The aim should be, while retaining the ink caught by the burr, to remove all the smudginess and heavy tone *between* the lines. This can best be done by repeated hand-wiping of the plate from all directions while the plate is fairly warm. Dry-point printing—or rather the preparing of the plate for the press —is thus a much slower process than etching printing, as so much more careful hand-wiping is required. "Retroussage" should be sparingly used, as the ink on the burr is easily smudged. A soft paper shows a dry-point to most advantage.

Because of its very simplicity, dry-point is a peculiarly "autographic" medium, very sensitive to the display of the temperament of the artist. All etched work bears a strong family resemblance, and still more so work with the burin. But a collection of the best dry-points shows an astonishing difference in the mere appearance of the lines. This is the great fascination of the craft, as a peculiarly personal style has been attained in it again and again. It is as capable of as many styles as drawing itself, to which indeed it is the nearest of all methods of making prints. There is no chemistry to overcome—no accidentals—the old gibe, levelled at etching, of "a blundering art" does not apply. If the student studies carefully the dry-points of Rembrandt, Whistler, Haden and Rodin, the immense range and possibilities of the medium should be clearly grasped. The inimitably natural stroke of the first, the sweeping "silky" line of the second, the abrupt strokes so suggestive of painters' colour of the third, the chisel-like cutting of the fourth—

there is no range comparable to this in any other system of making prints, and new triumphs of individual method in dry-point may yet have to be recorded.

DESIGN

DESIGN is the arrangement of lines or forms which make up the plan of a work of art with especial regard to the proportions, structure, movement and beauty of line of the whole. A design may be naturalistic or wholly the abstract conception of the artist. Its structure is related to the structure of the frame and the rendering of the subject, but not to the structure or anatomy of the subject itself. A design may be successful which is incorrect in every detail of anatomy. Design in one sense is synonymous with composition, and has to do with all the arts, though more pronounced in the applied arts than in the fine arts.

The Japanese artist Korin arrived at much of his design through the selection of certain parts of purely natural arrangements which were simplified and selected as typical, but which were rendered in a naturalistic manner. Much of modern design is not so made up, but consists of gross distortion for the overstressing of structure or movement, with a complete loss of other characteristics. This type of design is so close to caricature that it often detracts rather than adds to the beauty of a work of art.

Design is concerned not only with typical movement but also with typical rhythms. Through the medium of parallel master strokes or accenting of repeating movements, rhythms are set up which should, like the rhythms of great poetry, accent the meaning and express a crystallization of the personality of the artist, and at the same time of his subject as seen through his eyes. Just as in "The Raven" by Poe, we have the summing up of all of Poe's mood in his work and at the same time have the summing up of the expression of all human despair in the bird's recurring "Never more," so in the design of a master of the graphic arts will be found accents and rhythms which build the mood he wishes to establish. Design is to the graphic arts what verse form and rhyme are to poetry: the ladder up which

246

it climbs to the heights. Design can exist without colour, but just as there can be design in line and mass so there can also be design in colour, based upon the distribution of harmoniously blending or contrasting tones; when design is present in both line and colour the two must work together to further the effect of the conception. Every element of art can be designed separately and in relation to the other elements. Thus there can be structural design, movement design, outline design.

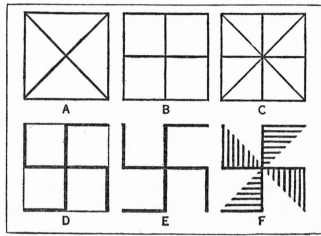

FIG. 52.—PROGRESSIVE STEPS IN THE FORMING OF A SWASTIKA WITHIN A SQUARE

Teaching.—In the teaching of design it is often helpful to have the student cut out various pieces of paper representing the main areas to be used and move them about within the size area, cut out of the centre of another piece of paper, upon which he is to work. When these have been arranged to his satisfaction, lines should be thrown in which tie the whole together; and finally, with these established areas and lines to guide him, work can be begun. The Chinese artist does this mentally as he sits contemplating the silk upon which he is to paint, for he has trained his mind to remember the arrangement once he has decided upon it. The student can teach himself to do this, but it is well to begin with the more objective method.

It is interesting to note that in given areas only a certain number of effective designs are possible, and that man has hit upon them in every part of the world without intercommunication. Scientists have tried to prove a common origin for the race because of the almost universal use of the swastika, but many children who have never seen this sign arrive at it spontaneously, when left to decorate squares. The steps are simple (*see* fig. 52):

(1) The corners, which catch the eye quickest for a starting point, are

247

joined; (2) the sides; (3) both are combined and before long, in the age-old attempt to represent movement, the spurs are discovered and all sorts of variations follow. The "wave" or "vine" or "running" border is developed in like manner, because it is the most obvious way to decorate a narrow space between parallel lines. We usually find (A) the geometrical treatment (fig. 53); (B) the curve with open areas which are soon (C) filled with spots as-

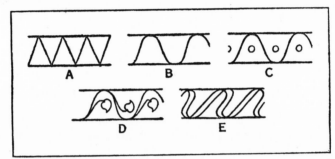

FIG. 53.—DEVELOPMENT OF WAVE, OR VINE, DESIGN WITHIN PARALLEL LINES FROM SIMPLE GEOMETRICAL FORM

suming the shape of leaves on a vine as time goes on (D) and, an excuse for their being is demanded. Finally, as in (E), the movement is increased and it becomes on many Tzu Chow vases of China a leaping rather than a running border, representative of waves from which the fiery dragon ascends.

Development.—The typical Persian ogee design has an interesting origin which is demonstrable on existing vases. In fig. 54 (A) is shown the old

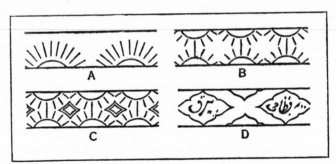

FIG. 54.—PROBABLE EVOLUTION OF TYPICAL PERSIAN OGEE DESIGN FROM OLD ZOROASTRIAN MOTIF

Zoroastrian motif of the rising sun which only loosely filled the border; other suns were introduced at a still earlier period. In a further attempt to build the border together a design was inserted between them, which sometimes held written characters and finally, as the religion is developed, the suns disappear and ogee patterns are fitted together, becoming a typical national motif.

248

DESIGN

Design is, therefore, old and has been thought of for many thousand years, and the student does well to acquaint himself with early examples found in various parts of the world. It is almost as difficult to create a new design as it is to discover a new geometric principle; but another element enters design, and, once having learned it as one would learn geometry, there is available, instead of a cold, mathematical deduction, a vehicle for the expression of one's personal sense of beauty.

ORIGINALITY

MODERN USE has tended to associate design with the word "original" in the sense of new or abnormal. But the end of design is utility, fitness and delight. If a discovery, it should be a discovery of what seems inevitable, an inspiration arising out of the conditions, and parallel to invention in the sciences. The faculty of design has best flourished when an almost spontaneous development was taking place in the arts, and while certain classes of arts, more or less noble, were generally demanded and the demand copiously satisfied, as in the production of Chinese porcelain, Greek vases, Byzantine mosaics, Gothic cathedrals and Renaissance paintings. Thus where a "school of design" arises there is much general likeness in the products but also a general progress. The common experience—"tradition"—is a part of each artist's stock in trade; and all are carried along in a stream of continuous exploration. Some of the arts, writing, for instance, have been little touched by conscious originality in design, all has been progress, or, at least, change, in response to conditions. Under such a system, in a time of progress, the proper limitations react as intensity; when limitations are removed the designer has less and less upon which to react, and unconditioned liberty gives him nothing at all to lean on. Design is response to needs, conditions and aspirations. The Greeks so well understood this that they appear to have consciously restrained themselves to the development of selected types, not only in architecture and literature, but in domestic arts, like pottery. Design with them was less the new than the true.

For the production of a school of design it is necessary that there should be a considerable body of artists working together, and a large demand from a sympathetic public. A process of continuous development is thus brought into being which sustains the individual effort. It is necessary for the designer to know familiarly the processes, the materials and the skilful use of the tools involved in the productions of a given art, and properly only one who

249

practises a craft can design for it. It is necessary to enter into the traditions of the art, that is, to know past achievements. It is necessary, further, to be in relation with nature, the great reservoir of ideas, for it is from it that fresh thought will flow into all forms of art. These conditions being granted, the best and most useful meaning we can give to the word design is exploration, experiment, consideration of possibilities. Putting too high a value on originality other than this is to restrict natural growth from vital roots, in which true originality consists. To take design in architecture as an example, we have rested too much on definite precedent (a different thing from living tradition) and, on the other hand, hoped too much from newness. Exploration of the possibilities in arches, vaults, domes and the like, as a chemist or a mathematician explores, is little accepted as a method in architecture at this time, although in antiquity it was by such means that the great master-works were produced: the Pantheon, Santa Sophia, Durham and Amiens cathedrals. The same is true of all forms of design. Of course the genius and inspiration of the individual artist is not here ignored, but assumed. What we are concerned with is a mode of thought which shall make it most fruitful.

MONOTYPES

A MONOTYPE is a unique print, taken either by passing the metal plate on which the picture has been done through a printing press, like an etching or engraving, or by hand-rubbing, like a woodcut, which is less effective, or, perhaps better still, by rubbing with an ivory or bone paper-knife. By the last process the paper can be lifted now and again, so that the progress of the print may be watched, and more or less pressure exerted where it is necessary to emphasize the gradations of dark or light, for the print is really an emotional effect, and it must not be forgotten that the plate has not been engraved at all. The subject has been either painted direct in oils or thick inks at a single sitting, or the plate has been thinly covered with ink or dark paint, not too oily, then the subject has been gradually evolved by the manipulation of the lights with the finger, a rag, or a brush, to suggest form by

EXAMPLES OF THE DRY–POINT TECHNIQUE

Dry-point is generally classed as a variety of etching, though actually a kind of engraving. In dry-points no acid is used on the plate, as in pure etching, but the lines are hollowed out of the copper with a sharp pointed instrument. The raised edge of copper turned up by the tool is called the "burr." This, in the printing, produces the soft velvety effect peculiar to dry-points

1. "Weary" by James Abbott McNeill Whistler, finished in 1872
2. "Christ Healing the Sick" (the "Hundred Guilder Print") by Rembrandt. An etching of his middle period (1640–50) retouched with dry-point
3. Portrait of Arnold Tholinx by Rembrandt, 1656
4. Portrait of Victor Hugo by Auguste Rodin (1840–1917)

5. Portrait of Henri Becque by Auguste Rodin
6. Portrait of Victor Hugo by Auguste Rodin
7. "Third Avenue" by C. W. R. Nevinson, contemporary British
8. "The Vista" by Rembrandt, 1652
9. "La Route d'Emmaus" by J. L. Forain, contemporary French

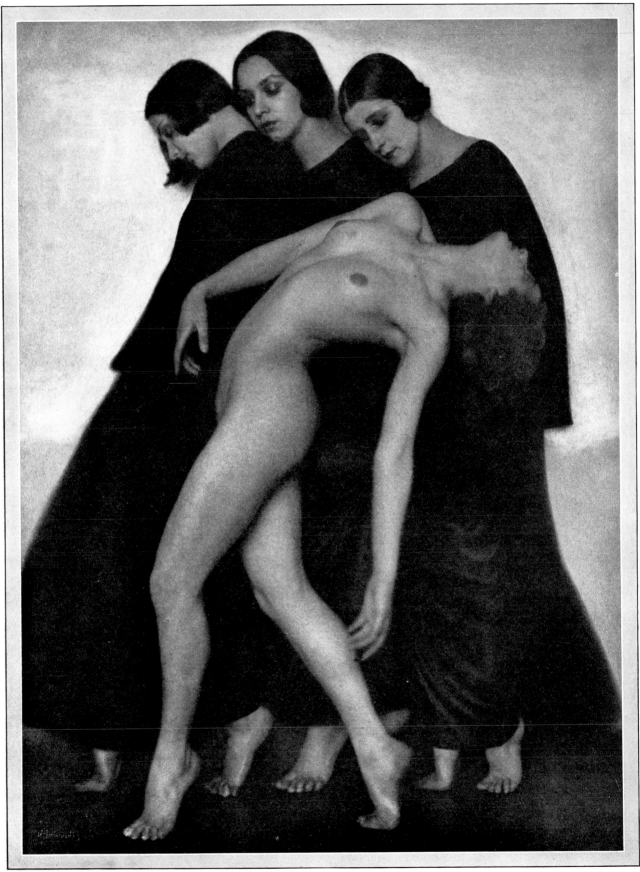

A PHOTOGRAPHIC STUDY IN MOVEMENT

A study by Dr. Rudolph Koppitz of Vienna; an important print, one copy of which has been acquired by the Tyng Foundation Trustees, for the permanent collection of the Royal Photographic Society. It is remarkably beautiful because of the strong massing of the figures, and for the rhythm expressed in the curved composition of the four heads, the sweep of curve of the body, and the pattern of the feet

a full range of tone, as the lights are scraped away in mezzotint. A mono-type resembles a mezzotint in effect, with its rich velvety blacks, and subtle half-tones, but to ensure a successful print, it must be taken while the paint is wet. Since only one print can be obtained, the method seems scarcely worth while, except for the fun of the thing. In recent years, many artists have amused themselves with it. Indeed, Sir Hubert Herkomer was an en-thusiast, and with his natural zest for experiment he dusted the plate with powder, to suggest the effect of a grain; then he made a mould or electrotype, so that impressions could be taken, but it then, of course, ceased to be a monotype.

ART

IN ANY ATTEMPT to arrive at a clear and comprehensive definition of the meaning of art it is necessary to disregard all philological or etymological der-ivations which, in the past, have led to much confusion of thought and to an expansion of the human activities embraced by this term, which oversteps the limitations imposed upon it by the modern conception of its meaning. We are not concerned with the meaning attached to the word Art, or its Greek, Latin and German equivalents, in the past, which was so vague that almost all attempts to define it led to contradictory and often diametrically opposed conclusions, but with the more restricted and purely æsthetic interpretation put upon it by modern thinkers.

The old meaning, in its widest sense, of the Greek τέχνη, the Latin *ars*, the German *Kunst* (derived from *Können*), implied skill and ability, ac-quired through patient practice and directed towards a definite end, whether this end be æsthetical, ethical or useful. According to their aim the arts would thus be divided into Fine Arts, Arts of Conduct, and Liberal Arts, the Fine Arts being concerned with the attainment of the beautiful, the Arts of Conduct with the good, and the Liberal Arts with the useful.

In the modern and more restricted sense the term art applies only to those human activities which tend towards an æstheticism—in other words, the Fine Arts—and although, in a figurative way, we speak of the art of cooking, the art of the chase, the art of living, the art of war, and so forth, neither cooking, nor hunting, nor living, nor warfare would ever be seriously included in a list of the arts which embraces the static arts—architecture, sculpture and painting, with their subdivisions—and the dynamic arts—music, poetry and the drama (rhetoric).

Many attempts have been made to explain the essential nature of art, the quality which distinguishes art from all other manifestations of human activity, but most of them lack clearness, do not cover the whole field, or are capable of being extended to non-artistic activities. A number of writers on æsthetics, from Plato and Schiller to K. Lange, recognizing the non-utilitarian, immaterialistic character of art, explain it as a form of play—a theory which cannot be reconciled with the now generally accepted notion that superstitious fear of the unknown forces of nature is one of the main springs of artistic creation in primitive man who, by the productions of his art, tries to placate the mysterious hostile powers or to create symbols of stability and rest in the bewildering turmoil of the universe.

Equally unsatisfactory, in the light of modern speculation is the *Einfühlung* (empathy, *q.v.*) theory, first advanced by Herder and elaborated, among others, by Vernon Lee, which, whilst throwing valuable light on the true nature of æsthetic enjoyment, does not supply a complete solution of the problem presented by the investigation of the basic constitution of art. Neither is this solution to be found in Croce's equation of art and intuition, nor in Santayana's "objectified pleasure"; less still in the entirely fallacious popular definition of art being nature seen through a temperament. Tolstoy came nearer the truth in insisting upon emotional impulse as indispensable to all artistic expression, but went sadly astray in the elaboration of his theory.

It is scarcely necessary to insist upon the fallacy of such popular notions as the identifications of art with the representation of nature, or, worse still, of the beautiful in nature. Art is not representation, but interpretation; and it is not too much to say that art begins where the artist departs from strict imitation of nature, imposing upon her a rhythm of his own creation, according to his own sense of fitness. Nature is the artist's inexhaustible source of inspiration, but the laws which govern the work of art are wholly independent from the laws of nature. If the Pastoral Symphony is a sublime work of art, it is because Beethoven, far from imitating the sounds of nature in the manner of "programme music" (which more often than not is but remotely connected with art), expressed the emotions awakened in him by intimate communion with nature in terms of abstract rhythm dictated to him by his inspiration and controlled by that perfect craftmanship which is essential to the creation of a work of art.

ART AND NATURE

IT IS TRUE that the arts of painting and sculpture, less abstract than the art of music, necessitate a higher degree of verisimilitude to nature; but it is equally certain that the æsthetic appeal of the painter's or sculptor's work, though enhanced by the pleasure of recognition and association with familiar visual experience, is based on abstract qualities akin to the qualities of music, the difference being merely the medium—sound in the one case, form and colour in the other. But whereas our ears are trained to be susceptible to the rhythmic combination of sounds and to accept the musical work of art without probing into the representational meaning of these sounds, the æsthetic education of our eyes has been comparatively neglected. Instinctively we turn to the painting or piece of sculpture with a feeling of curiosity as to its meaning. Instinctively we compare it with our own experience of natural appearance and are apt to make its verisimilitude the criterion of its artistic merit, disregarding, at first sight at least, the abstract rhythm of form and colour which distinguishes the work of art from the mechanical imitation of nature. The associations of the subject are apt to blind us to the essential art qualities. If the Japanese painter looks at a landscape through his straddling legs with his head lowered to the level of his knees, it is because, through seeing his subject upside down, he is not led astray by the associations of the various "incidents" that constitute the landscape, and his attention is riveted upon the pure pattern of colours and forms. For the same reason many Western painters, in the course of their work, at times turn their canvas upside down in order to be able to concentrate on the abstract qualities of the design, which are obscured by "life-like" representation.

If representational truth were the criterion of the work of art, a good photograph would have a better claim to this title than an Egyptian statue, a torso by Michelangelo, the *Primavera* of Botticelli, or a landscape by Claude or by Cézanne. Yet photography has no place among the arts, even though the photographer may, by his tact in selection, give evidence of a good deal of artistic taste. It does not rank among the arts, because it has to accept

253

nature uncontrolled and unmodified. And it is just that power of control and purposeful modification—*vide* the broad simplification and relations of planes in the Egyptian statue; the amplified muscles and heightened vitality of the Michelangelo torso; the graceful arabesque line of Botticelli's decorative painting; the orderly classic arrangement of the features in Claude's landscape; the deliberate architectural building up and accentuation of volumes in the Cézanne—that constitute the artistic significance of these works.

The function of art is the creation of beauty. Indeed, it may be said that there is no beauty outside art, or, to be more exact, no beauty that has not been revealed by art. Nothing in nature is either beautiful or ugly, for beauty and ugliness are not positive attributes of matter, but matter is invested with these attributes by the artist's emotional reactions to some outside stimulus. Beauty thus resolves itself into objectified aesthetic emotion. The artist has the power to make this emotion visible or audible to others, and to make them partake of his pleasurable excitement. We become aware of beauty and acquire the habit of transferring it from the work of art to the aspect of nature which was the source of its inspiration. We learn to see beauty in a tree, in a mountain, and even in things which, before the artist had opened our eyes, left us cold or even repelled us. A toothless old hag becomes beautiful under Rembrandt's magic touch, because he saw his subject emotionally and taught us to see it in the same way. It is doubtful if anybody found anything but dinginess and "ugliness" in the mist and fog of the Thames-side in London before Whistler, by the work of his brush and the poetic imagery of his "Ten o'clock Lecture," invested the murky London atmosphere with permanent beauty.

To go farther back, it is extremely doubtful whether the otherwise highly cultured anthropocentric Greek mind that evolved the ideal type of human proportions, which to this day remains the standard of perfection, was capable of discerning any beauty in the inanimate world. The Greek artist aimed at a perfection of symmetry and rhythm which was beyond the reach of nature. When, therefore, he borrowed any forms from nature, he evolved from them a stylistic formula representing the ideal type of these forms—an ideal which has no counterpart in actual existence. Greek ornament, architectural and otherwise, owes its origin to this attitude.

Until the dawn of the Renaissance in Italy the beauty of mountain scenery was a closed book to the mediaeval mind. A mountain was a thing to be shunned, an impediment to traffic, a source of danger and fatigue. Even a poet of the stamp of Petrarch found it necessary, in a long letter, to plead, as an excuse for his eccentricity in undertaking an unnecessary mountain expedition—an almost unheard-of adventure in his days—the example of Philip of Macedonia, who had ascended Mount Haemus in a similar spirit of enterprise. But this letter, which fills ten printed pages, whilst containing much information about the hardships, dangers and fatigue of the expedition, and theoretical reflections which might as well have been penned at the desk in his study, includes no hint of emotional response to nature in her most majestic moods, no description, no word of aesthetic appreciation. Petrarch in this proved himself the child of his time. Mountains only became beautiful in the eyes of mankind after Giotto and his followers had introduced them into their pictures to replace the traditional gold backgrounds of early mediaeval art. Art had then once more fulfilled its educational mission.

That beauty is not an attribute of nature, but of art, or of the artist's mind, need scarcely be demonstrated. If it were not so, it would be an immutable value, not subject to fluctuations. Yet, not only does the ideal of beauty change with successive generations, but it varies with races and individuals. It is only the beauty values set up by art that remain permanent, and their appreciation is largely a matter of artistic education. To define art as the attainment of the beautiful would, therefore, only be substituting one term for another, and would necessitate the even more elusive definition of the beautiful. Clive Bell's "significant form" as the determining factor of all art does not take us any further, for this "significant form" is only beauty in a new disguise. It would be as difficult to establish where exactly form becomes significant or where beauty begins.

Beauty, although the aim of art, has thus to be eliminated from any plausible and receptable definition of art. To find such a definition it is necessary to trace the common denomination of the infinitely varied manifestations of human activity which legitimately come under the heading of art, the peculiar characteristic which distinguishes the work of art both from the product of natural forces and of purely industrial activity. What is there in common between, say, a Gothic cathedral, a Beethoven symphony, a Greek vase, a Rembrandt etching, a Giotto fresco, a Shakespeare sonnet, the Ludovisi "Throne of Venus," the stained glass windows of Chartres cathedral, a Benin bronze, an Ispahan carpet, and a Euripedes tragedy, to explain their being accounted as works of art, whilst no such claim could be advanced for a coloured photograph, a cast of the human figure from life, the tawdry mantel ornament of factory production, a piece of doggerel verse, or a rubbishy ballad?

THE PLACE OF CRAFTSMANSHIP

THE DEGREE of expressional power acquired by the mastery of craftsmanship, the greater or lesser intensity of the emotional urge, and the varying skill in adjusting the rhythmic relations of lines, colours, forms, sounds or words, distinguish the masterpiece from the inferior artistic production.   It is for this reason that Leonardo da Vinci and Michelangelo and Rembrandt stand for all time as supreme masters, whilst their imitators, notwithstanding all their executive skill, are relegated to a comparatively insignificant position in the hierarchy of art.   The mysterious smile of the Mona Lisa becomes a meaningless smirk when perpetuated in innumerable versions by apt pupils of the stamp of Gianpietrino.   The muscular accentuation and amplification of Michelangelo's heroic sculpture assume an almost ludicrous aspect in Bandinelli and other Italian sculptors of the mid-16th century, because the generation that stood under the spell of the master's genius annexed—and often distorted to the verge of caricature -his forms without having experienced the emotional impulse to which these forms owed their existence. Their relation to Michelangelo finds a counterpart in the attitude of the early 19th century pseudo-classic sculptors to Pheidias and Praxiteles.

Craftsmanship is the handmaiden of art, but is, in the popular mind, often confused with art.   Innumerable pictures are produced, year by year, by painters who are endowed with a certain amount of technical skill, but who lack the power of expression because they have nothing to express— copies of nature, painstaking or careless, as the case may be, but devoid of the three elements of art: emotion, expression and rhythm.   Such pictures are no more entitled to be reckoned as works of art than the rows of featureless, ill-proportioned brick houses in the working quarters of a modern manufacturing town can claim to be regarded as examples of architectural art.

The function of art is almost as difficult to define as the meaning of art. The main purpose of art is to give pleasure; and for this reason art is held by many to be a useless luxury for the idle.   From a materialistic point of view art certainly is useless, in so far as it produces nothing of a strictly utilitarian character.

Yet art is, and has always been, an indispensable need of humanity.   It is implanted in the soul of the child, as in that of primitive man.   It is as necessary as articulate speech. It is indispensable to civilization. It is the art of each race that gives its civilization its distinct character and rhythm. It reflects, if it does not actually condition, the whole manner of life of a nation or period. Life and art are closely, inseparably interwoven, but life passes—the life of individuals and the life of nations—and art remains. It is the only thing that is permanent; and our knowledge of the past, of civilizations that have flourished and disappeared, is derived almost entirely from the fragmentary relics of their art. It is not from printed books that we visualize and form our estimate of the life, culture and character of ancient Egypt, Assyria, Greece or Rome, but from the ruined buildings, carved stones, half-decayed bronzes, fragments of pottery, frescoed walls, personal adornments and household objects dug out of the ground by the excavator's spade, which are of far greater and more lasting significance than the transitory effects of great wars and revolutionary political changes. History becomes a living reality to us through art. Without it, it would be a dead letter. Above all, art brings pure pleasure into the humblest life. It is a source of exaltation that raises us above the sordid realities of everyday existence. Without art, life would be intolerable, inconceivable. The human imagination requires food as imperiously as the human body, and art is the inexhaustible spring from which our imagination draws sustenance.

PHOTOGRAPHIC ART

THE MODERN TENDENCY in photography in the hands of both amateur and professional exponents is to employ the camera as a means of artistic expression. No consideration is being taken here of the widespread applications of photography in scientific and technical directions. It is more in reference to its position in the realms of art that this article is written. The appeal to the eye is greater than the appeal to the emotions through any other sense, and in this respect photography occupies a unique position as a maker of pictures. Many thousands of individuals are producing photographs, with the ulterior object of their appeal to the eye as pictorial representations of incidents of interest. Unfortunately, a very large majority of those who use the camera are not artists; in this way the prestige of photography as an art is apt to suffer.

Photography can be regarded as an art in precisely the same way that any other graphic process can be regarded as an art when it is dealt with and conducted by an artist. The process is really a medium of expression, and the camera, lens and sensitive material merely the tools employed. The true artist who seeks to express himself can, within the limitations of his tools and material, do so in any medium that appeals to him for the purpose, and the measure of success that attends the result a work of art is entirely the measure of the ability and inspiration of the artist. It is recognized that photography has limitations that are imposed by the apparatus employed. When these are recognized, the camera becomes a most facile instrument as a means of expression, and the main idea of picture making in photography is the same as that put forward by the artist with any other medium. It is, in brief, that the individual with something to say is never inarticulate. He may find paint, or music, or the pen most responsive for his expression. Photography, with its remarkable ease of production, has solved the difficulty for many.

In 1840-1853, Daguerreotype and Calotype were very popular, and a Scottish artist, D. O. Hill, made a series of portraits in Calotype in 1844–1845, which are still regarded as remarkable examples of pictorial portraiture. From that time onwards, a great variety of investigations and experiments were conducted, and the work steadily progressed towards simplification. An outstanding development was the introduction of the gelatine process; dry plates were regularly used and the foundations of modern photography were laid. From this time onward the progress became very rapid, as both the materials and the apparatus were being steadily improved. Printing processes increased and cameras were simplified.

Colour Photography in Art.—The photography of coloured objects received attention in the early stages of the history of photography, when it was observed that the tones rendered in monochrome on the photographic plate were not true comparative renderings of the originals, the blue end of the spectrum being rendered practically as white, and the red end of the spectrum practically as black. This irregular sensitiveness to different colours continued until Dr. H. W. Vogel found that the addition of certain dyes to the silver salt in the sensitive emulsion for plates made them more sensi-

PLATE II

PHOTOGRAPHIC ART

A BRIDGE IN MONTENEGRO

A landscape photographic study by Alexander Keighley, Hon. F.R.P.S. Printing medium, bromoil. The well-chosen angle from which the old bridge is taken gives great depth of perspective to the subject. The background is well blended in, the reflections break up what would otherwise be a rather flat foreground. As a result of the low viewpoint, the stonework looms high enough to make the single arch and its deep shadow the logical centre of the composition

A SEA BANQUET

A seascape by F. J. Mortimer, F.R.P.S., a leading English photographer. Printing medium, bromide. There is a fine blending and graduation of the perturbed sea and the stormy sky. The flock of birds is caught at such a point that it forms a sweeping curve guiding the eye to the crest of the highest wave, the picture's intended centre of attention. The movement of the wings of gulls is beautifully expressed in the clattering of those in the foreground and the easy sweep of the gliding birds in the background

tive to yellow and red. This was the foundation of orthochromatic and panchromatic plates and films as they exist to-day. However, colour photography, that is, photography in natural colours, has proceeded on other lines, and may still be regarded as being in the experimental stage.

Processes in which coloured results have been achieved have also been arrived at in cinematography, as well as in printing processes, in which the colours have been entirely under the control of the producer of the print and can hardly be regarded as colour photography at all.

Printing Processes.—In recent times, printing processes have also been perfected and others have appeared in which personal control has placed great power in the hands of the worker for pictorial effects. In regard to the direct printing processes, one of the earliest silver methods in which the silver salts were incorporated with albumen, is no longer employed. Gelatine has taken the place of albumen and printing-out-papers have been of the variety known as gelatine-chloride. In these, chloride of silver and gelatine have formed the base of the emulsion coating the paper, the image has been printed out beneath the negative and subsequently toned. Still more recently, bromide and gaslight papers have been the most popular printing media, the former being paper coated with an emulsion of bromide of silver, and the latter with chloro-bromide of silver. Both of these are known as development papers, the image being latent after the exposure and has to be chemically developed to produce a visible image. Many varieties of chloro-bromide papers are in use to-day and are proving extremely popular printing media for pictorial workers, both amateur and professional.

On the "control" processes, gum-bichromate was popular for a period and is still used by some pictorial workers. In this process, paper is coated with bichromatised gum and a suitable pigment. After exposure under a negative, the parts that have not been acted on by light and rendered insoluble, are washed away in water. The personal control in the result is entirely in the hands of the worker, according to the desired result. To a certain extent this process is similar to the carbon process, in which pigment and bichromatised gelatine are coated on paper, and after exposure beneath a negative, the tissue is placed in contact with another support and the image developed in hot water by dissolving away the unacted-upon gelatine.

The most recent developments in control processes have been in oil and bromoil, the former being founded on the action of light on bichromatised gelatine, which is coated on to plain paper, exposed under a negative, and then soaked in water. The parts that have not been acted on by light absorb water in proportion to the light action. In this condition, those parts of the print which have been acted upon by light, and represent the shadows of the original subject, can be made receptive to an oily pigment when dabbed on with a suitable brush, and the picture thus built up in pigment. The original drawing of the photograph is retained, but the tone values are entirely under the control of the operator. In the bromoil process, a print on bromide paper is bleached in a solution in which bichromate salt appears, the bleached image taking on the same qualities when soaked in water as the printed bichromate image in the oil process, and pigment is applied in the same way.

The carbro process is a development of the carbon process in which the same principle applies, and both carbro and bromoil processes have become very popular among pictorial workers in photography, not only on account of the control in the final result that is placed in their hands, but from the fact that the prints can be made from enlargements on bromide paper made from small negatives.

In amateur work in particular, small negatives with subsequent enlarging on to bromide paper produce finished results, either in that process or in bromoil, that account for a large proportion of modern exhibition work. All the tendency to-day is towards simplifying and making smaller and more effective the apparatus for the pictorial worker. The portable hand-camera with speeded shutters, large aperture lenses, and high-speed plates and films have rendered the production of negatives of high quality possible for the multitude, while in the hands of the expert, the most perfect tools are available for use.

Controlled Processes.—The real factors that decide the success of a picture by photography are those which occur before the exposure is made and after the negative has been developed. The use of accurate apparatus, intelligently used with a knowledge of its limitations and with the employment of the right type of plate or film, is a matter within the scope of practically anyone. For the production of pictorial work which may rank as art, the mental outlook that precedes the taking of the photograph and the manipulative processes that occur in the making of the final print, will determine the artistic quality of the result. The selection of subject, choice of viewpoint and due consideration of the lighting effect are three elements of picture making, where the trained artist has the advantage, and it is in these respects

260

that the photographer who is an artist can make the most of his subject, using the apparatus thereafter merely as a recording instrument to secure in a fraction of time the picture that has been visualized. The photographer, therefore, who is by instinct an artist, or who has had an art training, is more likely to make photographs that can rank as art than the snapshotter without these qualifications. After the plate has been exposed and the negative developed, it is in the production of the final print that the artist again finds scope for individuality. The same negative mechanically printed, on the one hand, or treated with care and thought by an artist to produce a beautiful picture by a controlled process, on the other hand, can be two widely different things. It does not necessarily mean from this that controlled printing processes employed indiscriminately, and without very definite knowledge of the final result required, will produce a picture; there is much evidence to the contrary. But many of the finest pictorial results by photography that rank high in pictorial art have been produced by one of the various controlled processes when employed by a worker who is an artist.

Bromoil Process.—Of these processes, probably the one most widely employed at the present time is the bromoil process. Bromoil has much in its favour for every worker who desires to express individual feeling and control in a pictorial photograph, and has the great advantage that, unlike many other photographic processes in which considerable control is possible a finished print on a large scale can be made with perfect facility from a small negative taken with a pocket camera. The artist, therefore, who is equipped with a small but reliable camera, and a knowledge of the picture he requires, can produce with its aid exhibition pictures of large dimensions impractical before the introduction of the bromoil process.

In the bromoil process the original negative, which should be of good quality, with the correct range of tonal values, is enlarged to the desired size by one of the ordinary methods of enlarging on to ordinary bromide paper. This enlarged bromide print then forms the basis of the bromoil print. The print, after developing, fixing and washing, is treated with a special bleaching solution which has the quality of converting the black and white silver image in the gelatine of the bromide print into a bleached image with, at the same time, a tanning action on the gelatine. This tanning action is in direct ratio with the tones of the original image. Thus, the darkest part, or shadows, of the picture become the parts that receive the greatest tanning action, the half-tones less in proportion to their strength, and the high-lights very little, or not at all. The subsequent pigmenting of the image with a greasy ink is regulated by the absorption of water in the gelatine. Where the image has been tanned or hardened by the action of the bleacher, there is not much absorption of water; whereas in the high-lights where the tanning action has not occurred, a considerable amount of water is absorbed, and those parts in turn reject the application of the greasy pigment, whereas the hardened portions, or shadows, will "take" the pigment, and so on through the entire range from darkest shadow to high-light. The pigment is applied with a specially made flat-topped mop-shaped brush with a dabbing action, and the image is built up in pigment in any colour and any strength, according to the desires or ideas of the artist. The original outline of the image is retained, but the tones are entirely under the control of the worker. One may thus lighten shadows or darken high-lights, according to taste, and as it is largely in the matter of tonal values that many photographs suffer in quality, the amount of control that such a process places in the hands of the artist is considerable.

The working details of the above bromoil process are as follows:—The original bromide print, which may be an enlargement or made by contact, should be on any good quality bromide paper that is suitable for the process. Most manufacturers of bromide paper now market a special "bromoil" paper, as some papers are "over-coated," or for other reasons are unsuitable. The print, fully developed and thoroughly fixed and washed, should be of good quality, and preferably fixed in a plain (not an acid) fixing bath of hyposulphite of soda. It may be bleached wet as soon as the washing is concluded, or it can be dried before applying the bleaching solution.

The following is a good formula for the bleaching solution:—

Copper sulphate	1 oz.
Potassium bromide	1 oz.
Potassium bichromate	60 grains
Hydrochloric acid	6 minims.
Water	20 oz.

For use, one part of this solution should be diluted with three parts of water. To bleach the print it should first be placed in water for a minute until limp and the surface evenly wetted, the water poured off and the bleaching solution poured evenly over the print. In from three to four minutes, the black and white image is converted into a faint brownish image. When fully bleached, the print should be thoroughly washed for a quarter of an hour and then fixed for ten minutes in a plain hypo bath, containing 2 oz. of hypo to 20 oz. of water. This is followed by a final washing of a quarter of an hour. The bleached, fixed and washed print should then be dried, and although it is possible to proceed with the pigmenting immediately after washing, better results are obtainable by first drying.

To prepare the bleached print for pigmenting it should be soaked in water at a temperature of 65° Fahr. for about half an hour. This will permit the gelatine to absorb water in inverse proportion to the shadows of the original image. The print, after soaking, is placed on a pigmenting pad consisting of several thicknesses of wet blotting paper laid evenly on a hard surface such as a sheet of glass. The wet pigmenting pad is necessary to keep the print in the correct moist condition during the application of the greasy ink.

The wet bleached print is now carefully blotted with fluffless blotting paper until the surface is dry, and the image will be observed in the gelatine in very slight relief. The high-lights which have absorbed most water have a distinct shine, while the shadows are matt in appearance. The pigments employed are specially prepared for the purpose and are similar in character to ordinary artists' oil colours, but are much stiffer. They are obtainable in practically any colour and in different degrees of hardness, but a very hard or stiff ink can be softened by using the medium sold for the purpose or "megilp." The brushes are also specially made for the process and are approximately in the shape of a horse's hoof, with a slightly domed surface, and are usually made of fitch (pole-cat hair). It is possible to use brushes made of other hair and even of hog hair, but these are generally too coarse for fine work. One or two large brushes and some small ones are necessary for different parts of the work. To apply the pigment a little of the colour should be taken from the tube and spread on a piece of glass or similar hard surfaced palette. A medium sized brush, which should be held lightly in an almost vertical position, is dabbed on the pigment and the dabbing continued on the palette until an even film of colour has been spread. The brush is then dabbed on to the surface of the prepared print, where it will be found that the pigment will adhere to those parts which formed the original image, whilst the high-lights reject the ink. From now onwards, the process is a matter of application of the pigment to the surface of the print, building up the image tone by tone until the complete picture is made visible in pigment. A certain amount of practice is necessary and desirable before the correct action for applying the pigment is acquired; but when it has been acquired, the pigmenting of a comparatively large print becomes a simple matter that is entirely under the control of the worker, who is thus able to reconstruct the subject with stronger tones where required, or high-lights filled in where necessary. A slow pressing action of the brush will tend to add more colour, while a quick hopping action will remove it. The colour should always be applied freely, and by continuing to work on the surface the texture will become finer until the right depth of tone is reached. Stronger shadows are produced by using a harder ink, which will tend to produce contrast, whilst softer inks should be used to tone down high-lights, and to make a more even tone over the entire picture. The pigmented print should be allowed to dry naturally in a warm atmosphere, and the surface should not be touched until the pigment is hard, when final spotting and cleaning up can be undertaken.

Bromoil Transfer Process.—A further development of the bromoil process, producing final prints of great beauty in pigment on plain paper, is bromoil transfer. This, as its name implies, consists of transferring the pigmented image to another base of selected paper. In this case the pigmented print, while still wet, is placed in contact with the new base, and between suitable supports (thin metal plates), is passed through a roller press under considerable pressure, similar to an etching press. If the paper is in proper condition the pigmented image is transferred from the bleached bromide print to the new base. If the transferred image is not sufficiently strong, the original print can be repigmented and a supplementary pull made for strengthening the transfer, care being taken to secure correct registration. Pictures produced in the bromoil transfer process are thus in permanent pigment on a permanent base, and comparable in the method of production with pictures in other graphic media in which an inked-up plate is pulled in a press.

Process and Expression.—Apart from the progress in processes, apparatus and materials, the individual side of photography has grown even more rapidly, but it must be admitted that, as in all other realms of art, the individual with strong personal proclivities in regard to the rendering of any particular subject matter, is always independent of the process. The peculiar advantages of photography for recording incidents, textures and subjects, beautiful *per se*, should have more than a passing claim on the attention of all who may regard it solely as a means of expressing artistic thought. There is, nevertheless, a tendency nowadays to confuse the process with the expression. To the artist, the latter is the first consideration; the photographer who is not an artist is concerned chiefly with the process, and it is with this clear division of interest that one has an opportunity of comparing results. To know the man is frequently to know his work; but on the other hand, the product does not always betray the man. The imitative faculty which the fatal facility of the camera has so readily engendered, renders the simulation of an accepted convention a matter of ease for the unoriginal. The same facility has, however, the saving grace that it enables the beginner with something original to say, to express himself nearly as well as the expert with but a few stock phrases.

The great increase in the number of photographers, both those who are attracted merely by the ease with which a picture is made, or the artists who have pictorial intentions, has been productive of vast numbers of photographic pictures; yet the original workers in the art who have produced the best pictures at various times remain pre-eminent. The multiplication and simplification of photographic processes have done much to smooth the path for the modern worker, and if a photographic exhibition of fifty years ago, or even a quarter of a century ago, could be reconstituted and compared with the representative modern display, the work of the real artist would still emerge, although the work of the rank and file would be obviously of a much higher level. There is now a sure base for further advance. The many methods that have been explored should leave no doubt as to the particular one that suits the requirements of the subject, or the mood of the worker, and here is one of the most accessible of the many different paths of progress. The development of the more plastic processes of photography, such as gum-bichromate, and bromoil, have converted photography into a vehicle both for the imaginative vision and for the trained hand, not content to copy outward appearances simply but aiming also at an inner significance. The camera is likely to become in an increasing degree an instrument for the artist.

The progress towards perfection in pictorial photography is undoubtedly one of difficulty for many, but there are those to-day who have nearly attained it. There are three problems to solve for the worker who is an artist and would use the camera to express his art; the technical problem embodying the choice and mastery of the process that is most fitting to individual requirements; the problem of artistic vision, involving all the subtleties of tone perception, values, light, atmosphere and selection; and then there is the question of expression, in which are comprised such matters as decorative and appropriate compositions, emphasis and simplification.

ILLUMINATED MANUSCRIPTS

ILLUMINATION, in art, is a term applied to the embellishment of written or printed text or design with colours or gold and, rarely, with silver. The old form of the verb "to illuminate" was "to enlumine," and 13th century laymen who practised the art were called "enlumineurs." While the term should be strictly applied to the brilliant book-ornamentation which was developed in the middle ages, it has been extended, by usage, to the illustration and decoration of early mss. in general.

The decisive changes in the history of the book are similarly turning points in the art of illumination. The production of precious illuminated mss. survived the introduction of printing by nearly a century. So far as we know, the art of decorating mss. did not create new forms through a development based on writing, but rather it took over pictures and ornaments from other forms of art. The written pages appear at first simple and unadorned, even where the parchment is coloured and the writing is in silver or gold; then simple enlarged initial letters and calligraphic ornament; in the Codices richly adorned title-pages and brilliant displays of ornament in the Canon-tables of Gospel mss. The form and position of the pictures vary exceedingly. Sometimes the illustrations are placed haphazard in the picture borders, in the text, or as framed pictures in the text; they may also occupy full pages, or in the form of a running band in the Codex above or below the text, or, as in the roll, running in a continuous series of pictures from end to end.

Illumination in Antiquity.—The little surviving from the first great period in the history of illumination which reached to about the 4th century, consists of numerous fragments of papyrus rolls. Such fragments include the ancient *Egyptian Book of the Dead*, in which the illustrations are either dashing drawings or coloured pictures. The only fragmentary examples of

266

PLATE IV

PHOTOGRAPHIC ART

PHOTOGRAPHS, (3) COPR. PIRIE MAC-
DONALD, (4, 6) COPR. CONDE NAST
PUBLICATIONS, INC., N.Y., REPRINTED
FROM VANITY FAIR

MODERN PORTRAIT
PHOTOGRAPHY

1. Baron von Hünefeld, by Nicola Perscheid; a portrait showing the use of light on the background, and a good composition in half-length
2. Ignace Paderewski, by Arnold Genthe, suggesting an almost Rembrandt-like quality, with fine composition and modelling in head and shoulders
3. George Russell (AE), by Pirie MacDonald; showing the face alone with fine modelling but less interesting composition

4. Evelyn Brent, by Edward J. Steichen; a striking portrait, with dramatic lighting
5. Georgia O'Keeffe, by Alfred Stieglitz; a study of the face alone, with good composition achieved through the use of hat, collar, and light in the background
6. Leopold Stokowski, by Edward J. Steichen, with interesting light effect and a modern background

PASTEL

EXAMPLES OF PASTEL

1. Self-portrait by Quentin de La Tour (1704–1788), French. 2. "Portrait of a Lady with Flowers in her Hair" by Rosalba Carriera (1675–1757), Italian. 3. "The Ballet Dancer" by Henri Matisse (1869–   ), French. 4. "Auguste Rodin" by Henry Tonks (1862–   ), English. 5. "The Violet Note" by J. A. M. Whistler (1834–1903), American. In the Isabella Stewart Gardner Collection, Boston. 6. "The Toilet" by Hilaire G. E. Degas (1834–1917), French. 7. "Lapis Lazuli" by J. A. M. Whistler (1834–1903), American. In the Isabella Stewart Gardner Collection, Boston

illustrated rolls of the classical period were found in Egyptian excavations, and our knowledge of this period, as a whole, is very slight. The most ancient and important of these are the fragmentary copy of the *Iliad*, on vellum, in the Ambrosian library, Milan (variously assigned to the 3rd and 5th centuries), of which there are 58 pictures of various sizes, obviously the remains of a magnificent ms.; the small Virgil at the Vatican (Lat. 3,225, 4th century) with pictures set off in a simple frame and inserted in the text, all of which are considered to have been based on Augustan models; and the later Vatican Virgil (*Codex Romanus*, Lat. 3,867, 5th or 6th century), the work of an artist who evidently did not understand his model's technique in painting and who was, therefore, incapable of copying it.

Illumination of Christian Books in the East.—Christian illumination dates back to the times to which the few early profane illuminated mss. in our possession belong. The number of ancient Christian illuminated mss. in Greek or in oriental languages is very small.

Other Theological and Profane Manuscripts.—Among illuminated theological or profane mss. which survive in the original, the most important is the Dioscorides (early 6th century) in Vienna. Few of the manuscripts are dated and localized and many important to early Christian art are preserved only in mediaeval copies; even those actually written in early Christian times may not be originals, but merely copies. Only on this basis can we explain why the Viennese Genesis, made up of various series of illuminations, is closely allied to the Codex Rossanensis, which belongs to another stage in the development of the style. The style is determined mainly by paintings of late antiquity based on Hellenistic models influenced by indigenous art (Coptic, Syrian, etc.).

Miniatures in the Middle Byzantine Period.—The development in Byzantium cannot be traced clearly until after the iconoclastic controversy. As art flourished again, the works of the Byzantine Renaissance, as it is called, began to be produced. To this renaissance belong those Codices which hand on works of late antique or early Christian times, partly in accurate copies, partly in free imitations (Joshua-roll, Kosmas Indikopleustes), Psalters like that at Paris (Grec. 139). On the other hand, the typical middle Byzantine art modelled its style on monumental art.

Although Constantinople decided the trend of artistic production, illumination was also cultivated outside the capital. As practised in the monasteries of Athos, its importance was far-reaching. From the 11th century a school of miniaturists developed in Russia, the works of which are, at first, scarcely to be distinguished from those of Byzantium. The Menology at the Vatican is the only Byzantine ms. in which each miniature is signed by the artist. The style in the later works, and especially in the productions of the monasteries, became dry, but still it persisted, not only through the Latin conquest (1204–61), but it was also capable of a rebirth after the restoration of the empire under the Palaeologues (1261).

Western Illumination in Early Christian and Carolingian Times.—Few early Christian illuminated manuscripts of Western origin have survived. A comparison between the Quedlinberg Itala fragment in Berlin of this period and the Virgil of the Vatican (Lat. 3,225) proves that the scriptoria which produced it also executed Christian illuminated mss. The affinity between the two is extraordinarily close; the style is clear and simple in character; the pictorial conception gives evidence of naturalness and it is without a trace of the Byzantine spirit. There is evidence that style quickly deteriorated in the West, but the process cannot be traced in detail.

The most important original ms. is St. Augustine's Gospels at Corpus Christi, Cambridge (Nr. 286) which was probably executed in Lower Italy. The Ashburnham Pentateuch at Paris is of a different type; its 19 miniatures are stylistically and iconographically unique, and indicate a connection with oriental models; they are possibly of Spanish origin. These mss. bear witness to a survival of late antique and early Christian art in the West. By comparison, the mass of the mss. produced in the monasteries of the Frank and Lombard kingdoms in the 7th and 8th centuries have quite a different character. Among the large number preserved only a few have figurative representations. Illuminated Bibles or Gospels hardly occur at all. Ornament, in general, is restricted to initials and decorated pages, a method of embellishment based on the art of the *scribe*, not of the *painter*. Compared with the simplicity of the text in late antique mss., it is a complete revolution. Part of the material originated in upper Italy and south France, apparently in the early 7th century. Later, the art was transplanted to central and northern France. The majority of the mss., and especially those richest in decoration, arose in north France in the latter half of the 8th century, *i.e.*, not until the Irish and Anglo-Saxon arts of illumination were already highly developed.

In Britain two fundamentally different tendencies must be distinguished, the Irish and the English. The development in England was determined by the Roman mission and by the close relations kept up between the Italo-

Saxon churches and monasteries and Rome itself. In the 8th century, from which period a series of splendid mss. have been handed down, the artists endeavoured to continue the early Christian figurative tradition in stiffly outlined forms, and at the same time displayed rich decorative splendour in the Irish fashion. The most important works of the Canterbury school are S. Augustine's Psalter with a portrait of David (British Museum) and the Codex Aureus in Stockholm.

Irish Illumination.—In spite of numerous contacts with England, Irish illumination is a world apart. It is one of the most interesting phenomena in the whole range of mediaeval art. In the art of illumination it represents, perhaps, a climax never again reached. It is the more remarkable in that it suddenly appears before us, fully developed, without any preliminary stages and with no source to which it can be traced. The three chief Irish works are the Book of Durrow (Dublin, Trinity college, A. 4, 5.), the Book of Kells (*ibid.* A. 1, 6) and the Lindisfarne Gospels (British Museum Cotton, New D. IV.). The Book of Durrow (*c.* 700) is pure Irish in style; the Book of Kells (for which the date 700 has been disputed in favour of a later period) shows traces of foreign ornamental ideas, and the Lindisfarne Gospels (written soon after 700), have pictures of the Evangelists, which are not Irish in style, but are only explained by the influences of the Italo-Saxon monasteries. The contrast arises from the refusal of the Irish artists to attempt naturalistic representation in order to make as free play with the figures of a picture as if they were calligraphic designs, that it is often difficult to see what these plaited figures really mean. This anti-naturalistic method of representation stands in sharp contrast to the whole range of classical antique art in all its derivations. Irish mss. show a richness of decoration unparalleled, so far as is known, up to that time. The various Gospels are preceded by whole pages with carpet-like designs, and the initials at the beginning of the text grow and spread until they, too, cover the whole page.

The Carolingian Renaissance.—Simultaneously with the reform of writing, a project of Charlemagne, there arose a number of new schools of painting which aimed at restoring the connection with antique and early Christian art. The chief works probably did not arise before the beginning of the 9th century; they include the Gospel-book of Ada (? Charlemagne's sister), at Trier, after which we call all these works the Ada-group. These mss. include rich Canon-tables, pictures of the Evangelists and of their symbols under large arcades, symbolical representations of the Church, the Fountain of Life, etc. Obviously there is an ancient pictorial tradition, which we can trace back, on the one side to Syria, on the other to Italy and England. The colouring is varied and splendid, the figures dramatic in movement, the faces fine and full of expression, the outlines of the figures rich in style. On the whole, the treatment, with its sharp and clear outlining of form, shows more of the spirit of drawing than of painting. All this points to models of high artistic importance.

Of a group of schools where work is in decided stylistic contrast to the Ada group is the Palatine school of Aix-la-Chapelle. Its chief work, the Gospel-book of Charlemagne, is preserved among the Crown treasures at Vienna. The treatment is altogether pictorial, the colouring fine and simple without being too varied. The plain style of embellishment, with the greatness of conception in the figures and the soft pictorial treatment, point to early Christian models. This tendency is continued in the school of Hautvillers, where a Gospel-book at Epernay town library was made for Ebo of Reims (816–35). Significant changes of style have set in however; the broad pictorial technique has made room for a hatched treatment, so that it has been supposed that the artist had been accustomed to using a drawing-pen. The style is that of the Utrecht Psalter, which has great affinity with later Anglo-Saxon work, and which subsequently exercised a strong influence on development in England. The Utrecht Psalter (Utrecht University library), is at once the most magnificent and the strangest production of Carolingian art. The composition with landscape like stage-scenery reminds one of early Christian models (Joshua-roll). Without a doubt, the Utrecht Psalter has some connection with early Christian art. Nevertheless, it is an essential creation of Carolingian times. The school of Tours was at its prime towards the middle of the 9th century under the lay abbot, Count Vivian. The Gospel-book destined for the emperor Lothaire is the most important work (Paris B.N., Lat. 266). The Tours mss. took over from early Christian models a large number of Bible illustrations, and introduced them into mediaeval art. A quite distinctive style marks the works of the Franco-Saxon school. It shows, unmistakably, a continuation of the Irish and Hiberno-Saxon school, enriched by Carolingian elements. Its strength is based entirely on ornament and it is notable for having spread the art of the initial as developed in England and Ireland.

Anglo-Saxon Illumination.—Anglo-Saxon illumination began to flourish once more under King Edgar (*c.* 960). The new style, based on Carolingian

ILLUMINATED MANUSCRIPTS

BLANCHE OF CASTILE AND SAINT LOUIS, KING OF FRANCE

Leaf from a *Bible Moralisée*, showing portraits of Blanche of Castile and her son, Saint Louis, king of France. This reproduction is from the original French manuscript, executed in the first quarter of the 13th century, now in the Pierpont Morgan library, New York

art, suddenly makes its appearance completely developed, in the works of the Winchester school. It is one of the most original and attractive in the whole range of mediaeval art. The artist is not satisfied by normal movements of the neck or head, so the line of the neck is unnaturally prolonged and curved; the draperies appear as if driven by a gale of wind, and end in fluttering points; the seams are broken into numberless, small folds. From the standpoint of correctness, much fault might be found with these figures, but as the expression of immense spiritual force they excite our wonder. Anglo-Saxon art, too, reaches its climax when it dispenses with painting in thick colours and contents itself with sketch-like drawings, which may be tinted with various light colours. The chief work of the early period is the Benedictional, which Bishop Aethelwold (963–984) caused to be written, by the scribe Godeman (Chatsworth library).

One of the most important seats of Anglo-Saxon art was at Canterbury. A copy of the Utrecht Psalter (Brit. Mus. Harl. 603) is supposed to have been executed there. More than three hands worked at it, so it must have been made in a large scriptorium. The Anglo-Saxon style remained full of life until the middle of the 11th century. It was not confined to England; during the 10th century it crossed the Channel. There the style appears in many works in such freshness and spontaneity that it is likely that Anglo-Saxon artists had emigrated to France. Of this type is the Evangeliar (Boulogne library, No. 11) written at the Abbey of S. Bertin. In northern France there arose, side by side with the illuminations influenced by the Anglo-Saxons, other mss. which, independent in style, are full of intense expression.

The Ottonian Renaissance.—The Ottonian Renaissance flourished in Germany about the same time as the Winchester school. Its political background was the renewal of the Holy Roman Empire by Otto I. Within a few decades an almost inconceivable abundance of magnificent mss. was produced, which we can allot to a number of different schools. These schools differ exceedingly in character, according to whether the artists used Carolingian models or went back direct to early Christian. Middle Byzantine art, too, begins to exercise its influence at this period. The great number of pictures in the Ottonian mss. springs from these various sources. All these schools, on the other hand, are very creative in ornament. They used whole page illuminations with a purple ground and richly formed initials of golden foliated branch work, similar to those found occasionally in Carolingian times, especially in the Metz school. In all the schools of the Ottonian period, painting with thick colours prevails. In the works of the golden age of Ottonian art we notice the intention to approach the illusionistic conception of the late antique. But these endeavours are soon frustrated, and at the beginning of the 11th century decline sets in. The painting becomes more mediaeval in character, the background of the pictures is divided up by ornamental and coloured stripes, for which occasionally the Byzantine gold background is substituted. One of the most prominent centres of artistic activity was the monastery of Reichenau, situated on an island in Lake Constance.

Romanesque Illumination in England, France, Germany and the Low Countries.—Middle 11th century illumination stands at the parting of the ways. Anglo-Saxon schools and the German Ottonian Renaissance were dying out, and so the connection with antique painting disappears. From now onwards the whole of the West is governed by a style based on linear, not pictorially treated, outline-drawing, for which colour is used to tint the surfaces in the flat, with only slight modelling of forms. Art abandons the last reminiscences of the illusionistic manner of the late antique, in which the picture was based on a reality seen either bodily or in the mind's eye. The mediaeval style, which now establishes itself, dispenses with illusion, it gives us the different components of the pictures, *i.e.*, the figures and whatever else is necessary to understand the action, but releases them from contact with natural space. Even the background has chiefly an ornamental importance. A gold ground becomes more and more popular, or border and background consist of a system of frames. This manner of representation permits the artist to pack the most complicated ideas into a picture, if only he has created the corresponding frame to hold the conceptions together, and this tendency now completely dominates the art of illustration. A counter movement is only to be seen in Byzantine art which never altogether lost contact with the antique, and which preserved formulas from the illusionistic age. In the 12th and 13th centuries Byzantine influence penetrated further and further forward into Italy and obtained a strong hold in Germany.

In the West of Europe, especially in northern France and in England, Byzantine influence may also be traced, but it was powerless to check the development which led to Gothic painting, and which was furthered most of all by the art of stained glass. For technical reasons, stained glass, with all its beauty of colour, can never know real modelling; it is based on outline-drawing in the proper sense of the word. It had an extremely strong influence on the method of painting, described above, in which numerous figurative representations are combined within a system of frames. Already, in the 12th, and especially in the 13th century, many illuminated mss. show evident traces of having been imitated from stained glass.

Anglo-Norman Illustration.—Soon after 1100 we find various Anglo-Norman scriptoria at the height of their power. Their productions are chiefly enormous Bibles, separate books of the Bible with commentaries, and especially the Psalter. The style abandons the lightness of Anglo-Saxon times. It is now based on stiff linear designs filled up with opaque pigments of harsh colour. The figures are, especially early in the 12th century, heavy and awkward. A little later the style becomes more spirited. The initial ornaments are astonishingly rich in invention and design, and they are enlivened with numerous fantastic forms of men and animals in strange colours.

Bury St. Edmunds produced the first of the large Bibles so characteristic of the 12th century. Winchester again became, about the middle of the 12th century, the seat of an important school. It produced the Psalter of Bishop Henry of Blois (British Museum, Nero C. IV.).

The wave of Byzantine art had now reached England also and the deeply agitated style with its singular types is replaced by an almost classical conception of art. The chief work of this tendency is the Winchester Psalter of the British Museum. Well-proportioned forms of measured placidity and solemnity of movement meet us in these pictures. Of the greatest importance is the latest copy of the Utrecht Psalter, which was only finished afterwards in Italy (Paris B.N. Lat. 8846).

Continental Schools.—Our knowledge of the history of miniature in France is altogether much slighter than in England. We know of the quick rise and decline of an important scriptorium at Cîteaux, the founder of which was Abbot Stephen Harding. Numerous mss. with most peculiar decoration, especially initial letters of quite fantastic formation, emanate from Limoges and western France. The productions of monasteries in Belgium and northern France are extraordinarily numerous. Many of these are dated and indicate the names of the artists. In the eastern part of this territory, a style approaching the Rhenish predominates, while towards the west, where the narrowness of the straits provided a natural connection with England, the Anglo-Norman affinities already mentioned make their appearance.

In these districts, also, we can establish the presence of a strong Byzantine influence in the critical period round about 1200.

In Germany the development of art, after the Ottonian Renaissance, varied in the different territories. In the south-east, the Middle Byzantine influence, already perceptible in the early 11th century, now became permanent.

In the western and northern districts of Germany Byzantine influence was not so powerful in the 12th century. One work, however, the famous *Hortus Deliciarum* of the abbess Herrad of Landsberg, in Alsace, occupies a position of its own on account of the unusual illuminations it contained. (The original perished in 1870.) Pure pen-drawing had spread in all directions. On the lower Rhine and in north Germany some miniatures were executed in opaque pigments. These are clear and calm in style, and at times they rise to an extraordinary height of monumental dignity, *e.g.*, in the Gospel Book of unknown origin at Paris (B.N. Lat. 17,325) or the Hildesheim mss. of the 12th century (Hildesheim, Ratman Missal, etc.).

With the beginning of the 13th century Byzantine influence extended its power over almost all the country, and its style displays great restlessness. In the latter part of the 13th century the desire to create original forms and to express passionate feeling was so strong that the style was often positively distorted. The Byzantine tendency attains its zenith in the Gospel-book of the town hall at Goslar, and the Missal (Pierpont Morgan's library), executed in the first third of the 13th century. Immediately after the middle of the 13th century numerous fine works were produced, especially in south Germany, where refined Byzantinesque style predominated (Psalter, Munich, Staatsbibl. Lat. 3,900).

Gothic Illumination in France, England, Germany and the Lower Countries.—In the first half of the 13th century a complete change came over French illumination which transformed the fundamental ideas of book-ornamentation. It is based, to begin with, on the cultivation of a refined and dainty style which caused the contrast between miniatures in Gothic mss. and the art of monumental painting to appear sharper than ever before. It rested, moreover, on the closer assimilation of picture and text, so that the historiated initial becomes predominant in Gothic mss. When the miniature remained independent, it bears the character of a small medallion or of a quatrefoil. The initials, however, expand more and more until they have twined themselves all round the pages of text. Figures dispersed at random in the margin, called drolleries, although they may represent any sort of object conceivable, introduced a new style of embellishment on which all development to 1500 is founded. Paris is regarded as the birth-place of the new style. Several mss. are designated as the property of Queen Blanche or of St. Louis, among them the Psalter of the Arsenal library in Paris. It is the first to show the substitution of medallions for the usual rectangular series of pictures. From other books it is still clearer that the illuminators are keeping very close to the example of stained glass windows, from which they borrow the complicated arrangement of the medallions.

Great as is the advance made by the mss. of the *Bible moralisée* and the allied mss., they had not yet produced the pure type of Gothic ms. Many other miniatures, however, display a strongly dramatic and restless style, which has a certain affinity to contemporary German work rather than with French Gothic. A number of splendid mss. which are supposed to emanate from Salisbury, are illustrated in this style. Early English examples include the magnificent pictures of the Apocalypse at Trinity college, Cambridge. A great new style, which was to oust all the previous tendencies in France and England, was created under the strong influence of monumental art in Paris about the middle of the 13th century. Its chief works are the Psalters written for St. Louis or other member of the royal family (Paris B.N. Lat. 10,525) and the liturgical mss. executed for the Ste. Chapelle. These works combine two qualities, firstly, the greatest simplicity of style, in that they work out the pure Gothic line, and secondly, a marked attention to reality in ornament and in architectonic details, in costume, etc. It is very difficult to distinguish between French and English work of this period. In spite of numerous English traits we can probably localize in Paris the Psalter of the municipal library at Nuremberg and the Psalter of Queen Isabella, Edward II.'s wife, at Munich. Queen Mary's Psalter at the British Museum is, beyond dispute, an early 14th century English masterpiece. In the work of the East Anglian school can be seen the gradual giving up of Gothic outline-drawing for the sake of a broader pictorial treatment. Its most singular characteristic is extravagant richness of ornamentation displayed in the large border-frames of the decorated pages, interlaced with figures of every shape and kind. In Parisian illumination the characteristic style of the miniaturist, Jean Pucelle, shows the change unmistakably. From now onwards we can follow in the miniatures of the mss. the development of modern painting. The fundamental revolution in style which takes place during this period can only be explained on the assumption of Italian influence arising out of the close connection between Italian and French art, based, in its turn, on political and dynastic relations and the transference of the papal court to Avignon. This may account for the fact that one of Pucelle's masterpieces, the Breviary of Queen Jeanne of Navarre (Yates Thompson collection), contains certain miniatures that can only be understood as imitating Italian pictures of the Trecento.

From the middle of the 14th century onwards, the naturalistic tendency becomes more and more powerful. For this period the phrase, "the naturalism of head and hand," has been coined. Its influence is seen most clearly in the dedication-pictures, where the elements of portraiture in the persons represented, as *e.g.*, Charles V., are unmistakable. In religious pictures, however, Gothic idealism continued until the beginning of the 15th century. The miniatures executed for Charles V. are often set in *quatrefoil* frames, and grey monochrome (grisaille) is preferred to painting in colours. The decisive change in the direction of modernity may best be studied in the mss. illuminated for Charles V.'s brother, the duke of Berry. The name of André Beauneveu, of Valenciennes, is given for the Psalter at Paris (B.N. Fr. 13,091), that of Jacquemart de Hesdin for the Prayer Books at Paris (B.N. Lat. 919) and Brussels (B.R. 11,060–61). In these mss. there is a change in the borders, the dainty sprays of ivy, which had hitherto sprouted loosely over the margins, now completely fill them up, and new *motifs* add to the wealth of ornament. In the miniatures we can see the old Gothic tradition gradually being displaced by Italian art, with a rapid progress in naturalism. The new art reaches its climax in the second decade of the 15th century in two mss. begun for the duke of Berry, which must be classed, beyond dispute, among the most magnificent illustrated books of all times. The unfinished Prayer Book at Chantilly (called, according to the Inventory, *Très riches Heures du duc de Berry*), was illuminated by Pol de Limbourg and his brothers. Pictures which remind us of famous Italian mural paintings stand side by side with faithful representations of reality, as *e.g.*, the Calendar-pictures with the views of the duke's castles or the genre-like February snow-landscape. We are taken a step further by the Prayer Book begun for the duke of Berry, but after his death continued for Count William IV. of Bavaria-Holland. In the pictures of William IV.'s time the Italian style has been completely replaced by a style so near to that of the brothers Van Eyck that some of the best pictures have been attributed to them. The

276

miniatures of the two last-named mss. are invaluable to the history of painting.

Spanish and Italian Illumination in the Middle Ages.—Spanish and Italian illumination had only a slight share in the Renaissance movement on which Carolingian, Ottonian and Anglo-Saxon art was based. In Spain, as in Italy, tendencies prevailed, during this period, which can best be compared with the Franco-Saxon school. The Spanish mss. of the 9th to 11th centuries display a rich, but fantastic decoration in which early Christian and Moorish elements are mixed. The figures are anti-naturalistic, reminding one of the Irish style. The most singular Spanish creation is the great series of illustrations to Beatus of Liebana's Commentaries on the Apocalypse which have survived in many copies from the 9th (?) to the 12th centuries (the oldest in the Yates Thompson college, a later one in the P. Morgan library).

The character of Italian illumination varies extremely in the different Italian territories, according to their relations with East and West. A curious blend of contrasting tendencies is to be seen in the book-ornamentation of the Benedictines at Monte Cassino in the 11th and 12th centuries. Here Hiberno-Saxon, Ottonian and Byzantine stylistic elements are intimately combined. Southern Italy made a speciality of Exultet-rolls, as they are called, *i.e.*, mss. adorned with miniatures and written in the form of rolls. Various Italian monasteries produced, from the 11th to the 13th centuries, gigantic Bibles, some of which show a singular beauty of initial which was afterwards imitated in the 15th century. The origin of these Bibles is partly to be sought in Tuscany, where, in the reign of the margravine Matilda, works of a pronounced original character were produced, *e.g.*, the Gospel-book which Matilda presented, in 1109, to the Abbey of Polirone (P. Morgan library). During the 13th century, Italian illumination in the large university towns of northern Italy developed freely and in a manner quite its own. Legal text-books, Bibles, etc., were executed and taken by the students all over Europe. Moreover, the 13th century produced a new type of book, the immense choir-book, which was everywhere used at church services. In general, large miniatures are rare in Italian illuminated mss. Most have only historiated initials, but these are drawn out to great length and spread out over the margins in branch and leaf work. Drolleries were added very early, so that one feels inclined to assume that they made their way to the North from Italy. All this, however, does not exhaust the importance of

Italian miniature. Just as in mural and panel painting, Italy was foremost in diffusing the Byzantine style.

We must not overlook the immediate influence of the Crusades in causing an interpenetration of the Western and Byzantine elements. In the Latin kingdoms of the Orient, there were executed for churches and princes magnificent mss. in which such a mixture of styles was inevitable, *e.g.*, the Psalter of Queen Melissenda of Jerusalem (British Museum), the Missal of the Holy Sepulchre church at Jerusalem (Paris), and many others. Similar works probably emanated from those districts of Italy which were particularly exposed to Byzantine influence. We may, perhaps, put in this class the Missal at Madrid. A similar mixture of style is evident, in a much coarser form, in the Epistolary, written in 1259 at Padua (cathedral treasure). About 1300 a large number of Byzantesque illuminations were produced at Bologna, which are distinguished by copious border-decoration, with figures in the pseudo-classic style. Splendid works of this kind are the Bibles at Paris (B.N. Lat. 18) and at the British Museum (Add. 18,720).

During the 14th century, throughout Italy's busy scriptoria, as at Naples, where French influence is noticeable, numerous mss. rich in miniatures were produced (Bible, subsequently Leo X.'s, now Berlin, Kupferstich-Kabinett). Only rarely can we connect miniatures with the artists who painted on panel. A Virgil in Milan and the Ufficio di San Giorgio in the archives of S. Peter at Rome, are assigned to Simone Martini of Siena.

Miniature Since the 15th Century.—Many illuminated mss. of the later 15th and 16th centuries surpass in wealth of pictures and magnificent embellishment, even the works from the time of the duke of Berry. Their place is finally taken in the 16th century by black and white. The splendid miniatures of the 15th and 16th centuries are, like those of the preceding period, chiefly destined for princes and great courtiers. Three large centres of production are prominent: Flanders (Ghent, Bruges); France (Paris, Tours); Italy (Florence, Ferrara, etc.). Illumination in this period acknowledged no restriction on its choice of subject. The Books of Hours, indeed, still played an important part, but, besides these, there were profane mss. of an incredible variety, among which the Chronicles on the one hand, and the Romances on the other, are prominent.

Flanders.—In the generation following the Van Eycks it can only rarely be proved that painters on panel had a hand in illumination. We know a number of miniaturists from their works or from documents, *e.g.*, Jean le

Tavernier, Willem Vrelant, Loyset Lyédet, Philippe de Mazerolles, the Bening family. About the middle of the 16th century the activity of the Flemish scriptoria seems to have died out. It is important to note Simon Marmion, unsurpassed in landscape (Book of Hours, British Museum Add. 38,126). A master belonging to the circle of Roger von der Weyden is called after the Romance of Girart de Roussillon Jean le Tavernier, who adorned the Conquêtes de Charlemagne executed for Philip the Good (Vienna, Staatsbibl. 2,549). His second masterpiece, the Chronicle of Hennegau, is at Brussels. (Brussels, B.R. 9,066.)

France.—The production of French mss. during the 15th century will not bear comparison with the Flemish. In connection with the mss. of the duke of Berry, there is the Bedford Missal (British Museum) and the Salisbury Breviary in Paris, with its numberless miniatures. About the middle of the 15th century Jean Fouquet, the most important personality among the French miniaturists, makes his appearance. He died about 1480, at Tours, where he had lived before and after his journey to Rome (between 1443–47). Attested works of his are parts of the *Antiquités Judaiques* at Paris, and the miniatures cut out from the *Heures d'Etienne Chevalier* at Chantilly. Fouquet's art has a touch of the Renaissance which otherwise shows affinities with Flemish naturalism. The miniature survived under Francis I., and even into the time of Louis XIV.

Germany.—In Germany, in the 15th century, illustration passes a humble existence in monasteries and scriptoria which engage in large-scale manufacture of mss. (Diebold Lauber in Hagenau.) In contrast with this mass production, there are the splendid mss. of the emperor Maximilian. The finest is the superb border, executed by Dürer and other great German artists, in a copy of the Prayer Book printed by Schönsperger (Munich, Staatsbibl. and Besançon).

Italy.—In Italy the renaissance in the mss. begins with the introduction of the *scrittura umanistica*, which goes back to the model of the fine Italian mss. of the 11th and 12th centuries, from which was also taken the scroll-work design in the frames enclosing the pages of text. Illumination does not really flourish until the middle of the 15th century, when there arose, almost always in connection with the luxury of courts, a number of studios which created a new style and new decorative forms. As in Flanders, the artists are seldom identical with the painters on panel, although, for example, the great art of Mantegna is reflected in miniature. In northern Italy, Milan and Verona were two of the centres. A masterpiece is the Book of Hours of Bona of Savoy, widow of Galeazzo Moria Sforza, duke of Milan, which afterwards came into the possession of Charles V. (British Museum Add. 34,924.) In the Ferrara school, where a number of miniaturists worked for the ducal family of Este, Taddeo Crivelli takes the first place (Borso d'Este's Bible, 1455–62, Modena). The most important miniaturist under Borso's successor, Ercole I., is Martino da Modena (Ercole I.'s Breviary at Vienna). Miniature-painting in central Italy was chiefly concentrated at Florence; Francesco d'Antonio del Cherico, with Attavante degli Attavanti, were the two chief miniaturists.

PASTEL

PASTEL, the simplest of all methods of laying colour upon a flat surface. The colours used consist practically of the pure powder colours; whereas in other methods, the colours have to be mixed with some medium, the immediate result often being that the tone of the colour is lowered, and even if on drying the original tone is restored, as in fresco (*q.v.*), the artist while at work can only calculate what the picture will look like when dry. In pure pastel as the colour is put on so it remains. The disadvantage of pastel is that its life is precarious, not because its colours are more fugitive than in other methods but because it remains on the surface of the paper, liable, unless protected by glass, to be rubbed off by any chance touch. On the other hand, if certain precautions are observed during the course of applying the colour it is able to resist violent shocks.

Pastels are made up into cylinders or pencils with the least amount of adhesive (a gum) necessary to hold the particles of colour together in the lightest possible manner, so that a touch of the pencil on the surface of the paper leaves an impression. Pastels, as sold by the modern dealer, are usually arranged in a series of tones, the darkest pencil consisting of the pure colour; all the other pencils of the series are mixed with white to a greater and greater degree as they ascend the scale toward the lightest. Thus the artist has a certain number of tones ready to use at once.

280

PASTEL

Pastel can be applied as a pencil, *i.e.*, by means of lines or short touches, or it may be rubbed. By far the best way of rubbing pastel is with the pad of the tip of the finger; if stumps are used they are apt to remove most of the powder. Speaking generally pastel should not be fixed, the use of the fixatives at once alters its character; it is converted into a painting and all the tones are lowered, and the beauty of the surface is at once destroyed. It becomes like a butterfly's wing dipped in water. No fixative is satisfactory, but one, which serves its purpose, is a weak solution of parchment, size and water blown on with a spray diffuser from a considerable distance.

Sometimes a very little fixative may be used in the early stage as this prevents a heaping up of the powder, the fixative making what is there firmly and thinly adhere to the paper, but the final touches must be pure pastel. It is easy by loading pastel upon the paper to reach the end of the possibility of this method, therefore, above all, the artist must learn to apply the powder very thinly and to keep the colours as much as possible clear and defined. A dirty mess is the end of a good many pastels.

Pastel has most distinctly a character of its own and should be used with an understanding of what it can do and what it cannot do. It should not be used to imitate oil-painting which it certainly cannot do without entirely altering its natural character. It should be considered as a method of applying colour, which owing to the practical absence of a medium is higher in tone than in any other method, thinly to the surface of the paper so that as in water-colour the actual paper itself may occasionally play a part in the design. With this knowledge of its proper use, very beautiful results can be obtained. It is an excellent method to use when a portrait is required, but better for small portraits than large; a life-sized head in pastel is seldom satisfactory and generally becomes overloaded with colour. It cannot pretend to the carrying power of oil-painting; it may be described as a more humble medium and, therefore, is not to be employed in large designs.

HISTORY

THE INVENTION of pastel, which used to be generally called "crayon," has frequently been accredited to Johann Alexander Thiele (1685–1752), landscape-painter and etcher of distinction, as well as to Mme. Vernerin and Mlle. Heid (1688–1753), both of Danzig. But the claim cannot be substantiated, as drawing in coloured chalks had been practised long before, *e.g.*, by Guido Reni (1575–1642), by whom a head and bust in this manner exists in the Dresden Gallery. Thiele was perhaps the first to carry the art to perfection, but his contemporary, Rosalba Carriera of Venice (1675–1757), is more completely identified with it. The Dresden Museum contains 157 examples of her work in this medium, portraits, subjects and the like. Thiele was followed by Anton Raphael Mengs (1728–1779) and his sister Theresia Mengs (afterwards Maron, 1725–1806), and by Johann Heinrich Schmidt (1749–1829).

Holbein, Watteau, Boucher, Greuze, John Raphael Smith and Sir Thomas Lawrence all made use of the coloured chalk. In 1747 Nattier (1685–1766) showed a pastel portrait of M. Logerot in the Paris Salon, and his son-in-law, Louis Tocqué (1696–1772), soon followed with similar work. Hubert Drouais (1699–1767) had preceded his rival Nattier in the Salon by a single year with five pastel portraits, and Chardin (1699–1779) followed in 1771. This great master set himself to work in emulation of Quentin de la Tour (1704–1788), who in spite of the ability of his rivals may be regarded as the most eminent pastellist France has produced. His full strength as a portrait-pastellist is to be gauged in the collection of eighty-five of his principal works now in the museum of St. Quentin. Then followed Simon Mathurin Lantara (1729–1778), who was one of the first to paint pastel-pictures of landscapes.

Two Swiss painters had considerable influence in spreading the use of pastel—the experimentalist Dietrich Meyer (1572–1658), one of the first to make designs in coloured chalks (and reputed inventor of soft-ground etching), and Jean Étienne Liotard (1702 or 1704–1788), one of the most brilliant pastellists who ever lived. Two of his works are world-famous, "La Belle Chocolatière de Vienne," executed in 1745, now in the Dresden Museum, and "La Belle Liseuse" of the following year at the museum at Amsterdam. The latter is a portrait of his niece, Mlle. Lavergne.

Crayon-painting was practised in England at an early date, and John Riley (1646–1691), many of whose finest works are attributed to Sir Peter Lely, produced numerous portraits in that medium. Francis Knapton (1698–1778), court painter, was a more prolific master, and he, with William Hoare of Bath (?1707–1792) who had studied pastel in Italy, prepared the way for the triumph of Francis Cotes (?1725–1770). Then for the first time pastel-painting was fully developed by an English hand. Before he became a painter in oil Cotes had worked under Rosalba Carriera, and, although he was rather cold and chalky in his tones, he produced portraits, such as his

282

"Mr. and Mrs. Joah Bates" and "Lord Hawke," which testify to his high ability. He was, however, far surpassed by his pupil, John Russell, R.A. (1745–1806), who brought the art to perfection, displaying grace and good expression in all his pastel work, whether portrait, fancy picture, historical subject, group, or "conversation-piece." Romney (1734–1802) in his single pastel portrait, a likeness of William Cowper the poet, showed that he might have excelled in this medium, which, indeed, was particularly suited to his tender manner. Hugh D. Hamilton (c. 1734–1806) of the Royal Hibernian Academy, Ozias Humphry, A.R.A. (1742–1810), Richard Cosway, R.A. (1742–1821) and his wife Maria Cosway (1759–1838) are among the better known English pastellists. Daniel Gardner (?1750–1805), whose pictures in oil have often been mistaken for Reynolds's, and Gainsborough's, gave rein to his exuberant fancy and his rather exaggerated taste in compositions. Gardner marked the deterioration of the art, which thereafter declined, Henry Bright (1814–1873) being almost the only pastellist of real power who followed him. Bright's landscapes have probably in their own line never been surpassed.

Since 1870 there has been a revival of the art of pastel, the result of a better understanding and appreciation on the part of the public. The art of pastel, as M. Roger Ballu expressed it, "was slumbering a little," until in 1870 the Société des Pastellistes was founded in France and met with ready appreciation. With many artists it was a matter of "coloured chalks," as, for example, with Millet, Lhermitte and Degas in France, and with Whistler in England. With the majority the full possibilities were seized, and a great number of artists abroad then practised the art for the sake of colour, among whom may be mentioned Adrien Moreau, A. Besnard, Émile Lévy, Machard, Pointelin, Georges Picard, de Nittis, Iwill, René Billotte, Jozan, Nozel, Raffäelli, Brochard (mainly upon vellum) and Lévy-Dhurmer in France; in Belgium, Émile Wauters (who has produced a great series of life-sized portraits of both men and women of amazing strength, vitality and completeness) and Fernand Khnopff; in Italy, C. Laurenti, P. Fragiacomo and Giovanni Segantini; in Holland, Josselin de Jong; in Germany, F. von Lenbach, Max Liebermann and Franz Stück; and in Norway, Fritz Thaulow.

America has also been closely identified with the revival of the art. Among the American painters who have been successful in the use of pastel are: Mary Cassatt, Thomas W. Dewing, Robert Blum, Jerome Myers,

W. J. Glackens, Albert Sterner, Everett Shinn, J. Wells Champney and James Alden Weir.

In England the revival of pastel dates from 1880, when the first exhibition of the Pastel Society was held in the Grosvenor Gallery. The exhibition was a *succès d'estime*, but after a while the society languished until, in 1899, it was reconstituted, and obtained the adhesion of many of the most distinguished artists practising in the country, as well as of a score of eminent foreign painters. In that year, and since, it has held exhibitions of a high order; and intelligent public appreciation has been directed to the work of the most noteworthy contributors. Among these are E. A. Abbey, R.A.; M'Lure Hamilton, J. M. Swan, R.A.; J. Lorimer, R.S.A.; A. Peppercorn, R. Anning Bell, J. J. Shannon, R.A.; Sir James Guthrie, P.R.S.A.; H. Brabazon, Walter Crane, Melton Fisher, Edward Stott, A.R.A.; S. J. Solomon, R.A.; and W. Rothenstein.

ILLUSTRATION

ILLUSTRATION, in art, a picture which tells a story. On the walls of the temples and tombs in Egypt are many pictures which tell a story. These pictures are bound by conventions to such a degree that the individuality of the artist is lost in the imposed formula. There is no drama as we understand it. An exalted personage is simply represented proportionately larger than his fellows. Attitudes and gestures are prescribed. Yet they tell a story and to that extent they are illustrations, but they are more than that: they tell the story of a whole people, of a people's faith and hope and life. They are generic. They do not deal with incident. If one finds two people playing a game, it is an incident in the whole life of all the people and tells the story of that people and a game—not of two definite individuals at a moment in one special game with the specific incidents that attend that particular moment among all others. An illustration is a story-telling picture of a specific incident and its weakness lies in this very thing: that the greater idea is often secondary to the less. Yet in most illustrations, of fiction especially, the picture deals with the lesser idea.

284

ILLUSTRATION

The illustrator's work is the complement of expression in some other medium. A poem can hardly exist which does not awaken in the mind at some moment a suggestion either of picture or music. The sensitive temperament of the artist or the musician is able to realize out of words some parallel idea which can only be conveyed, or can be best conveyed, through his own medium of painting or music. Similarly, painting or music may, and often does, suggest poetry. It is from this inter-relation of the emotions governing the different arts that illustration may be said to spring. The success of illustration lies, then, in the instinctive transference of an idea from one idea to another; the more spontaneous it be and the less laboured in application, the better. The mind must be aware of an underlying unity, yet without being intellectually conscious of it.

Greece and Rome.—Proceeding another step, to the decorations on Greek vases, we have a more decided association between literature and pictorial art. We have a great legacy of poetry, picture and sculpture derived from Greece. There was a great theme—the heroes, the gods and demi-gods. The many legends and stories made them living beings, understandable because of their human qualities, inspiring because of their magnificence. These extraordinary myths filled the minds of all the people, for the story tellers went about reciting to those who could not read. All of the people perceived splendour in these heroic adventures—physical adventures, of course—and they magnified their heroes into an ideal.

A poet or an artist appears to be an individual, developed by his race, whose business it is to go out and see beauty and come back and tell about it. His business is to go out and see with the eyes of his own people, of his own time, of his own country and to show to them the things they love or reverence in a manner intelligible to them.

To the Greeks, the hero was a glorious human creature; inevitably their artists were moved to sculpture and to an ideal, an ideal which sought to show how magnificent man might become. Their honest service in this respect to their race leaves them unrivalled through all the centuries that have elapsed. Inspired they surely were, but inspired wholly by the passionate impulse of their time. When the draughtsman came along to decorate the vases of his people his motive was usually a simple association of those same heroes, gods and goddesses in one picture, containing, indeed, the essential surroundings, but always governed by the racial delight in perfected humanity. The poets told the same stories, so that to-day the sculpture, the picture and the play or poem mutually illuminate one another. Though not designed to illustrate any special line or poem, the pictures become illustrations of the finest type, generic rather than specific.

The Roman artist began to see landscape and introduce it into his wall paintings, usually to increase the apparent size of the garden upon whose enclosing walls his pictures were usually painted.

The Christian religion provided the next tremendous impulse toward visual art. Again all eyes were turned in one direction, all aspirations toward one glory and all reverence toward the sacred personages who suffered that they might bring to the humble masses no less than to the exalted individuals the wonderful message. For the Founder of the Christian religion had made the multitude worthy in its own eyes. He proclaimed their kinship with God and convinced them that they were beloved children of a loving, omnipotent Father in Heaven with Whom they should dwell, after this life of trial, in glory forever.

To a people treated like beasts of burden, driven and trampled upon, such a revelation was of tremendous import. The individual's right to prosperity and happiness here in this world naturally had not yet occurred to the many. They were taught that resignation, contentment and labour for their masters was the service for which they should receive the Divine reward in Heaven. The poet and the artist, born and bred of the peoples under that impulse, did as they were bound to do. They showed to the multitude the thing it reverenced and longed to see. The artists of that day were the sons of the multitude, and sharing in the beliefs of that multitude. They set forth in their paintings that which filled their own hearts no less than the hearts of all men moved by the same revelation.

Gradual Development.—The whole thing became a driving desire to make visible a great drama. They began to perceive the possibility of the dramatic composition which preserved the just proportions, and yet permitted the emphasis to fall upon the important incident in the picture which is known as the "centre of interest."

Composition was not unknown before this time, but it was a composition of design entirely, owing nothing to tone and very little to light and shade. Rarely, in even the best examples of vase paintings, is great action attempted. Generally, the figures express themselves in simple gestures, so that no intolerable suspended motion is noticeable. The Italian painter, finding himself confronted by the necessity to depict dramatic moments full of activity, devised new methods of composition. The suspended moving body or drapery, conforming to realism, is made to flow upon a line in the composition in such a manner that it is no longer a painfully maintained posture, but a part of the rhythm of the composition, an expression of extreme grace and of beauty.

Year in and year out that development went painfully on. They strove mightily, those men; they worked to exhaustion. They had but little to work with, compelled as they were to invent their own materials, colours, brushes, whatever they needed. In the early years of the attempt to reveal to their own eyes, and those of their people, a vision glowing of the spirit, they had nothing with which to do it. They could not draw, they could not paint; they recognized perspective but vaguely and they lacked general knowledge. But they had a story to tell in pictures and they themselves lay under an urgent need to see the visualization of their own dream. It was a story of the spirit—which is beauty. They painted a message from heart to heart. Any man, standing before these old treasured pictures, who is unable to let them appeal directly to his emotions, as is the case with music, can never hope to see them nor to understand why they are treasured.

As time went on jealousy and rivalry arose. The secrets of the craft were carefully guarded. A painter of great ability was crowded with commissions, which were often commands. Daylight was precious. Every moment was needed upon his compositions. He surrounded himself with pupils and from among these he chose helpers according to their ability. Thus came into existence the journeyman-apprentice, who reached his greatest development during the last century. He was the pupil of great technical skill, direct observation and little imagination. He was sent out to get facts. A group of trees was needed for some part of an important composition. He was sent out to make a study of it—not only the group of trees with meadow and clouds, but accurate information of branch and twig, with the pattern of leaf, the modelling of the trunk and the facts about the spreading roots with the plants growing between. He came back with definite knowledge, precise information which the master painter used as he saw fit. He chose what he needed, simplifying it into harmony with its importance in the picture, discarding what was irrelevant. The master painters were great illustrators, and it is from among them that arose the immortal few who are known as the Old Masters, because of the grandeur of their vision and the splendour of their expression of it.

And then the association of picture and its subject-text bound in the same volume came into being in the form of the illuminated manuscript. The same story and the same sincerity inspired these little pictures, truly works of art, though small and painted upon the page of a book and definitely designed to harmonize with the page and with the elaborate initial letter of which, frequently, they were a part. Some of them were superb masterpieces. The size of a picture matters little. If, however, the subject idea is unworthy of a great effort, the picture made too large, and with the inevitable elaboration, appears even more trivial than if proportioned appropriately.

Portraiture.—In ancient portraiture, incidental to all this early art, one seems to observe evidence that likeness primarily was sought. In Egypt imposed conventions prevented any real development of characteristic portraiture, or perhaps the artist was so trained to convention that it was not possible for him to free himself from its influence. Nevertheless, there are examples, small statues and statuettes, which are portraits of individuals, of definite character. Greek portraits, however, painted on small panels, seem meagre studies of character, but were probably sufficiently good likenesses. During the Renaissance portraiture came very much alive, emerging from hampering tradition and convention, until, in the 17th century it reached a magnificent expression. It became a realistic study of character, which was food for imagination. Painting his portrait, the artist came to know the man. He found, as he and everyone else already knew, that men are very much alike, and entirely different, in real life; he discovered that it could be expressed in art. Self-defence had taught everyone to discern the mood of another. Everyone knew at once whether another was about to strike, to smile, to speak a word of kindness; now the artist began to discover it in terms of his craft. He discovered that he could envelop the characters of his picture in an emotional atmosphere. He perceived in the hat and gloves left by his sitter on chair or table a likeness to their owner and that if they were used in a picture these adjuncts would have something to say as to the character of the man. When he came to paint the genre (*q.v.*) picture, he saw to it that the things belonging to his subject character were exactly the things with which this individual would inevitably surround himself. That is a part of illustration which requires imagination, knowledge and understanding derived from close and habitual observation. Imagination here is spiritual vision. This vision once possessed, aided by all his various funds of knowledge, the artist will perceive how an Individual whose character he has studied

288

and come to understand will behave in a given situation. It amounts to a vision of orderly events inevitable for that individual.

The religious story had been told, and while it continued to appear, and still often does, it was no longer in demand to the same extent. The artist was free to choose his subjects where he would, to descend gradually from that height to which the hunger, need and will of his race had driven him. Perhaps the most impressive example of this hangs in the museum of the Louvre. Huge paintings tell the story of the marriage of a man and a woman, but the man was king of France, Henry IV., and the woman a princess of Italy, Marie de' Medici. To the consciousness of that time such nuptials were great and impressive affairs, symbolic and resplendent with the grandeur of nations. Realistic pictures, however gorgeous, would be merely pictures of the pageantry of the event. The artist's task, however, was to make the significance of the event immortal.

Here is another instance where the artist was in accord with the convictions and motives of his time. He may have hated that particular king, but he and all men worshipped kings. To him and to all men this particular episode was of divine moment and significance. The gates of heaven opened; gods and angels with all their attributes of Power, Principalities and Virtues were present at the ceremonial, bearing aloft, in order to magnify those two royal mortals above mankind, the insignia of their isolation. That is what the pictures tell us.

To this artist, learned in his craft, it was not a very troublesome problem. The art and science of composition taught him how to use every incident in his pictures—numberless attendant figures; the profuse ornament of landscape and cloud; luxurious draperies, architecture, banners, armour—extraordinary in their number, variety and form; to exalt the two principal personages upon the apex of his design and convey that, while in the midst of many, they were solitary, unapproachable, beings apart. Previously he had painted many portraits, landscapes, studies of all kind in astonishing numbers. He had used his countless studies in countless paintings of every sort. He employed many hands besides his own. Nevertheless, he invented and designed his group of pictures as a whole, supervised and brought it into being. They were great inventions, for his imagination was apparently concerned with another aspect of the matter: it was busy with his audience—not in vanity, but in the *completion of his theme*. His business was to convey an idea to the world. He was not realizing a vision of his own and so, in his imagination, he viewed his growing designs with the eyes of the world, inventing his means step by step. Whether he, specially, was hated, whether he was bitterly regarded by jealousy are things aside. His world was with him in this task which it had commanded. He worked for a great audience, for the generations, for all time. He was not at the mercy of the turning page descending into oblivion with a trivial story.

Later Development.—It is not to be understood that no great works of art have occurred since that time. But the times were changing. Democratic ideas began to seep in and spread. New seas and continents were being discovered. Shipping, commerce, international intercourse vastly increased. Wealth was increasing rapidly until it became more than a motive, an ideal. The artist, of necessity sensitive to the psychology of his time, inevitably sensed this ideal. Being no longer under command of church and noble he was free to sell his talents to the highest bidder. He did and became often both politician and courtier, frequenting and contriving that he might frequent, the places whence commissions came. For the palaces of the rich, artists painted huge compositions, many of them splendid but of frivolous thought upon tawdry subjects. Not all of them did this, for some were the spiritual descendants of the great masters; they went back to the countryside. There they painted pictures so full of charm, of beauty and of poetry that they still hold our wonder.

The religious subject in pictorial art is not of paramount importance, nor is any subject. War and the ambitions of men have provided the opportunity for many great paintings. As to the written title of a picture, it is a mere label. The subject is what the passion of his race has taught the artist to think about it. Because the poet, the artist and the inventor—which is to say the poet—is born supremely sensitive to racial motive, he has led in thought and has imagined into material existence the things of its need and desire.

Imagination is the power of creative vision which gives direction to intellect. It is the business of intellect to find means whereby this vision is given material existence. In finding these means intellect must refer again and again to imagination for new directions until the dream comes true.

There is another sort of imagination: a primitive imagination busy with fears and reprisals. It is the mother of superstition and has troubled the mind of man with a terror of natural phenomena. He cowered before the wind, retreated in dismay before the rising waters in the spring-time and

EXAMPLES OF VARIOUS TYPES OF RENDERINGS

1. Carbon pencil drawing on cameo paper: made to visualize a proposed structure; effect of mass remaining dominant in spite of thoughtful delineation of detail; sense of relation to surroundings. By Chester B. Price. **2.** Crayon drawing: made to visualize proposed structure; arbitrary handling of tone values, details and entourage resulting in an unusual impression of mass. By Gilbert P. Hall. **3.** Wash: made to visualize a proposed structure; grasp of architectural factors, sensitive feeling, conveyed through a cultured technique. By H. VanBuren Magonigle

Plate II   RENDERING, ARCHITECTURAL

BY COURTESY OF (1) B. G. GOODHUE

EXAMPLES OF RENDERINGS, VARIOUS AS TO MEDIUM, USE, CONTENT AND STYLE

1. Water colour: made to convey general impression of a proposed structure in relation to its natural surroundings; adequate consideration of material reality of the general scene; architectural elements handled impressionistically with detail omitted; pictorial values predominating; emphasis on atmosphere and colour. By Birch Burdette Long

2. Lithograph: made to vivify an historical subject; cautious delineation of material facts; intelligent exaggeration of scale, conveying emotion of dignity, mystery, spaciousness. By David Roberts (1796–1864)

3. Pencil drawing, with wash: made to visualize proposed structures; fine discrimination between essentials and details, resulting in a convincing sense of reality both as to structural and human factors. By Thomas R. Johnson

4. Water colour over pencil layout: made to visualize proposed interior; fidelity to material detail. By Houghson Hawley

5. Pencil drawing on tracing paper with water colour used after mounting: made to visualize proposed addition to existing structure; complete comprehension of architectural factors conveyed by a perfected technique. By Otto Eggers

6. Water colour and pencil: straightforward sensing of material facts, intelligent subduing of detail to dominant, absence of emotional bias resulting in credible visualization. By Cyril Farey

shuddered at thunder, whispering that it was the voice of an angry god or the roar of some demon. As he grew weary of his fears man developed a courageous creature who was not afraid to take his life in his hand, to go out and see; one who would be satisfied with nothing but the truth, who would not stop till he knew it. He went out upon his mission and came back and reported that these things are inevitable results of natural law—dangerous but not malignant. Having begun, he can not stop, for the will of the race is that he must go on. We call him the scientist; his reports are called scientific facts; but scientific fact is the statement of the operation of natural law and natural law must be obeyed in art as well as in life.

Learning to Draw.—If any one turns to these pages in the hope that he will find a suggestion how to proceed, let him remember that, like the primitive artist, he has already in childhood scratched the uncertain image upon a slate. Let him take as his model the labour of the artist from that remote primitive time until he attained to his greatest stature.

First he learned to draw a figure; then he strove to make that figure beautiful; then, expressive. He laboured with nature to learn the laws of composition. He came into the lamplight and went out into the sunshine to know about light and shade. He studied atmosphere and the moods of nature. He learned to present an individual with his characteristic possessions and the psychology of his relations with others. He mastered these things thoroughly—then dismissed the troubles of ignorance and painted his picture. This impersonation of all artists lived for many centuries through all the turmoil of the great march of mankind. He is immortal. We are part of him. Without the understanding which came through his long life we can do little. His life has left its record. Learn to know it.

The laws of composition are written down. Learn them. The scientist has sought till he found the laws of light; he has arranged the simple formula of perspective; these are material means which nature provides and imposes. We must know them.

The artist has always told a story of some sort; let it be the simple statement that "Silver is Beautiful with Blue." That is theme enough for a masterpiece of colour. Perhaps it may be that "A Tree against Clouds is a Beautiful Design." That is theme enough for a masterpiece in black and white.

The Work of the Illustrator.—If stories are told in words, however skillfully elaborated and explained, one must refer to one's own observation and experience to perceive the motive of the author. That reference to the writer's observation, conveyed in words of one's own experience and vision, is generic illustration. Many persons have had no opportunity for parallel experiences with the author. Many have not the power of original observation. But the majority can associate the two when someone shows them how. That is the work of the illustrator.

No modern illustrator worthy of the name fails to realize that he is working for the people who buy that medium of distribution of story and picture which we call a "magazine." He is paid by so small a fraction of the amount expended that his work is bought for virtually nothing. He is under command of the whim of no one man. But he is under command. So were his forbears. They were under command of the whim of power. One of the greatest, a *sculptor*, was commanded by peremptory authority to *paint* the ceiling of the Sistine chapel. He spent three years lying on his back to work upon it and eased his bruises by writing plaintive sonnets and querulous letters to his father complaining that the work was vile and would not be accepted.

We of the present are under command only of the necessity imposed by a vast organization of which we voluntarily form a part. That the story and picture may reach the millions who wait upon a certain day, a great, complicated organization of men and machines must work constantly and without interruption. The illustrator becomes a part of that organization when he accepts a commission. He does not have to accept it; he may refuse; but once undertaken it must be done within a given time that all the processes may function at their best and the printed work delivered where and when it is expected. This is not arbitrary; it is inevitable.

Consider the editorship of the grand epoch of art. The labour of years was unveiled—the cold churchman stalked before it seeking heresy. The partisan peered into its corners for offence. Woe to the poor artist if either was found! The editor of to-day is all concern in his attitude toward the artist, providing a chair and kindly words; this is found to be more humane than the accusation of heresy and a cell under the leads.

The work of an illustrator is of the present, now. Art is of its own time, looking forward. It derives its knowledge and power of comparison from the past, but its real inspiration from its own time. It is a sad thing to find an artist to-day so possessed with admiration of one of the great of the past that he endeavours to depict his own times, not as the dead genius might do

292

now, but as he did then: whispering an unintelligible echo of stalwart tones reverberating with the meaning of the past. Times have changed. Little of the expression of the past applies to the present. There is no motive now, in any one direction, to impel a living pictorial art.

Mankind is making machines, discovering new laws and forces, applying them to his entertainment. Art, too, is an impulse of nature and it also is being used for entertainment. Born of the multitude, the artist must serve the multitude; if it so commands, he serves by leading it. And if it should have a great dream he must present it pictorially. If the public desires tawdry decorations, he will be bullied or cajoled into making them. If it demand entertainment he must help provide it. Increasingly specialized, used for meagre ends, he has therefore almost ceased to be—sleeping, perhaps, to be awakened at the call of a new need. Buildings go up and are torn down after such brief existence that mural paintings are but vaguely used—the easel picture has little reason to be—it is too heavy for our temporary walls. The exhibition gallery continues to house for its appointed time the dwindling work of the journeyman-apprentice. The real place for pictures seems to be the page of the magazine. The times demand it; it appears inevitable. Possibly this is only a phase.

It is the illustrator's business to give his best. The public will not help him, because it cannot. It behooves the illustrator to become a scholar; to know; to put all he is and has into his work; to study his story, not merely read it. He must do it alone, for himself; no one cares. If his work is up to publishing standards in craftsmanship it will be used. Editors will not help him with drastic criticism, or demand his best. He must work alone and for himself—that is what "art for art's sake" means now. It is true he will be paid a handsome sum; but it is also true he will be paid just as much for work not his best. Here is a spiritual problem. He must do his best, for himself, alone, rejoicing if three persons in the million realize it. He must be a strong man.

The Illustrator's Problems.—To-day the conditions are utterly different from any hitherto confronting the artist. Instead of some single motive he has many. Wide spread democracy encourages everyone to get for himself whatever he most desires. Universally that is wealth. Everyone works for wealth and in his leisure seeks amusement, entertainment, demanding of the arts that they provide it.

If a universal motive is a compelling theme for the artist then this uni-

293

versal struggle for wealth should surely supply it. If it is, then it appears to have developed, by almost equally universal patronage, a new art: the motion picture. It may be significant that the most popular, and therefore successful, motion pictures dwell lavishly upon great wealth, the effort to gain it—within or without the law—or else upon broad comedy. The motion picture might be regarded as illustration in its most elaborate form; but it is not. It is an art alone, and like all arts, best when it tells its own story in its own terms, borrowing from no other.

In the life of to-day there is another new thing. We are conscious of enormous forces that can be made to obey. We are aware of tremendous machines developing an energy equal to an army division, to several army divisions! We have ceased to fear the forces of nature and we have learned that if we obey natural law we may use the unlimited power nature's forces supply. These huge machines move in simple rhythm; ponderous creatures, impersonal, obedient, whose soulless grandeur has given a character to the times. Their significance is power. Some of us shudder at it, some exult, and it moves deeply the emotions of others.

In the presence of these new beings, made by the hands of men, traditional beauty of graceful curves, with the delicate harmony of colour, becomes a cloying sweetness, out of key. The painter has made an effort to express his sense of all this. Therefore we have had a procession of "schools": the cubists, the futurists and many others have made efforts to get into tune with the age. The painter tried geometrical forms; he tried brutal evasions of actuality of form and colour. He sought desperate means indeed. He sought to express the thing he felt—he did not seek to find some new thing to sell. For the painter has tried to stand firm upon integrity and to be faithful to traditions.

Whenever an individual perceives a new and real thing and tells about it, immediately he is surrounded by followers, enthusiasts, incapable of, or lacking the courage of original vision, but quite able to see when shown, and courageous enough to follow. *They* are sincere. *They*, in turn, are followed by imitators. The imitator sees only the thing that has been done and he sees it but superficially, copying the mannerism more often than the manner and never apprehending the underlying motive at all. Nor does he care. His purpose is to sell what he can while the public interest in the original remains. He it is who destroys that public interest, for his stature is soon apparent, and his stuff is rejected. The pity of it is that he brings about a

294

misunderstanding of the whole effort; a few see the work of the original while the many are informed of it only through meaningless imitations.

Modern Tendencies.—The foregoing is a bare outline of the history of illustrative art, from the first intimation scratched on stone to the present difficult situation. A few centuries ago a knowledge of the history of art was not so important to the artist. His work had to do only with his own people, people who believed as he did, thought as he did and only desired to have these things shown to them. No one knew or cared how the Jew in Palestine dressed and lived in Biblical times, so the Italian painter arrayed the Biblical characters in the Italian costume of his day. To-day we have another state of affairs altogether.

The camera has gone into every corner of the world and has brought back cold, precise facts. The reporter and the investigator have gone wherever the camera has gone; they have come home with more facts, and with explanations of the camera's pictures. This is knowledge; the newspapers and magazines send it to everybody. The important question to the artist, no matter whether he paint pictures for the galleries or make them for the magazines, is: what have this wide spread knowledge and the countless photographs got to do with *him?* Shall he go into competition with the camera? The camera in the hands of an artist-photographer is a formidable opponent. Can he meet it on its own terms, on its own ground? He cannot. In a fraction of a second it will defeat his labour of weeks.

The taste of the world demands pictures. It demands paintings, illustrations, photographs; it has seemed to declare definitely when and where it desires to see one or another. It would appear, then, that the painting and illustration has something the photograph lacks. On the other hand when people desire to see in a picture what is lacking in painting or illustration they turn to the photograph. The camera can only report what is before it; it can report with exceeding beauty, at times, but it can only report. The artist can create and he can select from the manifold beauties of nature what he will, to incorporate with his creation. To the artist then, it would seem that the deliberate message of the world appears to be that *he* is expected to create and to let the camera report.

Those artists (called inventors) having knowledge of the findings of scientists, have responded superbly to this demand and have created marvellous works. The creations of the inventors have absorbed the attention and the interest of the world almost to the exclusion of pictorial arts except where these contribute as luxurious accessories, or means of entertainment and amusement. Illustrations are seen by both the "classes" and "masses." They are seen by those capable of discrimination and of appreciation. It behooves the illustrator to respect his "audience."

Illustration may become a great art, but to become a great art it must be creative. It cannot hope to compete with the camera in the reporting of facts. It has no business with the outer shell of things at all. It deals with the spirit. Dealing with the psychological aspects is a great opportunity and a serious handicap. Presupposing a pictorial presentation of the relations of people, the telling of the story is inevitable. A great and simple story, akin to truth, or a poor and trivial one, akin to meagre facts, may be told of the same incident—depending upon the insight, the vision of the artist. The nature of the story portrayed is the measure of the artist who portrays it. It makes no difference that he may be most accomplished in his craft. Though he may draw with marvellous skill, though his composition be perfect, though his detail be faultless, if his conception is trivial and his thought upon it slight, then his technical excellences betray him the more and his work is a mere virtuosity, empty and meaningless.

The outward form given to an inward vision depends upon composition. Technical skill merely develops that outward form and is governed by composition which, in its character, must possess the emotional meaning of the vision and speak directly to the emotions. It has been said that the artist struggled with nature to learn the laws of composition, and after that he devised rules for it. One should know, then, the fundamental natural law so that he may, at need, disregard the rules.

The meaning of emotional character of form in composition may be illustrated by referring directly to human experience. Mankind has looked with awe upon the mountains for countless generations. The effort to cross them taxes his utmost powers and has cost much in pain and death. The vast pyramidal forms of mountains stand in his imagination as a sign of majesty. In composition the pyramidal form is used sparingly, only when the emotion of majesty, of grandeur, is to be conveyed. Man has long looked upon tall trees with respect and has endowed them with personalities; he has bowed low before temples stately with tall columns. Tall lines in composition are used to express dignity. The sombre greys of storm clouds, full of thunder, have terrified us since the infancy of the race. Cloud forms, subtly introduced into a composition, suggest impending evil. Primal man was probably colour-blind; he learned to see colour slowly. Perhaps he recognized red first, his own blood, seen in pain in the midst of fierce passions of rage and fear. Feeling this to be true, would it not seem strangely out of harmony to paint a sweet and motherly woman in a scarlet gown?

If the illustrator has not parallel experience with the writer he cannot march beside him, but must follow, presenting inconsequential, quasi-photographic, external repetitions—a faint accompaniment, indeed—of what the author has written. The illustrator must be a person of wide knowledge, that he may have understanding; of wide sympathy, that he may know the people whom he is to picture; of creative imagination that the story may be real in his vision. To maintain such an ideal in the face of the difficulties which confront him is almost impossible, and necessitates a rare devotion to his work.

A magazine has been defined as a medium for the distribution of story and picture. It is sold at a trifling price. The publication of it at this trifling price involves a vast organization having contact with innumerable interests and bound by contracts written and implied. It *must* appear on the day when it is due to appear, otherwise these contracts are broken. Some contracts are with advertisers. Were it not for the advertisements carried in its pages the single number, to the single subscriber, would cost a hundred times or more the amount he now must pay. It is the money paid by the advertiser which makes it possible for the person of small means to have the work of the ablest writers and artists presented to him every month or week. To combine the labour of so many brains and hands that this punctuality may be maintained occupies most of the waking consciousness of publisher, editor, writer and artist. There is no eight-hour day for them.

In the necessity for such punctuality lies the exhausting handicap for the illustrator. Difficult situations must be met. Fair play sometimes forbids him from exercising his right to decline work in which he is not deeply interested. This has been called "commercializing" art, but it is not; it is complying with a need. In the lives of the old masters there were parallel instances. To return to the incident of the Sistine chapel, Michelangelo, who painted the decorations for it, was commanded by the whim of a powerful old man, and he was obliged to obey. The illustrator of to-day is commanded by a necessity involving countless individuals over the whole country. To obey such demands requires knowledge so completely in mind that it can be set forth at once—either that or evasion. To be obliged to work far into the night, day after day, is no unusual experience. "Overtime" is a word unknown to the illustrator, the writer, the editor. Few of them can be bribed by money to the exhausting work which their love of it, for its own sake, makes them gladly do.

The illustrator's first obligation to himself and to his public is a complete understanding of the story for which he is to make illustrations. One reading of it is rarely enough. If there are any allusions to things he does not know, he must learn them. Often such allusions, if understood, suggest an entirely new conception of the story. Material inaccuracies are of slight importance. The spirit and the meaning of the story are the important things. What the author thinks about it does not matter to the artist, nor does it matter what the editor and the public think about it. What the artist himself thinks about it is all-important to him and to the public. To depict that is his reason for being.

ARCHITECTURAL RENDERING

ARCHITECTURAL RENDERING is a pictorial art whose object is to visualize architectural conceptions. When an architect is employed to design a building, it is desirable that he provide his client, in advance, with an accurate impression of the appearance of the proposed structure. Since words cannot adequately convey the architectural story, paintings or drawings are employed to render it, as it were, clear to the eye; they serve as a kind of communication. This is the most familiar application of the art; and, when so used, rendering may be defined as the medium whereby the renderer communicates a sense of the reality of a structure in advance of its concrete materialization. Occasionally, however, the architect has a rendering made in the course of his own work and as an aid to his own study. When an architectural conception first forms in the background of his mind, it has, of necessity, a certain nebulous character. But with the effort of expressing it on paper, in actual lines and tone values, it emerges, so to speak, and crystal-

PROGRESSIVE VIEWS OF A RENDERING

A rendering by Hugh Ferriss, showing: 1. Lines drawn, tentatively suggesting a mass in space. 2. Additional lines added as material for tone values. 3. Lines rubbed together with paper stump, producing tone values to confirm indication of mass. 4. The form further modelled by use of kneaded eraser on right hand planes. 5. Principal subdivisions of the mass delineated, also by use of (1) pencil, (2) paper stump and (3) kneaded eraser. 6. Minor items introduced, same process. (*See* section of article on *Procedure.*)

PLATE IV

RENDERING, ARCHITECTURAL

RENDERINGS IN VARIOUS MEDIUMS

1. Engraving: structural factors, accurately sensed, recomposed with a virile imagination, conveying powerful emotional impression. By Piranesi (1720—76). 2. Pencil drawing, coffee wash: made to visualize a civic project; primarily concerned with the architectural conception, yet adequate attention given to pictorial values. By Eliel Saarinen. 3. Etching: imaginary composition on historical motif; highly stimulating impressions. By William Walcot. 4. Pastel: selection of architectural factors from an existing building; thoughtful composition of subject matter, affectionate attention to technique. By T. de Postels. 5. Pencil: example of a one minute sketch made to convey an architect's conception to his assistants; attention centred on essentials of the design (which were later constructed as sketched). By Cass Gilbert

lizes. When so employed, rendering serves as a definite step in the evolution of architectural conceptions.

Rendering has a third use; viz., in connection with already existing buildings. When so used, renderings—as distinguished from the miscellaneous paintings and drawings that refer only incidentally to architecture—have, as their chief or sole concern, to render clear the strictly architectural nature of the subject. By this selection of architectural factors, they may enable the layman to grasp the significance of a building more readily than when faced by its multitudinous and irrelevant details. At the same time, they may serve as a faithful record of the historic course of architectural design. In these three ways, rendering fulfills a recognized function, and has done so over a long period.

In the last quarter of a century, there has developed an aspect of architectural and engineering practice that involves rendering on a more extended scale—town and city planning (*q.v.*). A comprehensive plan for the future building development of any large community is never the conception of a single mind; many minds must collaborate in it. Nor is it materialized in a few years, but in many years. In these circumstances, it becomes impractical for its whole purport to be carried only in any single given mind, or for an accurate image to be postponed until the whole long scheme has been consummated. The various contributory ideas and suggestions must be assembled, in definite terms, on the paper or canvas of the rendering, in order that the prophecy may assume sufficient reality to serve as a criterion and a guide.

Another factor, which more clearly reveals the contemporary field of rendering, is that Western architecture, as a whole, is passing through a period of transition and, therefore, of experiment. It is true that the practice of many of the most prominent architects is to continue constructing mere copies, or very slightly modified copies, of those classic styles which, in their impressionable years, they were led to regard as being the very body of architectural culture; their effort is to emulate the classic designers in all respects, save, perhaps, the latter's logic, sense of congruity and ability to fashion novel forms. Their public, accordingly, has been wont to feel the presence of architecture only in a building to which the architect has added a Greek colonnade, a Roman dome or a Gothic spire. In all this, professional rendering has been able to play but a small part, since the picture has been regarded as an end in itself simply to be made as attractive as possible; it could scarcely be employed as a means of rendering forth a new truth, more especially as the appearance of these styles of architecture has been known for centuries.

In recent years, however, definite changes have occurred in methods of construction and the manufacture of materials, as well as in the general social and economic situation; and one notices that in the larger centres of Western civilization a distinct type of designer is making his presence in the architectural profession more and more strongly felt. These designers are inspired not so much by the traits of an architectural heredity as by the needs of contemporary environment. For them, the tremendous environmental changes that have occurred imply and demand a corresponding change in the architectural approach. They do not—to choose one example—employ a new material, steel, to support façades, which have developed in other materials and can be logical only therein. They are engaged, briefly, in developing new types of architecture. Certain limitations lie upon these practising and experimental architects. It is sometimes too hazardous to test a novel conception by actually carrying it out in a building which, whether a success or a failure, must stand for many years. But the conception may be quite thoroughly tested in a series of conscientious renderings. For example, the modern American zoning laws involved a radical departure in the general forms of buildings, and into the strange spaces created by these laws some architects proceeded without pause to force the classical images with which their minds were filled. More cautious architects sought to discover the basic structural types that the laws admitted; for this purpose, renderings were employed. Another limitation is that the projects of architects are practically bound by the ideas and the financial resources of their clients; they cannot actually build in advance of their clients' prepossessions. In renderings, however, they may freely express their real intentions, and these renderings, when duly exhibited can, and in fact do, make a distinct contribution to the progress of architectural design. A third limitation is that no practising architect, however fortunate, has time to build more than a very few influential buildings during his lifetime. He may, however, record himself in soundly fashioned drawings and paintings whose content, though at first existing in only two dimensions, may, in due time, be realized in three.

In addition to the functions thus far mentioned, rendering has a rôle to play in what is doubtless the greatest concern of architecture—the psychological influence it exerts on human life. A few people, it is true, are fully conscious of the impressions that they receive in the face of noble buildings;

'the more pertinent and important fact is that the vast majority of human beings are continually, if unconsciously, influenced by the architectural forms and spaces with which they come in contact. Architects themselves are often unaware of the extent of this influence; that is to say, the influence which is unconsciously received is unconsciously initiated. Perhaps it is in consequence of this that the haphazard and miscellaneous architectural scene which is presented by most modern cities, and which is constantly before the population, is left to impress the corresponding qualities upon the human psyche. On the other hand, there have been periods in the past—the "great periods" of architecture—when the designers must have been quite aware of the influence, and utilized it for conscious purposes. In the Gothic cathedrals, for example, there is embodied, in terms of form and space (terms safely beyond the vicissitudes of any particular church) a potent and lasting influence for the betterment of mankind. Buildings of the first category—depressing or distracting buildings—are legion; those of the second—buildings which arrest or elevate—are rare. But the more significant forms may be repeatedly delineated and interpreted in drawings and paintings by whose agency they may be widely exhibited, published and, so to speak, broadcast. Rendering, in short, by allying itself with the conscious and objective forces in architectural work, may serve, by paraphrase, to bring home the laconic message of architecture.

To sum up, rendering has six principal objects. The first three have long been recognized: to convey advance realizations of proposed structures, to aid in crystallizing ideas in the architect's mind and to interpret the architectural significance of existing structures. The other three remain largely for future development: to serve as criterion and guide in city planning, to assist in evolving new types of architecture and to strengthen the psychological influence of architecture on human values.

Whichever of these objects a given rendering is to serve, the renderer —having comprehended *why* the drawing is being made—is faced with two fundamental considerations. The first is to grasp *what* is the nature of the architectural subject to be rendered, to so ponder it as to exclude non-essentials. The second is *how* to employ the various devices of draughtsmanship so as to communicate this realization to others. Between these two items—the nature of the subject and the process of rendering—there exists the distinction between ends and means, and it is important that the renderer have this distinction clearly in mind at the outset.

GRAPHIC ARTS

As a matter of common practice, this distinction is often not made. The painting or drawing is often regarded as being an end in itself, and discussion of it centres, in consequence, on purely technical questions: interest of composition, nicety of line, cleverness of brushwork, etc. Many such works are contributions to the subject of technique and justify the enthusiasm of technicians; but, lacking architectural significance, they are not, strictly speaking, architectural renderings.

It is also a common practice to regard rendering as indeed a means but to substitute for its authentic and natural ends, ends that are special or perverted. For example,—as in the Beaux Arts curriculum—projects are often rendered in elevation *i.e.*, (the representation is of but one façade of the building as this would appear were the eye directly opposite each and every point thereon). This, obviously, produces a form which can exist only on paper; it is not the form which the human eye would perceive in the building itself. Such a treatment serves a purpose, in that an architect, when reading its conventionalized and inexact statement, can translate it, in his trained mind, into at least an approximation of the truth. But just because it requires a translation, and is, in itself, foreign to reality, it may be classified as a special practice.

Another common practice, of a different category, is to accomplish, by means of a picture, an end which is positively opposed to architectural fact. The renderer may be called on to exaggerate certain aspects of a proposed building in order to create a more favourable advance impression; or to exaggerate certain factors of an existing building in a way to advertise them. The architect or advertiser may wish such a rendering as a result of deliberate calculation or because his personal interest in particulars is so great as to obscure from his view the real appearance of the building in its entirety. In any case, the executing of such commissions falls rather into the class of commercialized art and may be excluded from a discussion on rendering.

The twofold criterion of values remains to be applied to all renderings: first, comprehension of the architectural essentials involved in the subject; second, effectiveness in pictorial communication.

ESSENTIALS TO BE RENDERED

Mass.—From the renderer's point of view a building is, in the first place, a material mass. While it is not, in actuality, a mass in the sense that a mountain is a mass, *i.e.*, it is not a solid, nevertheless the effect of solidity is essential to it.   And while, in constructing a building, this effect may be the last to be realized, in drawing a building it is logically the first.   The renderer must realize the presence of mass before he can fully realize the presence of any appurtenant form.   It may be likened to the clay which a sculptor must grasp before any particular shape can be given or any details modelled.   The first necessary attribute of a convincing architectural rendering is, correspondingly, an adequate suggestion of mass.   Without this primary effect of solidity, all details which may be delineated later must appear without body and the presentation as a whole must lack substance.

Form.—Being imbued with a sense of the substantial nature that his subject, in general, possesses, the renderer addresses himself to a study of its particular form.   It is generally taken for granted that if accurate floor plans and elevations are available, an accurate image of the building can be produced by following the rules of perspective draughtsmanship—those rules are said to have originated with Leonardo and are commonly accepted as being correct and comprehensive.   The fact is, however, that there is considerable question as to how forms really look.   It is quite doubtful if the system of perspective draughtsmanship which we accept as a science, is more than a convention—a convention which, indeed, is usually of great help to accurate representation and yet, in numerous instances, is a specific hindrance.   The forming, in the human eye of images of buildings appears, in fact, to involve factors with which we, as renderers, have not yet adequately dealt.

The Single Viewpoint.—One item to be considered in this connection is that, in laying out perspectives the draughtsman habitually assumes that the subject is being viewed from a single viewpoint.   He establishes, on his draughting board, a specific point, termed the "viewpoint" and his operations proceed from this base.   But this assumption is inadequate to the extent that the appearance which a building actually produces on a one-eyed man is inadequate as compared to that produced on a two-eyed man.   In some cases, the discrepancy is not remarkable—as, for example, small forms viewed at considerable distances.   But, in forms which are closely scrutinized, the discrepancy becomes pronounced; there is a definite lack of the three-dimensional quality to the single-eyed vision, and there is a corresponding flatness to the general run of perspectives laid out from the single viewpoint.

The Stationary Viewpoint.—A second item is that a draughtsman in laying out his perspective assumes, according to the convention, that his single viewpoint is stationary.   In reality, however, an observer in forming his image of a building, assumes a series of viewpoints. In seriously studying a building, one will purposefully view it from many different angles; but even if the interest is only casual one will instinctively look at it more than once—always from a viewpoint which is, of necessity, slightly altered. In all cases, it may be said that the image which the observer takes away with him is not the single first impression received from a literally stationary viewpoint, but is a composite of several distinct impressions. This composite quality of the image is an essential which demands the renderer's attention: how he may, by a cunning draughtsmanship, convey this aspect of the case is considered in this article under the heading of "Procedure."

The foregoing consideration involves a problem that often appears in rendering; viz., one is often faced with the necessity of choosing between a truthful pictorial statement of the building which is being drawn and a truthful statement of the viewpoint which happens to have been chosen.

It is usually held that when a viewpoint has once been selected, it is demanded by honesty that all items of the scene (including adjoining buildings) must be delineated exactly as they appear; that if one arbitrarily makes alterations (as, for example, showing adjoining buildings less prominently than they actually are) he is guilty of "faking." Undeniably, many renderings are "faked"; at the same time, there is a distinction to be made. If the alteration has been made for the purpose of conveying a more favourable impression than the actual scene, then the charge of misrepresentation is, obviously, sustained. It often happens, however, that a building possesses a very important feature which, while entirely visible from many points of view, may happen to be screened from the particular point of view that has been chosen. For instance, a building may possess a certain buttressing member which gives its tower integrity, and which may be visible from many viewpoints, but this member may be hidden from the chosen viewpoint by some extraneous and perhaps temporary obstruction. We may assume at the same time, that the renderer's commission is to depict the building as truthfully and completely as possible in a single drawing. In such a case, it would appear that he is not so much permitted as actually required to slight incidental facts of his viewpoint in favour of the essential facts of the subject which he is viewing.

Perspective of Vertical Lines.—Another item demanding the renderer's attention is that all effects of perspective which a building presents to the human eye apply to its vertical as well as to its horizontal extension. Although this is obviously so, the current convention of perspective generally disregards it, the horizontal lines, only, being drawn to meet in a "vanishing point," but the vertical lines being arbitrarily drawn parallel to each other. In the case of very low buildings, the discrepancy is not important; but in the cases, now so numerous, of very tall buildings, the inaccuracy is serious. The convention not only produces distorted drawings, but so habituates onlookers to distortion that they become disinclined to recognize normal appearances.

Method of Construction.—The renderer may, to a considerable degree, express in his drawing such differences of appearance as exist, for example, between a building of solid masonry and one of steel grille construction. His medium allows considerable variety of indication of texture characteristic of stone, brick, terracotta, glass, etc.

Atmospheric Conditions.—Buildings are, of necessity, seen through a physical atmosphere and a suggestion of reality obviously cannot be conveyed in a drawing in which an atmospheric condition is not convincingly suggested; some renderings, for instance, fail by conveying the suggestion that the subject was viewed through a vacuum.

The important question of colour belongs to a general study of the painter's art.

In addition to these material factors, an architectural subject presents others of a psychological nature. A realistic rendering may, indeed, be produced by dealing honestly with only the physical facts; an authentic rendering, however, demands a realistic treatment of intellectual and emotional aspects as well. In this connection, the following experiment is illustrative. An exact perspective was laid out of the form of the Woolworth building, using the architect's blue prints as a basis. A second study was made, sketching from the building itself from an exactly corresponding viewpoint. The building was then photographed from this viewpoint. On comparing the three results it was found that the principal proportions were different in each case. The more striking conclusion was that none of them conveyed the sense of structural logic which the disposition of the steel members themselves conveys to the thoughtful observer; none of them suggested the emotion of soaring aspiration which the form itself suggests to the human onlooker. It becomes, indeed, one of the chief concerns of the renderer to comprehend the nature of the architectural idea which his subject embodies, the trend of thought the architect has expressed. Similarly, the renderer must especially aim to appreciate the emotional tone, the particular mood, of his subject. On entering these outlying psychological domains rendering, like the other arts, may attain its happiest freedom of movement. Yet just here, unfortunately, it must evade competent technical guidance. We have many paintings and drawings which succeed in conveying an isolated thought or an isolated emotion; but too often we find that the renderings which have attained this success have paid in distorted material proportions.

Viewed in this way, renderings as a whole fall into certain rather well-defined groups. The largest, and most familiar, includes those in which the renderer has made a competent presentation of the material facts, but has failed to include any of those elements which, in architecture, stimulate the mind and arouse the emotions. It is as though he worked only with his hands, neither his thought nor feeling having been involved. The result is correct but chilling. A second group is that in which only an emotional aspect of the subject has been fully rendered, just as a third is that in which only an intellectual aspect has been emphasized. Such works, generally labelled "impressionistic," "futuristic," etc., often convey what was intended yet fail of permanent value in that they distort or omit the physical facts of the case. If, for example, the subject be a mausoleum which has, in actuality, an atmosphere of solemnity, such a rendering may—perhaps in a few dark washes—convey an emotion of solemnity but leave the mausoleum itself in doubt. Or, if the subject be a tower notable for its logical growth, the rendering may—perhaps in a few cold lines—suggest logical growth but refer to no particular tower. There follow, naturally, three further groups in which the result is more appealing or convincing: that in which the material facts have been accurately presented in a thoughtful manner; that in which they have been presented with appreciable emotion; and that in which, while the material facts have been presented inexactly, a clear architectural thought appears accompanied by deep feeling. The ideal, which would constitute a seventh group, would be to convey the material, the emotional and the intellectual facts in the same rendering.

Why renderings should fall into these various groups is probably not difficult to ascertain: they do so by following the various personalities of the renderers. A draughtsman naturally draws that aspect of a building which he is by habit inclined to appreciate. From one renderer, we shall almost always get a very correct and cold drawing; from another a very bold and incorrect drawing. This suggests the reason why a perfectly balanced rendering has never been produced. It also suggests a point of interest to the student of rendering. It may well be that he will develop his art not simply by cultivating whatever tendency he happened to exhibit in the beginning, but, rather, by seeking to add to his forces some tendency which was not habitual to him. For example, if he is in the way of being an excellent draughtsman, he might seek to acquire an emotional appreciation of architecture in addition; just as, if he has always had strong feelings about buildings, he might seek to comprehend the pure logic by which all architectural masterpieces are given form. When thus regarded, rendering becomes, for the renderer himself, not so much a matter of self-expression as of self-development.

PROCEDURE

To answer the remaining question—*how* to make a rendering—it is necessary, since there are numerous equally promising methods of procedure, to describe the method employed in a specific case. In the case of the rendering reproduced in fig. 1–6 of Plate III. the procedure was as follows:—

A sheet of mounted Whatman paper 27 by 40 in. was tacked to a slightly larger drawing board and placed on a vertical easel. The draughtsman standing before the easel, made the assumption that, for the moment, the paper represented *space*. With the intention of introducing into this space, the presence of *mass*, a number of lines were lightly sketched in, using a 3B Wolff crayon (*see* fig. 1). These lines fall into three groups, according to their direction; they proceed, respectively, from three previously assumed "vanishing points." They serve the draughtsman as an adequate notation of the three-dimensionality which characterizes any mass in space. While sketching these generalized lines, he emphasized such as would tentatively indicate the particular form that he intended to give the mass—the form which, until now, had existed only in his mind. The next step was to confirm and solidify these outlines by introducing tone values—produced by drawing, rapidly, a number of freehand lines across the areas to be shaded (*see* fig. 2) and rubbing these lines together into a tone with a gloved finger or a paper "stump" (*see* fig. 3.) In the rendering now under consideration, the degree of solidity which was desired at this stage was effected by producing three general tones—the background being the darkest, the planes of the building which face toward the left being intermediary, and the planes which face toward the right being the lightest. The last tone was produced by cleaning the areas with a "kneaded" eraser (*see* fig. 4).

307

GRAPHIC ARTS

At this point, the draughtsman had before him a visualization, vivid enough for his own purposes, of the basic form of the building. His next step was to identify, in his mind, the principal subdivisions of his preconceived design and to indicate, on the paper, these modifications of the basic form. This involved a repetition, at a smaller scale, of his previous procedure; that is to say, he first sketched in the minor forms in line and then solidified them with tone values, using glove, stump and eraser. At this point another tone value was added to contribute further to the effect of solidity; *i.e.*, the cast shadows (*see* fig. 5). The same process of indicating form in line was repeated again and again—each time dealing with a category of smaller forms—until the building appeared in that degree of detail which seemed best calculated to serve the purposes for which the drawing was undertaken (*see* fig. 6).

Of renderings of this sort, it might be said that the draughtsman begins his task in this spirit: he is, metaphorically, facing a building which, although it exists in its entirety, is completely hidden from him in a mist or fog. As he approaches his subject, however, he begins to discern the principal outlines of its mass. Soon its secondary and tertiary features appear. He is free to continue his approach until the most minute details have become plain. Nevertheless, it is important that he halt at that point where his subject has revealed all that is essential to his inquiry.

The numerous other methods of rendering, all equally useful, can best be studied in reproductions of actual renderings; such material, with explanatory notes, is shown in the accompanying plates. They all point to the same conclusion—the draughtsman's best procedure is first to delineate the essentials of his subject, then to build all indication of detail on this foundation.

BIBLIOGRAPHIES

DRAWING

Francesco Bertinatti, *Elementi di anatomia fisiologica applicati alle belle arti figurative*, Torino: P. Marietti, 1837, i. v. 8. Atlas fol. 43 pl.

Richard Lewis Bean, *Anatomy of the Use of Artists*, London: H. Renshaw, 1841, 8. 47 pp., 10 pl.

William Wetmore Storey (1819–95), *The Proportion of the Human Figure*, According to a Cannon, for Practical Use. London: Chapman & Hall, 1866, roy. 8. 3 p. 1., 63 pp., 7 tab.

Robert Fletcher, *Human Proportion in Art and Anthropometry*. Cambridge: M. King, 1883, 37 pp., 4 pl. 8.

William Rimmer, *Art Anatomy*. London: Kegan, Paul, Trench and Co., 1884. fol. 2 p. 1., 81 pl.

Julius Constantin Ernst Kollmann (1834–1918), *Plastische Anatomie des menschlichen Körpers, für Küntstler und Freunde der Kunst*. Leipzig: Veit und Comp., 1886, roy. 8. By the professor of Anatomy at Basel. Illustrated with lithographs from hand-drawings, photographs from the nude, ethnic studies of facial features arranged on echelon, etc. The text, like Hyrtl's, is of unusual historic interest, and includes special chapters on the anatomy of the infant, human proportions, and ethnic morphology. Among the models used are Sandow, Rubenstein and other celebrities.

Edouard Cuyer, *Anatomie Artistique du Corps Humain*. Planches par le Dr. Fau, Paris: J. B. Ballière et Fils, 1886, vii.-208 pp., 17 pl.

Charles Rochet (1815–1900). *Traité d'Anatomie, d'Anthropologie et d'Ethnographie Appliquées aux Beaux-Arts*. Paris: Renouard, 1886. xii.–276 pp. Illustrated by pen drawings (in black and white and colours) by G. L. Rochet.

Paul Richer (1849–   ), *Anatomie Artistique*. Description des formes exterieures du corps humain au repos et dans les principaux mouvements. Paris: E. Plon, Nourrit et Cie., 1890, fol. viii., 110 pl.

Physiologie Artistique de l'Homme en Mouvement. Paris: O. Doin, 1895, 8. 335 pp., 6 pl.

Paul Richer (1849–   ), *Nouvelle Anatomie Artistique du Corps Humain*, Paris: Plon. 1906. sm. 4 vi.–177 pp.

Ernst Wilhelm Brucke (1819–92), *Schönheit und Fehler der menschlichen Gestalt*. Wien: W. Braumuller, 1891, 8. 1 p. 1., 151 pp. By the professor of physiology at Vienna. A book of unusually attractive and informing character, illustrated with 29 small woodcuts of singular beauty by Hermann Paar. English translation 1891.

Charles Roth, *The Student's Atlas of Artistic Anatomy*. Edited with an introduction by C. E. Fitzgerald. London: H. Grevel & Co., 1891, fol. viii.-50, 34 pl.

BIBLIOGRAPHIES

Arthur Thomson. *A Handbook on Anatomy for Art Students*. Oxford: Clarendon Press, 1896. 8. A work of solid merit which has reached its fourth edition. Illustrated with superb photographic plates of the nude, in brown tone, each plate having opposite a schema of the underlying muscles, with legends. The male and female models were chosen not for excessive muscularity, but for all-round symmetry and proportion. Far and away, the best model treatise on the subject in English.

Carl Heinrich Stratz, *Die Schönheit des weiblichen Körpers*, Stuttgart, F. Enke, 1898. A treatise on artistic anatomy, based upon direct photography of female models.

Der *Körper des Kindes*. Für Eltern, Erzieher, Aertze und Künstler. Stuttgart: F. Enke, 1903, 8. xii.—250 pp., 2 pl. An admirable study of surface anatomy of the female body in children, illustrated by photographs from the nude.

James M. Dunlop. *Anatomical Diagrams in the Use of Art Students*, arranged with analytical notes, and with introductory preface by John Cleland. London: George Bell & Sons, 1899, rov. 8. 4 p. 1., 72 pp. Illustrated with parti-coloured drawings and photographs.

George McClelland. *Anatomy in Its Relation to Art;* an exposition of the bones and muscles of the human body, with especial reference to their influence upon its actions and external forms. Philadelphia: A. M. Slocum Co., 1900, 4. 142 pp., 41 1., 126 pl. Illustrated by 338 original drawings and photographs made by the author. The drawings are mostly rude diagrammatic sketches. The photographs are elegant, well-selected album-pictures of the nude, many of them duplicating the poses and thus demonstrating the excellent anatomy of many antique and modern statues.

Robert J. Colenzo. *Landmarks in Artistic Anatomy*. London: Bailliere, Tindall and Cox, 1902, sm. 4. vi. (i.–1)—56 pp. 6 outlines pl.

Robert Wilson Shufeldt (1850–   ). *Studies of the Human Form*, for Artists, Sculptors and Scientists. Philadelphia: F. A. Davis Co., 1908, roy. 8. xxxi.—664 pp. Illustrated by photographs of nude models.

Sir Alfred D. Fripp and Ralph Thompson. *Human Anatomy for Art Students*, with drawings by Innes Fripp and an appendix on comparative anatomy by Harry Dixon. Philadelphia: J. B. Lippincott Co., 1911, 12. 296 pp. Contains 151 illustrations, among which are 23 effective photographs from the nude.

John Henry Vanderpool (1857–1911). *The Human Figure*. London, 1913, 8.

Edwin George Lutz. *Practical Art Anatomy*. New York: Charles Scribner's Sons, 1918, 8. vii.—254 pp. Illustrated with very rudimentary outline drawings by the author.

George B. Bridgman. *Constructive Anatomy*. Pelham, New York. Bridgman Publishers 1919—213 pp. il. 400 bds.

George B. Bridgman. *The Book of One Hundred Hands*. Pelham, New York. Bridgman Publishers 1921—172 pp. il. 400 bds.

George B. Bridgman. *Bridgman's Life Drawing*. Pelham, New York. Bridgman Publishers 1924—172 pp. 2 il. 300 bds. Edward C. Bridgman; Geo. B. Bridgman (Pelham, N. Y.).

PERSPECTIVE

R. W. Ware, *Modern Perspective* (1894); V. T. Wilson, *Freehand Perspective* (1900); W. P. P. Longfellow, *Applied Perspective for Architects and Painters* (1901); W. H. Lawrence, *Principles of Architectural Perspective* (3rd ed., 1908); D. M. Norton, *Freehand Perspective* (1924); W. W. Sturtevant, *Mechanical Pictorial Drawing* (1927).

BIBLIOGRAPHIES

BATIK

C. E. Pellew, *Dyes and Dyeing* (1913); P. Mÿer, *Batiks, and How To Make Them* (1919); C. F. Lewis, *A Practical Handbook on Batik, the Art of Wax Pattern Dyeing* (1924); D. Réal, *The Batiks of Java* (1924); J. A. Loebèr, *Das Batiken Eine Blüte idonesischen Kunstlebens* (Oldenburg 1926). *See also* Report by Dutch Government, *Die Batik-Kunst in Niederlandisch Indien.*

LITHOGRAPHY

W. D. Richmond, *The Grammar of Lithography* (1878); E. Duchatel, *Traité de la Lithographie artistique* (1893, 2nd ed., as *Manuel de Lithographie artistique pour l'artiste et l'imprimeur,* 1908); A. Curtis, *Some Masters of Lithography* (1897); C. Wagner, *Alois Senefelder, sein Leben und Wirken* (1914); J. and E. R. Pennell, *Lithography and Lithographers* (1915).

A. Senefelder, *A complete course of Lithography* (1819, trans. by A. S. Ackermann) history from 1796 to 1816, translated by J. W. Muller, published as *The Invention of Lithography* (1911); C. Harrap, *Transferring* (1912), the practice of transferring to stone and metal as applied to planographic printing; D. Cummings, *Handbook of Lithography* (1919), a practical text-book for lithographers; F. T. Corkett, *Photo-Litho Offset Printing* (1923), a collection of brief articles by various authorities; H. J. Rhodes, *The Art of Lithography* (1924), a modern textbook giving a survey of the various processes; C. Halbmeier, *Senefelder and the History of Lithography* (1926); C. Harrap, *Offset Printing from Stone and Plates* (1927).

CARICATURE

J. P. Malcolm, *Historical Sketch of the Art of Caricaturing* (1813); T. Wright, *History of Caricature and Grotesque in Literature and Art* (1865); Champfleury (Jules Fleury), *Histoire de la Caricature (antique et moderne),* and other volumes by the same author (1865, etc.); J. Paxton, *Caricature and other Comic Art* (1878); J. Grand-Carteret, *Les Mœurs et la Caricature en Allemagne, etc.* (1885); *Bismarck en Caricatures,* and numerous other volumes by the same author (1890) etc.; G. Everitt, *English Caricaturists and Graphic Humorists of the Nineteenth Century* (1886); Armand Dayot, *Les Maîtres de la Caricature française en XIX° siècle* (1888); Arsène Alexandre, *L'Art du rire et de la Caricature* (1893); M. H. Spielmann, *The History of Punch* (1895); Georges Veyrat, *La Caricature à travers les siècles* (1895); A. Brisson, *Nos Humoristes* (1900); E. Bayard, *La Caricature et les Caricaturistes* (1901); E. Fuchs, *Die Karikatur der europäischen Völker* (1901); A. Filon, *La Caricature en Angleterre* (1902); R. de la Sizeraine, *Le Miroir de la Vie, la Caricature* (1902); A. B. Maurice and F. T. Cooper, *The History of the Nineteenth Century in Caricature* (1904); C. E. Jensen, *Karikatur-Album etc.* (Copenhagen, 1904–08); P. Gaultier, *Le Rire et la Caricature* (1906); E. Rasi, *La Caricatura e i Comici Italiani* (Florence, 1907); J. Frances, *La Caricatura Española Contemporanea* (1915); C. R. Ashbee, *Caricature* (1928).

POSTER

C. M. Price, *Posters* (1913), *Poster Designs* (1922); H. C. Duce, *Poster Advertising* (1912); P. V. Bradshaw, *Art in Advertising* (1925); Alexander, Spielman, Bunner and Jaccaci, *The Modern Poster* (1895); P. Pollard, *Posters in Miniature* (1897); J. Pennell, *Liberty Loan Poster* (1918), an essay on the poster. Books containing examples of the work of dis-

311

BIBLIOGRAPHIES

tinguished poster artists include: Prof. H. K. Frenzel, *Ludwig Hohlwein* (1926); H. Furst, *Frank Brangwyn* (1924); J. Klinger, Cosl-Frey and Willrab, *Poster Art in Vienna* (1923); E. McKnight Kauffer, *The Art of the Poster* (1925). *The Poster*, the national magazine of outdoor advertising and poster art, is issued monthly in Chicago by the Outdoor Advertising Association of America.

BOOKS

General: A. W. Pollard, *Fine Books* (London, 1912); H. Bouchot, *Le Livre*, trans. by Bigmore, *The Book: Its Printers, Illustrators and Binders* (London, 1890); G. H. Putnam, *Books and their Makers during the Middle Ages* (New York, 1896); R. B. McKerrow, *An Introduction to Bibliography* (Oxford, 1927); Sir Frederic Kenyon, *Ancient Books and Modern Discoveries* (1927); M. Audin, *Le Livre: Étude technique et historique* (Paris, 1927).

Before printing from type: T. Birt, *Die Buchroll in der Kunst* (Leipzig, 1907); W. Schubart, *Das Buch bei den Greichen und Römern* (Berlin, 1907); F. Madan, *Books in Manuscript* (London, 1920); H. Guppy, *Stepping-stones to the Art of Typography* (Manchester, 1928); T. F. Carter, *The Invention of Printing in China and its Spread Westward* (New York, 1925); W. L. Schreiber, *Handbuch der Holz und Metallschnitte des XV. Jahrhunderts* (Leipzig, 1926–27).

Printed books, general and early: T. F. Dibdin, *Bibliotheca Spenceriana*, a descriptive catalogue of the books printed in the 15th century, in the library of George John, Earl Spencer (London, 1814–15); E. G. Duff, *Early Printed Books* (London, 1893); S. Morison, *Four Centuries of Fine Printing* (London, 1924); A. W. Pollard, *Early Illustrated Books* (London, 1893); "The Art of the Book," *Studio*, special number (London, 1914); *Times Literary Supplement*, special printing numbers (London, 1912, 1927); *Gutenberg Festschrift* (Mainz, 1925); C. J. Sawyer and F. J. Harvey Darton, *English Books, 1475–1900* (1927).

Printed books to-day: S. Morison, *Modern Fine Printing* (London, 1925); O. Simon and J. Rodenberg, *Printing of To-day* (London, 1928); L. Pichon, "Modern French Book Illustration," *Studio*, special number (London, 1927); H. Loubier, *Die neue Deutsche Buchkunst* (Stuttgart, 1925); W. Morris, *The Ideal Book* (London, 1908); Modern Book Production, *Studio*, special number (1928).

Periodical and other publications: *Transactions of the Bibliographical Society* (London); *The Fleuron*, a journal of typography, vol. i., 1923 *et seq.*; *The Imprint*; *Gutenberg Jahrbuch*, vol. i. (Mainz, 1926 *et seq.*); *Arts et Métiers graphiques*, vol. i. (Paris, 1927).

W. A. Dwiggins, *D. B. Updike and the Merrymount Press* (1924); F. Warde, *Bruce Rogers, Designer of Books* (1925); D. C. McMurtrie, Ruth Grannis, and others, *Walter Gilliss, 1855–1925* (1925); W. Gilliss, *Recollections of the Gilliss Press* (1926); *The Merrymount Press, Its Aims, Work and Equipment* (1927); G. P. Winship, *The Merrymount Press* (1928); W. Ransom, *Private Presses and the Books they have given us* (1928).

CRAYON

Joseph Meder, *Die Handzeichnung. Ihre Technik und entwicklung* (1919); Harold Speed, *The Practice and Science of Drawing*.

ETCHING

G. Pauli, *Inkunabeln der Radierung* (Graphische Gesellschaft, Berlin, 1906 *seq.*); K. Zoege von Manteuffel, *Die Radierung*; M. C. Salaman, *The Great Etchers from Rembrandt to*

BIBLIOGRAPHIES

Whistler (London, 1914); H. W. Singer, *Die moderne Graphik* (2nd ed., Leipzig, 1920); Sir Frank Short, *The Making of Etchings* (London, 1888).

A. Bosse, *Traicté des manières de graver* (1645; 3rd ed., enlarged, 1745); W. Faithorne, *The Art of Graving and Etching, wherein is expressed the true way of Graving in Copper* (1662); Anon., *History and Art of Engraving* (1747; 4th ed., 1770); J. H. Green, *The Complete Aquatinter* (1801); M. Lalanne, *Traité de la Gravure à l'Eau-Forte* (1866; Eng. trans. with notes by S. R. Koehler, 1880); P. G. Hamerton, *Etching and Etchers* (1868); F. S. Haden, *About Etching* (1878); S. R. Koehler, *Etching: an Outline of its Technical Processes* (1885); F. S. Haden, *The Art of the Painter-etcher* (1890); W. Strang and H. W. Singer, *Etching and Engraving* (1897); F. Wedmore, *Etchings* (1911); A. Whitman and M. C. Salaman, *The Print-collector's Handbook* (1912); J. Pennell, *Etchers and Etching* (1920); A. M. Hind, *A History of Engraving and Etching from the 15th Century to the Year 1914* (1922); W. P. Robins, *Etching Craft* (1922); E. S. Lumsden, *The Art of Etching* (1925); W. Shaw Sparrow, *British Etching from Barlow to Seymour Haden* (1926); J. Laver, *A History of British and American Etching* (1929).

MEZZOTINT

A. Browne, *Ars Pictoria* (1669); J. Evelyn, *Sculptura* (1662), with the first mezzotint ever published in a book, a head of the Large Executioner, by Prince Rupert; J. C. Le Blon, *Coloritto* (1737); H. D. Chelsum, *A History of the Art of Engraving in Mezzotinto* (Winchester, 1786); G. K. Nagler, *Künstler-Lexikon* (München, 1835–52); L. de Laborde, *Histoire de la Gravure en manière noire* (1839); J. Maberly, *The Print Collector* (1844); T. H. Fielding, *The Art of Engraving* (1854); S. Redgrave, *Dictionary of Artists of the English School* (1874); W. G. Rawlinson, *Turner's Liber Studiorum* (1878); P. G. Hamerton, *The Graphic Arts* (1882); J. C. Smith, *British Mezzotinto Portraits* (1883); Sir F. Short, *On the Making of Etchings* (1888); Sir H. von Herkomer, *Etching and Mezzotint Engraving* (1892); H. Paton, *Etching, Drypoint, Mezzotint* (1895); H. W. Singer and W. Strang, *Etching, Engraving and other Methods of Printing Pictures* (1897); Sir F. Wedmore, *Fine Prints* (1897); A. Whitman, *Masters of Mezzotint* (1898); J. Frankau, *John Raphael Smith* (1903); C. J. Davenport, *Mezzotints* (1904).

CALLIGRAPHY

H. Jenkinson, *The Later Court Hands in England* (Cambridge, 1927); H. Jenkinson and C. Johnson, *Court Hand Illustrated* (Oxford, 1915); E. A. Lowe, "Handwriting" in Crump-Jacob, *Legacy of the Middle Ages* (Oxford, 1926), illustrated, admirable summary of development closing of minuscule with the Humanistic period; F. Madan, *Books in Manuscript* (London, 1895); E. Crous and J. Kirchner, *Die Gotischen Schriftarten* (Berlin, 1928); P. Jessen, *Meister der Schreibkunst* (Stuttgart, 1925); A. Prunaire, *Les Plus Beaux Types de Lettres* (avec avant-propos de Claudius Popelin et Preface par Anatole France) (Paris s.d.); S. Morison, *The Calligraphical Models of Ludovico degli Arrighi surnamed Vicentino* (Paris, 1926); Luca di Pacioli, *De Divina Proportione* (Venetiis, 1509), reprint of text (with introduction) in Constantin Winterburg, *Fra Luca Pacioli, Divina Proportione* (Quellenschriften für Kunstgeschichte u. Kunst-technik des Mittelalters u. d. Neuzeit, Wien, 1889); A. Dürer, *Unterweysung der Messung mit dem Zuckel und Richtscheyt in Linien, Ebnen und ganzen Corporen* (Nuremberg, 1525) and *Of the Just Shaping of Letters* (New York, 1917), translation by R. T. Nichol of that portion of the *Unterweysung* dealing with the construction of letters; G. Tory, *Champfleury* (Paris, 1529); *Champfleury* (New York, 1927), English translation by George B. Ives; G. Manzoni, *Studii di Bibliografia Analitica* (Bologna, 1882); S. Morison

313

BIBLIOGRAPHIES

and A. F. Johnson, *Fleuron, The,* Nos. 2, 3 and 4 for articles on early italics (London, 1924–27); R. Blanco y Sanchez, *Arte de la Escritura y de la Calligrafia* (Madrid, 1920); D. M. de Servidori, *Reflexiones sobre la Verdadera Arte de Escribir* (Madrid, 1789); E. Cotarelo y Mori, *Diccionario Biográfico y Bibliográfico de Caligrafos Españoles* (Madrid, 1913–16); T. Torio de la Riva y Herrero, *Arte de Escribir* (Madrid, 1798); M. Dubois, *Histoire abregée de l'Écriture* (Paris, 1772); N. Duval, *Nouvelle Méthode pour Apprendre Facilement L'Art de toutes les Ecritures usitées dans le Royaume* (Paris, 1750); W. A. Smith, *"According to Cocker," The Progress of Penmanship from the earliest times* (Paisley, 1887); J. Bonzon, *La Corporation des Maîtres-Ecrivains sous l'ancien Régime* (Paris, 1899); J. Grand-Carteret, *Papeterie et Papetiers de l'ancien temps* (Paris, 1913); W. Massey, *Origin and Progress of Letters* (London, 1763); S. Morison, *Caractères de l'Ecriture* (Paris, 1927), valuable bibliographical and other details (in the style of Massey, *q.v.*); F. Aeffens, *Lateinische Paläographie,* (Trever, 1908); E. F. Strange, *The Writing Books of the Sixteenth Century;* E. Johnston, *Writing,* and *Illuminating and Lettering* (London, 1906); E. Johnston and A. Eric R. Gill, *Manuscripts and Inscription Letters* (London, 1911); R. Bridges (edited by), *English Handwriting,* with thirty-four facsimile plates and artistic and paleographical criticisms, by Roger Fry and E. A. Lowe, S.P.E. Tract No. xxiii. (Oxford, 1926); M. Gorce, *Cours de Calligraphie* (Paris, 1921); H. Nélis, *L'Écriture et les Scribes Bibliographiques* (Brussels, 1918).

LINE ENGRAVING

Adam Bartsch, *Le Peintre Graveur,* 26 vols. (Vienna, 1803–21); J. D. Passavant, *Le Peintre Graveur* (supplement to Bartsch), 6 vols. (Leipzig, 1860–64); F. Lippmann, *Der Kupferstich,* 3rd ed. (Berlin, 1905); Paul Kristeller, *Kupferstich und Holzschnitt in vier Jahrhunderten* (Berlin, 4th ed., 1922); A. M. Hind, *A History of Engraving and Etching* (3rd ed., revised, 1923), with full and excellent bibl. Technique:—A. Bosse, *Traité des manières de graver* (Paris, 1645), later editions revised by C. N. Cochin fils, 1745.

Particular countries and periods:—Max Lehrs, *Geschichte und kritischer Katalog des deutschen, niederlandischen und französischen Kupferstiches im 15. Jahrhundert* (Vienna, 1908), etc. (in progress); M. Geisberg *Die Anfänge des deutschen Kupferstiches und der Meister E. S.* (Leipzig, 1908), and *Kupferstich der Frühzeit* (Strasbourg, 1923); A. M. Hind, *Catalogue of Early Italian Engravings in the British Museum,* 2 vols. (London, 1910); F. Courboin, *Histoire de la Gravure en France* (Paris, 1923–26).

BARK-CLOTH

P. Hambruch, *Oceanische Rindenstoffe* (Oldenburg, 1926) gives a summary of the Pacific industry. For a review of this and further references, as well as a description from the Garo hills, see *Man 5, 6* (1927). For Uganda *see* J. Roscoe, *The Baganda* (1911) and *The Banyankole* (1924).

ENGRAVING

Guide to the Processes and Schools of Engraving, issued by the British Museum.

WOODCUTS AND WOOD-ENGRAVING

William A. Chatto, *Treatise on Wood Engraving* (London, 1839); W. J. Linton, *Masters of Wood Engraving* (1889, Privately Printed); W. J. Linton, *History of Wood Engraving in America* (1884); George E. Woodberry, *History of Wood Engraving* (New York, 1883);

BIBLIOGRAPHIES

Frank Weitenkampf, *How to Appreciate Prints* (New York, 1907 and 1921); Frank Weitenkampf, *American Graphic Art* (New York, 1912); Frank Weitenkampf, *Wood Engraving of Today* (New York, 1917); Laurence Binyon, *Catalogue of Japanese and Chinese Woodcuts in the British Museum* (London, 1916); Laurence Binyon and J. J. O'Brien Sexton, *Japanese Color Prints* (London, 1923); *Modern Woodcuts and Lithographs* (London Studio, 1919); *Prints and Their Production* (*A Bibliography*), New York Public Library (1919); Malcolm C. Salaman, *Woodcut of Today* (The *Studio*, London, 1927); Herbert Furst, *The Modern Woodcut* (London, 1926).

TYPOGRAPHY

See bibliographies of PRINTING and PRINTING TYPE: also E. G. Gress, *American Handbook of Printing* (N. Y. 1907); H. Fournier, *Traité de la Typographie* (new ed., 1919); C. T. Jacobi, *Printing* (6th ed., 1919) F. Thibaudeau, *La Lettre d'imprimerie* (2 vols., 1921), and *Manuel français de typographie moderne* (1924); G. Milchsack, *Gesammelte Aufsätze über Buchkunst und Buchdruck* (Wölfenbüttel, 1922); A. W. Unger, *Die Herstellung von Büchern* (Halle, 1923); L. E. Brossard, *Le Correcteur typographe* (Tours, 1924); S. Morison, *The Art of the Printer* (1925); F. C. Collins, *Authors' and Printers' Dict.* (6th ed., 1928); J. C. Oswald, *Hist. of Printing* (1928).

STIPPLE AND CRAYON ENGRAVING

Malcolm C. Salaman, *Old English Colour-Prints* (Special Winter No. of *Studio*, 1909), *Old Engravers of England* (1906), *Eighteenth Century French Colour-Prints* (1913); Julia Frankau, *Eighteenth Century Colour-Prints* (1900; 2nd ed. 1906); Campbell Dodgson, *Old French Colour-Prints* (1924).

PEN DRAWING

J. Pennell, *Pen Drawings and Pen Draughtsmen* (New York, 1920); A. L. Guptill, *Drawing with Pen and Ink* (New York, 1928).

BOOK-PLATES

The curious in the matter of book-plate composition will find it treated in the various volumes of the Ex-libris Series. *See* also A. Poulet-Malassis, *Les Ex-libris français* (1875); Hon. J. Leicester Warren (Lord de Tabley), *A Guide to the Study of Book-plates* (1880); Sir A. W. Franks, *Notes on Book-plates, 1574–1800* (1887); Friedrich Warnecke, *Die deutschen Bücherzeichen* (1890); Henri Bouchot, *Les Ex-libris et les marques de possession du livre* (1891); Egerton Castle, *English Book-plates* (1892); Walter Hamilton, *French Book-plates* (1892), *Dated Book-plates* (1895); H. W. Fincham, *Artists and Engravers of British and American Book-plates* (1897); Count K. E. zu Leiningen-Westerburg, *German Book-plates*, Eng. trans. by G. R. Denis (1901); Clifford N. Carver, *Book-plates of Well-Known Americans* (Princeton, N. J., 1911); George W. Fuller (ed.), *A Bibliography of Bookplate Literature* (Spokane, Wash., 1926).

DRY-POINT

W. P. Robins, *Etching Craft* (1922), pp. 163 *seq.*; E. Lumsden, *The Art of Etching* (1925), pp. 18, 46, 127 *seq.*

BIBLIOGRAPHIES

ART

Plato, *Republic;* J. C. F. von Schiller, *Briefe über die ästhetische Erziehung des Menschen* (trans. G. J. Weiss, in *Philosophical and Aesthetic Letters of Schiller* (1845); G. Semper, *Der Stil* (1860–63); G. W. F. Hegel, *The Philosophy of Fine Art* (trans. F. P. B. Osmanton, 4 vols., 1920); B. Bosanquet, *Introduction to Hegel's Philosophy of Fine Art (Ästhetik)*, trans. with notes and prefatory essay (1896); Herbert Spencer, *First Principles*, ch. xxii. (1862, later ed., 1910); H. Taine, *De l'idéal dans l'art* (1867), *Philosophie de l'art en Grèce, Philosophie de l'art en Italie, Philosophie de l'art dans les Pays-Bas* (1865–69); trans. J. Durand, *Lectures in Art*, 5 vols. (1889); E. Véron, *L'Esthétique* (1883); C. Fiedler, *Der Ursprung der Künstlerischen Tätigkeit* (1883); E. Grosse, *Die Anfänge der Kunst* (1894); G. Santayana, *The Sense of Beauty* (1897); L. Tolstoy, *What is Art?* (1899); K. Gros, *Die Spiele der Menschen* (1899); trans. E. L. Baldwin, 1901, *Die Spiele der Tiere* (2nd ed., trans. E. L. Baldwin, 1898), *Ein leitung in der Ästhetik* (1902); Grjö Hirn, *The Origins of Art* (1900); Benedetto Croce, *Estetica* (1900); Th. Lippo, *Grundlegung der Aesthetik* (1903–05); V. Lee and C. A. Thomson, *Beauty and Ugliness and other Studies in Psychological Aesthetics* (1912); P. Gaultier, *The Meaning of Art* (1913); Clive Bell, *Art* (1914); W. Worringer, *Abstraktion und Einfühlung* (1919), *Form probleme der Botik* (1922); De Witt H. Parker, *The Analysis of Art* (1926).

PHOTOGRAPHIC ART

H. T. Bailey, *Photography and Fine Art* (Philadelphia, 1918); H. R. Poore, *Pictorial Composition* (New York, 1914); P. L. Anderson, *The Fine Art of Photography* (Philadelphia, 1919), *Pictorial Photography—its Principles and Practice* (Philadelphia and London, 1923); F. C. Tilney, *What Pictorialism Is* (New York, 1924); A. Hammond, *Pictorial Composition in Photography* (Boston, 1920); J. W. Gillies, *The Principles of Pictorial Photography* (New York, 1923); F. C. Tilney, *The Real Pictorialism* (London); Antony Guest, *Art and the Camera* (London); A. J. Anderson, *A.B.C. of Pictorial Photography* (London); H. P. Robinson, *Pictorial Effect in Photography* (London, 1893); *Picture Making by Photography* (London); G. Schweitzer, *La Première Année de Photographie* (Paris); C. Duvivier, *Le Procédé à L'Huile* (Paris); C. Puyo, *Les Procédés Aux Encres Grasses* (Paris); E. J. Wall, *The Dictionary of Photography* (Cambridge, 1925), *Photographic Facts and Formulas* (Boston, 1924); J. Cassell, *Cassell's Cyclopaedia of Photography* (London); A. E. Garrett, *The Advance of Photography: Its History and Modern Applications* (London, 1911); A. Watkins, *Photography: Its Principles and Applications* (London, 1911); H. P. Maskell, *Photography* (London, 1911); E. S. King, *Miscellaneous Photographic Investigations* (1912, Harvard University, Astronomical Observatory. Annals. Vol. 59, No. 10); W. L. F. Wastell, *Progressive Photography;* C. E. K. Mees and M. S. Schramm, *Monographs on the Theory of Photography*, from the Research Laboratory of the Eastman Kodak Company (New York, 1921); W. D. Bowman, *Photography* (London, 1924); A. Hammond, *Pictorial Composition in Photography* (American Photographic Publications, 1920); F. J. Mortimer, *Photograms of the year, 1925–1926* (American Photographic Publications, 1927); W. Nutting, *Photographic Art Secrets* (New York, 1927); L. Derr, *Photography* (New York); C. R. Gibson, *Photography and Its Mysteries;* J. S. Adamson, *Retouching and Finishing for Photographers* (New York, 1925); R. C. Bayley, *Complete Photography* (new revised edition, New York, 1923); *Photography Made Easy* (American Photographic Publications); H. C. Jones, *Photography of To-day* (Philadelphia); W. Wallington, *Chats on Photography* (Philadelphia); A. Watkins, *Photography* (New York); A. E. Courady, et al., *Photography as a Scientific Implement: a Collective Work* (New York,

1923); H. N. Durham, *Colouring of Photographs*, Lantern Slide and Other Transparencies with Artists Colour Oils (F. Weber Co., Philadelphia).

ILLUMINATED MANUSCRIPTS

The most convenient book of reference is: H. Omont, *Listes de recueil de facsimilés et de reproductions de mss. conservés à la Bibl. Nat.* (2nd ed., Paris, 1912). Numerous articles of the highest importance are scattered through the scientific periodicals.

1. General:—I. A. Herbert, *Illuminated Manuscripts* (London, 1911); C. Couderc, *Les Enluminures des Mss. du Moyen-Age* (Paris, 1926); A. Michel, *Histoire de l'Art*, contributions from Leprieur, Haseloff, Millet, Durrieu, Bernath (Paris, 1905 *et seq.*); M. Bernath, *Die Malerei des Mittelalters* (Leipzig, 1916).

2. Reproductions:—Comte de Bastard, *Peintures et Ornements des Mss.* (Paris, 1832–69); G. Leidinger, *Meisterwerke der Buchmalerei aus Mss. der Bayerischen Staats-bibl. München* (Munich, 1920); H. Martin, *Les Joyaux de l'Enluminure à la Bibl. Nat.* (Paris, 1926); G. Warner, *Illuminated Mss. in the British Museum* (1899–1903); *British Museum Reproductions of Illuminated Mss.* (1923); *Schools of Illumination* (1914–26).

Great Britain and Ireland:—E. G. Millar, *English Manuscripts Illumination from the 10th to the 13th Century* (Paris, 1926); *English Illuminated Manuscripts of the 14th and 15th Century* (Paris, 1928); I. A. Bruun, *Celtic Illuminated Mss.* (Stockholm, 1897); E. G. Millar, *The Lindisfarne Gospels* (London, 1923); E. Sullivan, *The Book of Kells* (London, Paris, New York, 1920); O. Homburger, *Die Anfänge der Malerschule von Winchester* (Leipzig, 1912); Warner and Wilson, *The Benedictional of St. Aethelwold* (Roxburghe Club, 1910); M. R. James, *The Trinity College Apocalypse* (Roxburghe Club, 1909); S. C. Cockerell, *The Gorleston Psalter* (London, 1907); I. van den Gheyn, *Le Psautier de Peterborough* (Haarlem, 1906); G. F. Warner, *Queen Mary's Psalter* (London, 1912); J. A. Herbert, *The Sherborne Missal* (Roxburghe Club, 1920).

France:—Lauer, *La Miniature en France des Origines au 13ᵉ Siècle* (Paris); H. Martin, *La Miniature en France du 13ᵉ au 15ᵉ Siècle* (Paris, 1923), *Les Miniaturistes Français* (Paris, 1906) and *Les Peintres des Mss. et la Miniature en France* (Paris, 1909); Oursel, *La Miniature du 12ᵉ Siècle à l'Abbaye de Cîteaux* (Dijon, 1926); Graf Vitzthum, *Die Pariser Buchmalerei* (Leipzig, 1907); Cockerell, *A Psalter and Hours Executed before 1270 for a Lady connected with St. Louis, probably his Sister Isabella of France* (London, 1905); Comte P. Durrieu, *Les Antiquités Judaiques et le Peintre Jean Fouquet* (Paris, 1908), and *Le Boccace de Munich* (München, 1909).

Low Countries:—Byvanck and Hoogewerff, *Noord-Nederlandsche Miniaturen* (1922–25); A. W. Byvanck, *La Miniature Hollandaise* (Paris, in prep.); Comte P. Durrieu, *La Miniature Flamande* (Paris, 1921); F. Winkler, *Die flämische Buchmalerei* (Leipzig, 1925); Comte P. Durrieu, *Les Très Riches Heures de Jean de France Duc de Berry* (Paris, 1904), and *Les Heures de Turin* (Paris, 1902); G. Hulin de Loo, *Les Heures de Milan* (Brussels and Paris, 1911).

Germany:—F. Jacoby, *Die Deutsche Buchmalerei* (Munich, 1923); A. Goldschmidt, *Die Deutsche Buchmalerei* (I. die Karolingische, II. die ottonische) (Florence and Munich, 1928); M. Bernath, *La Miniature Allemande de la Période des Othons jusqu'au. 16ᵉ Siècle* (Paris, in prep.); Sauerland u. Haseloff, *Der Psalter Erzbischofs Egberts in Trier* (Trier, 1901); G. Swarzenski, *Regensburger Buchmalerei* (Leipzig, 1901), and *Salzburger Malerei* (Leipzig, 1913); H. Ehl, *Die ottonische Kölner Buchmalerei* (Bonn u. Leipzig, 1922); A. Merton, *Die Buchmalerei in St. Gallen* (Leipzig, 1912); E. F. Bange, *Eine Bayerische Malerschule* (Munich, 1923); A. Haseloff, *Eine thüringisch-sächsische Malerschule* (Strasbourg, 1897); K. Loffler,

BIBLIOGRAPHIES

Schwabische Buchmalerei (Augsburg, 1928); K. V. Amira, *Die Dresdener Bilderhandschrift des Sachsenspiegels* (Leipzig, 1902 and 1924).

Italy:—*See also* the respective histories of art by Bertaux, Marle, Toësca, Venturi. P. d'Ancona, *La Miniature Italienne du 10° au 16° Siècle* (Paris, 1924); *La Miniatura Fiorentina* (Florence, 1914); P. Toësca, *La Pittura e la Miniatura nella Lombardia* (Milan, 1912); G. F. Warner, *The Gospels of Matilda, Countess of Tuscany* (Roxburghe Club, 1917); Graf Erbach-Fürstenau, *Die Manfredbibel* (Leipzig, 1910).

Spain:—W. S. Cook, *La Miniature Espagnole* (Paris, in prep.); W. Neuss, *Die Katalanische Buchmalerei* (Bonn u. Leipzig, 1922).

PASTEL

See Karl Robert [Georges Meusnier], *Le Pastel* (Laurens, Paris, 1890); J. L. Sprinck, *A Guide to Pastel Painting* (Rowney, London); Henry Murray, *The Art of Painting and Drawing in Coloured Crayons* (Winsor and Newton, London). Among early works are: John Russell, R. A., *Elements of Painting with Crayons* (1776); M.P.R. de C.C., *Traité de la peinture au pastel avec les moyens de prévenir l'altération des couleurs* (Paris, 1788); Rosalba Carriera, *Diario degli anni 1720 e 1721 scritto di propria mano in Parigia*, etc. (Giovanni Vianelli, Venice, 1793, 4to); Girolamo Zanetti, *Elogio di Rosalba Carriera, pittrice* (Venice, 1818, 8vo). *See also* Henri Lapauze, *Les Pastels de M. Quentin de la Tour à St. Quentin*, *preface by Gustave Larroumet* (Paris); George C. Williamson, *John Russell, R.A.* (London, 1894).

ILLUSTRATION

Henry Blackburn, *The Art of Illustration* (London, 1894); J. W. G. White, *Children's Books and their illustrators* (Studio 1897–98); T. Kutschmann, *Geschichte der deutschen illustration* (Goslar, 1899, 2 vols.); A. W. Pollard, *Old Picture Books* (London, 1902); Walter Crane, *Of the decorative illustration of books old and new* (London 1905); S. T. Prideaux, *Aquatint Engraving* (London 1909); A. W. Pollard, *Fine Books* (London 1912) and *Early Illustrated Books* (15th–16th centuries; London 1917); Geoffrey Holme, E. G. Halton, and M. C. Salaman, *Modern Book Illustrators and Their Work* (Studio 1914); Joseph Pennell, *The Graphic Arts* (1920, Chicago 1921), and *Pen Drawing and Pen Draughtsmen* (N.Y. 1921); Karl Schottenloher, *Das Alte Buch* (Berlin 1921); E. J. Sullivan, *The Art of Illustration* (N.Y. 1921), Universal Art Ser.; (Ed.) Césare Ratla, *Gli adornatori del libro in Italia* (Bologna 1923); Frank Weitenkampf, *American Graphic Art* (N.Y. 1924); Léon Pichon, *The New Book-illustration in France* (The Studio, 1924); Louise Norton Brown, *Block Printing and Book Illustration in Japan* (N.Y. & London 1924); Joseph Pennell, *Adventures of an Illustrator* (Boston 1925); Aubrey Beardsley, *Uncollected Work* (N.Y. 1925); L. S. Olschki, *Le Livre Illustré au XV° siècle* (Florence 1926).

ARCHITECTURAL RENDERING

David A. Gregg, *Architectural Rendering in Pen and Ink* (1891); F. F. Frederick, *Architectural Rendering in Sepia* (1892); Frank A. Hays, ed., *Architectural Rendering in Pen and Ink* (1915); A. L. Guptill, *Sketching and Rendering in Pencil* (1922); H. V. Magonigle, *Architectural Rendering in Wash* (1926); A. L. Guptill, *Drawing with Pen and Ink* (1928). Articles on architectural rendering have also appeared in the following magazines during the years indicated: *Arts and Decoration* (New York, 1920); *Pencil Points* (New York, 1921–25); *Architecture* (New York, 1923).

318